IWO JIMA

This book is dedicated
to all the Americans at Iwo Jima,
of every race and creed, and to
the memory of the 6,821
who gave their lives

"Victory was never in doubt. Its cost was. . . . What was in doubt, in all our minds, was whether there would be any of us left to dedicate our cemetery at the end, or whether the last Marine would die knocking out the last Japanese gun and gunner. . . ."

—Major General Graves B. Erskine
at the dedication of the
Third Marine Division Cemetery at Iwo Jima,
March 14, 1945.

FIRST VINTAGE BOOKS EDITION, June 1986

Copyright © 1985, 1986 by Bill D. Ross

Library of Congress Cataloging-in-Publication Data

Ross, Bill D.
Iwo Jima: legacy of valor.

Reprint. Originally published: New York: Vanguard,
1985.
Includes bibliographical references and index.
1. Iwo Jima, Battle of, 1945.   I. Title.
D767.99.I9R67   1986   940.54′26   85-40665
ISBN 0-394-74288-5

Cover photograph is from the original black and white by Joe Rosenthal,
AP/World Wide Photos

Manufactured in the United States of America

IWO JIMA

LEGACY OF VALOR

BY

BILL D. ROSS

VINTAGE BOOKS
A DIVISION OF RANDOM HOUSE
New York

"Here lie officers and men, Negroes and whites, rich men and poor—together. Here are Protestants, Catholics, and Jews—together. Here no man prefers another because of his faith or despises him because of his color. . . . No prejudices. No hatred. Theirs is the highest and purest democracy."

—From a eulogy by
Chaplain Roland B. Gittelsohn
Iwo Jima, March 14, 1945

CONTENTS

AUTHOR'S NOTE

For thirty-six days in early 1945, nearly 75,000 United States Marines were locked in epic struggle with 22,000 Japanese troops defending to the last man a seemingly impregnable flyspeck Pacific island called Iwo Jima.

Newspaper headlines and radio broadcasts trumpeted the story as it unfolded. An historic flag-raising photograph made atop Mount Suribachi was to etch the monumental combat into American history alongside Antietam and Gettysburg, and make it perhaps the best-known battle of World War II—certainly of the Pacific conflict.

In the passage of years, in the birth and maturing of new generations and the emergence of other events crucial to civilization's present and future, the conquest of Iwo Jima has become a diminishing footnote to history, largely remembered by military history buffs and a vanishing legion of aging Marines and other men who did battle there.

But the fact remains: Iwo Jima was a landmark of mass courage and individual valor. It was a battle the likes of which mankind most probably will not witness again.

So perhaps this is the moment to chronicle and attempt to recapture the essence of a pivotal time in American history and to refocus some measure of thinking about patriotism, devotion to duty, and self-sacrifice—sometimes cloudy and even questionable virtues in many minds since Korea and Vietnam.

In the 1,364 days from the Pearl Harbor attack to the Japanese surrender, with millions of Americans fighting on global battlefronts, 353 men received the Congressional Medal of Honor, the nation's highest decoration for valor "above and beyond the call of duty." Of these, 27 were for actions at Iwo Jima, thirteen posthumous.

As with most bloody military operations, questions persist about the human cost of Iwo and its strategic worth in the downfall of Japan. Casualties can perhaps best be described by numbers—in only 36 days 25,851 Americans, most in their teens or early twenties, of whom 6,821 were killed, died of wounds, or were missing in action. Of the twenty-thousand-plus Japanese garrison on the eight-and-a-half-square-mile chunk of volcanic ash and stone, 1,083 were taken prisoner and survived.

Iwo Jima in American hands meant that 24,751 Army Air Corps crewmen would be saved from ditching disabled aircraft in the icy waters of the north Pacific with an almost certain loss of most of them. By war's end, 2,251 emergency landings had been made on the island by B-29 Superfort bombers.

And Iwo gave the United States a forward airbase at the front door of the Japanese homeland, a bastion that cleared the way and made feasible the dropping of atomic bombs in Hiroshima and Nagasaki to win the war.

Iwo's conquest also was the stage for constant conflicts and high drama among the commanders who planned and led the invasion. It was a military classic of shrewd and tenacious resistance by a cunning and dedicated Japanese general and his suicidal forces. The losses they inflicted on the Americans generated a swirling controversy in the States that marked the demise of the Marines' top general in the Pacific.

Nearly four decades have passed in the writing of this book; not as a full-time effort, but as it has simmered and churned through the years. It began on Iwo where I was a twenty-three-year-old combat correspondent sergeant with the Third Marine Division. It took some small substance and form in such far-flung locales as the comforts of post-war Japan and in the bitter combat conditions of Korea as an Associated Press reporter.

Thoughts, notes, and words were strung together as an AP man in Washington during the final years of President Truman's administration, and later in dismal hotel and motel rooms from Bloomington, Indiana, to Manhattan and Hollywood while on myriad, now-forgotten writing and other assignments. And finally to a workroom in the basement of a rambling house in New Jersey, where a white, one-eyed poodle named Casey is a constant companion as I write.

This isn't a personal memoir—I never fired a shot at a Japanese I could see—but recollections of that faraway place and time are reflected in the book's outcome. The work and help of countless people made it possible; I am in debt to all of them. My sole hope of repayment is that it meets with their approval.

They are those who previously have written about the battle: the authors of several excellent books; the civilian reporters who were

1

Pearl Harbor, in early fall of 1944, bristled with military might marshaling for the climactic battles in the conquest of Japan. And on September 7—thirty-three months to the day since the Japanese attack—Admiral Chester William Nimitz assembled his admirals and generals to make final plans for the invasion of Iwo Jima.

No one was more certain of victory than the admiral. This had not been the case on the bleak 1941 Christmas Day when he had flown from the mainland to take over a shattered command under direct orders from President Roosevelt. The Commander in Chief was sure the fifty-six-year-old soft-spoken Texan was the only man who could rebuild the shambles of the fleet and use it to turn the tide of the war in the Pacific.

Nimitz wasn't awestricken by the assignment's smothering responsibility or the promotion to four-star rank that came with it—but he was surprised. The President had passed over twenty-eight admirals senior to him on the Navy's sacrosanct promotion list to make him the new CinCPac, the Navy's acronym for Commander in Chief, Pacific Fleet.

As the Navy's personnel chief, Nimitz believed his forty-year career already had reached its zenith. He had been headed for high command since September 7, 1901, when he entered the U.S. Naval Academy at sixteen, the youngest plebe in his class. A plainsman from cattle country, he didn't know the bow of a warship from its stern. But four years later he graduated seventh among 158 shavetail ensigns.

It wasn't long before Ensign Nimitz's talents were put to use. His first duty was in China; World War I found him as chief of staff to the commander of the United States Atlantic Submarine Fleet. After the armistice, Nimitz did traditional duty aboard cruisers, battleships, and aircraft carriers. But his deepest loyalties remained with destroyers and submarines—"the tin-can fleet and the silent service"—where he always felt more at home with the close camaraderie of the smaller crews.

In 1939, now a three-star rear admiral, Nimitz headed the Bureau of Navigation, then the Navy's curious name for its manpower branch. In many respects, it was the most crucial and demanding post in the service, since Nimitz had the final word on the assignment of all officers and men in a burgeoning fleet he was convinced would soon see combat duty in global waters.

Thirteen turbulent days after the Pearl Harbor attack, the new CinCPac packed a battered Gladstone traveling bag and headed for the war. His only traveling companion aboard the Pennsylvania Railroad's Capital Limited was Lieutentant Junior Grade A. Arthur Lamar, highly capable and devoted aide, who would still be at the admiral's side when the Japanese surrender was signed.

Vice Admiral W. S. Pye, a friend from Annapolis days, met the new CinCPac at Pearl Harbor. There was no honor guard, no ceremonies—only a handshake and a few words of greeting. Then, in a nondescript 1940 black Chevrolet sedan, a Marine driver took them along little-traveled back roads to Pacific Fleet Headquarters near the crest of an extinct volcano called Makalapa, the Hawaiian word for "flashing eyes."

An unnerved and dispirited staff waited for them in the map-lined conference room on the top deck of a four-story concrete building painted battleship gray. With its oblong shape and towering radio antennae, it bore a vague resemblance to a landlocked man-of-war.

Eighteen days earlier, the assemblage of brass had watched in angry frustration and bewilderment, powerless to strike back, as the Japanese attack roared about them. In the intervening time they had worked around the clock to gird against fresh enemy onslaughts that were expected momentarily. Now they were certain heads would roll and careers would be shattered—wherever the blame might lay.

They didn't expect Nimitz's bombshell.

"There will be no changes," he said in his characteristically quiet tone. "I have complete confidence in you. You've taken a terrific wallop, but I have no doubts as to the ultimate outcome." The first of hundreds of Nimitz's war councils at Makalapa, and one of its most tense, was over in five minutes. With few exceptions the team would remain intact until war's end. While it was an inherited staff, the admiral *did* have full confidence in it—not necessarily as individual officers, but as integral cogs in the military staff system, with himself as the final decision maker.

Makalapa was well suited to Nimitz's temperament. He had a

penchant for brisk walks, preferably up and down hills, and a passion for secrecy. Like many Texans, he was a crack pistol shot. Each morning before his rapid two-mile hike, he peppered away on a private target range behind headquarters. A watchful Marine sentry stood at parade rest to warn passersby that firing was in progress.

Work at Makalapa was carried out under strictest security. The place was nonexistent in official press releases and communiqués. Intelligence officers trembled at mere mention of the name. Taxi drivers refused to make the half-hour trip from downtown Honolulu to "the Hill" at any price, fearful of immediate arrest by burly Marines patrolling the area and guarding the gates.

Makalapa, its exalted occupants, and their work were no secret to correspondents. But they respected the tight mandate of security; they wrote neither about the place nor of what was happening behind the twelve-foot-high chain-link fence surrounding it. Stories were datelined "Admiral Nimitz's Headquarters" or "CinCPac Naval Headquarters." Its location might have been Catalina Island off the coast of southern California as far as people back home knew from news stories or radio broadcasts.

In talks among themselves, reporters dubbed Nimitz's staff "The Mad Monks of Makalapa." The irreverence stuck; for the rest of the war it surfaced in conversation among newsmen and all ranks of servicemen in the Pacific—except, of course, among the Monks themselves.

2

Nimitz had no illusions about what he faced as CinCPac in the early months of the war. It was a desperate life-or-death holding action with no hope of immediate help. President Roosevelt had made this clear in a one-on-one post-midnight conference in the Oval Office when the admiral was given his assignment. Nimitz must defend Hawaii and fight, for months and possibly years, with what remained of decimated United States military power in the Pacific.

Japanese naval forces outnumbered the American fleet by more than two to one in aircraft carriers and battleships. Odds were even more formidable in the number of submarines, destroyers, cruisers, troop transports, and other support craft. And the President had left no doubt that the war in Europe would have priority in manpower and all the other resources to contain and defeat the Axis powers.

So even if the Japanese juggernaut could be stopped, it would be a long time before the United States could produce the ships, planes, tanks, guns, ammunition, and the thousands of other necessities to fuel an offensive fighting machine. And millions of men would have to be drafted, outfitted, trained, and transported to the battle-zones before victory was more than a promise. But on Christmas Day of 1941, the Monks of Makalapa began to think about the first steps on the long journey that would lead to Tokyo Bay and the unconditional surrender of the Japanese on the yet-to-be-built *Missouri*. The invasion of Iwo Jima was 785 days away, and it was unlikely that anyone at Makalapa knew the island existed, much less the epic role its conquest would have on the history of World War II.

Nimitz knew help ultimately would come if his outnumbered and outgunned fleet could somehow halt the Japanese sweep across the millions of miles of Pacific Ocean they controlled. If that miracle couldn't be brought off, the whole matter was academic.

Fate had blessed the United States in one way when the Japanese struck Pearl Harbor: the lucky happenstance that the fleet's two aircraft carriers were at sea. The *Lexington*, and its screen of escorts, was ferrying a Marine fighter squadron to Midway Island. The *Enterprise*, and its force of three cruisers and nine destroyers, was steaming five hundred miles west of Hawaii on course for Honolulu after shuttling twelve Grumman Wildcat fighters and their Leatherneck pilots to Wake Island.

In the desperate days, weeks, and months that followed, these ships and planes and men were the nation's flimsy shield against further enemy attacks. And fresh blows were expected against Hawaii at any time Tokyo wanted to flash the signal. But the signal never came.

Why weren't Pearl Harbor and the other battered installations on Oahu hit again while the Americans were virtually defenseless? Was it because enemy warlords hadn't planned beyond the sneak hit-and-run attack? Did the Japanese high command believe the Americans couldn't recover from the debacle? that the Pacific fleet was out of action forever? that the United States would sue for peace? Was it because Japan was so heavily committed elsewhere on the Asian continent and in the south Pacific that it didn't have the ships, planes,

PART ONE

Prologue
to
Invasion

there, and whose dispatches and broadcasts told the day-to-day story for millions of people back home; and those in the Marine Corps who wrote official battle reports and other documents. And there are hundreds of conversations with men who fought at Iwo Jima and the recollections of what they did, saw, and said—especially my combat correspondent and photographer comrades, three of whom were killed and thirteen wounded during the campaign.

What follows is an attempt to come up with something of value in telling of a proud chapter in American history. Perhaps the result isn't in the vernacular and organization of military or academic historians. Some details most certainly will not mesh with other versions of the happenings. And the deeds of many units and individuals who gave greatly to the victory will not have been told in full or may have been missed in the recounting. It is an inadvertency for which I apologize. But if readers gain a deeper insight into the battle, and what motivated the men who fought it, the book will have fulfilled its purpose.

It meant much of intrinsic worth, then and now, to have been with the Marines of Iwo Jima. One in three were killed or wounded in upholding the traditions of the Corps. I left the island very grateful to be alive and in one piece—and very proud. Forty years later, my feelings haven't changed.

—B. D. R.

Somerset, New Jersey, 1985

and men to deliver a final coup de grâce? Or was the Imperial General Staff in Tokyo simply too cautious?

With Great Britain driven from the European mainland and expecting a German invasion at any time, with Holland, Belgium, and France defeated and occupied by Nazi legions, who was to halt total Japanese conquest of the Pacific? Only Nimitz's shadow of a fleet and fewer than two hundred obsolete Army Air Corps bombers and fighters stood in the way.

Historians still ponder and debate why the Hawaiian Islands were not invaded. The answer remains arcane, but one thing is certain. If Pearl Harbor and the other bases on Oahu had been captured, the Japanese would have had a free hand across the entire Pacific from Asia to Australia, and the front door of the United States mainland would be open to attack—even to an invasion attempt.

3

If Admiral Nimitz had a Japanese counterpart, it was the perceptive and brilliant Admiral Isoroku Yamamoto, Commander in Chief of the Combined Imperial Fleet. He was the mastermind of the Pearl Harbor attack, acutely aware of the industrial potential of the United States and the overpowering strength of American manpower in a prolonged war.

"Unless the American fleet is put out of action by 1942, the balance of power will shift to the United States and that will be the end," Yamamoto warned the Imperial War Council in early 1941 when he first presented his strategy for victory. The Japanese must hammer the Hawaiian Islands with a fatal blow, then capture Midway Island, invade the Aleutians at the tip of Alaska, and be poised for landings on the West Coast of the United States.

"If we succeed in this, and bring about the destruction of the American fleet," the admiral told his fellow warlords, "the United States will negotiate a peace and leave Japan a free hand in China, Southeast Asia, and the Pacific Ocean. That is our one great hope."

At the beginning, Yamamoto's clock of conquest ticked with alarming accuracy. In the first six months of 1942, disaster after disaster befell the United States with frightening speed and repetition. Wake

Island, Guam, and the Philippines were quickly overrun, with General Douglas MacArthur escaping to Australia with his family and entourage, leaving his troops behind to surrender at Corregidor. The Aleutians were invaded, and Alaska threatened.

Powerful Japanese pincers snipped off Malaya, Borneo, and the oil-and-tin-rich Dutch East Indies. The enemy took Guadalcanal in the Solomon Islands, and most of New Guinea. Singapore was seized from the British, and a giant striking force was set to invade Australia. Crippling new American naval losses came in a series of fierce sea battles in the south Pacific.

Each thrust was according to the timetable of Yamamoto's master plan; nothing was helter-skelter, each move dovetailed and had a well-defined purpose, and each success brought Japan one step closer to achieving its aims. Since it had first launched its audacious adventure in Manchuria in the mid-1930s, the goal was to seize the sources of raw materials needed to feed the staggering consumption of an exploding population and meet the skyrocketing demands of a homeland rapidly industrializing and arming to the teeth.

By late May Nimitz knew a major and decisive battle would come soon that could quickly determine the outcome of the war.

Long-range Navy Catalina flying boats and submarines operating deep in enemy waters flashed word that Yamamoto had assembled a gigantic strike force in the central Pacific. It was moving at twelve-knot speed toward battle at an undetermined place and time, and something momentous would surely happen somewhere north and west of Hawaii within a week.

But if the Americans must face the enemy while still outnumbered and outgunned and unsure of winning, they had a powerful edge unknown to the Japanese. Cryptographers among the Monks of Makalapa had broken the secret Japanese naval code and were monitoring every radio transmission between Imperial Fleet headquarters and Yamamoto's flagship. Combining coded intercepts with an intuitive sense of where he would strike if he were the enemy commander, Nimitz set an ambush.

The stage was set for the Battle of Midway.

It began in the morning haze of June 3, 1942.

For the next forty-three hours, the outcome of the war in the Pacific hung in shaky balance.

It was apparent why the Japanese wanted, and must have, Midway. Its capture would send a new shock wave of anxiety across the American home front. But it meant much more: a Japanese-held Midway would give the enemy tight control of the sealanes between the United States and Hawaii, and the south Pacific and Australia. Pearl Harbor and what remained of Nimitz's fleet would be within easy range of land-based bombers. And it would be the rendezvous point for carrier-based attacks against the West Coast—and even landings on the mainland.

Yamamoto's fleet was still five hundred miles away when the battle was joined. It was a minor, but highly significant, air-sea scrimmage with no losses to the Americans and minor damage to the Japanese. But Yamamoto had no intention of breaking off the action even if the Americans knew where he was. Confident that his armada could take the objective, the fleet sailed on through the night. It was just over the horizon at dawn of June 4 when hell broke loose.

Marines flying twenty-five stubby, obsolete Brewster fighters found the formation twenty miles at sea. The carriers had turned into the wind and were launching interceptors when the day's marathon dogfights began. Minutes later, Japanese bombers razed everything above ground on Midway.

It was familiar business to many of the Japanese pilots—they had ravaged Pearl Harbor. They leveled every building on the flat, barren atoll, and hit a gasoline dump and many gun emplacements in the first bombing run. Smoke from the blazing fuel climbed thousands of feet into the cloudless sky as the planes swung around and headed for the carriers for more fuel and bombs. The only thing the Japanese hadn't pummeled was the airstrip; they expected to be using it within hours.

As the morning skies came ablaze in brilliant sunlight, the battle erupted in furious confusion. Nimitz had sent the *Enterprise* and *Yorktown* to stations between the island and the invaders when radio intercepts told him what Yamamoto was trying to do. Now the American carrier planes joined in the mad scramble to keep Japanese troops from landing and put the force to flight.

It was a stand-off until early afternoon, when Nimitz played his trump card; the *Hornet*, with its fighters, dive bombers, and torpedo planes, swarmed into the savage action. The carrier and its screen of escorting destroyers had sped to the scene at thirty-knot flank speed after launching Lieutenant Colonel James H. Doolittle's Army bombers in their raid on Tokyo in that first American offensive action of the war.

Swirling dogfights cluttered the skies. Japanese interceptors darted and dove among American planes aiming at every ship below them. Billowing parachutes, friend and foe, blossomed and swayed in the gentle wind as pilots bailed out of planes tumbling out of control. Flaming aircraft splashed into the sea.

Bright yellow life rafts of downed Navy and Marine pilots bobbed like polka dots on the gentle ocean swells. Here and there, Japanese floated in life jackets, but most had gone down with their planes. Heavy black smoke climbed thousands of feet, signals that the enemy's scheme to conquer Midway had failed.

As darkness came slowly, all of Yamamoto's carriers were sunk or aflame before plunging to the ocean's two-mile depths. Downed Americans, awaiting rescue in rafts and Mae West life jackets, were eyewitnesses to the incredible panorama. They watched Japanese planes circle for hours in a futile search for a place to land, until motors coughed and died as fuel ran out. In addition to the carriers and their planes, the Japanese lost a heavy cruiser, nine destroyers with nearly three thousand sailors, and most of the troop transports and their men.

In the last hours of battle, an anonymous Navy communications man penned a couplet that ultimately found its way to Admiral Nimitz. It allegedly was an urgent dispatch from a desperate aircraft carrier commander to Yamamoto. It read: "Send aid/Send it fast/Have lost face/Am losing ass."

Aboard *Yamoto,* the admiral surveyed the violent seascape with bewilderment, then stoically accepted defeat after two days of give-no-quarter combat. He signaled all ships still fighting to break off. The mauled armada scattered at top speed to the north and west toward Japanese waters, and the solemn and broken commander went to his cabin to pray for guidance and beg forgiveness from Emperor Hirohito.

Not only had a monumental battle been lost, but the Japanese had failed to land one man on Midway's beaches and, in Yamamoto's own words, "our one great hope for a negotiated peace" had vanished.

Midway was not without sobering cost to the victors. The carrier *Yorktown* and one of its destroyer escorts were sunk. Three hundred and seven men, most of them pilots and air crewmen, were killed or missing; 152 planes were lost. But Americans henceforth would think and speak of Midway as the place where valorous and outnumbered men wiped out Japanese strategy, and bought time to fire up the military might of the United States.

There was no doubt in Yamamoto's mind that the war would continue, but henceforth it would be a losing cause. The United States might still be on the defensive everywhere, but now he was certain that Japan's one main chance of capturing Hawaii, of slicing the Pacific sealanes, of attacking the West Coast, had been destroyed. Now it was just a matter of time before the Americans could gain the ultimate victory. Of this the admiral was certain.

The meaning of Midway's loss was soon clear to the Imperial War Council in Tokyo. Enemy forces continued for a time to consolidate conquests in southeast Asia and the south Pacific, but the days of rampant aggression came to an abrupt halt. There were further crippling setbacks for the Americans in south Pacific naval battles, but these were without lasting consequence; they were engagements fought by the Japanese in desperate attempts to hold the fruits of halcyon days of earlier victories.

Now the United States swung slowly, purposefully, to the attack. Each new campaign was bigger, more complicated, more costly, and always crucial as the long journey to Japan began. Marines invaded, suffered heavy casualties, and seized key strongholds: Guadalcanal, Bougainville, Tarawa, Kwajalein, Roi-Namur, Guam, Saipan, Tinian, and Peleliu. The Army beat back, then contained and defeated, the enemy in the jungles and mountains of New Guinea and snuffed out the threat of an Australian invasion. General MacArthur massed troops for the return to the Philippines.

Less than a year after Midway, Yamamoto—the brave, brilliant, realistic strategist and commander who had two fingers missing from his right hand—would die in the flaming crash of a transport plane, the victim of an aerial ambush by long-range Army P-38 fighters off Rabaul in distant New Britain.

Americans knew to the minute the time and place to shoot down his unarmed aircraft—a coded message had been intercepted with the flight plan and timetable. As at Midway, the supposedly secret information was put to devastating use. When told of Yamamoto's death, Nimitz called him "a tenacious and shrewd foe who did his job, sometimes too well to suit me."

4

Thus, on September 7, 1944, thirty-three months to the day after the Pearl Harbor attack and exactly forty-three years after he had entered the Naval Academy, Admiral Nimitz was meeting with his staff.

Allied forces were on the offensive on all fronts of the global war. Germany was being devastated by round-the-clock thousand-plane American and British bombing raids, and its ground forces were caught in a gigantic nutcracker with the United States Third Army slashing ever more deeply into the Fatherland from the west, and a five-million-man Russian steamroller assaulting it from the east.

American naval forces ranged virtually unmolested over millions of miles of the Pacific and had bottled up the Japanese fleet now guarding the sea approaches to the home islands. General MacArthur had mounted a mammoth island-hopping campaign to clear the way for the Army's invasion of Leyte and the liberation of the Philippines.

Victory in Europe still was the top priority of the Allies, and it must be won before they could unleash their overpowering military might against the Japanese. But the Joint Chiefs of Staff in Washington knew the Pacific conflict was about to enter its climactic months. And they were acrimoniously split over strategy for the momentous final moves to bring about the downfall of Japan.

Fundamental and deeply rooted differences in basic military concepts of how to win the Pacific war were compounded by the simmering personal hostility between Admiral Nimitz and General MacArthur. Each believed his strategy was the best, least costly, and quickest way to victory—and each sought the mantle of Supreme Commander in the invasion of Japan.

General George C. Marshall, chairman of the Joint Chiefs and the grand generalissimo of the Allies' globe-girdling war effort, was caught in the middle, a man on a tightrope attempting to balance the towering ambitions and military thinking of his two most brilliant and headstrong commanders in the Pacific.

MacArthur's strategy was the more grandiose. It called for the recapture of the entire Philippine archipelago and the seizure of

Okinawa and Formosa to protect his flanks, and then the landing of a million-man force on the Chinese mainland. From there would be mounted the final invasion and conquest of Japan.

Nimitz's scenario was more direct and possibly less sure of success, but he was ready to take the chance. It envisioned a herculean amphibious operation surpassing anything in history, even D-Day in Europe; a direct seaborne assault spearheaded by Marines to establish a beachhead on Kyushu, the southernmost of the Japanese home islands.

Unchallenged control of the skies over Japan and the thousands of miles of ocean approaches to it were vital to the success of both schemes. And the Joint Chiefs demanded several months of saturation air bombardment of Japanese industrial centers and military installations before *any* invasion would be approved.

They were convinced that CinCPac had the enemy fleet in hand— barring an unforeseen disaster. But Japanese airpower was still a matter of deep concern, especially with thousands of kamikaze planes and their legions of suicidal pilots ready to wreak havoc among American invaders.

Immediate strategy of the Joint Chiefs, regardless of whether their final imprimatur was on the MacArthur or Nimitz invasion scheme, was to bomb and burn the Japanese heartland with pulverizing air attacks. To do the massive job, hundreds of giant B-29 Superfort bombers were arriving each month in the war zone from the States with battle-ready crews. The four-motored behemoths were nearly twice as big, had more than double the range, speed, and armament— and carried several times the bomb load—of the B-17 Flying Forts and B-24 Liberators that were devastating Germany.

With the Marines' conquest of the Marianas in late June and most of July 1944, the United States had broken the last line of major island defenses guarding the approaches to Japan from the south—and had gained a land mass capable of handling massive numbers of Superforts. Within weeks, Army engineers and Navy construction battalions hacked out and paved three-mile-long runways where there had been palm trees and jungles among the lush hills of Guam, Saipan, and Tinian.

Even before the dirt scrapers and concrete mixers had finished, B-29s flew their first missions from the bases: small-scale daylight raids against Tokyo, Yokohama, and half-a-dozen other targets.

The bomb run to Japan was no milk run. It was, at best, a dangerous and fatiguing round trip of three thousand miles. At worst, it was hell in the skies that claimed heavy losses—casualties so severe, in fact, that General Curtis E. LeMay, commander of the 20th Air Force, said they couldn't be sustained for long.

Iwo Jima was the major reason. There was no way to skirt the island; it was halfway to Japan from the Marianas and squarely athwart the only direct flight path to targets. With Iwo Jima in Japanese hands, every mission was a cliffhanger. The island's primitive radar station worked well enough to give interceptors time to take off, gain altitude, and ambush Japan-bound formations with devastating losses. Fierce fighter attacks and deadly antiaircraft fire, triggered by word of impending attacks flashed by wireless from Iwo, would again hit the Superforts after they had made their bombing runs.

Crippled American planes trying to get home were easy targets for enemy pilots lurking in the skies around Iwo, and bombers based there made almost nightly harassing raids on Saipan's airfields.

This would end with Iwo's capture. So, in early July, General Marshall ordered that the island must be taken by mid-January, 1945. Then, instead of being an early-warning station and a base for enemy fighters, it would be a haven for shot-up Superforts, as well as those short of fuel for the 723-mile flight back to the Marianas. There were other important considerations: Iwo in American hands would provide an airbase for fighters to protect B-29s on the last dangerous leg of missions, and would secure the eastern oceanside flank of invasions of Okinawa and Formosa—if and when they were mounted.

Despite Marshall's edict, there was powerful behind-the-scenes maneuvering in Washington to scuttle Operation Detachment, the code name for the Iwo Jima invasion. It came from high Army brass, dissident members of the Joint Chiefs who didn't see eye-to-eye with their chairman, and various congressmen and senators. Their position was backed by a small but loud-voiced coterie of newspaper publishers led by William Randolph Hearst and Colonel Robert R. McCormick, the bombastic owner of the formerly isolationist *Chicago Tribune*. It was sparked by their determination to see MacArthur—and not Nimitz—named Supreme Allied Commander in the Pacific as Eisenhower was in Europe; and to make certain that the flamboyant general's plan to invade Japan was used to win the war.

When Admiral Nimitz learned of the contretemps, he sent a top aide to MacArthur's headquarters in Australia with a personal invitation to meet at Makalapa to reconcile their clashing strategies. The envoy waited for two days to see the general, and was given a thanks-but-no-thanks reply; the general was too busy planning his return to the Philippines to fly eight thousand miles to Hawaii.

But to confidants he made no secret of his real reasons: he was thoroughly disgruntled by the whole idea; he felt that a journey to CinCPac headquarters would undermine and weaken the status of his command; and that his proud public image would be tarnished in the nation's press by making it seem he was subservient to Nimitz. And since the Joint Chiefs already had told him to start planning Operation Causeway—the invasion of Formosa—after the Philippines campaign, he was certain this meant the Iwo Jima assault would be scrapped—General Marshall's order to Admiral Nimitz notwithstanding.

So the Monks of Makalapa met without MacArthur to set in motion the cumbersome military machine that would put the Marines ashore at Iwo. Two of the Army's most respected top brass—Lieutenant Generals Simon Bolivar Buckner and Millard F. Harmon—were there. To Nimitz's surprise, both put their strongest endorsement on the plan to take Iwo Jima and to abort the MacArthur proposal for Formosa and China.

While the careers of both would be enhanced under the general's plan, they were solidly against it for valid military reasons. In the Formosa campaign, Buckner was slated to lead the United States Tenth Army, a force of 250,000 troops, with Marines in the assault to take the beachhead. But he thought it would be impossible to muster that much manpower and the equipment and logistical support to conquer the 13,890-square-mile island of six-million-plus inhabitants just across a narrow straight from the Chinese mainland, where the Japanese had an estimated one million combat troops. Thus, he opted for Iwo. Within a year he became the highest ranking American killed in action during World War II when an artillery shell slammed down on his hillside command post during the battle for Okinawa.

Harmon was the highest ranking Army Air Corps general in the Pacific, and was as close to MacArthur as anyone outside his intimate clique; but the venture made no sense to him. The most logical way to shorten the war, he felt, was to batter Japan with saturation air

raids, and Iwo Jima's capture would give B-29s the clear flight paths
to bomb and burn the enemy homeland into submission. "I see no
advantage whatsoever," he said, "in the capture of Formosa."

The conference ended shortly before noon. Nimitz, with his welcome and unexpected Army support, was ready to speed ahead with
Operation Detachment. But he was in a quandary. MacArthur was
poised to begin the Philippines campaign and deep in the planning
of the Formosa adventure—despite what the admiral thought. And
with winning the war in Europe still the first priority, the Pacific
theater was hard-pressed for many of the vital necessities of combat.
There just weren't enough men and ships and ammunition and equipment to wage simultaneous battles on both Iwo Jima and Formosa.
To Nimitz, it must be one or the other.

There was only one way to resolve the dilemma: to put the question to the Joint Chiefs in a face-to-face confrontation. Nimitz was
aboard the flying boat *Mars* at daybreak for the flight to the mainland
and a hastily called conference at Treasure Island in foggy San Francisco Bay. Admiral Ernest J. King, close confidant of President Roosevelt, Chief of Naval Operations, and the Navy's man on the Joint
Chiefs, was waiting.

King's reputation for irascibility and hard questions was justified.
He had flown all night from Washington. The trip was bumpy and he
was in a foul mood. Storm flags were flying from the outset as the
CNO made it clear that he wanted to invade Formosa, as did the Joint
Chiefs; he intended to change General Marshall's mind about the Iwo
affair. But the Navy's top boss also was known for open-mindedness,
and Nimitz set out to make his case.

Nimitz, in his quiet way, laid out the strategic thinking, hammered hard with the endorsements of Buckner and Harmon, and was
backed up in his presentation by Rear Admiral Raymond A. Spruance
and Captain Forrest P. Sherman. Spruance was the admiral's shaker
and mover, trusted long-time friend, and his second-in-command.
Forty-three-year-old Sherman was Spruance's number two and headed
the Fleet War Plans Division. His summary was later described by
Nimitz as "a masterful job that carried the day." When the five-hour
meeting ended, the Monks of Makalapa had changed King's mind.

It was another uncomfortable fourteen-hour flight back to Washington, but Admiral King, who hadn't been to bed for three days, flew
back that night. At ten o'clock the next morning he recommended in

a special meeting with the Joint Chiefs that the assault on Formosa
be canceled and Iwo Jima be invaded as ordered by General Marshall
in the first place. King told them why he had changed his mind; the
war planners agreed to a man with Nimitz's reasoning.

The decision was flashed to the Monks in San Francisco. It went
to General MacArthur in Australia where, aides later said, he now
began to have serious doubts about being named Supreme Allied
Commander, Pacific, and to believe the invasion of Japan would be
Nimitz's show.

Again the *Mars* flew Nimitz to Pearl Harbor where, with Spruance
and Sherman, he told the other Monks what had happened: Iwo Jima
was next on the timetable of what he smilingly called "the Tokyo
Express."

5

Had they known of it, the Japanese high command wouldn't have been
surprised by the decision. The warlords had felt for months that an
attempt to take Iwo was inevitable, and that if it fell, there was no
way to keep the Americans from assaulting the home islands. With
the downfall of the Marianas and the capture of the last bastions of
the main defense line in the central Pacific, Emperor Hirohito had
ordered an all-out build-up of Iwo Jima. He personally selected the
one general he deemed divinely suited to make the volcanic outcropping an impregnable fortress.

For nearly four centuries, no one, not even the Japanese, had
paid much attention to Iwo Jima and the two smaller islands that made
up what some geography books called the Bonin Islands and others
the Nanpo Shoto—the Japanese words for Volcano Islands. They were
first charted in 1543 by a Spanish sea captain, Bernard de Torres.
They were visited in 1673 by an English explorer named Gore, who
called Iwo Jima "Sulphur Island" because it reeked of the vile-smelling
mineral. Hanging down like a crescent from Honshu Island, the archipelago lies from 650 to 700 miles almost due south of Tokyo Bay.
In addition to Iwo, the chain consists of Haha Jima and Chichi Jima.

A Russian named Krusenstern had stopped at Iwo in 1805 but
hadn't bothered to claim it for the czar. Captain Reuben Coffin, of

the whaler *Transit* out of Nantucket, anchored at Haha Jima in 1823 and claimed it for the United States. Commodore Matthew Perry of the United States stopped at Chichi Jima in 1853. Seeing the possibilities of the entire Nanpo Shoto as coaling stations and supply bases for ships then starting to ply the Pacific in growing numbers in quests for international trade and whales, he wanted to plant the American flag. But Congress would have nothing to do with Perry's idea or Coffin's claim.

Foreigners came to Chichi Jima in 1827 when the island was settled by a polyglot mixture of adventurers from Hawaii. They claimed British sovereignty, but were led by Nathaniel Savory from Massachusetts. The group included families of Englishmen, Portuguese, Italians, and Hawaiians. Until World War II put an end to it, descendants celebrated Washington's Birthday and the Fourth of July, but didn't bother to observe national holidays of other homelands. The events always were marked with fireworks, picnics, speeches in English, and a proud display of the American flag.

Japan finally made formal claim to the Nanpo Shoto in 1861 in a move never challenged by other nations, and piecemeal colonization began in 1887. Fewer than one thousand pioneers ventured out of Japan, and the islands remained obscure outposts, producing sulphur and small amounts of sugar cane. But even then, they were considered part of the homeland and were governed as Tokyo's most remote suburb.

Japanese soldiers first appeared early in the twentieth century, and the islands were placed off-limits to foreigners. During World War I, Chichi Jima had been armed with several batteries of naval guns and had a wireless and weather station. These installations remained after the armistice of 1918—a small but vital backwater outpost for Japanese forces guarding the southern approaches to the home islands.

So security-minded were the Japanese that in 1937 a large sign was posted in Japanese and English at Iwo's East Boat Basin, the only place on the island where people and supplies could be landed. It read:

"Trespassing, surveying, photographing, sketching, modeling, etc., upon or of these premises without previous official permission are prohibited by the Military Secrets Protection Law. Any offender in this regard will be punished with the full extent of the law." Marines found the warning, bullet-pocked and weathered, when they landed.

On December 7, 1941, the Nanpo Shoto was garrisoned by 1,400 troops, all on Chichi Jima. Iwo Jima became the headquarters and focal point of activity in 1943; it was the only island suitable for airfield construction, and work started on Chidori, the first of three airstrips.

After Kwajalein and Eniwetok were seized in February, 1943, Iwo's build-up accelerated. With the fall of the Marianas, it went into high gear: an around-the-clock grind with soldiers and sailors, and a battalion of Korean laborers burrowing miles of tunnels and building hundreds of concrete gun emplacements, bunkers, and pillboxes at a frantic pace to make the island impregnable.

To put all the pieces together and make them work, to plan and command the defenses of the island fortress, came Emperor Hirohito's hand-picked general. He was Lieutenant General Tadamichi Kuribayashi, a man cast in an historic military mold.

Five generations of his ancestors had served in the armies of six emperors, and he carried the tradition with pride and zealous dedication. Because of Kuribayashi's training, discipline, desire, and devotion to duty and the Emperor, Hirohito was certain he was the right warrior, at the right place and at the right time, to save Japan from the disgrace of invasion and defeat. As the Americans would find at frightful cost, he was to perform exceedingly well.

Kuribayashi was husky, even for a samurai warrior. He weighed just under two hundred pounds, all of it hard muscle, and carried it on a five-feet nine-inch frame—somewhat tall for a Japanese. Thirty of his fifty-three years had been spent at duty stations and military schools in Japan, at embassies in the United States and Canada, and commanding combat troops in the victorious sweep of Manchuria and China.

Kuribayashi was a thirty-seven-year-old captain and deputy military attaché at the embassy in Washington in 1928. For the next two years he crisscrossed the United States in almost constant travel— time spent in observing Americans and practicing his fluent English in such diverse locales as Buffalo, New York, and the U.S. Army Cavalry School at Fort Bliss, Texas, where he studied the then important tactics of horse-mounted combat.

Brigadier General George V. H. Mosely, commandant of the school, gave the likable captain an inscribed portrait when he returned to his homeland. "With high regards and esteem," the inscription read. "I shall never forget our happy association together in America. Best wishes to you and Japan." The memento still hangs, with other treasured memorabilia, in the home of Kuribayashi's son in a small home on the outskirts of Tokyo.

Captain Kuribayashi was devoted to his family and unhappy that Japanese policy kept his wife Toshii and young son Taro from being with him on his travels in the United States. Twice a week he wrote them chatty letters, often embellished with excellent sketches of places he had seen and people he had met. In one more serious than usual, he said:

"The United States is the last country in the world Japan should fight. Its industrial potential is huge and fabulous, and the people are energetic and versatile. One must never underestimate the Americans' fighting ability."

Kuribayashi's first sight of Iwo Jima came eighty-eight days before the Monks of Makalapa made the final decision to invade the island. The previous night he had had a private farewell audience with Emperor Hirohito, an almost unheard-of honor for a commoner.

Before praying to his ancestors and begging their blessing and guidance on his mission, he wrote a final note to his brother. "I may not return alive from this assignment," it said in classic bold Japanese characters set down with traditional brush and black ink, "but let me assure you that I shall fight to the best of my ability, so that no disgrace will be brought upon our family. I will fight as a son of Kuribayashi, the samurai, and will behave in such a manner as to deserve the name of Kuribayashi. May my ancestors guide me."

At dawn he was the solitary passenger aboard a war-torn four-motored flying boat much smaller, slower, and older than Nimitz's *Mars*. With a crew of three, the lumbering plane was loaded with high-priority cargo—official dispatches, long overdue mail, some electronic gear, and urgently needed medicine to treat malaria and dysentery. Even without the threat of invasion, Iwo Jima was not a healthy place.

Admiral Teiichi Matsunaga, commander of Iwo's naval forces and the general's second-in-command, paced the East Boat Landing two miles north of Mount Suribachi on the black beach of coarse volcanic sand on the island's eastern shoreline. He had been waiting more than three hours—the exact time of the plane's arrival was unknown because of radio silence. The Japanese had learned a lesson from Admiral Yamamoto's death.

Matsunaga heard the drone of the motors; then the flying boat broke through the low-hanging gray clouds, banked around the summit of Suribachi, and landed in the choppy waves of the ocean three hundred yards offshore. Kuribayashi knew from photographs and briefings what to expect. And there it was: ugly and small.

From the air it looked like an overdone pork chop, or an off-color and lopsided pear with Suribachi at the stem. The island was sweltering hot by day, and bone-marrow cold at night. Where giant boulders didn't dominate the landscape, steaming sulphur beds and shifting volcanic ash left little chance for vegetation—just a few scrub trees, some dwarf brush, and no trace of fresh water anywhere.

By 1943, Iwo was armed to the teeth. Its garrison carried 5,170 troops. Chidori Airfield bristled with fifty-two first-line fighter planes. The island had an arsenal of fourteen large navy coastal defense guns, thirteen heavy artillery pieces, 4,652 rifles, more than two hundred light and heavy machine guns, and thirty twin-mounted antiaircraft weapons. Manpower and firepower would mushroom in the months ahead as the island braced for the inevitable.

Kuribayashi knew why he was on Iwo Jima. Emperor Hirohito had made his assignment clear, and his briefings by the Supreme War Council left no doubt about Iwo's importance and the extreme gravity of the situation. Iwo Jima must be defended to the death of the last man. It was not only of far greater importance than its size indicated, but it was part and parcel of the home islands. If Iwo Jima fell to the Americans, it was inevitable Japan would fall too.

Tadamachi Kuribayashi, the samurai warrior, knew this as he marched in solemn cadence up the slope of the dirt road. The only sounds were the gentle lapping of the surf and the muted stride of Matsunaga and an eleven-man honor guard of stalwart Imperial Marines marching a respectful three paces behind the general.

They were escorting him to his new headquarters. Like Admiral Nimitz's at Makalapa, it was on an extinct volcano.

February 19, 1945. H-hour minus twenty minutes: First waves of Higgins boats begin run to shore. (*Robert R. Campbell*)

"Bombs Away!" photo may have been a pre-invasion security leak. (*U.S. Navy*)

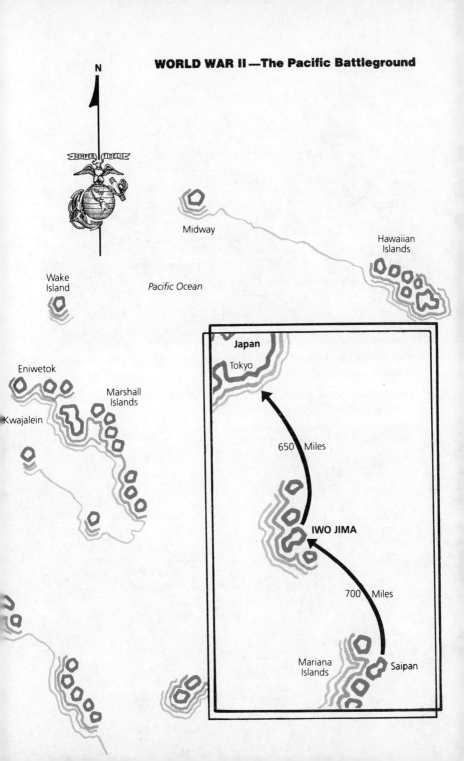

WORLD WAR II — The Pacific Battleground

N

SEMPER FIDELIS

Midway

Hawaiian
Islands

Wake
Island

Pacific Ocean

Eniwetok

Marshall
Islands

Kwajalein

Japan

Tokyo

650 Miles

IWO JIMA

700 Miles

Mariana
Islands

Saipan

Five-inch guns of destroyer fire at Japanese positions on Iwo as assault is launched. (*Arthur J. Kiely, Jr.*)

H-hour plus ninety minutes: LSMs with tanks and troops head for the beaches. (*Arthur J. Kiely, Jr.*)

D-Day minus three: troop transports, part of the U.S. invasion armada of some five hundred ships, steam toward Iwo. (*Arthur J. Kiely, Jr.*)

H-hour minus thirty minutes: first wave of amtracs leave line of departure. (*Arthur J. Kiely, Jr.*)

H-hour minus five minutes: pall of smoke covers Iwo as amtracs near beaches. (*U.S. Navy*)

"Howlin' Mad" Smith at final press briefing before D-Day. *Right foreground, left to right*: Kelly Turner, James Forrestal and Harry Hill. (*Arthur J. Kiely, Jr.*)

PART TWO

A Gathering
of
Warriors

1

Hawaii's soft trade winds had chased the morning showers and low-hanging clouds to sea. At Pearl Harbor, below the heights of Makalapa, the weather was muggy. The humming fans barely stirred the already hot and sticky air that comes to the islands in late fall. It was a few minutes before eight o'clock, and Admiral Nimitz's staff had already started on the day's schedule.

Nimitz, a stickler for punctuality, long hours, and hard work, was forty-five minutes into his dispatches and papers. He had already fired a pleasing score on the pistol range, hiked a brisk four miles—tail-wagging pet schnauzer Makalapa at his heels—before arriving at his sparse office at the Navy Yard's submarine base. An American flag and his admiral's colors flanked his desk, behind which was a big steam pipe. The only other decoration was an autographed photograph of President Roosevelt.

While the admiral was keen on the convivial niceties and relaxation of after-hours social life, liked his cocktails before dinner with nightly guests at Makalapa, symphony records playing softly in the background, during the day he was strictly business. There wasn't a couch or a visitor's chair in his office. Those who came to see him stood before his desk, stated their concerns, and quickly moved out. If they had a question or a problem, they usually left with an answer.

A week had passed since the decision had been made to invade Iwo Jima, and Nimitz had called a conclave of the men who would command the operation. Fifteen paces down the corridor, Ray Spruance was deep in paperwork at a long stand-up desk built to his specifications. Known as the "quiet admiral" because of his disdain for publicity, he would go to Iwo in command of the battle.

In cubicles and two large "bull pen" rooms, junior officers scanned overnight dispatches from the mainland, from ships and submarines at sea, and from faraway islands in the battlezone. They were a conglomeration of Navy men, Marines, and a scattered few from the Army; cryptographers and intelligence officers, communications men, experts in weaponry and logistics, doctors making plans to treat the wounded, other people to see that the dead were collected and buried, clergy and finance officers, censors and public relations men—all with the special backgrounds and skills to run a giant, cumbersome military machine.

How well their work was done could mean victory or disaster before the first shot was fired across the beaches. So the planners had begun to determine the needs of battle: thousands of men, countless numbers of tanks and bulldozers, mountains of artillery shells and millions of rounds of rifle and machine gun ammunition, enough food and supplies to fill the larder of a medium-sized city in the States. And an armada of ships to carry the cargoes and deliver them to the target on schedule.

Seventy-three mass-produced Liberty and Victory transports would haul the troops and combat necessities. Each would have rations for sixty days, 6,000 five-gallon cans of water, gasoline for twenty-five days for all vehicles, 5,263 pounds of grease, ammunition for all assault troops and weapons aboard, bandages and medicine for thirty days, maintenance materials for all weapons and vehicles, spare parts for communications equipment, and thirty days of general supplies for all troops.

The weight for each Marine was 1,322 pounds, and every item was needed. Paper and pencils. Blood plasma and bandages. Matches and maps. Bullets and batteries. Holy water and white crosses. Splints and shoelaces. Spark plugs and smoke pots. Dog food and garbage cans. Welding rods and asphalt-making machines. Flashlights and flares and fingerprint ink. Carbon paper and house paint. Blankets and light bulbs. Toilet paper and socks. Duplicating machines and movie projectors. The Fifth Division would carry 100,000,000 cigarettes and enough food to feed the population of Atlanta, Georgia, for a month. On Iwo Jima there was no supermarket or shopping center around the corner.

Despite the staggering detail in planning and mounting an invasion nearly four thousand miles away—and the fact that two-thirds of the assault force would travel that distance and farther—Nimitz faced more serious problems.

He knew it would take his first team to capture Iwo Jima: the coterie of hard and tested battle commanders who had made the long trek northward through the Pacific since the darkest days of Guadalcanal and won an unbroken chain of victories. Above all, he realized that ultimate success at Iwo Jima would be in the hands of the Marine assault troops—dedicated young men would have to take the island in bloody head-on combat.

But he had much more than Iwo Jima on his mind. Despite the burgeoning might of the Navy—it now had 1,161 warships, most of them in the Pacific—he still felt the United States didn't have enough men and ships and planes and ammunition to cover millions of miles of ocean and to carry out simultaneously more than one invasion.

But as things were developing, two invasions *would* be roaring at the same time: MacArthur's in the Philippines, and the Marines' at Iwo. The fleet's battleships and carrier task forces must constantly roam the seas to guard against possible forays by the still-potent Japanese navy. And massive carrier attacks and seaborne shelling were on the schedule to blast Tokyo Bay as a prelude to the Iwo landing.

It all came down to one inescapable certainty: Nimitz wouldn't be able to hammer Iwo Jima with the pre-invasion naval bombardment needed to take the beaches without heavy losses. This was only part of the admiral's predicament. Even more serious was the interservice and personal animosity and bickering among members of his top brass— the very team of warriors who must mastermind and lead the campaign. And always, simmering just below the boiling point, was his skittish relationship with MacArthur.

Vice Admiral Richmond Kelly Turner was going to Iwo in tactical command under Ray Spruance. Kelly Turner was the hard-driving three-star ramrod of the assault, a job he had done in every Marine landing beginning at Guadalcanal. Rough, tough, aggressive, and abrasive, he was "Terrible Turner" to the officers and men who had suffered his ire, and to most war correspondents.

Rear Admiral Harry W. Hill was the two-star commander of Task Force 53. He would see that the Marines got to Iwo in the largest armada of American naval craft so far sent to battle in the Pacific. He liked being known to reporters, and to his officers and men, as "Just Plain Harry," a quiet, competent, unobtrusive counterbalance who could often smooth hackles ruffled by Turner's violent temper.

Rear Admiral W. H. P. Blandy had command of Task Force 52. Its job was the pre-invasion softening up of the beachhead, and knocking out the enemy's big guns both on Mount Suribachi and in the center of the island. "Spike" Blandy knew his work—he had been at

Normandy, and had covered all the Marine landings in the central Pacific.

And there was Lieutenant General Holland M. Smith, top Marine commander in the Pacific.

He was "Howlin' Mad" Smith in the headlines, news stories, and often harsh editorials back home, as well as to the troops of the Fleet Marine Force who fought the battles. But "my Marines," as he constantly called them, were devoted to the Old Man. When they spoke of him as "Howlin' Mad," it was with a warm smile and a chuckle— a sharp contrast to their reference to "Terrible Turner."

Smith's nickname had followed him for forty years, since his days as a second lieutenant in the Philippines. Though he was exceedingly loud-spoken, often profane, and tough when he thought the situation demanded, he contended that the "Howlin' Mad" tag was more the result of its similarity in sound to his given name—Holland McTyeire— rather than to his disposition.

At sixty-two, he was the oldest three-star combat general in the armed services. Because of age and serious diabetes, it had taken the personal intervention of President Roosevelt to get the aging warrior sent overseas to command men in battle. The Commander in Chief knew a fighter when he saw one, and he was determined to have Smith despite repeated calls for his scalp.

It was always the same reason: terrible Marine casualties—especially after the bloody invasion of Tarawa, where 3,056 Second Division men were killed or wounded in seventy-two hours of combat in November 1943. Loud demands for Smith's dismissal came from families of many servicemen, but usually not Marines; from some members of Congress; and some newspapers, notably those published by William Randolph Hearst and Robert R. McCormick. "Butcher...cold-blooded murderer...indiscriminate waster of human life" were the scathing words used in McCormick's *Chicago Tribune* demanding that the general be removed from his command.

Smith took the heat with outward calm; it came with the job. But he felt deep inward pain and monumental frustration at what he saw as misdirected and often politically motivated attacks by foes of the Marine Corps and the President, whose eldest son was a Marine with battle stars and decorations earned in combat.

The murderous villain, the wanton killer of young men, Smith knew, was the war itself. And it was especially tragic and costly in the islands of the Pacific, where each campaign meant crossing reefs and lagoons in tiny landing craft and hitting exposed beaches in the face of blistering enemy fire; of rooting out the Japanese from heavily entrenched blockhouses and bunkers in frontal assault; of always carrying the battle to the enemy who were dug in and waiting. Let those at home believe he was to blame if they wanted to, he had broad shoulders. But let them remember that he was devoted to his men— and they to him; and that he had shared with them the dangers and rigors of combat, and wept long and openly over their suffering and losses.

Before and after every campaign, "Howlin' Mad" went to the mat with Ray Spruance and Kelly Turner about pre-invasion naval bombardment and air support—or the lack of it. "If the Marines had received better cooperation from the Navy our casualties would have been lower," he said in a savage condemnation of Navy brass after the war. "More naval gunfire would have saved many lives," he declared. "I had to beg for gunfire, and I rarely received what the situation called for."

The chasm between Smith and the admirals was not just over naval gunfire and air support; it involved even thornier matters of bitter personality conflicts and steaming interservice rivalries. The depth of the split was kept locked in the secrets of Makalapa until after the war, when Smith published his memoirs.

"The Navy transported us, landed us and protected us against Japanese naval and air attack," he wrote. "We could not have reached the islands without the Navy, but at that point their duties should have ended." The general didn't name individuals, but Spruance and Turner always went with the assault forces, and the inference was clear: "Instead they tried to continue running the show. . . . It was admirals who wanted to be generals who imperiled victory among the Pacific islands."

Smith was often at loggerheads with Nimitz. He believed the admiral personified an ingrained Navy state of mind that looked down on the Marine Corps as a poor relative, and that it must always be treated as such. He thought Nimitz too protective of the Monks; he called them Nimitz's "myrmidons," and believed some should be sacked for glaring incompetence. His autobiography painted the CinCPac as a nervous opportunist.

"Never an exuberant man, he could work up, in his quiet way, an extremely pessimistic mood," the truculent general said. "Admiral Nimitz was riding to fame on the shoulders of the Marines, so what did he have to worry about? The Japanese were on the run. Nimitz couldn't lose. He knew the Marines would win. If we didn't, he probably would be yanked out of his job and perhaps the Army would be in command."

Smith didn't hide his feelings from Nimitz. Any hint of deception or the Machiavellian was totally foreign to his character and beneath the dignity of an officer and gentleman, a devout Methodist from Alabama. Nimitz was stung deeply by Smith's outbursts; he resented them, and thought the general often hit below the belt. But he abided "Howlin' Mad" Smith as General Eisenhower did the peccadilloes of "Blood 'n' Guts" George Patton in Europe, and for the same reason. Both were fighting generals who could and did win battles.

Nonetheless, the admiral was finding the general a heavy cross to bear. He was sure he suffered from severe military myopia; couldn't understand the vast scope of the Pacific war and how it was being won; that he had a mental block to armed forces unity—a vital necessity.

In many ways, Nimitz was right. The Joint Chiefs had been told in no uncertain terms that the Army wouldn't let its forces ever again serve under Smith's command as they had at Roi-Namur and in the Marianas. During those battles, "Howlin' Mad" had cashiered two Army generals for not moving fast enough against the Japanese. The Army's lack of aggressiveness, Smith said, was costing the lives of "my Marines" and needlessly prolonging the fighting.

But despite the gaping breach, the in-fighting, the personality clashes, *this* was Nimitz's first team; and whenever the Japanese were faced in battle, it functioned with fantastic precision and dedication. Individual differences would again be buried to plan and achieve the conquest of Iwo Jima; for each man was a deep-rooted patriot, a dedicated military professional.

Nimitz's first team didn't stop with these top men. The assault force would be led by generals and colonels, all veterans of earlier battles. Most had won their combat spurs as young second lieutenants in the great engagements in France in World War I. They had honed their military skills as captains and majors in the testy "banana wars" of the Caribbean and Central America in the 1920s and early thirties, and now wore the eagles and stars of battle commanders who had met and defeated the Japanese in the Pacific.

Major General Harry Schmidt, called "the Dutchman," would be ranking commander ashore during the battle. His Fifth Amphibious Corps would be the largest force of Marines ever in combat. The troops were from the Third, Fourth and Fifth Marine Divisions. Like Schmidt himself, division commanders were two-star generals.

Graves B. Erskine would lead the Third; its men had driven the Japanese from Bougainville and Guam in costly campaigns. Clifton B. Cates would have the Fourth, proud conquerors of Roi-Namur, Saipan, and Tinian. Keller E. Rockey was CG of the Fifth. It was to see action for the first time, but it was heavily manned with officers and noncoms who had fought and been wounded at Guadalcanal, Tarawa, and other bloody battles, had recovered, and were assigned to the fledgling division. Others were rotated from home leave and were on another tour of combat duty.

Now Admiral Nimitz had assembled the planners and movers for the first of three final conferences before D-Day. In a soft voice more suited to a blue-chip corporation's wood-paneled board room than the map-covered war chamber of Makalapa, he outlined the battle plan.

General Smith chomped an unlit cigar, pale blue eyes impassive behind gold-rimmed glasses, as the CinCPac ran down a check list of radio intercepts, late intelligence reports, and current reconnaissance photos made from aircraft and submarine periscopes. They confirmed a frantic build-up of the island's already formidable defenses. The campaign had to mesh with General MacArthur's final push to recapture the Philippines, he said, and it must dovetail with landings on Okinawa slated for the first week in April. Because of these operations—all demanding heavy commitments of battleships, aircraft carriers, cruisers, and destroyers—Smith, like Nimitz, felt it would be impossible to pound Iwo Jima with the pre-invasion bombardment necessary before the Marines landed.

One of the Monks recalled glancing at "Howlin' Mad" at that moment. "The general scowled and slowly removed his glasses with one hand and the cigar with the other," he told a friend years later, "and began speaking with his slow Alabama drawl."

"This will be the bloodiest fight in Marine Corps history," Smith said in a low voice, looking straight at Nimitz. "We'll catch seven kinds of hell on the beaches, and that will be just the beginning." He brushed squinting eyes and replaced his glasses. "The fighting will be fierce, and the casualties will be awful, but my Marines will take the damned island."

There was dead silence; the war room seethed with tension. The general still glared at the admiral. "How much bombardment will we get before H-Hour?" Smith wanted to know.

Nimitz turned to Spruance for the answer. "Three days," he said. Surprisingly, there was no explosion from "Howlin' Mad." But his face flushed, and he bristled with controlled rage as his glare shifted to Spruance.

"Damn it, Ray, three days won't do the job." The words came out softly. "I need at least ten days of battleship and cruiser and carrier plastering. Otherwise the carnage will be unbelievable. God knows our losses will be horrible regardless of what we do." Spruance didn't respond, and Nimitz remained impassive. The matter was out of his hands; there was little, if anything, he could do. He would ask the Joint Chiefs to hold off D-Day for thirty days from the now-scheduled January 20th. This might give time for more aerial bombardment, but it wouldn't free any more naval firepower. There simply wasn't any more to be had, Nimitz said.

General Schmidt made a final plea for at least eight days of shelling, but to no avail, although Nimitz did appear to give a little: Iwo Jima would get a maximum of four days of pre-invasion naval softening; and that, only if the weather was perfect. Otherwise it would be three.

Smith fought to control his bitterness, and Schmidt was more disheartened than he'd ever been in thirty years as a Marine. But they both accepted the inevitable; Nimitz and Spruance had made their decision, and the Marines would have to do what they must do: take Iwo Jima's beaches, and the island, with whatever the Navy gave them. General Smith would again suffer the epithets and be accused of wasting lives. He would carry to his grave the bitter conclusion that ten days of shelling and more carrier-based bombardment before D-Day would have saved thousands of Marines.

Nimitz called two more sessions of the planners and commanders, and there was a smidgen of good news for the Marines at the final conference. The Joint Chiefs had pushed back Iwo's D-Day for one month. But this was final; there would be no turning back.

Iwo Jima would be invaded February 19, 1945.

2

An invasion is like an avalanche; once started, it must run its course. Now it was up to the Marines to take the island. They would have to take it the hard way: with riflemen and tanks and artillery, pillbox by pillbox, bunker by bunker in close combat. The ultimate weapon would be a young man with a bayoneted rifle.

Major General Julian C. Smith, who was at Tarawa as the Second Division's commander, once put the picture in sharp perspective during a turbulent session with the Monks. "Even though you Navy officers do come in to about one thousand yards," he said, "I remind you that you have a little more armor. I want you to know that Marines are crossing the beach with bayonets, and the only armor they'll have is a khaki shirt."

Troops had been training for months for Iwo. For them, life was boring, rugged, and stereotyped. Its formula was rigid and simple: rigorous training for combat; then invasion of another island; then more training, followed by another invasion of another island. Unlike Europe, where Americans liberated cities and countries and enjoyed the rewards of conquering heroes, the Pacific was a sad and different story.

Liberty was almost unheard of; there was nothing to do anyhow— no place to go, nothing to see on the remote disease-infested jungle islands where the Marines had their tented base camps. Entertainment was a nightly outdoor movie, rain or shine—and it rained much of the time; the same films were repeated so often that bored viewers repeated dialogue, word for word, with the actors. If a USO show came, it was second-rate. The pattern was always the same unless you were wounded and flown stateside for hospitalization and treatment. Then, after recuperation and thirty days' leave, you'd most likely be sent back to the Pacific—and more combat—unless wounds were serious enough for a man to be invalided out of service.

Marines never knew where, or when, they would fight next; but they knew they would have to take another "rock" no one ever heard of, and that buddies would be wounded and killed; that they might be among the casualties, and, if they were lucky, live. They were told code names of the operations; this time it was Operation Detachment; the target, "Island X." And they were told this campaign would be rough—"rougher than a corn cob," as one colonel put it. Only just before D-Day, when they were aboard transports en route to the beachhead, would they learn the identity of the objective and where it was.

On Maui, the lush and mountainous island seventy-five miles southeast of Honolulu, the Fourth Division got the word: "Saddle up and move out." It went to the Fifth Division on Hawaii, the Big Island, the same distance beyond Maui. The Third Division, 3,021 nautical miles away on Guam, was alerted: "Wind up training and embark by the first week in February."

Veteran "old salts" sensed that the next operation would be a "real man-killer, no pun intended," in the words of a gunnery sergeant who'd fought at Guadalcanal. Ruggedness of training, always back-breakingly strenuous as another campaign neared, was the clue.

Troops were pushed harder than ever before in field problems with flamethrower teams and demolitions men. Every day, on each of the islands, the men scrambled up steep slopes, rehearsing frontal attacks against mock pillboxes and bunkers. They trained under live fire from artillery, mortars, and machine guns, and zooming Marine dive bombers added further realism to the exercises. Thirty-mile forced marches, with full combat packs and weapons, added stamina to men already in top shape. It was a dawn-to-dusk schedule that sometimes went through the night, tailored to harden and hone them for Iwo's wicked terrain and defenses.

Battalions and regiments blessed with heavy contingents of old-timers were at peak efficiency. But each division embarked for Iwo with 2,650 replacements, men overseas only a matter of weeks. With them it was a different and worrisome matter. Two hundred and fifty were new second lieutenants, fresh from platoon leaders' school at Quantico, Virginia. Troops were recruits straight from boot camp with little advanced combat training, or older Marines from desk jobs at stateside posts. Eight thousand men facing a baptism of battle gen-erated deep concern, from General Smith down to the platoon level.

Many replacements were less than a year from civilian life, some of them bitter, angry, and confused over being drafted into the Marine Corps. Being in the Army or Navy, they felt, offered a better chance of living. Many had wives and children and were in their late twenties or early thirties—old men for Marines.

Combat cram courses were given the replacements before boarding ship, but it was a tragically futile experience. It was hoped that at Iwo they could work in relatively safe shore parties unloading cargo. But from the first hour of the invasion, losses were so heavy that the new men were flung immediately into savage fighting, where lack of combat knowledge made many of them instant casualties. Countless numbers were hit before learning the name of their nearest comrade, much less that of their commanding officer.

On Christmas Day, vanguard elements of the Fifth Division boarded the attack transport *Athene*. Many of the 27,518 residents of Hilo, the island of Hawaii's only large town, cheered as the troops marched to the docks. The Big Island was proud of its Marine division, and hoped it would be back soon with most of the men safe. On Christmas Eve they, and the Fourth Division on Maui, had dined in scrumptious style. "Feeding the lambs and sending them to slaughter," said a sardonic oldtimer.

Troops far-sighted enough to hoard beer from scant rations of four bottles a month used it to cap celebrations. Grapefruit or pineapple juice, laced with sick-bay medicinal alcohol, packed a wallop of Christmas cheer for a lucky few; they had friends among Navy corpsmen and doctors. Chapels were crowded for midnight services, but many men just took it easy.

The Third Division also had its Christmas spread, but for its troops more training was still ahead. Since they were fifteen hundred miles nearer Iwo, they wouldn't embark for another five weeks.

On December 27, the Fourth Division came down from Camp Maui, fifteen hundred feet up Haleakala, the world's largest active volcano. A blessed handful from the division had liberty in Honolulu when five transports put in at Pearl Harbor to load more ammunition.

Streets were jammed with servicemen and civilians. Bars jumped with loud chatter and jarring juke boxes and were wall to wall with people paying sky-high prices for drinks. In every saloon there were at least ten men to every woman. Unless you came very early, or waited in a very long line, you couldn't squeeze into the packed USO or YMCA. Overpriced hamburgers and hot dogs quickly sold out at lunchrooms. Seats were filled in every movie house. But even if liberty meant nothing more than walking the narrow streets and watching people and flashing neon signs, it was good to see civilization. Many would never see it again.

Before weighing anchor for the rendezvous area off Saipan, Fourth and Fifth Division assault troops made final rehearsal landings on Maui's southeast coast and on Kahoolawe, the smallest island in the Hawaiian chain, but five times larger than Iwo Jima. Like most dry runs, the exercises were chaotic.

Several transports ran into bad weather and didn't arrive in time to send landing craft to the beaches. Ubiquitous amphibian trucks, officially designated as DUKWS and universally known as "ducks" because of their ability to operate at sea and ashore, weren't put in the water; it was deemed unwise to expose their cargoes of ammunition to salt-water corrosion. Offshore reefs and choppy waves scuttled plans to land tanks and artillery.

The brass was not overly distressed. Like people in show business, they believed in the axiom that "a poor dress rehearsal means a good opening." It had happened that way in the past, and all hands hoped it would hold true at Iwo Jima.

By the first week in January, Fourth and Fifth Division ships had vanished from the islands. It would be forty days before Marines aboard them would feel land under their feet. Then it would be the tortuous black sands of Iwo Jima, and the island would be shaking and roaring with explosions from General Kuribayashi's big guns and heavy mortars.

As the Marines finished training and headed for Iwo, the Japanese worked night and day to make the island even more impregnable, but it was already feeling the might of American naval and airpower. The island was blasted December 8 by the heaviest air attack so far in the Pacific war, when 212 heavy bombers and long-range fighters plastered Chidori Airfield and heavy naval gun emplacements. All returned to the Marianas without loss; the Japanese lost six interceptors.

On Christmas Eve, Navy cruisers delivered an unwelcome package. Four moved to within a mile of shore to unload two thousand rounds of eight-inch shells. The enemy responded Christmas night with a six-plane bomber strike against Saipan. They eluded the island's radar, destroying four B-29s and damaging another eleven. Navy cruisers were off Iwo again on December 27 and fired another twelve hundred rounds of eight-inch shells, sinking two small freighters near shore. There was no retaliation this time against Saipan; nor would enemy planes ever again hit the Marianas.

The battle for Iwo Jima had been joined. There would be no letup until the island was invaded and conquered. Beginning with the December 8 attack by B-29 Superforts and B-24 Liberators, the island would be pummeled for seventy-two consecutive days by aerial bombardment or spasmodic, but heavy naval shelling from close-in off-shore.

During the first eleven days of January, Army bombers hammered Iwo in daylight with 15,000 tons of explosives. The first battleship, the brand-new *Indiana*, in action for the first time, appeared off the island on January 25 and fired 1,300 sixteen-inch shells into it in daylong salvos. The same day four cruisers slammed another 1,300 eight-inch rounds on the shuddering target, sweeping the beaches and Chidori Airfield from end to end. Air photos showed nearly five thousand craters on one square mile of rubbled terrain, and other attacks came daily from the sea or air until troops hit the beaches on H-Hour of February 19.

But to what ultimate result? General Smith said the air strikes and Navy shelling were virtually meaningless, and minced no words in his critique: "All this added up to a terrific total of destructive effort which the uninitiated might expect to blast any island off the military map, level every defense, no matter how strong, and wipe out the garrison," his memoirs said. "But nothing of the kind happened. Like the worm which becomes stronger the more you cut it up, Iwo Jima thrived on our bombardment. The airfields were kept inactive by our attacks and some installations were destroyed, but the main body of defenses not only remained physically intact but they strengthened markedly," he wrote.

As General Kuribayashi braced for the inevitable, Admiral Nimitz moved his headquarters and staff to Guam. Although Guam had become a powerful base, it was still in the war zone. Nimitz wanted to be nearer the action, to keep tight control over the steamrolling events about to unfold at Iwo and the other operations to follow on the timetable for Japan's downfall.

Nimitz again lived atop a commanding hill with a view—this time, the bustling town of Agana, the island's capital. His quarters were not as plush as those at Makalapa, but they were more than adequate. He had a low-lying clapboard house with four bedrooms and four baths opening on a courtyard facing toward Tokyo, landscaped with Kentucky bluegrass and flower beds. The combination living and dining room, in which the admiral entertained nightly, was twenty-five by thirty-five feet. But no such posh accommodations housed "Howlin' Mad" Smith or other visiting Marine brass. They were quartered in two-deck Quonset huts farther down Nimitz's aerie known as CinCPac Hill, where the inhabitants at its top still were called the Monks of Makalapa.

Twelve miles across the island, the Third Division had its base camp in a coconut grove above crescent-shaped Ylig Bay, a magnificent and picturesque inlet with a fine beach. The days were hot, but nights were comfortably cool and mosquito-free—welcome changes from the insufferable earlier tent camps in the south Pacific.

General Erskine had commanded the division's 21,000 men since their conquest of Guam. He was forty-six, the youngest two-star general in the Marine Corps. As a teen-age company bugler from Columbia, Louisiana, he had served in the Army on the Mexican border before getting second lieutenant bars and shipping overseas as a Marine in World War I. Twice wounded, he wore eleven decorations from the United States and France when the armistice was signed—awards for valor in the battles of Château-Thierry, Belleau Wood, Soissons, and Saint-Mihiel.

When out of earshot, officers and men called Erskine "The Big E." He knew of the sobriquet and was proud of it; but not when, in black humor, they called him "Graves Registration" Erskine for his role as "Howlin' Mad" Smith's chief of staff in the bloody battles of Tarawa, Saipan, and Tinian. "The Big E" came not entirely from his physique, although he was just under six feet tall and was solidly muscular, but from his strong will, tough discipline, fairness, and the fact that he had the solid respect of his troops and officers. He could be described as ruggedly handsome, and was soft-spoken most of the time, but he could cuss with the best. His pale blue eyes flashed with a cold glint when he was angry, but his smile was gentle and disarming.

Captain Louis Heyward, a movie actor before joining the Corps after starring in a film about Leathernecks, once said of Erskine: "He looks like what Central Casting in Hollywood tries to find when they need the ideal Marine general for a film." To General Smith and other friends, he was Bobbie Erskine for some reason no one seemed to know.

Erskine was General Smith's stalwart right hand, protégé, and confidant before taking the Third Division. Together they had trained the men, planned and ramrodded landings from the bitter cold of the Aleutians to the torrid heat of the south and central Pacific. Because of the hectic and often turbulent days as Smith's shaker and mover, Erskine had a keen insight into how the Old Man thought, and what he expected of the Marines at Iwo; possibly more so than did Rockey and Cates.

In the battle plan, the Third was the floating reserve; it would be eighty miles at sea on D-Day, ready to land if called in. Iwo's beaches were too small to take three divisions abreast in the assault, and the landing zones would be jammed with men and equipment as it was. There was the outside chance that the Third wouldn't be needed at all, that the Fourth and Fifth could take the island with their 42,000-plus men. When first casualty reports came from the beachhead, the pipe dream vanished.

3

Nearly five hundred ships were anchored off Saipan by the second week in February. From shore to horizon of Magicienne Bay, vessels of every size and description waited to sail the last six hundred miles to Iwo Jima. Nearly a hundred were attack transports and LSTs (landing ship tanks) with the men and their combat gear for the assault. Others were supply ships camouflaged in weird zigzag stripes of gray. They arrived at the staging area singly, in two and threes, and in small unescorted convoys. Some sailed from West Coast commissioning shakedown cruises with little danger from submarines or rampaging warships: what was left of the enemy fleet was hemmed in, protecting the home islands.

Missing from the armada were battleships and heavy aircraft carriers. They were steaming off Japan, with screening cruisers and destroyers, in the war's heaviest naval foray so far—a mighty sweep against Honshu Island to unleash thousands of two-ton shells and launch hundreds of bombing and strafing air strikes against enemy targets.

But much of everything else in the fleet was there: four communications ships bristling with radio equipment and carrying the generals and admirals commanding the invasion; LSTs and their loads of tanks and amphibious tractors and troops; tankers low in the water with 10,000,000 barrels of gasoline; two glistening white hospital ships with bright red crosses painted on their hulls; fleet oilers; escort aircraft carriers, and gunboats. There were ammunition ships, minesweepers, and seaplane and submarine tenders—something of almost everything in the fleet, including a converted ferry boat, all needed to land and support the invasion.

On Lincoln's Birthday, Marines went through a last dry run before leaving Saipan behind. They clambered down cargo nets to bobbing landing craft, circled for a time in the choppy sea, and then began the run to shore. Bow doors opened on the ugly LSTs, spewing out amtracs with troops and weapons. Air cover roared over the beaches in low-level mock attacks on make-believe fortifications. But two things were different from what would come at Iwo: there was no answering enemy fire, and the landing craft veered off before reaching shore and returned to their mother vessels.

Two days later, Magicienne Bay was empty of ships. The armada lifted anchor at dawn and steamed over the horizon on an almost due-north course at twenty-knot speed. Seventy-two hours later the Third Division followed from Guam.

General Kuribayashi knew the Americans were coming; was certain invasion was only days away. The day the invaders left Saipan, he ordered all beach positions manned and ready for action.

It was never learned how the general got his information. All but a few Japanese records were destroyed during the battle, and the answer went with them. Perhaps it was a shrewd guess based on the Japanese commander's keen knowledge of what it would take to mount an invasion of Iwo—and the extent of the naval might the Americans would throw into such an operation.

Task Force 58 had passed within fifty miles of Iwo on its way to sear Honshu in a massive raid. It was impossible to hide its 116 ships from Iwo's radar station, primitive though it was. And it is more than likely that an air spotter from Iwo saw the armada of eight battleships, sixteen aircraft carriers, fifteen heavy and light cruisers, and seventy-seven destroyers speeding northward.

Or was the tip-off an official announcement from Admiral Nimitz—a crack in his secrecy shield, which the Japanese had monitored when it was broadcast to the United States from powerful radio transmitters on Guam? Nimitz personally had scrawled out the statement in longhand and ordered its release to the press. Communiqué No. 259 read:

"Vice Admiral Marc A. Mitscher is in command of a powerful task force of the Pacific Fleet, which is now attacking enemy aircraft, air bases, and other military targets in and around Tokyo. This operation has long been planned, and the opportunity to accomplish it fulfills the deeply cherished desire of every officer and man in the Pacific Fleet.

"Surface units of the Pacific Fleet are bombarding Iwo Jima. Aircraft of the Strategic Air Force, Pacific Ocean Areas, are bombing Iwo Jima and nearby positions in the Bonin Islands. The fleet forces are under the tactical command of Admiral R. A. Spruance, Commander, Fifth Fleet."

It was the first time Iwo had been mentioned in a communiqué, and perhaps Kuribayashi simply put two and two together. Or had the Japanese, from a cave in the hills of Guam, somehow learned the date and destination, and radioed it to Tokyo, and thence to Iwo? Had the leak come from spies on Maui or Hawaii? Or in Honolulu? The mystery remains.

A glaring breach of security did occur on December 22. The *Honolulu Advertiser* published two dramatic photographs released by the Army Air Corps. One caption read "Bombs Away!" and showed American bombers over a target. Without doubt, it was Iwo Jima. Mount Suribachi was easily identified, as was Chidori Airfield. Nimitz's chief censor blasted the offending public relations officer the next day, and complained loudly to the embarrassed editor: "Any man familiar with 'Island X' maps and who saw the newspaper photos couldn't help but know our destination." But knowing the destination of the invasion force and getting the information to Kuribayashi was another matter still unresolved.

"Island X" maps were used widely during troop training, minus specific details about location, but showing the shape and small size of the target. In the bars of Honolulu, there was the usual loose talk about the upcoming campaign, but this had happened before other invasions without jeopardizing the outcome. Nonetheless, a rumor was planted that Formosa was the next invasion objective, but no one seemed to believe it.

A Japanese diary found on Iwo said four divisions and a brigade of Marines would try to invade no later than February 19—the exact D-Day. A captured corporal told of a widespread belief that five divisions would be in the assault force. Tokyo Rose, in her propaganda broadcasts widely listened to by Marines, correctly named specific units headed for Iwo.

If Admiral Nimitz had known of the frightening accuracy of Kuribayashi's intelligence—or lucky guess—he had neither the inclination nor authority to abort the invasion plan. Everything was in motion. The timetable was too tight.

As the seventy-mile-long convoy churned north, Marines felt a chilling drop in temperature. "The men aboard this ship are old hands at transport life," wrote Technical Sergeant Alvin M. Josephy Jr., a twenty-six-year-old Marine combat correspondent who in postwar years would become editor of *American Heritage*.

"Most of them have been in the Pacific more than two years," he continued. "They have ridden transports in and out of action from the Solomons to the Marianas. Every few months they leave their camps, hike to the beach, and embark for another island nearer Japan. Nevertheless, there is a difference between this trip and all the others that preceded it. This one has taken us out of the tropics for the first time since we left the States and it is cold."

But it was still warm enough during the day for men to sun themselves on deck. They did calisthenics, read, played cards and checkers and chess, shot dice, talked, argued, cleaned rifles and other weapons, checked and rechecked ammunition, waited in chow lines, washed clothes, wrote letters home, cussed and discussed women, recounted pleasures and disappointments of ancient liberties and leaves, reviewed training exercises, studied maps and models of the island— anything to chase boredom and escape anxiety.

At night, talk and activities went on below decks until "lights out" blared through loudspeakers. Topside, the skies were clear, the sea was smooth, and a bright quarter-moon failed to dim the sparkle of millions of stars. Hundreds of Marines had slept on deck on previous operations to escape the stifling heat of berthing compartments. But not now; it was too cold.

At dawn, February 16, Iwo Jima was three days away and shrouded in low-hanging clouds and pelted by rain squalls. During the night, Admiral "Spike" Blandy's pre-invasion bombardment force had moved to within six miles of shore. His six battleships were the venerable "old ladies" of the fleet: three were pre-World War I coal burners and three had been salvaged from the sludge of Pearl Harbor. Now all were modernized and refitted and packed a powerful punch; turrets mounted a total of seventy-four 12- and 15-inch guns. On station with the battlewagons were five heavy cruisers and ten destroyers. Twenty-five miles to the southeast, ten baby flattops were set to launch planes when the weather lifted.

Blandy flashed the signal at 8:00 A.M.: "Commence firing!"

Each ship knew its targets in advance. Iwo was gridded in numbered squares, each square assigned to a specific ship. Every known major position was numbered and listed in a master index. When a target was demolished, it was checked off the chart on Blandy's flagship *Estes*.

The methodical system faced a devastating stumbling block: the weather.

Blandy had orders to shell only when targets could be identified and impacts seen by air spotters. But ten minutes after the first shells landed, visibility fell to near zero and all bombardment ceased. Only when clouds and rain lifted did shelling resume in brief salvos; but hoped-for heavy bombardment never came. Just eight planes took to the skies from the carriers to make strafing runs on Chidori Airfield and Mount Suribachi.

For thirty minutes, forty-two B-24 Liberator bombers from the Marianas circled the island ten thousand feet above the cloud layer. Unable to spot targets, they flew back without dropping a bomb. At sunset, Blandy's ships moved thirty miles offshore to spend the night; they would try again in the morning.

Seventeen targets were checked off the master list. But nearly seven hundred were undamaged, packed with firepower and troops waiting for the Marines. The first of the three alloted days of pre-invasion softening-up was a tragic failure.

It was a different, happier story for Spruance and Mitscher and

Task Force 58 off Tokyo Bay. Blessed with perfect weather for two days, carrier planes demolished thirty-seven buildings of the Nakajima Aircraft Company's complex, forty miles northwest of Tokyo, and knocked down 117 interceptors. American planes were back the next day, plastering airfields and naval installations, bombing and strafing other aircraft plants, and hitting coastal shipping. Foul weather wiped out the third day, and the fleet headed for Iwo Jima.

Admiral Nimitz announced the results of the massive raid against the Japanese homeland in a special communiqué: 332 enemy planes shot from the skies, 117 destroyed on the ground, a small aircraft carrier left burning, a destroyer and five small merchant ships sunk, and extensive damage done to shipping and military installations. Forty-nine American planes were lost and nine pilots saved.

Nimitz hailed the rampage as "a victory as historic as it is decisive in the heart of the enemy's defenses" and predicted that "our future operations will hurt the enemy even more." He meant the Iwo invasion, but didn't say so. All hands were impressed except those close to the downed Navy pilots—and "Howlin' Mad" Smith. He wondered why at least part of the fleet hadn't stayed at Iwo to add big guns and planes to the pre-invasion bombardment.

Seventy civilian correspondents were aboard Admiral Turner's flagship, the *Eldorado*. Some had been with the Marines on other beaches, and had a good idea what was ahead. Others were newcomers to the Pacific and used to the relative comforts of the European theater; many would cover the battle from shipboard. Reporters represented the wire services, radio networks, metropolitan dailies, and magazines; a sprinkling of newsmen came from Europe and Australia.

On D-Day minus three, they gathered in the steaming wardroom for a final news briefing before the landing. Turner stood at the podium and waited a few minutes before beginning to speak. He was a constant nightmare to browbeaten Navy public relations officers, whose duties he never understood or wanted to.

Turner's dealings with correspondents were always brusque, often approaching the feud level. He tolerated reporters and photographers as little more than excess baggage on a military operation. He had once asked Nimitz to ban them from the fleet, but the admiral turned him down. Oldtimers, who knew the "Terrible Turner" of earlier campaigns, were taken off guard by his opening words:

"It is the express desire of the Navy Department that a more aggressive policy be pursued with regard to press, magazine, radio, and photographic coverage of the military activities in the Pacific Ocean areas," he said in a stilted manner, as if he didn't believe his own words.

He gazed at his self-defined antagonists over steel-rimmed glasses, his black beetle brows and thinning gray hair giving him a stern judicial look, and continued:

"We feel that photographers are not evil. Correspondents we also have the highest regard for. They take the same chances we do. We expect facts in stories to be verified. The opinions correspondents express are their own. That's between them and the American people. Censorship will be liberal except for technical information." So far he was making few new friends with his professorial tone; he was, after all, still Kelly Turner. He turned to the specifics of Iwo Jima:

"The defenses are thick. The number of defenders there is considerable and well-suited to the size of the island. It is, I believe, as well-defended a fixed position, particularly an island position, as exists in the world today. We expect losses. We expect losses of ships and we expect losses of troops, and we believe they will be considerable. We are taking steps, as far as our knowledge and skill and intent are concerned, to reduce these losses as far as we can, to as low a figure as we can. But we are going to have losses. However, we expect to take the position."

General Smith nodded agreement, but showed no other reaction as Turner took a seat next to him. But as Smith listened he must have recalled his pleas for ten days of shelling, and wondered if Turner believed what he said about "taking steps, as far as our knowledge and skill and intent are concerned, to reduce these losses as far as we can." "Howlin' Mad" wasn't convinced he did.

Brigadier General William A. Rogers, Harry Schmidt's chief of staff, traced the assault scenario with a pointer on a large map. He outlined the plan of attack, listed day-by-day objectives, and predicted "the enemy will try to do his utmost to keep us from establishing a landing and consolidating our beachhead." The morning of D-Day plus one, he feared, would see the Japanese send a massive pre-dawn banzai charge against the Marines if the beachhead had been taken.

Colonel Edward A. Craig, operations officer for Schmidt's Fifth Amphibious Corps, took his turn at the podium. "We expect to have eight thousand men ashore the first hour, and by nightfall we hope to have in excess of thirty thousand on the beach," he said.

Now it was General Smith: "It's a tough proposition. That's why my Marines are here." The Old Man paused and fingered his glasses. "The Japanese, in my opinion, will have a mechanized defense. Every man, every cook, baker, and candlestick maker will be down on the beaches, somewhere, with some kind of weapons." And then: "We may have to take high casualties on the beaches, maybe forty percent of the assault troops. We have taken such losses before and, if we have to, we can do it again." Casualties *would* be heavy on the beaches, but not as high as the general expected.

The Old Warrior sat down. Perspiration showed under his arm pits and his eyes were misty; this was his last campaign. He and "my Marines" would never again be in combat under his command. He had taken them as far as the high command would let them go together on the long road to Japan. Orders to this effect hadn't yet come from Nimitz, but Smith knew they would. After Iwo, he would be a figurehead: a desk general, and maybe not even that; maybe just a retired armchair general.

General Schmidt was next. Never an outgoing man even in a small group of friends, he had few words. "We are not sending boys to do a man's job," he said, disregarding the age of most of the troops but not their dedication. "We are going to get after them quick," the craggy Nebraskan promised. "General Smith has always said 'Get on their tails and keep on their tails.' What we're going to do is to take their tails away."

Seated in the front row with Turner and Smith, and listening intently, was a man in Navy khaki. He was without service insignia or rank or the shoulder patch of correspondents. Navy Secretary James V. Forrestal had come aboard at Saipan for his first eyewitness view of a Marine invasion. He stood up and began speaking. His manner was almost shy, but his words were strong and forceful:

"It has been said here that you are honored to have me present for this operation. Quite the reverse is true. It is a high privilege for me to see in action the quality of leadership America has produced." But the millionaire Wall Street financier knew who would meet the cost of winning the battle. "In the last and final analysis," he said, "it is the guy with the rifle and machine gun who wins the war and pays the penalty to preserve our liberty." He paused to select the right words for what he said next. "My hat is off to the Marines. I think my feelings about them is best expressed by Major General Julian Smith. In a letter to his wife after Tarawa he said: 'I never again can see a United States Marine without experiencing a feeling of reverence.'"

Except for the hum of overworked fans, there wasn't a sound as he sat down. The blur in General Smith's eyes was gone; now they were sparkling, and he had a tight, proud smile on his face.

Kelly Turner elaborated on censorship restrictions; no mention would be allowed about Japanese kamikaze suicide planes, napalm fire bombs, Navy frogmen's underwater demolition teams, or new weapons and equipment. "Are there any questions?" he asked. From a correspondent in the back row: "When's the next boat back to Pearl Harbor?"

The admiral ignored the attempt at humor and closed the briefing. "I hope you get many good stories," he said, "and I hope that you don't get many sensational ones." After a few minutes the wardroom emptied. "Howlin' Mad" left alone, turned down a passageway, and walked slowly to his cramped stateroom, there to think about what would happen to the Marines in the hours and days ahead.

"I was not afraid of the outcome of the battle," he later told Percy Finch, an Australian correspondent and old friend. "I knew we would win. We always did. But contemplation of the cost in lives caused me many sleepless nights. My only source of comfort was in reading the tribulations of leaders described in the Bible. Never before had I realized the spiritual value, the uplift and solace a man on the eve of a great trial receives from the pages of that book."

4

Admiral Blandy was on the bridge of the *Estes* at dawn of D-Day minus two. The weather was perfect for bombardment and flying: smooth seas, gentle breezes, and cloudless skies. Maybe the guns and planes of his task force could make up for lost time; make a dent in the master index of targets they couldn't find in yesterday's low over-cast and pelting rain. They certainly would make a determined effort.

Firing commenced at 8:40. The battleships *Nevada*, *Idaho*, and *Tennessee*, three of his six "old ladies," slammed opening salvos into the beaches and slopes in front of Chidori Airfield from two miles offshore. The cruiser *Pensacola* was 750 yards off Suribachi, and blasted its base from pointblank range.

Twelve rocket-firing minesweepers, small and wooden-hulled, were even closer to shore. They darted back and forth, almost in the surf at times, probing for reefs, shoals, steel spikes, anything that could stop landing craft before hitting the beach. In the gentle swells between the battleships and the cruiser, three destroyers and a dozen gunboats closed toward the island at full speed, belching shells and five-inch rockets as they came.

Furious action erupted everywhere—a violent sea-land battle in the making. Before noon, the Navy would lose more ships and men than on D-Day in Europe. Thousands of sailors from ships offshore scanned the incredible scene with disbelief.

Giant orange fireballs, erupting geysers of black sand and rubble, and heavy gray smoke hid the beaches and obscured much of the island. But only a few shells splashed harmlessly among the battleships, and the *Pensacola* and minesweepers were so far unmolested. It was all too easy.

General Kuribayashi watched from his headquarters in the high ground north of the airstrip. Was this a feint or the real thing? For him this was decision time. He wouldn't expose his concealed gun emplacements needlessly; he was certain American reconnaissance planes hadn't spotted all of them. But if this was the invasion, he wanted the Americans to know they wouldn't land without fierce opposition and heavy losses. His gunners waited for orders to open fire.

The general decided the invasion had begun.

He believed the flotilla of rocket-firing gunboats and the angry escort of destroyers were the first wave of assault Marines. But instead of combat troops, the gunboats carried fifty-man crews and 102 Navy and Marine frogmen from Underwater Demolitions Teams in swimming trunks, face masks, tennis shoes, and fins. They were moving toward shore, armed only with combat knives and small satchels of explosives, to make a final check of surf conditions and to see if the bottom was clear.

Less than 250 yards from the beaches the gunboats were smothered by an avalanche of shelling: enemy coastal defense guns, heavy artillery, rockets, and heavy mortars. In ninety minutes, every vessel in the tiny armada was hit, some more than a dozen times. Forty-three crewmen were killed and 153 wounded before the battered remnants finally escaped under a smoke screen.

Gunboats weren't big enough to have names, only numbers. And frantic radio calls told the unnerving story—by the numbers—of what was happening. 471 asked "where do we go" for medical help. Engines had been knocked out on 441, and it was dead in the water. 457 was sinking fast. 469 took multiple hits and was flooding. 438's bow gun had been blown away. 459 was anchored, afire, and needed a tow to survive. 466 was in the same terrible fix. 473 blazed from bow to stern with nearly two hundred holes in its hull.

An artillery round cut down five men manning the forty-millimeter bow gun of 449 and blew the weapon into the sea. As it crashed into the water, bubbling the surface like a kettle of boiling oil, another blast demolished the conning tower and killed twelve men.

A third explosion sent hot shrapnel into the body of 449's skipper, Lieutenant Junior Grade Rufus H. Herring. The twenty-five-year-old North Carolinian fought for the next thirty minutes to stay alive and save his first command. Blood gushed from three deep wounds as he steered toward the *Terror*, where the stricken little boat was lashed to the destroyer's side.

There wasn't an unwounded man aboard, and Herring refused to be hoisted to the *Terror*'s deck until the last of twenty men still alive were taken from his craft. For seventeen of 449's sailors, there was no need to hurry; they died at their guns. Herring was barely conscious, and rescuers found him propped against empty shell casings at the base of the shambles of the conning tower. A Congressional Medal of Honor would be waiting when he recovered from his wounds.

Unaware of what was happening to the gunboats, the UDTs swam toward shore in a zigzagging line stretching two miles from Suribachi to the northern end of the beach at the East Boat Landing. They were between fifty and a hundred yards apart, and were underwater as much as possible. When they surfaced for breath, they could see Iwo looming closer; their bobbing heads, gulping to fill lungs with air, brought torrents of enemy machine gun and sniper fire, and heavy mortar barrages.

Shortly after eleven o'clock, several frogmen crawled out of the water to collect soil samples for examination aboard ship and implant a small sign. It read: "Welcome to Iwo Jima." For the first time in more than a century, Americans were on Iwo Jima for a few minutes;

two days later thousands more would come to stay longer. What the swimmers found beneath the waves was both good and bad news; the bottom was firm and clear of obstructions right up to the shoreline, but just a few yards from shore the surf was nearly six feet high. Navy coxswains would have a hard time keeping landing craft on the beaches when Marines stormed the island.

"These men proceeded with their assigned tasks in a 'business as usual' fashion," an official report said later; factually correct, but something was lost in translation from deeds to words. No mention was made of the bravery of the unarmed sailors and Marines who also went to the front door of the battle in icy water under a deluge of enemy fire.

It was business as usual for Ensign Frank J. Jirkla. "What the hell, we're getting paid for it," he smiled before tumbling into the water for the swim to shore. Shortly after noon, he lost his legs when artillery hit the gunboat that picked him up after the mission. But casualties were amazingly light among the UDTs: two men. One cut himself on Futatsu Rock, two hundred yards off Suribachi, where he placed a flashing acetylene torch to aid landing craft and LSTs in finding the beach. Carpenter's Mate First Class Edward M. Anderson was missing, last seen swimming near the base of Suribachi with a mortar barrage bracketing him.

During the mad melee while the frogmen were in the water, the cruiser *Pensacola* laid down constant covering fire into Suribachi, and enemy batteries answered with heavy salvos. Just before 10:30, as she turned to escape the murderous shelling from 250 yards offshore, six heavy artillery rounds slammed into the vessel within three minutes. One blast wiped out the ship's combat information center. Commander Austin C. Behan, the executive officer, and sixteen other men were killed. Another 127 sailors were wounded when exploding ammo boxes demolished three forward gun turrets. The Kingfisher scout plane was blown from its catapult as damage control teams battled to halt the fire so that the 514-foot vessel could limp out of range.

Minutes later, the *Tennessee* took a minor hit. Six men received slight wounds as the battleship swung to within 750 feet offshore to lay down smoke to hide the stricken gunboats. Moments later, less than a hundred yards away, a shell found the destroyer *Leutze*, also making smoke and fishing survivors from the sea. Seven men were

killed and thirty-three wounded, including the skipper, Commander
B. A. Robbins

With the mauled remnants of the gunboat flotilla and the damaged
Pensacola and *Leutze* as far as possible out of harm's way, Admiral
Blandy's big guns opened up again. Planes from the escort carriers
Bismarck Sea, *Wake Island*, and *Lunga Point* made roaring low-level
strafing runs and unloaded five-hundred-pound explosives and napalm
bombs along the eastern edge of the airstrip.

The center of the island was pummeled with 126 tons of frag-
mentation bombs by sixty-two B-24 Liberators from the Marianas.
But, as "Howlin' Mad" Smith had observed, "Like the worm which
becomes stronger the more you cut it, Iwo Jima thrived on our bombardment." Still undamaged were hundreds of concealed blockhouses,
bunkers, pillboxes, and caves, all crammed with firepower and gunners
and troops waiting for the assault. And time was running out: Marines
would hit the beaches in less than thirty-six hours.

General Kuribayashi watched the one-sided land-sea battle and
was pleased. He radioed Imperial Army Headquarters in Tokyo that
the Americans' first attempt to invade was beaten off, but he knew
they would be back. That night Radio Tokyo told the homeland: "On
February 17 in the morning, enemy troops tried to land on the island
of Iwo. The Japanese garrison at once attacked these troops and re-
pelled them into the sea."

Praise and encouragement were flashed to Kuribayashi from Admiral Soemu, Commander in Chief of the Combined Japanese Fleet:
"Despite very powerful enemy bombings and shellings, your unit at
Iwo coolly judged the enemy intentions and foiled the first landing
attempt and serenely awaits the next one, determined to hold Iwo at
any cost. I am greatly elated to know that, and I wish you to continue
to maintain high morale and repulse the enemy, no matter how intense
his attacks, and to safeguard the outer defenses of our homeland."

D-Day minus two was a spectacular display of American naval
might; but on balance, it was little more than an expensive show of
firepower. Admiral Blandy's ships blasted the island with 11,243 rounds
of explosives and rockets—in all, some three thousand tons of steel
and TNT. Carrier planes laced the beaches and Chidori Airfield with
machine gun and rocket fire, and slammed napalm into Suribachi's
base, rugged slopes, and summit in 226 sorties. But General Kuri-

bayashi's defenders gave more than they took; losses inflicted on the gunboats, and the damage to the other warships, tilted the scale of the day's fighting heavily in his favor.

When firing ceased at 6:21 P.M. and the ships moved over the horizon for the night, air photos told the sad story. Of twenty known blockhouses on the terraces above the beaches, three had been knocked out. Dozens of reinforced pillboxes, bristling with machine guns and mortars, were in hummocks just yards from water's edge; a handful were destroyed. Casemented artillery and naval gun positions on Mount Suribachi's base and steep slopes were hardly touched. The cliffs around the quarry above the East Boat Landing, honeycombed with concrete fortifications armed with antitank guns and heavy naval rifles, were deadly as ever. On the plateau north of the beaches, hundreds of other dug-in defenses were unscathed, and more were undiscovered than known.

That night on the *Estes*, a troubled Blandy and his staff studied the last photos made before sunset and decided on new tactics.

Instead of concentrating only on known targets and ticking results off the master index, battleships and cruisers would come close in; would saturate the beaches, the terraces, the airstrip, and Suribachi with every gun in the armada. It would be a day-long, last-ditch massive bombardment to neutralize the landing zones before the Marines faced the Japanese and their weapons on the beaches.

Lieutenant Colonel Donald M. Weller, the Marines' gunfire officer on Blandy's staff, gladly endorsed the scheme, but he also had another suggestion: postpone D-Day for twenty-four hours.

Despite the Joint Chiefs' edict that the landings must be made on February 19, Admiral Spruance had given Blandy the option of an extra day's softening bombardment if he felt he needed it. Fearful of Kelly Turner's ire, Blandy turned to the admiral, who vetoed any such idea and said increasing bad weather might jeopardize the entire operation. Spruance was still with the task force off Tokyo Bay and couldn't be consulted, so Blandy rejected Weller's plea.

There was nothing for the Marine to do but acquiesce; he was a low man on the totem pole of command. "Never mind the artillery, mortars, and antiaircraft guns still undestroyed; never mind the inland blockhouses and pillboxes that would bar the way later," he wrote a friend after the battle. "Decision: Clear the beach defenses and the coast guns commanding the beaches."

At dawn of D-Day minus one, weather gave every sign of again becoming a potent ally of the Japanese. Visibility was fair, but turned poor as frequent rain squalls moved through. But Blandy had no thought of letting the elements slow the attack.

At 7:45 he flashed the order to the battleships: "Close on the beach and commence firing!"

For the next five hours the *Tennessee*'s batteries were seldom silent. Salvo after salvo roared into the cliffs and the quarry above the East Boat Landing. The *Idaho*, five hundred yards off Suribachi, did everything it could to silence the naval guns at its base and the heavy artillery on the slopes. The *New York* and *Nevada* hammered the terraces behind the beaches, blasting every suspicious hummock they could spot. Cruisers and destroyers and rocket-firing gunboats laid down screaming nonstop barrages throughout the day as the armada tried desperately to level targets missed earlier, and to give the first waves of Marines a fighting chance to survive.

Air strikes were again hampered by the weather. Carrier planes flew only twenty-eight sorties, and many of their napalm bombs failed to detonate. Rocket attacks and low-level machine gun strafing of Chidori Airfield did little except kick up geysers of dirt and dust. A flight of B-24s from the Marianas might as well have stayed on the ground; once more, they couldn't find Iwo under the cloud cover, and flew back to Saipan with bombs still aboard.

When the ships ceased fire at 6:21 and again withdrew for the night, air photos showed little real change in General Kuribayashi's defenses. Sixteen more blockhouses and seventeen additional coastal defense guns had been destroyed. Of a certainty, an unknown number of pillboxes and other small positions were silenced, but hundreds of dug-in, heavily armed and fortified emplacements were untouched. And time had run out to destroy them before D-Day.

By sundown, Iwo Jima's seascape was an eerie sight.

Not a ship was in view. It was as if the war had forgotten the island; as if both sides had given up a senseless struggle and decided to call off the battle. Not so. General Kuribayashi knew that invasion was inevitable; that the Americans would be back in the morning with another mighty show of force. And he would be ready.

Aboard the *Estes*, Spike Blandy again looked at the latest reconnaissance photos and sent a signal to Kelly Turner on the *Eldorado*:

"Though weather has not permitted complete expenditure of entire ammunition allowance, and more installations can be found and destroyed with one more day of bombardment, I believe landing can be accomplished tomorrow as scheduled." Blandy and his fellow gunfire officers weren't going to cross the beaches in the morning as were the Marines, with khaki shirts their only armor. But he felt the bombardment had done all it could under the circumstances.

Marines aboard the attack transports and LSTs at the point of the assault strike force—the troops who would spearhead the invasion— obviously were unaware of Blandy's passed option for one more day of pre-invasion shelling. But the next morning, caught in the slaughter of enemy fire on the beaches, they were dead certain that not nearly enough had been done by the Navy to wipe out the violently reacting Japanese and their defenses, and the Marines were bitter.

So was a livid "Howlin' Mad" Smith, who would never forget or forgive the fact that Blandy's battleships had retired for the night with hundreds of shells still in ammunition lockers.

D-Day eve was always a time of mixed and conflicting emotions among men about to smash head-on against the enemy on a beachhead certain to be savagely contested. It was Sunday night. Chaplains held church services in wardrooms and messing quarters. But attendance was low—most of the men were finishing letters home, giving battle gear another check, and girding themselves, as best they could, to face the coming ordeal.

In a crowded troop compartment of one of the ships, some men tried to resolve, as Alvin Josephy reported, "a never-settled argument between sailors and Marines about who leads the rougher life." Marines said that sailors had clean sheets aboard ships, with no mud or foxholes, and better chow. Sailors replied that they were more often in combat, usually in dangerous waters where, at any time, they could be sunk by submarines, mines, or planes. But according to a little coxswain who would take Marines ashore in a Higgins boat, "neither life is soft."

Scattered among the invasion fleet were the frogmen whose mission had triggered General Kuribayashi's quick reaction and his report to Tokyo that the Americans' first attempt at invasion had been repulsed. They had been pulled from the sea by any vessel they could reach when the gunboat flotilla was obliterated, and now waited for transportation back to the Marianas to get ready for the Okinawa campaign.

One group was aboard the attack transport *Blessman*. Their work at Iwo Jima was done; they showered, had evening chow, and were talking about the hectic day, some from bunks in the crowded berthing compartment, others standing, others sitting on the deck.

Shortly after 10:30, a low-flying kamikaze roared across the island from the northwest. He had no specific target—any ship would do. He dropped one bomb and was shot flaming from the sky; but the one-hundred pounder crashed through the *Blessman*'s deck and exploded among the UDTs; two were killed and twenty wounded, along with eleven of the ship's crew.

In his cabin on the *Eldorado*, Holland McTyeire Smith, Lieutenant General, United States Marine Corps, once again read his Bible and prayed. Before putting out the bunk light and closing his eyes, he read aloud from a small blue card the ship's chaplain had passed out to all hands. The words had been written in 1642 by another old warrior, Sir Jacob Astley, about to lead his troops in the Battle of Edge Hill in England's bloody civil war:

> *O Lord! Thou knowest how busy I must be this day:*
> *If I forget Thee, do not Thou forget me.*

And so the warriors had gathered off Iwo Jima for a battle to rival the carnage of Antietam and Gettysburg.

H-hour plus five minutes: Fifth Division troops under murderous fire as they swarm ashore on Red Beach I. Minutes later, "Manila John" Basilone was killed. (*Joe Rosenthal*)

Immediately behind are troops of the 27th Regiment as they begin the drive to cross the island at the base of Suribachi. (*Robert R. Campbell*)

Pinned down Marines take fire from Surıbachi and from the terraces leading to the airstrip, suffering heavy casualties. (*Louis R. Lowery*)

H-hour plus twenty minutes: Fourth Division troops on Yellow Beach I are unable to move. Man in right foreground is Second Lieutenant Jim Lucas, a Marine combat correspondent who later would receive the Pulitzer Prize as a civilian reporter during the Korean War. (*Robert R. Campbell*)

Despite the devastating enemy fire, Marines move ahead toward Motoyama Number One, the first objective of the invasion. (*Robert R. Campbell*)

H-hour plus seventy minutes: beachhead is a junkyard that reaches from the base of Suribachi for two-and-a-half miles to the north. The surf and the Japanese combine to make Iwo Jima a deathtrap for Marines. (*Eugene S. Jones*)

Fifth Division Troops on Red Beach I move over the first terrace in the assault on Motoyama Number One. Deep black sand and withering enemy fire are common enemies. (*Henry Dreyfuss*)

Marine killed by a sniper's bullet through his helmet atop the terrace. (*Charles O. Jones*)

PART THREE

D-Day:
Curtain Time
in Hell

1

A soft seven-knot breeze from the north barely rippled the turquoise sea. A few scattered clouds dotted the rapidly brightening skies as dawn spread across the horizon. If ever there was an ideal day for invasion, this was it.

Surrounding the island was an armada that dwarfed any so far assembled in the Pacific war. Admiral Spruance, on his flagship *Indianapolis*, had arrived during the night to take command of the assault, and he had brought Admiral Mitscher's mighty Task Force 58 with him.

Stretching to the limit of sight, and well beyond, were 485 ships needed to land General Smith's Marines and support them in battle, once the beachhead was seized.

As the sun's first rays brought detail to the gray silhouettes of the invasion force, Admiral Turner appeared briefly on the bridge of the *Eldorado*. In tattered old bathrobe, he rubbed sleep from his eyes, scanned the island dead ahead and its steel ring of ships. Then he disappeared to launch the attack.

D-Day of any invasion begins early, slowly, and in seeming mass confusion. It gains overpowering momentum as intricate planning, training, and organization take hold. Then it explodes in a cacophony of thundering sound and destruction. The pattern was the same at Iwo Jima. General Kuribayashi and his troops could have felt only awe at the scene and known that the Americans had come in full force, with every intention of staying.

At 3:00 A.M., Marines were roused from bunks by clanging gongs and blaring loudspeakers: "Reveille! Reveille!" Few had slept soundly; most tossed fitfully through the night, others slept not a wink. And few took more than a few bites from steak breakfasts, the traditional last meal before assaulting the beaches.

At 6:30, Admiral Turner gave the order: "Land the landing force!"

The three-and-a-half hours had been an interminable wait for the men; but now everything would be governed by an unforgiving time-table set months before at Makalapa. Topside on transports, sailors opened hatches and swung out heavy booms to work cargoes of equipment and supplies. They lowered Higgins boats on their davits and slung nets over the side for Marines to clamber down, loaded with heavy packs and weapons, to waiting landing craft.

Troops on LSTs—the men who would be in the first waves— backed down steep ladders from troop compartments to cavernous tank decks, and climbed aboard amphibious tractors, the amtracs that would carry them to the beaches. Beads of sweat broke out on faces; jackets were soggy from the heat. Blue, swirling exhaust fumes from roaring engines clogged lungs and made eyes water. As each amtrac reached open bow doors, sometimes after thirty minutes of inching ahead, it clanked over the hump of the LST ramp and jerked down a cleated incline. The violent motion pitched men into one another, and those in front crashed into forward steel bulkheads. Once in the water, the amtracs made giant circles like covered wagons in a movie fight between cowboys and Indians, and waited for the signal to form waves and head for shore.

The last chance to clear the beaches with naval fire began at 6:40. It mounted in fury for eighty minutes as thousands of tons of hot steel and explosives ripped into the island. Every capital ship—eight battlewagons, nineteen cruisers, and forty-four destroyers—seemed to be firing at the same time. Each knew what it was expected to do: what targets to hit, the number of shells to fire, and the exact time to send them on their way.

Navy men and correspondents who had been at Normandy said the bombardment was mightier than that on D-Day in Europe. The island shuddered as if its slumbering volcano was coming to life. "Maybe the goddammed thing will blow up and sink into the ocean," a Marine on the *Eldorado* said, "and then we can all go home."

From offshore, men watched in awe. They could clearly track the arching trajectories of sixteen-inch shells from the battleships screaming through the sky. Each impact made a brilliant orange flash that vanished in a blanket of grayish-black smoke and billowing clouds of dust. Suribachi's mustard-brown slopes were hidden in the pall, its summit barely visible. The beaches, and the slopes behind them, were engulfed in falling cascades of dirt and debris. Giant craters were punched in Chidori Airfield, and the Motoyama plateau in the center of the island quaked.

Nine rocket-firing gunboats moved to within 250 yards of the East

Boat Landing and opened fire at 6:45. In thirty minutes, 9,500 of their five-inch missiles slammed into the cliffs around the quarry; blazing trails of white sparks and smoke marked the roaring flights to targets.

All firing ceased at five minutes past eight. It was time for the carrier planes to add their pulverizing punch. Four abreast in screaming dives from 10,000 feet, seventy-two Navy Corsair and Hellcat fighters and Dauntless bombers swarmed into action. They made low-level, three-hundred-mile-an-hour runs in a mad aerial circus, dropping bombs, firing rockets, and strafing with curtains of machine gun bullets. They crisscrossed the beaches, buzzed the terraces inland, and plastered the hills to the north, then zoomed up under full throttle to swing around Suribachi and make more passes in the pattern of destruction.

Lieutenant Colonel William A. Millington's all-Marine squadron waited for its cue to blast Suribachi and the landing zones. When the Navy pilots headed for carriers to refuel and rearm, the Leathernecks took over. Forty-eight gull-wing Corsairs peeled off from their circling rendezvous at 5,000 feet and followed the flight leader's orders. "Go in and scrape your bellies on the beach," he told the pilots.

Men on the jammed decks of transports, others in Higgins boats or in amtracs disgorged from LSTs, watched and wondered how any Japanese could survive. "They're givin' 'em hell," a corporal from Missouri said. "I'd hate to be in those bastards' shoes!" His buddy from Brooklyn agreed. "You bet your ass," he said. They cheered and pounded each other on the back as the last planes headed seaward.

With skies clear of aircraft, naval bombardment started again at 8:25. It was thirty-five minutes until H-Hour. In that time, another 8,000 shells smothered the landing zones. It was now or never if the beaches were to be cleared of Japanese resistance. In five minutes, sixty-eight amtracs would cross the Line of Departure and begin the 4,000-yard, half-hour run to shore.

The awesome job of the first wave of amphibian tractors was to get ashore, smash any enemy positions they could find on the beaches, grind fifty yards inland, and set a defense perimeter for the landing force. No assault troops were in the seven-ton steel-sided landing craft—only a three-man crew to operate it and man a 75-millimeter howitzer and three machine guns.

Six waves of amtracs carrying the first Marine riflemen would follow from 250 to 500 yards apart and land at five-minute intervals.

Each wave would have 1,360 men. Hundreds of Higgins boats would come in succeeding lines with thousands of men to consolidate and expand the beachhead, and to slash across Iwo's narrow neck at the base of Suribachi.

Four regiments—the 23rd and the 25th of the Fourth Division on the right, and the 27th and 28th of the Fifth Division on the left— were the spearhead.

Prosaic names were given the seven landing zones on the two miles of black sand from Suribachi to the northern cliffs around the quarry: Green Beach, Red Beach I, Red Beach II, Yellow Beach I, Yellow Beach II, Blue Beach I, and Blue Beach II. As place names in history they couldn't match Omaha, Utah, Nevada, and the others at Normandy. But to the Marines, Iwo's beaches would never be forgotten.

High tension rode with the men as they churned toward shore. Across the ramp of one Higgins boat, in foot-high letters, were the words "Too Late To Worry." Troops peered intently over spray-drenched gunwales of the bouncing craft and wished they were some-where else—anywhere else.

They wore freshly laundered olive green fatigues sprayed with disinfectant. Men in early waves had covered their faces with a white cream to protect against the possibility that the Japanese would meet the assault at the shore with a wall of flames fed by underground fuel lines. Steel helmets were camouflaged with a light brown cloth cover; the Marine insignia of globe and anchor was emblazoned on left breast pockets; rank was stenciled on sleeves; and last names, likewise, across the back of dungaree jackets.

Troops carried their weapons and two heavy knapsacks of gear, as well as a gas mask, a rolled blanket, and a poncho. All had extra socks and dungarees, toilet supplies, and cherished photographs and letters; many had Bibles in jacket pockets.

Corpsmen toted fifty-one pounds of battle dressings, morphine, sulfa, and a small kit of surgical knives and scissors. Mortar men were saddled with a backbreaking 122 pounds. Battle baggage of riflemen, machine gunners, communications squads, flamethrowers, and dem-olitions men varied in weight somewhere in between.

Normal conversation was impossible in the landing craft; only yells were audible. One man might smile at his buddy with a self-conscious, tight-lipped grin of bravado and they would make shouted attempts at confidence-building banter. But most tried to control anxiety and fear—even battle-hardened oldtimers knew *no one* ever got used to a combat landing under fire.

Allen R. Matthews would always remember the ride to the blazing beach, although the sounds of battle were still faint as he made the trip. The roar of his amtrac's engines, and the clatter of its endless steel-belted tracks, all but drowned out even the thunderous blasts of sixteen-inch guns unless the craft was passing within yards of a cracking salvo from a battleship.

Matthews was a thirty-two-year-old private, the oldest man in his company, a father of two, and less than a year from civilian life; he'd been a political correspondent for the Richmond, Virginia, *Times-Dispatch*.

"I checked my gear carefully," he wrote of the anxious thirty minutes. "Canteen tops tightly screwed, yes; grenade pins bent sufficiently to keep them from being pulled accidentally, but not enough to hamper my pulling them when I needed to, yes; chamber and operating rod of my rifle free of dust, yes; oil and thong case and combination tool in my rifle, yes.

"And my personal possessions: the extra socks in the hip pocket with my handkerchief; my billfold was in the other hip pocket; the waterproof envelope in which I carried the pictures of my wife and family was secure; my fountain pen was clipped fast in my breast pocket; the extra cigarettes were in the gas mask carrier. I was afraid that I was showing my nervousness, and I felt that I wore too much gear, and I wondered how the BAR man could maneuver at all with his heavier weapon and his larger supply of ammunition."

A grinning corporal shouted in his ear. "They're really pouring it in, aint' they! I'd rather be out here going in than in there having to go through what they're having to go through." Another voice: "I wonder if we're drawing fire from the shore batteries?" Grins vanished, Matthews recalled, "and we all turned more anxiously toward the island."

Corporal Eugene S. Jones, on his way in with a flamethrower platoon, thought the island looked like a pinball machine, what with the streaking rockets and fireballs from exploding shells. "Biggest fuckin' pinball machine you'll ever see!" was the shouted answer to the eighteen-year-old from Sergeant Herbert Ginsberg.

From someone else: "It'll be like shooting ducks!" The loud re-

joinder: "But these sonuvabitchin' ducks'll be shooting back!" Sailors
waved and shook their fists and yelled at passing landing craft: "Go
get 'em, you beautiful glory hounds!" Marines smiled and waved back,
not hearing a word.

2

Ten minutes before H-Hour, B-24 Liberators made their final bombing
runs. It was another disappointing performance; of forty-four planes
that left the Marianas, fifteen made it to the island; the rest turned
back because of bad weather en route to the target. Those that did
find Iwo haphazardly unloaded just thirty-six five-hundred pounders.

So disenchanted was Admiral Spruance with the Seventh Air
Force's contribution to the pre-invasion bombing plan that, the night
before, he wanted to scrub the last mission. "Hell, Ray, we'll take all
the help we can get," General Smith said, and the raid, such as it
was, came.

Naval bombardment lifted from the beaches at 8:57. The first
wave of amtracs was less than six hundred yards from shore. Now the
thunderous shelling ripped the island four hundred yards up the terraces, and the range would lift farther inland every three minutes to
keep from hitting the troops.

Bill Millington's Marine pilots swarmed back for a final plastering
of Suribachi with napalm bombs. It was a spectacular show as their
Corsairs unleashed the oblong missiles that tumbled end-over-end
into the volcano's gun-infested sides and among the giant boulders at
its base. Big balls of flame and smoldering black clouds of smoke
erupted when the bombs exploded. But more than half didn't, and
bounced crazily along the rugged ground where riflemen later detonated the duds.

Radio circuits crackled with minute-by-minute reports from air
spotters. "Landing wave four hundred yards from shore!" the terse
voice of one said as the naval shelling moved inland, and Millington's
planes headed for the carrier *Wake Island* twenty miles at sea.

Marines would hit the beaches within minutes now, and they
would land on an island whose main defenses hardly had been dented,
much less destroyed. It was a tragic fact that seventy-two consecutive

days of air attacks and naval bombardment had barely diminished General Kuribayashi's power. Of 915 major installations on Iwo, fewer than two hundred had been silenced, and this didn't count literally hundreds of smaller but deadly strongpoints that would claim thousands of Marine casualties.

At 9:02 the flash came: "Boats on the beach!" It was two minutes behind the invasion timetable.

Men in the first wave of amtracs were amazed at how easy it had been to reach shore. They had no trouble with the three-foot surf and were taking only spasmodic small arms fire. But once out of the water, it quickly became a different story.

Machines lost buoyancy and traction as engines roared and steel treads cut foot-deep trenches in the loose black sand as they struggled to grind up the steep fifteen-foot terraces. To stay on the beach meant disaster; minutes behind were the first wave of assault troops who had to have room to scramble out of their craft and fight.

Congestion mounted like a Times Square traffic jam at theater curtain time. Some amtracs reversed gears to back a few yards offshore and lay down covering howitzer and machine gun fire. Others desperately churned in the water waiting for the mess to clear, but it got rapidly worse. Those on the slopes were head-on with a concentration of blockhouses and pillboxes they couldn't see. But still only scattered small arms fire pinged off the tractors' armored sides.

United Press correspondent William F. Tyree watched from a Navy spotter plane circling 1,000 feet over the scene. "It is systematic murder and destruction," his dispatch to 1,200 newspapers and radio stations said.

As Tyree watched, a Navy fighter plane was hit by antiaircraft fire in the smoky haze over Suribachi. The Hellcat trailed a bright flash of flame and a heavy plume of inky-black smoke, screamed skyward for an instant, then roared into the sea between the fourth and fifth waves of landing craft.

At 9:05, jammed radio rooms of every ship in the armada heard the message: "Assault troops on the beach!"

Amtracs were still moving as rear ramps slammed down and the first wave swarmed from them in a thin, surging line stretched along two miles of beach. They hit it on a dead run. First strides were easy, as momentum carried them a few yards. Then, suddenly, strides slowed to laborious shuffles as feet sank calf deep into soft, sucking, coarse black volcanic cinders. Each forward step left elephant-size footprints, and as men crossed the first narrow wet ribbon and flung themselves against the terraces, the going was worse.

Any mammoth ship-to-shore amphibious landing is the most complex and difficult of all military operations, and can become total chaos within minutes. Success or failure hinges on the first critical moments, and the attack can go either way, all depending upon the training and discipline of the troops. Now, on Iwo Jima's strange shore, order began to emerge as Marine tradition and combat skills took hold. Individuals started to form up in fire teams and squads, then in platoons and companies and battalions, as they became a fighting machine.

Colonel Harry B. Liversedge's 28th Regiment had a tenuous foothold on Green Beach near the base of Suribachi. Colonel Thomas B. Wornham's 27th was ashore on the Red Beaches and getting into position to push toward the southern end of the airstrip. Colonel Walter B. Wensinger and his 23rd Regiment held the center of Yellow Beach I and II, and were pointed up the terraces. On the Blue Beaches, in the shadow of the cliffs in front of the quarry, Colonel John R. Lanigan's 25th pulled its troops together for attack.

Wary Marines began to think that maybe, maybe, everything was going to be all right. They were ashore, and the landing, except for the black sand, was made with amazing speed and precision. Maybe, just maybe, most defenses were destroyed. After all, the Japanese were reacting with only small arms fire. First reports from shore to the *Eldorado* reflected the surge of optimism:

9:11—Colonel Wornham on Red Beach: "Landings on schedule. Casualties unexpectedly light. Proceeding toward airstrip against light resistance."

9:14—Colonel Wensinger on Yellow Beach: "Four waves ashore and moving inland. Taking moderate mortar fire."

9:17—Colonel Lanigan on Blue Beach: "Bogging down in heavy sand and steep terraces, but conditions generally favorable. Moving forward against airstrip under moderate fire."

9:19—Colonel Liversedge on Green Beach below Suribachi: "Troops ashore and moving to isolate volcano. Resistance moderate, but terrain awful."

General Kuribayashi wasn't surprised by what was happening— he had planned it that way. The key to his battle scheme was to let the Marines land and suck them into a gigantic ambush. His troops had been stunned and shell-shocked by the Americans' massive firepower, but now they were at their posts, ready to wipe out the invaders when he ordered. The shrewd samurai bided his time for nearly an hour.

Let the Marines land against light opposition. Make them lift naval gunfire and halt air support to avoid hitting their own troops. Give the Japanese time to shake off the effects of bombardment and bombing. Let the beaches pile up with men and equipment. Then cut off further landings with smothering artillery and mortar fire. Halt the flow of reinforcements to pinned-down Marines. Let outfits ashore bleed to death with casualties. Then push the invaders off the island.

Kuribayashi triggered the trap shortly after ten o'clock.

Sand hummocks, appearing as giant dead ant hills moments before, spewed machine gun fire from apertures hardly visible just above ground level. Mortars fell in cascades from hundreds of concealed pits. Heavy artillery and rapid-firing antiaircraft guns, barrels lowered to rake the beaches, slammed shells into oncoming landing craft and support vessels. Land mines, sown like wheat in a field, exploded in sickening blasts on the terraces as Marines stumbled across them. Fifteen-inch coast defense guns and large mortars rained down from Suribachi's base, slopes, and crater.

Every square yard of the beachhead was under methodical, deadly fire. There was no main defense line for the Marines to breach; it was like a giant sponge, every hole a separate hell. By now 6,200 men were pinned down on the 3,000-yard strip of sand—more than two Marines to every yard of shoreline. Boats were still trying to land— and troops wondered why; there was no place for more men to maneuver.

There was no way to dig a foxhole. As fast as loose volcanic ash was scooped out, the hole filled up again as in a bin of wheat. Men burrowed as best they could into the sand, or pressed against porous rocks, or hugged the sides of shell craters—anything for a shield from the withering enemy fire. When landing craft could, they backed off through the surf, but many were hit in the water.

Seven were demolished within five minutes and sank with tanks, trucks, and ammunition. Shore parties desperately tried to manhandle cargoes and keep the beachhead open. It was a losing attempt. When vehicles and artillery made it to shore, they were immediately mired to the hubs in the sand. Damaged Higgins boats and larger landing craft quickly filled with water that made them unmovable.

It was a scene of twisted hulks of boats, of burning jeeps and trucks and bogged-down cannon. And the early wounded: waiting painfully, patiently, for evacuation.

Two miles at sea on the *Eldorado*, General Smith and Admiral Turner monitored radio circuits that snapped with heavy static and cryptic messages from unit commanders over the sounds of battle. They'd shared the common bond of apprehension and concern before—especially during the bloody invasions of Tarawa and Peleliu—but never had the situation been more grave.

10:36—From Pat Lanigan's 25th Regiment at the northern end of the thin beachhead: "Catching all hell from the quarry. Heavy mortar and machine gun fire. Troops inland two hundred yards but pinned down." His men were looking up at cliffs nearly as formidable and heavily armed as was Suribachi.

10:39—From Walt Wensinger's 23rd Regiment in the center, hugging the terraces at their steepest incline along the sides of the airstrip: "Taking heavy casualties and can't move for the moment. Mortars killing us."

10:42—From Tom Wornham's 27th Regiment on Wensinger's left: "All units pinned down by artillery and mortars. Casualties heavy. Need tank support fast to move anywhere."

10:46—Harry Liversedge's 28th Regiment, struggling to cut off Suribachi from the rest of the island: "Nearly across the neck but taking heavy fire and forward movement stopped. Machine gun and artillery fire heaviest ever seen."

General Kuribayashi had sprung his ambush.

But it had a fatal flaw.

He had waited too long.

He had given the Marines an irretrievable hour before launching his counterattack. And during that hour, everything the Marines Corps was—well-trained, disciplined, proud, brave, determined men—showed the stuff of which it was made.

More than six thousand troops were on a tiny but functioning beachhead. They had a few tanks and bulldozers to cut lanes through the terraces to get the Shermans into firing position. They had some artillery; not very much, but enough to let the Japanese know it was ashore. They had something of everything needed to fight and survive for the time being. And they had faith that help would come; faith that, because they were Marines, they would pull through and win again.

Once more men started to move, spurred by Marine Corps tradition and individual valor. "The Marines have a way of making you afraid; not of dying, but of not doing your job," was the way Captain Bonnie Little, killed in action at Tarawa, said of the esprit de corps in his last letter home.

First it was one man lunging into the maelstrom of enemy fire; then twos and threes, then fire teams and squads, then larger units. Some landing craft survived the mortars and artillery to put more tanks and cannon on the beach. Marines fell in mounting numbers, their screams of pain cutting through the din of fighting, but others pushed inland from the shore, up the terraces, and over the top onto the airstrip runway. Still others rammed across the neck of the island at Suribachi's base. They crept and crawled, dodged and ducked, slithered and staggered—but they moved forward.

Sergeant Charles C. Anderson Jr. was mortally wounded early on Yellow Beach I. He lost both legs and an arm to a land mine, and was evacuated to an attack transport. In one of war's tragic ironies, his father was the ship's skipper. "I'm feeling pretty good, but I wonder how Mother will take all this," he whispered, and died in his father's arms.

When a Navy chaplain carried word to Mrs. Anderson at home in Washington, D.C., she asked: "Is it my husband or my son?" Given the answer, she said: "A force stronger than ours has taken charge." Then she dressed in a neat candy-striped uniform and reported for duty as a volunteer nurse's aide at Bethesda Naval Hospital.

Only family and close friends would know about Sergeant Anderson's death. But newspapers and radio broadcasts told millions of another D-Day loss—Gunnery Sergeant John Basilone. Already a Marine Corps legend as the first Leatherneck to be awarded the Medal of Honor in World War II, "Manila John" was leading his machine gun platoon through the fury of Red Beach II when a mortar cut him down.

In 1942, on a black October night in the steaming jungles of Guadalcanal, Basilone had single-handedly wiped out a company of

Japanese trying to overrun his position on the Tenaru River. With a Colt .45 pistol and two machine guns—one cradled in his arms after the other was knocked out—he stopped a screaming banzai attack and held out alone until dawn, when reinforcements came up. Nearly a hundred sprawled enemy dead were around his cut-off outpost.

Basilone was dark complexioned and handsome, had big ears like Clark Gable, and a wide grin. His Italian parents beamed with pride on a very special afternoon in 1943 when 30,000 well-wishers honored him at a gala celebration on the 2,000-acre estate of tobacco heiress Doris Duke near Raritan, New Jersey, his hometown.

"Manila John" blushed when news photographers snapped his picture while being kissed by a Hollywood starlet, smiled broadly when an oil portrait was unveiled in the tiny brick town hall, and was shyly grateful for the $5,000 war bond neighbors gave him. He turned down the bars of a second lieutenant. "I'm a plain soldier," he said, "and I want to stay one." From earliest memory, Basilone had wanted to be a professional fighting man. He had done a hitch in the Army before joining the Marines in 1940, and had served in the Philippines—hence his nickname.

To millions, Basilone was a hero, one of the first of the war, and could have remained stateside training troops and selling war bonds. Instead, he said farewell to his new wife, also a Marine, and joined the Fifth Division. Staying behind, he told buddies, would be "like being a museum piece." And it just wouldn't seem right, he said, "if the Marines made a landing on the Manila waterfront and 'Manila John' wasn't among them."

Now, with the invasion ninety minutes old, the intrepid sergeant had one thought. "C'mon, you guys! Let's get these guns off the beach!" he yelled at the gunners just behind, backs hunkered low and straining under heavy loads of weapons and ammunition amid the blistering fire. The wasplike whir of an incoming mortar sounded its eerie warning; then a shattering blast.

Basilone lunged forward in midstride, arms flung outward over his head. He and four comrades died in that instant. On his outstretched left arm was a tattoo: "Death Before Dishonor!" "Manila John" wouldn't see Dewey Boulevard again, but he had won the Navy Cross, the Marines Corps' second highest decoration for valor.

Other heroes took his place that day on Iwo Jima. One was Tony Stein, a twenty-four-year-old corporal from Dayton, Ohio, a hardened veteran of campaigns at Guadalcanal, Bougainville, and Vella Lavella, a tiny island of rain forests in the Solomons. His rampage came as Able Company of the 28th Regiment's First Battalion struggled to isolate Suribachi.

Stein and two other men—Sergeant Merrit M. Savage and Corporal Frederick Tabert—were at the point of the assault. Stein spotted a pillbox holding up the advance and went for it. His weapon was a one-of-a-kind machine gun fired from the hip in the swashbuckling style of a gunfighter in the Old West.

The husky corporal called it his "stinger," and it was unique. Stein had been an apprentice toolmaker before enlisting in 1942, and used his skills to fashion it from a scrounged machine gun from the wing of a wrecked Navy fighter plane. Spewing bullets in rapid bursts, the "stinger" and its gung-ho triggerman pinned the Japanese inside the pillbox while Savage finished them off with a demolitions charge.

In a sixty-minute shoot-out against nine other strongpoints, Stein killed at least twenty Japanese while Savage and Tabert covered him. When ammunition was gone, he shed steel helmet and burdensome shoes and dashed to the beach under savage fire to get more. He made eight round trips, shepherding a wounded Marine each time. On the ninth foray, he was slammed in the shoulder with chunks of shrapnel.

Captain Aaron C. Wilkins, the company commander, ordered him to the beach for treatment and evacuation. Stein talked him out of it, and stayed in the fight. At day's end, he and the "stinger" were still in action, battling the enemy in pillbox after pillbox, bunker after bunker, yard by yard, foot by foot, as the thin line of Marines drove a wedge across the island.

Tony Stein's Medal of Honor for his day's work—the Marines he saved and the Japanese he killed—was the first awarded to a Marine during the battle.

Lieutenant Colonel Jackson B. Butterfield commanded Stein's battalion. By eleven o'clock, three of its squads slashed the bitter seven hundred yards to the western shoreline and were immediately cut off in no man's land. It took three hours and heavy casualties to reach the isolated men and consolidate the flimsy line.

On Butterfield's left flank, less than a football field's length from Suribachi's base, Lieutenant Colonel Chandler W. Johnson's First Battalion was in trouble. It had landed at 9:35 in an early wave and

made good initial headway across the beaches and among the ravines
and boulders at the foot of the volcano. But by noon the outfit was
pinned under heavy mortar and artillery fire and could barely move
for several hours. It would be sundown before the First linked up
with the other battalions and consolidated the front.

Fifth Division tanks were trying to move to help Lieutenant Colonel Charles E. Shephard's Third Battalion, but were snarled in the
beachhead traffic jam. For fifty minutes, fourteen Shermans were
bogged down and taking blistering fire as shore parties and bulldozers
labored to get them out of the sand. When the tanks were finally able
to move in single file, they were easy targets for antitank guns. Within
three minutes, four took short-range direct hits from steel-piercing
shells.

Sergeant Thomas Grady Gallant of Chattanooga, Tennessee, saw
a round slam into one. "It punched through the cold armor plate as
a finger is punched through putty," he recalled, "making a hole all
the way through the thickest part." The crew died in what Gallant
remembered as "a jellied, liquefied mass blended into a viscoidal sticky
fluid" caused by exploding shells the tank carried.

Other Shermans braved the onslaught and clanked forward, their
cannon and machine guns laying down a shield of firepower for the
struggling infantry. With the tanks in support, the line crawled ahead,
and by late afternoon things were looking better.

Early twilight found Johnson's troops stretched along a precarious
front across the island at its narrowest point; they had made 350 yards
against the worst opposition any of the men had ever seen. Shepard's
battalion also hacked a narrow swathe from shore to shore and were
pointed north toward the airstrip, while Johnson's men pivoted south
to face Suribachi.

Both battalions had fought desperately throughout the day, but
the situation never was as precarious as that faced by Colonel Wornham's 27th Regiment battling for a toehold on the airstrip.

Ninety minutes after landing, the battalions of Lieutenant Colonel
John A. Butler and Major John W. Antonelli had clawed up the slope
to the eastern edge. Resistance was light until 10:45 when, as Antonelli
put it, "crap hit the fan in copious quantities." Moments before, they
were catching only small arms fire. Now, when Kuribayashi pulled
the plug, they were in the middle of the ambush and taking a deadly

fusillade of machine gun bursts and mortar fire from concealed by-passed positions in the hummocks.

Everywhere along the terraces, the picture had a deadly sameness. Shell craters were the only cover for troops. Tanks were stymied on the beach with desperately needed amtracs and their howitzer and machine gun support. Ammunition was running short. Casualties worsened by the minute, and any attempt to take the wounded off the slopes drew even heavier violence. There was no forward movement by 11:30, and the battalions were fighting to live from naked positions against overpowering odds.

Gaunt, lumbering, slow-talking Colonel Louis C. Plain, the 27th's executive officer, had fought the Japanese as a captain at Guadalcanal. Now he scampered from shell hole to shell hole to see what could be done at the front. Just as he reached the ridge, a machine gun chattered and he fell with deep wounds in the left shoulder and arm. He stayed in a crater for six hours, helping beat off the enemy, until he knew the line would hold. Then he crawled and rolled down the terraces and waited for hours with hundreds of others to be evacuated.

Confusion and devastation mounted by the minute on the beaches, and the effects of the near-chaos were felt two miles at sea. In the choppy waters, Higgins boats and larger landing craft—loaded with reinforcements, tanks, artillery, ammunition, trucks, cranes, medical supplies, bulldozers, fuel, and fresh water—circled the Central Command Boat and waited for a signal to head for shore.

But the beachhead was so cluttered with wreckage, so smothered in artillery and mortars, that only a trickle of boats could leave the area. Those that did were sent in one by one as debris was manhandled or winched aside or blown to smithereens by explosive charges.

Shortly after one o'clock, Admiral Turner accepted the inevitable. He closed the beaches until enemy fire slackened and something could be done to clear the monstrous logjam.

Nothing moved toward shore for nearly two hours. Finally, at 2:58, the calamitous situation had eased enough for six Fifth Division tanks to land, along with Lieutenant Colonel Daniel C. Pollock's First Battalion of the 26th Regiment. They swarmed into a morass of destruction and heavy fire; it took nearly two hours to get off the beaches. Before they reached the slope, two tanks were destroyed and the infantry was cut to pieces.

Lieutenant Colonel Donn J. Robertson's Third Battalion of the 27th Regiment was the last of the Fifth Division troops to land. They clambered down cargo nets to bobbing Higgins boats shortly after nine o'clock. It took nearly seven hours of circling before they were sent ashore. Many were seasick, and the hours of anxiety were made no easier when the men looked over the heaving gunwales and saw what was ahead.

When finally on the beach, they lumbered into a bedlam: bodies of dead Marines, hundreds of wounded awaiting evacuation, smoldering wreckage of boats, supplies, and equipment. The move up the terraces was as bad and deadly as ever; but by twilight they were along the edge of the airstrip and digging in for the first night on Iwo.

The Fourth Division's landing zones stretched north from halfway up the shoreline to the high cliffs above the East Boat Landing. Masses of reinforced concrete blockhouses armed with coastal defense guns and artillery, and a maze of bunkers, caves, and pillboxes packed with antitank and heavy machine guns, honeycombed the steep slopes.

From this high ground around the quarry, enemy firepower was zeroed in on the division's beaches and made them a roaring death trap that surpassed, if that were possible, the inferno around Suribachi where the Fifth Division was meeting the enemy for the first time.

But the Fourth's assault battalions had had relatively easy going until General Kuribayashi sprang the counterattack. Then, like their Fifth Division comrades, they were easy targets for the downpour of artillery, mortars, and concentrated machine guns.

Lieutenant Colonel Ralph Haas's First Battalion of the 23rd Regiment made slow headway against the searing artillery and mortars and found itself with another problem: a field of land mines. Major Robert H. Davidson's Second Battalion, on Haas's right, met the same savage resistance and obstacles as it punched toward the cliffs. Each minute brought more casualties to each outfit.

Lieutenant Colonel Hollis U. Mustain's First Battalion spearheaded the 25th's push toward the quarry. It fought through miserable terrain and violent enemy reaction to gain six hundred yards inland from the beachhead and up the slopes. Lieutenant Colonel Richard Rothwell's Second Battalion of the 24th, on Mustain's left, paid a ghastly price for its limited advance among the rocks and caves. Most of his company commanders and platoon leaders were gone by nightfall, the ranks of noncoms all but wiped out.

Captain Elwyn H. Woods just had time to move Item Company into action before he was wounded; by sunset, five more of the outfit's officers had been hit. Captain Thomas Witherspoon, K Company's commander, was cut down within minutes of Woods, and by 4:30 all of the unit's officers were dead or wounded. When the Second Battalion crossed the beaches, it had 954 people; that night fewer than three hundred were alive and unwounded.

Brigadier General Leo D. Hermle was the highest rank to land on D-Day. The Fifth Division's assistant commander had expected to be ashore by noon at the latest. It was three o'clock, shortly after the beaches reopened, that he made it and set up a command post in a sandbagged shell hole near the south end of the airstrip.

Hermle had been at Tarawa; had seen the horrible carnage; had marveled at the enemy fortifications; had shuddered at the flat terrain of the atoll and the bloody lagoon that surrounded it. Now he saw that Iwo Jima would be far worse. Reports from regiments and battalions quickly convinced him that it was pointless for General Rockey to land before the next morning. He advised the division commander to stay aboard the *Athene* until then.

3

Runners went out at five o'clock to all units from Hermle's CP: "Consolidate positions, button up for the night, and expect the worst."

Sunset came at 6:45. Everyone, from admirals and generals afloat to teen-aged privates ashore, believed there would be a screaming banzai sometime before dawn. Where, when, and in what force the enemy would strike was anybody's guess. But the counterattack had come every time and everywhere Marines had invaded; there was no reason to believe it wouldn't come on Iwo.

Sometime, somewhere during the night, the Japanese would counterattack—a massed mob of yelling troops, some drunk with sake, led by sword-swinging officers and armed with automatic weapons and hand grenades, charging with fixed bayonets in a desperate lunge to drive the invaders into the sea. What the Americans didn't know was that the banzai, for the first time in the Pacific war, wasn't part of the Japanese scheme of defense—not with General Kuribayashi in command and with thirty thousand Marines, with thousands of tons of equipment and supplies jammed on the beachhead, and with every square foot of it within easy range of every big weapon in its arsenal.

Darkness came quickly—twilight was gone by seven o'clock. Marines were dug in along the front and in shell craters on the slopes and shoreline, waiting for whatever came. Most shivered in the shallow holes in chilly forty-degree temperature. A lucky few were warm; digging had tapped seams of volcanic heat just below the surface.

Front lines were nowhere near D-Day objectives; the only key position in Marine hands was the quarry, and the hold on it was tenuous.

Men strained to catch any movement in the darkness, seeing movement that wasn't there. Bursts of rifle and machine gun fire crackled spasmodically. Tracer bullets marked their paths toward suspected Japanese positions, and many times Marines were unknowingly shooting at one another.

Enemy mortars and artillery fell without letup into the lines—a few rounds here, a few rounds there, but always enough to cause more casualties and make sleep impossible. To warn against infiltration and signal the start of a banzai, empty tobacco and ration cans were strung on heavy cord that stretched from foxhole to foxhole.

On the beaches activity was hectic. Shore parties worked in the eerie half-light of parachute flares fired from close-in destroyers to illuminate the front. Bulldozers roared and clanked, pulling pallets of supplies inland, cutting down terraces and carving roadways so tanks and trucks could move, winching wrecked equipment from the surf and sand, scooping out protective revetments for ammunition, fuel, and medical aid stations.

More than a thousand casualties had been evacuated before dark; but hundreds were still on the beaches, some on stretchers, others lying on ponchos on the sand. Many would die before they could be removed to hospital ships in the morning.

From five hundred yards offshore, gunboats laid down harassing fire on known enemy targets. Their bombardment went on throughout the night; by dawn more than ten thousand rounds of 4.2-inch high explosives had dropped just ahead of the lines and on the high ground in the center. Battleships added to the crescendo with intermittent salvos of 16-inch shells that screeched through the darkness and crashed to earth four miles away near Iwo's northern shore.

If any of the men in the lines or along the beaches could find surcease to their anxiety, it came from having lived and trained with men in the next foxhole or shell crater. They knew each other's faces, voices, temperaments, combat experience, family backgrounds, and from close comradeship they drew inner strength.

Second Lieutenant Cyril P. Zurlinden Jr. and Sergeant Roy Heinecke weren't this lucky.

Ashore since early afternoon to gather news copy and pictures from correspondents, and see that stories and negatives got to the *Eldorado* to be censored and sent stateside for publication, they hadn't seen a familiar face on the beachhead. They had more gear than most assault troops: personal knapsacks and weapons, a typewriter and camera, and a heavy seabag packed with copy and carbon paper, manila envelopes, several waterpoof canvas bags with PRESS stenciled across them, and a satchel of two-ounce bottles of hundred-proof brandy.

They had been side by side on Saipan before Zurlinden was given a field commission, and both were newsmen in civilian life—Zurlinden, an Associated Press correspondent in Annapolis, Maryland, where he was known as "Pete, the little round man that covers the Capitol"; Heinecke, a press photographer from Olney, Pennsylvania. They were pinned down for hours, but shortly before five o'clock fire became sporadic, and they started up the slope with the load of baggage, dragging the heavy seabag between them in the sand.

At sundown the lonely pair was two hundred yards nearer the ridge. They found a vacant crater, dug shallow foxholes in its bottom, piled packs and the burdensome seabag around the positions, and broke out blankets and ponchos to ward off the night's chill. Zurlinden was dozing when he heard Heinecke:

"Pete! The bastards are walking the stuff this way!" Shrapnel from exploding artillery zinged inches over their heads, and each barrage was coming near. "Why the hell can't they leave us alone?" Zurlinden complained.

Two shells slammed down a few yards away, sending black clouds of sand and hot steel over them. An instant later two more shattering blasts came. Zurlinden was blown skyward, then fell back into the crater in a cascade of dirt and shell fragments. He heard Heinecke yell that he'd been hit, and Zurlinden knew something was dreadfully wrong with his own body. He looked down and saw that his left leg twisted away from his body at a grotesque angle. He slumped back in sharp pain and felt the warm ooze of blood saturating his dungarees.

Both men had been in tight spots before, but never in anything like this. Zurlinden was grateful for two things: Heinecke had a cool head in any situation, and each carried two canteens—one filled with water, the other with brandy. He was swept by nausea, but found enough strength to unscrew the cap and take a long pull of the brandy. He felt better, and asked Heinecke what shape he was in.

"Got it in the legs and back," was the reply. "I can't stand up!"

"Get some sulfa powder on it," Zurlinden said. "My leg is gone."

He looked down again and thought he saw an extra limb and foot. The sight offended him; he had to get rid of the thing. He grabbed for it and tried to fling the bloody mess from the hole. It was his own leg, still attached to his body in a tangle of flesh and bone. He straightened the limb as best he could and tried to kill the agony and his stomach's demand to vomit by gulping down another slug of brandy.

Heinecke's foxhole had vanished in the rubble, and he painfully scooped out another while lying on his side. When it was done, he crawled to Zurlinden and they pulled a poncho over their heads to wait. They were lighting their cigarettes when the ground shook with another deafening roar from another shell. Heinecke's new foxhole was gone; they were saved only by the sand and knapsacks around them. For the rest of the night, they huddled under the poncho, shivering from a combination of the cold, the ebb and flow of fear, and their wounds.

Dawn was cutting through the overcast when another shell, this time a mortar, landed on the lip of the crater. Packs and seabag were blown to bits, but there was no further damage. Heinecke checked his wounds, found he could walk with a painful limp, and went for help. Four men came with a litter for the lieutenant.

Zurlinden kept his leg, and with steel braces it worked well enough for him to dance at his wedding a year later. After the war, he went back to newspapering and was a top reporter for *The Los Angeles Times*. Heinecke recovered fully, stayed in the Marine Corps, went to Korea and Vietnam, retired after twenty years' active duty, and became a foreign service officer of the State Department.

Zurlinden's and Heinecke's ordeal the first night on Iwo was commonplace. The situation was critical everywhere, but the business of war went on. Men on the front remained alert for the expected banzai; others labored to clear the landing zones and General Kuribayashi's guns fired so often and accurately that Admiral Turner was forced to close Yellow and Blue Beaches shortly after eleven o'clock for two hours.

Two hundred yards from the base of Suribachi, Colonel Liversedge studied his map of the sector by lantern light under a blackout tarpaulin that covered his shell hole command post, and issued orders for the 28th Regiment's morning attack against the obstreperous objective. A few feet away Lieutenant Colonel Robert Williams, his executive officer, shaved with a straight razor. His hand was steady as a steel beam as mortars landed thirty yards away. Neither man bothered to look up.

Since second lieutenant days, Liversedge—a tall man who moved with a loping stride—was known as "Harry the Horse" to his men and fellow officers. He had started in the war leading a raider battalion in the south Pacific, had fought at Tarawa and Saipan, and was decorated for leadership and bravery under fire. He was from Volcano, California, and, by strange coincidence, his men were now going after Iwo's own volcano landmark.

Up at the northern end of the beaches, Ralph Haas's battalion took more casualties as the enemy pounded it on the slopes leading to the quarry. Shortly after midnight, his CP was hit by mortars and the colonel and his operations officer, Captain Fred C. Eberhardt, were killed. Lieutenant Colonel Louis B. Blissard, the executive officer, crawled six feet from his hole and took command of the outfit. D-Day had cost it a third of its officers, and nearly forty percent of its troops.

Less than two hundred yards away, an artillery shell found the 25th Regiment's ammunition and fuel dump about an hour before dawn. Raging fires and thundering explosions lit up the rock-strewn landscape and brought down heavier fire. Exploding rockets and tracers zoomed skyward, and belts of machine gun bullets popped like an endless chain of giant firecrackers.

Lieutenant Commander W. W. Ayres, a regimental surgeon, found himself buried in a caved-in foxhole. He clawed free and began digging in the next hole for Major Leo A. McSweeney. His hands found a helmet; beneath it was the major, his lungs all but bursting. Ayres freed McSweeney's nose and mouth and kept digging. Burning ammunition exploded around them. The doctor pulled McSweeney out and they crawled away, gasping for air and ducking stray bullets.

Robert Sherrod, of *Time* and *Life* magazines, shivered through the hectic night in a foxhole halfway down the perimeter. He was an old hand; had been with the Marines at Tarawa and Saipan. At dawn, he looked from his shallow shelter and surveyed the scene.

"The first night on Iwo Jima can only be described as a nightmare in hell," he told millions of readers. "About the beach in the morning lay the dead. They had died with the greatest possible violence. Nowhere in the Pacific have I seen such badly mangled bodies. Many were cut squarely in half. Legs and arms lay fifty feet from any body." Eight dead Marines were in a crater not ten yards away. Two unexploded land mines were just on the other side of his foxhole. Within a hundred feet he counted some fifty Marines, wounded but still fighting.

On one of the attack transports offshore, Lieutenant Commander J. H. McCauley, of Los Angeles, finished surgery on his nineteenth casualty. He was proud of the last operation: he hated to amputate, and had saved the leg of a red-haired corporal. A doctor at the next table had performed brain surgery during the night. "First time I've ever tried that in a ground swell," he said. Their ship had expected to handle twenty casualties that day, at most; seventy-four was the total for the day and night.

D-Day plus one was beginning. Out on the *Eldorado*, General Smith took another look at the battle reports and wondered why there had been no banzai; why "every man, every cook, baker, and candlestick maker" hadn't met the assault on the beaches. "I don't know who is he, but the Jap general running the show is one smart bastard," he told correspondents.

General Rockey was ready to leave the *Athene* and open up Fifth Division headquarters ashore; likewise, General Cates of the Fourth on *Auburn*. Far to the southeast, General Erskine's command ship *Fremont* and the Third Division's LSTs and transports were rendezvoused. "The Big E" was sure the division would be used.

General Kuribayashi, from his concrete blockhouse headquarters in the high ground above the second airstrip, had informed Tokyo that Marines had landed and that he was slaughtering the invaders. With little cost to Iwo's defenses, his guns had maimed and killed Marines in dreadful numbers during the first eighteen hours. In all, 2,312 had fallen.

At the White House, President Roosevelt was told of the invasion and that the battle continued. He shuddered at the casualties. "It was the first time in the war, through good news and bad," author Jim Bishop wrote, "that anyone had seen the President gasp in horror."

Minesweeper delivers close-in D-Day firepower against shore batteries north of invasion beaches. (*Arthur J. Kiely, Jr.*)

Marines form human conveyor belts on D-plus two to unload supplies from LSTs on Red Beach II. (*U.S. Coast Guard*)

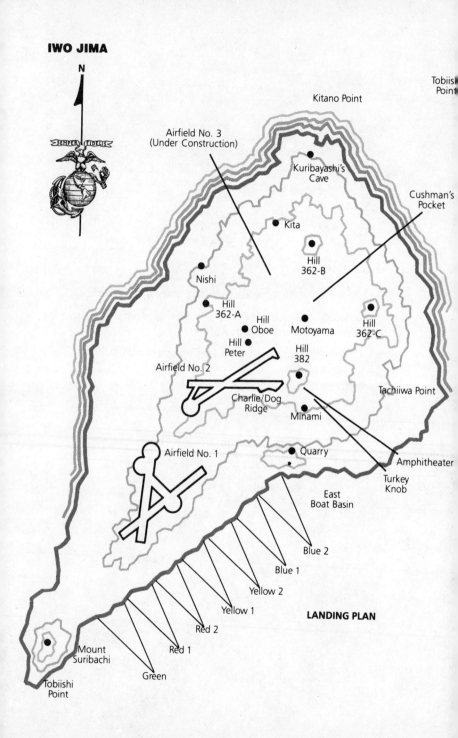

IWO JIMA

N

Tobiishi
Point

Kitano Point

Airfield No. 3
(Under Construction)

Kuribayashi's
Cave

Cushman's
Pocket

Kita

Hill
362-B

Nishi

Hill
362-A

Hill
Oboe

Motoyama

Hill
362-C

Hill
Peter

Hill
382

Airfield No. 2

Tachiiwa Point

Charlie/Dog
Ridge

Minami

Airfield No. 1

Quarry

Amphitheater

Turkey
Knob

East
Boat Basin

Blue 2

Blue 1

Yellow 2

Yellow 1

LANDING PLAN

Red 2

Red 1

Mount
Suribachi

Green

Tobiishi
Point

Suribachi

556 ft.

Hill 382

382 ft.

Kitano Point

Five Miles

D-Day Objective

Final Jap Pocket

D-Day Plus 14-35

D-Day Plus 14-35

D-Day Plus 5

Actual Line at D-Day's End

4th Marine Division

3rd Marine Division

General Direction   Attack

5th Marine Division

Green Beach I: H-hour plus twenty minutes. Marines advance under heavy machine gun and mortar fire. (*Robert R. Campbell*)

Burdened with heavy packs and equipment, communications men push inland from Blue Beach II. (*Obbie Newcomb*)

Thirty-seven millimeter gun unleashes support fire for troops assaulting the 556-foot volcano. (*James Cornelius*)

Flame-thrower Sherman tank burns pillbox near base of Suribachi as infantry waits to attack. (*Mark Kaufman*)

Marines from Chandler Johnson's battalion begin final drive to raise flag atop Suribachi, passing dead Japanese as they move out. (*Louis R. Lowery*)

LEFT - Marine artillery slams into enemy position as advance continues. (*Louis R. Lowery*)

RIGHT - Flame-thrower and infantrymen approach summit. (*James R. Lowery*)

PART FOUR

The Men of Suribachi and Two Flags

1

General Kuribayashi knew from the first that, when the Americans came, they would try to isolate and seize Mount Suribachi—it was simple military logic. Suribachi's 556-foot summit dominated the island's eight square miles of barren, volcanic rubble. It was an all-seeing eye to watch every movement on the island and direct pin-pointed bombardment on the invaders.

So he began on his first day on Iwo to fortify the maze of boulder-strewn gullies and ravines at the base, the honeycomb of caves on its steep slopes, and the huge crater at its crest.

By D-Day, Suribachi was as formidable as the famed Rock of Gibraltar. The wasteland at the foot of the volcano was studded with more than seventy camouflaged concrete blockhouses. Another fifty were concealed on its rocky sides, and many of these were connected by tunnels with hundreds of caves, mortar and sniper pits, and rein-forced pillboxes.

Two thousand troops defended Suribachi. They weren't Kuri-bayashi's best men; his elite forces held the deep main defense line across the island at its widest point two and a half miles to the north. He hoped the volcano would hold out for at least ten days to ravage the beaches with its own arsenal and direct fire for his other fortifi-cations in the northern highlands, positions from which to bleed the Marines to death with bombardment.

Following the Samurai's plan of defense, if Suribachi fell earlier, and the Marines pushed northward, the cream of the general's fight-ers—and his strongest defenses—still would slaughter the Americans.

Colonel Kanehiko Atsuchi commanded the Suribachi garrison. He believed he would die on the mountain; there had been too many close calls before D-Day when his headquarters rattled with near misses from bombing and naval gunfire. At fifty-six, he was the oldest colonel in the Imperial Army, and his battalion commanders were a motley group.

One was an aging lieutenant colonel passed over for promotion because of his years; one was a major with no combat experience; and two of the three captains had risen through the ranks without attending the Imperial Military Academy—a rarity in the Japanese army. But at Iwo, all fought valiantly and died with their troops. Six of Atsuchi's men survived the battle, huddled in a barbed-wire stockade at the volcano's base when the fighting ended.

Marines gave Suribachi the code name "Hotrocks," and clouds of steam did occasionally billow from its crater. Before the invasion, troops had heard rumors that heavy naval gunfire and air bombardment might set off a full-scale eruption of the slumbering mountain, but seismologists disagreed.

When "Harry the Horse" Liversedge and the 28th Marines went to work on Suribachi on D-Day plus one, his three assault battalions were across the seven-hundred-yard isthmus. But the ground they held was less than two hundred yards deep, and faced the enemy in two directions. Now they must surround the fortress before they could move up the slopes to the summit, while at the same time they had to push northward toward the airstrip. It took four bloody days to do the job.

"It's gonna be a helluva day in a helluva place to fight the goddamned war," Colonel Johnson said as his battalion jumped off at 8:30. The thirty-seven-year-old Naval Academy man came from Highland Park, Illinois, and was headed for high command if Iwo, or another invasion down the road, didn't claim his life. In earlier campaigns, his lackadaisical attitude toward personal danger flabbergasted even the bravest men, and the pattern continued.

On D-Day, he strode casually and erect up and down Green Beach, stub of a cigar in his mouth, exhorting his men: "Okay, you Marines, let's get the goddamned hell off this beach!" He was short and chubby, if not a trifle fat; not the tall, trim stereotype of a career Leatherneck officer. He flaunted regulations by wearing a faded cotton fatigue cap with upturned bill instead of a steel helmet. He didn't carry a knapsack, he didn't wear a cartridge belt, and disdained all combat gear except a Colt .45 pistol carried in his right hip pocket; he didn't even have a canteen.

Where Johnson was concerned, clothes didn't make the man— at least in combat. His superiors—and, more important, his men— knew he was all Marine, and that's what mattered. He was a stern disciplinarian, and could outlast any man on a thirty-mile training march; then he did tote a full battle pack to show he could. He had the mean look of a Marine bulldog when angry; a mellow, smiling, almost fatherly expression when in a good mood. His men were devoted and proud to be in his battalion; they would go anywhere, do anything he asked because they knew he'd be with them all the way.

Now Johnson was at it again, nonchalantly gesturing and pointing out enemy positions as the battalion moved around Suribachi's base from the east. The task at hand was his only concern. He has a devout believer in the centuries-old axiom of warriors that fear is a deadly contagion in battle, but that courage of combat commanders under fire can spark and flame the determination of men to fight beyond their limits. In the jargon of the still-to-come space age, Johnson and his men had "the right stuff."

Jackson Butterfield's battalion jumped off at the same time, pointed around the volcano from the west. His men thought the name sounded more like a professor's—or maybe a lawyer's or a minister's—than a veteran of hard fighting in the central and south Pacific. He had little of Johnson's devil-take-the-hindmost attitude, but his men knew he was fearless in combat; the outfit had been the first to drive across the isthmus and he had been in the thick of the action.

Charley Shepard's battalion was in reserve, taking on fresh men to replace casualties and mopping up die-hard strongpoints bypassed in D-Day's fighting. They didn't expect too much trouble, and weren't expected to take any new ground. But nonetheless they killed seventy-five Japanese in what often was close-in and bitter fighting.

There were no air strikes and no naval shelling before the jump-off; Japanese lines were too close to Marine positions. Tank support was also missing: eight were expected to spearhead the push, but they were sitting silent, out of fuel and ammunition. It took two hours to resupply the Shermans, and when they started to move, a storm of mortars hit them from Suribachi. Twice more they tried to join the attack; twice more they were bracketed by shelling.

By midmorning, the advance was from fifty to seventy yards, and it had been costly. Without help from the tanks, it was a case of frontal assault by riflemen and demolitions teams against well-entrenched and camouflaged positions. Shortly after eleven o'clock, the Shermans finally were able to grind into the melee. Newly landed artillery moved inland and commenced firing. For a time, the push slowly gained some momentum, but opposition was still fierce.

Even with the added firepower, the advance had sputtered to a halt by sundown, and Johnson and Butterfield ordered the men to dig in for the night. They had gained from 175 to two hundred yards, and lost twenty-nine men killed and 123 wounded—one fallen Marine for nearly every yard of new ground.

Another chilly night of anxiety engulfed men in their foxholes. Flares lit the sides of Suribachi and the narrow front as they slowly floated to earth under oscillating parachutes. Marines kept alert for any movement from the mountaintop, and Japanese on it fired periodic pyrotechnic signals to their artillery in the north that brought almost immediate response: heavy shelling of Marine positions. The all-night harassment made sleep beyond question, as did the constant threat of infiltration and the still-expected banzai. But, for the second night, it didn't come. General Kuribayashi was following his battle plan to the letter.

Again the Japanese got a potent, unexpected ally on D-Day plus two: the weather. During the night, the northeast wind swelled to gale force. Six-foot surf lashed the cluttered beachhead, and Admiral Turner ordered it shut down for the third time since H-Hour.

At daybreak fast-moving clouds looked heavy with rain. But visibility was good, and at eight o'clock forty planes came in from the carriers. They hit Suribachi and positions guarding its base for twenty minutes in wave after wave of rocket and machine gun fire and napalm. At 8:30, Johnson's and Butterfield's men took up the advance from where it had stopped. Shepard's battalion jumped off, headed in the other direction, northward, to deepen the hold across the island.

From platoon leader to private, the Third Platoon, Easy Company, Second Battalion, 28th Regiment, Fifth Marine Division was a microcosm of all Marines on Iwo Jima. Ethnic backgrounds, personalities, physical characteristics, civilian jobs, attitudes, and personal desires and ambitions were a cross section of every outfit fighting to take the island.

First Lieutenant John K. Wells's platoon was at the point of the push by Johnson's men. He was a twenty-three-year-old Texan, who carried a Thompson submachine gun with a forty-round clip of ammunition. Like his commander, he was on the flamboyant side; back in base camp he wore his khaki overseas cap at a jaunty forward tilt, and he spent more time mingling with his men than in officers' country.

Sun and wind had deeply tanned his strong features, making him look older than his years. It was his first time in combat, but when he stormed a pillbox on the beach, the troops were sure they had a leader who knew what he was doing. They called him "Tex" or "G. K." for Genghis Khan.

Ernest I. Thomas was Wells's platoon sergeant and second in command of the forty-five-man outfit, a twenty-year-old, hard-boiled, rough-talking former drill instructor at San Diego's boot camp. His men liked "Thomas the Tiger," a name given more in recognition of a self-proclaimed prowess as a lady-killer than for ferocity. "His growl is worse than his claws," they said.

Sergeant Henry O. Hansen was number three. The twenty-three-year-old platoon guide came from Somerville, Massachusetts. "The Count" was slender, just under six feet, and prided himself on a natty appearance in snappy dress blue uniform, khakis, or dungarees. The platoon called him "one helluva fighter," and he lived up to the billing on D-Day when he demolished four pillboxes and pulled three wounded men from no man's land in the process.

Sergeant Howard M. Snyder, from Huntington Park, California, was twenty-two, a squad leader with four campaigns behind him. "Maybe I'm crazy," he said before landing, "but I'm looking forward to this fight. I think it'll beat anything I've seen so far." Iwo met his expectations.

Corporal Harold P. Keller was from an Iowa hamlet incongruously named Brooklyn. He was a BAR man and, like Snyder, a veteran of four earlier landings—one from a submarine in a raid on Makin Island—and had been wounded at Bougainville. His combat record gave newcomers a feeling of security; he knew what war was all about, and how to survive.

The platoon called Corporal Everett M. Lavelle "Pappy." He was in his thirties, graying at the temples—the oldest man in the outfit—and had three battle stars. He came from Bellingham, Washington, and throughout the first night on Iwo, he said he had a constant thought: "Jesus, what a relief it'll be when morning comes." Now he wasn't so sure.

At eighteen, Private First Class James Robeson was the youngest member of the platoon. He, too, was from Washington, a town with the Indian name Chewelah, and looked younger than he was. Shaving wasn't yet a daily ritual, and his button nose was a perpetual victim of sunburn. Iwo was his first battle. His buddies called him "Chicken" or "Baby" or "Chick." He didn't mind the latter.

Sergeant Kenneth D. Midkiff was an easygoing mountaineer from West Virginia. He spoke in a soft drawl, was a former paratrooper, and had made three amphibious assaults before Iwo. The platoon felt comfortable around "Katie"; he was battle-wise and cautious and planned to return when the war was over to his native hills "to hunt, fish, and make some moonshine." He never made it.

Private First Class Raymond Strahm had three landings under his belt; four, counting Iwo. He had learned to use a parachute as a Paramarine, but, like Midkiff, always went ashore in a landing craft— all Marine parachute units disbanded before making a combat jump. A shade over six feet tall, Strahm was called "Little Raymond." The Chicagoan was the platoon's world-class poker player. The week before embarking, he'd cleaned out a big game back on Hawaii, won $3,700, and loaned losers ten dollars each.

Scholar of the unit was Corporal Robert A. Leader, a student at the Boston Museum of Fine Arts when he signed up. Red-haired, blue-eyed, fair-complexioned and tall, he had the reserve and practicality expected of a Massachusetts Yankee. Iwo Jima, for him, was a short and brutal experience.

On D-Day, sand from an artillery burst buried him completely; after what seemed like an eternity buddies dug him out, unhurt. Six days later he was cut down by machine gun fire during the fight for the second airstrip. This time, Harold Keller dragged him to safety and an aid station. Leader survived near-fatal stomach wounds, spent months recovering in a stateside hospital, and returned to school. He became, in postwar years, a well-known liturgical artist and Associate Professor of Art at Notre Dame University.

Private First Class Louis Adrain was a taciturn Spokane Indian from Wellpinit, Washington. Seeing no enemy troops on the beach, he asked: "Where's the reception committee?" Now, the morning of D-Day plus two, a sniper's bullet pierced his heart. He fell forward, wearing a borrowed dungaree jacket with another man's name across the back, weapon still firing.

One of the platoon could have missed Iwo. Private First Class John J. Fredotovitch was in Camp Pendleton's hospital in California when the Fifth Division was shipped out to Hawaii. He talked his way back to the outfit, and was now in action for the third day. Shortly before noon, mortar fragments bit into his left shoulder and upper left leg. For him the battle was over. His immigrant Russian-Polish parents in Oakland, California, were glad he was still alive.

Corporal Leonce Olivier could trace his ancestry back two centuries to the French Cajuns who came to Eunice, Louisiana, from Canada. "Frenchy" didn't trust the Garand M-1 rifle most infantrymen used; he thought the '03 Springfield, a pre-World War I vintage weapon, more accurate and reliable. His buddies weren't happy when he said, "This is gonna be worse than Tarawa," where he'd used the Springfield to win the Silver Star Medal for gallantry.

There were thirty-two others in the platoon—men like nineteen-year-old Private First Class Richard S. White, a devout Baptist from east Texas who yelled to a corporal as they moved forward, "You still an atheist?" A mortar exploded yards away and the answer came back: "I'm gonna start praying in the morning."

There were men like Platoon Sergeant Josephy McGarvey, a rabid baseball fan from Philadelphia. He crouched behind a bunker waiting for the mortar barrage to lift when one of his squad jumped into the hole: "You think the Phillies will win the pennant this year?" "I hope so," McGarvey said, and went about his business as the shelling lifted—business that would earn him the Silver Star.

And there was Private First Class Donald J. Ruhl.

He was twenty-one, came from Montana's cattle country, and was a maverick to the core. At base camp in Hawaii he often was in trouble—ignoring orders, arguing and fighting, the platoon's malcontent. But, like Tony Stein, he had the killer instincts of a cowtown gunfighter, and they showed on D-Day. In a one-man charge against a fiercely defended blockhouse, he killed nine Japanese, dragged a wounded Marine to safety through forty yards of no man's land, and spent the night alone in an enemy machine gun pit he had captured single-handedly; he wanted to make damned sure the weapon wouldn't be used against the platoon.

Now, on D-plus two, he and Sergeant Hansen were at the point of the struggling assault. By eleven o'clock they had worked to within a few yards of Suribachi's base when they spotted a camouflaged bunker and dove for cover. Ruhl raised his head above a boulder to get a better view and heard a sputtering hiss.

"Sonuvabitch! Watch out! Grenade!" he yelled to Hansen as it landed six feet away. He flung himself on the missile, his body taking the full impact of the explosion. In the only three days of combat he would ever see, Ruhl had earned the Medal of Honor and sacrificed his life to save his sergeant.

From a hundred different positions on the slopes of Suribachi, barking machine guns, screaming artillery, and crumping mortars seemed to be coming simultaneously along with the cries of "Corpsman! Corpsmannnnnn!" Wounded crawled, when they could, to any protection they could find. Stretcher bearers braved the scythe-like fire in desperate rescue attempts as the fighting roared on.

"Genghis Khan" Wells and four men hugged the sides of a shell hole in front of another bunker waiting for the mortars to lift. One slammed into the crater, and all were wounded in the blast. The lieutenant was groggy, bleeding profusely, but refused to leave the scene. He took a shot of morphine from Corpsman John Bradley and kept command of the platoon.

Corporal Charles W. Lindberg saw what was happening as Wells and the other wounded crawled behind the pillbox alive with machine gun fire. With his flamethrower he turned the enemy position into a roaring furnace. Two more pillboxes and a bunker were yards away; it took two minutes to flame them and their defenders. As the advance moved ahead, bullets still thudded around Wells as he screamed orders, but his strength ebbed and his wounds filled with sand as he fought to stay conscious. Yet it was another half hour before he turned the platoon over to Sergeant Thomas and made his way to the battalion aid station where litter bearers ducked mortars to take him to the beach for evacuation.

"Thomas the Tiger" knew what he had to do. He located three tanks and led them against several pillboxes and bunkers. The heavily reinforced positions were silenced in a furious firefight that cleared the way for the rest of the battalion to break through to the base of Suribachi; the area had been the soft spot in the defense line. Wells and Thomas received the Navy Cross for their actions; Lindberg, the Silver Star.

Action was fierce the rest of the day as artillery and mortars rained down from Suribachi, and enemy machine gunners and snipers raked the attacking troops in front of the slopes. At sunset things quieted down, but it was eleven o'clock before the line was consolidated and the men of the 28th dug in for another night.

Butterfield's troops had gained 650 yards; Shephard's, five hundred; Johnson's, one thousand. Marines now were in solid strength at Suribachi's north base and halfway around the volcano.

Chandler Johnson was pleased with his battalion's performance during the day, especially that of Wells's platoon. He'd been with them several times, moving among the ravines and boulders, pointing out positions, and prodding the men to keep going. "Stay in one place and the bastards'll kill you," he yelled at one point to a squad pinned down by mortars. That night he made a mental note that he'd found the right unit for the final push to take Suribachi's summit when the time came.

He couldn't have found more determined men; they not only had blasted open the way to the volcano's base, but in one day their platoon had become the most decorated in Marine Corps history: one man had earned the Medal of Honor, two would receive the Navy Cross, the second highest decoration awarded Marines; one would wear the Silver Star; seven would get Bronze Stars; and seventeen, Purple Hearts for wounds received in a single dawn-to-dusk action on a tiny chunk of forlorn real estate.

It was strangely calm early in the evening at the base of Suribachi. Men nearest the mountain could hear muffled chatter among the defenders as they moved about in caves on the slope, and there was the spasmodic tat-tat-tat, tat-tat-tat of machine guns and the cracking of rifles. There were still enemy artillery and mortars, but not as heavy as during the two previous nights.

Then, shortly after 2:00 A.M., Japanese infiltrators struck at Johnson's battalion—not in a screaming banzai, but in a well-organized raid. Mortars made a shambles of the attack before it had hardly begun, and sixty enemy intruders were killed in the barrage made more deadly by a thirty-minute firefight. On the western side of the volcano, where Shepard's men were dug in, twenty-eight more Japanese were cut down in a fierce ten-minute melee. Butterfield's men, alerted by the furor, expected something, but it never came.

2

D-plus three was George Washington's Birthday, a national holiday back home, but on Iwo few men remembered or cared. Overnight, the weather had turned miserable. A torrential cold rain soaked men to the skin, and jelled with the coarse volcanic ash to clog and jam weapons.

Meteorologists at Makalapa had warned about the weather at Iwo this time of the year. Their studies found that major storms often buffeted the island, that the skies were clear only twenty percent of the time, that forty-five percent of the days were cloudy, twenty-seven percent partly cloudy, and nine percent rainy. Now the heavy rain was driven by a twenty-knot gale that whipped up a pounding nine-foot surf. At 10:20 A.M., the beaches were closed again; it was useless to try to land reinforcements and supplies. Angry clouds hung below five hundred feet and hid Suribachi's crest.

But a battle can't wait for weather. At eight o'clock, despite the wind and the rain, the attack against Suribachi started again.

Tanks couldn't move in the hub-deep slush; artillery didn't fire because targets couldn't be spotted; there was no air support or naval shelling. So it was another dirty job for the infantry. They shivered under the driving rain and moved out against the dreadful terrain and the desperate, determined foe estimated by "Harry the Horse" Liversedge's intelligence officers to number six hundred still alive.

Drenched Marines assaulted foxhole after foxhole, pillbox after pillbox, bunker after bunker with rifle fire, grenades, flamethrowers, and demolitions. It was slow and dangerous work, but they made steady progress. An eleven-man patrol worked partway up the steep, rocky slopes searching for a route to the summit; naval gunfire and air strikes had wiped out existing trails.

While Johnson's men cleared out opposition around the eastern side of the volcano and battled up the slippery sides, Shepard's battalion bolstered the line in the center. Butterfield's outfit still slugged around the western side, bent on final encirclement of the fortress.

At 6:30 P.M., the push was halted for the day. Opposition had been heavy, but it had come in wild flurries, not in the sustained fighting that had marked previous days. In some ways the weather helped the Marines, exhausted from three days of bloody battle. With the near-zero visibility and curtains of rain, Japanese artillery and mortar fire were sharply reduced, not only around Suribachi, but across the entire island.

And it was now becoming apparent that the assault had taken its toll of the defenders and cut deeply into their ability to hold the mountain much longer.

Night was relatively quiet on the lines. No infiltrators. No savage firefights. The weather improved, and once again the beachhead was operational. Men, equipment, and supplies came ashore. Casualties were evacuated.

Offshore, aboard the *Auburn*, where General Smith now had his headquarters, losses were tallied. They were far worse than he expected, and, like President Roosevelt, he shuddered. In three days they amounted to 4,574 men killed and wounded. In the push to take the airstrip, and in the fighting for the high ground around the quarry, the Fourth Division had lost 2,517 on the beaches. The Fifth Division, on Green Beach and in the push to conquer Suribachi, had lost 2,057.

Chandler Johnson was busy long before dawn of D-plus four, briefing his company commanders on the day's plan of action. He was determined that Marines would be atop the volcano by sundown, and was trying to figure out the best way to get there. Shortly after daybreak he ordered out the first patrols. At eight o'clock, he sent a runner for First Lieutenant Harold Schrier, who had taken command of Wells's platoon during the night.

He pointed out to Schrier a possible route up the slopes. His orders were simple: "Take the platoon up the hill, and put this on top."

Johnson handed him a small flag—it measured fifty-four by twenty-eight inches—that First Lieutenant George G. Wells, the battalion adjutant, had brought ashore in a map case from the transport *Missoula*. Wells knew it would be wanted when the summit was taken.

Scouts from D and F Companies already were on the steep sides looking for a path to the crest and feeling out resistance. Sergeant Sherman B. Watson and three privates were surprised at how easy the the ascent was going—once out of the sliding rocks near the base the footing was good. George Mercer, who came from a small Iowa town, was amazed at the quiet. Louis Charlo, an Indian from Montana's sheep country, glanced over his shoulder at the spectacular view. Theodore White, a Kansas wheat farmer, expected that "all hell would break loose at any minute." So far they had met no resistance, and within forty minutes they were on the crest, peering into the cone. Still no Japanese, but they spotted several machine guns with neat stacks of ammunition nearby. It was 9:40 A.M. They scampered and slid down the slope to make their report.

Lieutenant Schrier, a lanky twenty-four-year-old veteran of a disbanded Marine Raider Battalion, was ready to move out with his men. They had stocked up with ammunition, replenished supplies of hand grenades and demolition charges, and flamethrowers were full of fuel. A radioman and two stretcher teams joined the forty-man patrol. So did Louis R. Lowery, a twenty-five-year-old staff sergeant photographer for *Leatherneck*, the official Marine Corps magazine.

They left in single file, moving at a fast clip until the climbing became steeper. They passed a Marine howitzer with two men sprawled across the weapon—it had taken a direct hit from artillery—as well as several dead Japanese, one of whom wore bright orange sneakers. As the slope steepened, the men stopped every few minutes for breath. Flankers went out to guard the column. At times when climbing became difficult, the ascent was on hands and knees. Several threatening cave entrances were passed, but there was no fire; nor were any live Japanese seen.

Marines below watched in astonishment. Offshore, men tracked the snake-like column through binoculars. One sailor on a transport said: "Those guys should be getting flight pay."

Schrier crested the summit first and called a halt. In thirty minutes the patrol had climbed half-a-thousand feet up what had been a death-dealing mountain for four days. Not a shot had been fired, not a man hurt. He peered into the crater, saw the unmanned machine guns, several destroyed rocket launchers, a number of mortar pits, and five artillery pieces. "Where the hell are the Nips?" he muttered aloud, and signaled the rest of the men to follow.

Harold Snyder, the sergeant who was "looking forward to this fight," was next over the lip. Harold Keller, the careful corporal from Brooklyn, Iowa, followed. Right behind was "Chick" Robeson, the platoon's teen-age "baby"; then came the scholar corporal, Robert Leader. They felt they were in the eye of a hurricane: it was all too

quiet—an eerie, frightening, almost deathly stillness. One man uri-
nated into the cone. "This is what I think of you sonsabitches," he
said.

Sergeant Thomas and about half the patrol, weapons primed for
firing, stood silhouetted on the skyline atop the rim. Others probed
down the crater's sides looking for Japanese. Several men scouted for
something on which to raise the flag.

Keller saw the first enemy. "The Nip started to climb out of a
deep hole with his back to me," he said in telling of the action. "I
fired three times from the hip and he dropped out of sight." The rifle
fire triggered an immediate torrent of grenades from several camouflaged cave mouths, and the Marines answered with bullets and grenades of their own in a short-lived scrimmage that ended as quickly
as it had begun.

While the melee was at its height, two men—Leader and Private
First Class Leo J. Rozek—had found a seven-foot length of iron pipe
from a rainwater cistern, and they attached the flag to it. No one in
the patrol bothered to check the time, but thousands of men below,
and aboard the ships of the offshore armada, knew to the minute when
it happened.

It was 10:31 A.M., February 23, 1945. An instant in history.

"There goes the flag!" shouted the Marines at the base of Suribachi.

Those on the beaches, who were aware of what was happening
and could see it, cheered the sight with their own shouts of jubilation.
Ships' radios crackled with news of the momentous event and flashed
it to those in the fleet who couldn't see it. General Kuribayashi, if he
saw Marines atop the mountain, must have known the end for Suribachi's defenders was at hand—something the Japanese on the volcano
already knew.

Lou Lowery focused his Rollecord camera to capture the historic moment: the raising of the first flag on Iwo Jima. Robeson,
crouching at the cameraman's side, refused to be in the picture; he
"didn't want to be a Hollywood Marine." As the flag blew almost hor-
izontal to the rocky ground, four members of the platoon were photographed: Schrier, Thomas, Lindberg, and Private First Class James
R. Nicel, a replacement who had joined the outfit that morning.

As Lowery clicked the shutter, a Japanese leaped from a cave
and opened fire on him and Robeson. He missed. Robeson didn't; his

BAR cut the enemy down in midstride. The body was grasped by its feet and dragged into the cave. An officer sprang from the entrance, snarling and swinging a broken sword in a giant half arc. Howard Snyder squeezed the trigger of his Colt .45. It misfired and the sergeant ducked for his life. A rifle burst from Private First Class Clarence B. Garrett stopped the one-man charge. But this was just the start.

Grenades came like hailstones from several caves. Marines sprayed the mouths with rifles and grenades, then flamethrowers moved in to burn the openings, and demolition blasts closed many almost as soon as they were flamed.

Lowery leaped to escape a grenade's explosion, and rolled and skidded fifty feet down the steepest slope. He was unhurt, and the camera, with its precious roll of film, was undamaged. His photo coverage of the campaign became an historical treasure in Marines Corps archives. After the war he stayed with *Leatherneck*, first as a six-striper sergeant and then as its civilian photographer director, until his retirement in 1982.

The frantic mini-battle was over in minutes. Within half an hour, Suribachi's commanding summit was serving the Marines as it had the Japanese—as an observation post. High-powered binoculars and electronic detection devices were in place, spotting enemy artillery whenever it fired anywhere on the island.

Lieutenant Schrier was puzzled as the platoon scouted the crater and nearby slopes for enemy positions. He wondered why the brief, sharp counterattack—the last organized resistance on Suribachi—hadn't come the instant the Marines moved over the crest. "We'd have been real dead ducks," he said. "They could've killed us all."

That afternoon, Sergeant Thomas and ten men inspected the cave from which the last attack had come. It burrowed nearly a hundred yards into the mountain; in it they found more than 150 dead Japanese. Most died by holding hand grenades to their stomachs and pulling the pins. Demolitions men blew the entrance to kill the overpowering stench and to give the enemy an unmarked mass grave.

Among the litter of documents the Marines found in the crater was one indicating that, the night before, about one hundred troops had left in the darkness in an attempt to sneak through Marine lines and join General Kuribayashi's main forces in the north. Only a handful made it, and they probably died in the fighting for the second airstrip.

Colonel Atsuchi's body never was found, nor were those of any of the other Japanese officers who most certainly were killed on the mountain with nearly two thousand of their men.

Several men on the beaches and near Suribachi's base, and at least one man aboard the hospital ship *Samaritan*, were more interested than most in the capture of the volcano's summit.

One was Chandler Johnson, watching from his CP. "Some sonuvabitch is going to want that flag," he told his adjutant, "but he's not going to get it. That's our flag. Better find another one and get it up there and bring ours back." A runner, a lisping corporal called "Wabbit," was sent scampering to the beach to see what he could find.

Fate had placed two others on Green Beach when the flag was raised. One was General Smith, and the other was the Secretary of the Navy.

"Holland, this means a Marine Corps for another five hundred years," Forrestal told the Old Warrior as they watched what was happening. "Howlin' Mad" nodded, his eyes filled with tears. Neither knew in advance that the final push to the summit was underway. Forrestal was on the beachhead because, over strenuous objections from Admiral Turner, he wanted to be there.

General Smith was there to be close to his Marines, and to be with the Navy's top man if anything happened; he didn't want to be safely aboard ship if Forrestal was hit by enemy fire. The beach was far from quiet: twenty-three Marines had been killed within the hour a few yards from where the brass stood. With them were two admirals, two of Forrestal's aides, and several reporters.

Forrestal wore khakis and a gray sweatshirt to break the cold, blustery wind. Both had steel helmets, were unarmed, and Smith wore a zippered combat jacket over fatigues. He chomped his omnipresent unlighted cigar and was "proud as hell to be wearing my Marine dungarees."

Platoon Leader Wells was aboard the *Samaritan* and raising seven kinds of hell to get ashore despite his wounds. "By God," he ranted, "they're my men, I'm sure of it, and I want to be with them and dammit, I'm going to be." An understanding doctor gave him a first-aid pack of sulfa and morphine, and the lieutenant hitched a ride on a press boat headed for shore to pick up correspondents' news copy. He limped to the start of the path up Suribachi and found Chick

Robeson and Private Robert E. Goode about to go to the top again. With arms around one another's shoulders, the trio labored up the steep slope to join the valiant platoon.

Colonel Johnson professed to be livid when he heard Wells was back on the mountain. He wasn't. "I was proud as hell of that young fighter," he told a newsman, and Wells kept his platoon to finish the mop-up of the crater.

Private Charles S. Rogers also had more than a casual interest in the flag-raising. He was nineteen, one of Johnson's men, and had been seriously wounded by mortars on D-Day. From his cot on the deck of the hospital ship *Solace* he could barely see the flag and wanted to lift himself for a better view. He couldn't make it, but he tried; his eyes misted and he was proud of the lump in his throat.

Joe Rosenthal was sorry he missed being with the platoon, but that's the way things often turn out. The thirty-three-year-old Associated Press photographer had been in the business a long time and knew, as he put it, "you win some, you lose some."

He'd been in the Pacific for a year, and had landed with the Marines at Guam and Peleliu, where he'd made a name for himself as a man who could make good pictures under fire. Before shipping out from AP's San Francisco bureau, he'd tried to enlist but none of the services would take him because of myopia so severe that he wore thick glasses, and had two extra sets with his photographic gear. He carried 150 pounds on a five-foot-five-inch frame and had a small mustache. Some friends said he resembled a French chef.

Rosenthal landed early D-Day afternoon on the Fourth Division's beaches and had made dozens of pictures of the fighting since then. He returned at sunset each day to the *Eldorado* to write captions and see that his negatives were aboard the courier flying boat to Guam, and to eat and sleep.

When he came ashore the morning of February 23, he trudged through the sand and up the terrace to Colonel Liversedge's command post. "Harry the Horse" told him Schrier's platoon already was on the summit, but Rosenthal decided to go up anyway; maybe he could get a panoramic shot of the island, or find something else worth shooting.

Two Marine photographers had the same idea, Sergeant William Genaust and Private Robert Campbell. Genaust was a motion picture cameraman with several rolls of sixteen-millimeter color film. Campbell had a Speed Graphic for black-and-white stills. The trio was about to begin the climb when "Wabbit" returned.

He was out of breath, but he had located another flag on LST 779 on the beachhead. It took several minutes to tell Ensign Alan S. Wood why he wanted it; with his excited, lisping speech he had trouble making himself understood. When Wood was able to decipher the Marine's mission, he gave him the ship's rarely used ceremonial flag. It was twice the size of the original, measuring eight feet by four feet, eight inches.

"Must be rough up there," the ensign said, as "Wabbit" nodded "yes" and took off in a dead run. He didn't want to catch hell from the colonel for being gone too long. Johnson immediately sent a man to the summit with the new flag, and he was there with several of the original flag-raisers when the trio of photographers arrived, huffing and puffing.

The new flag was immediately lashed to a longer length of pipe, and six Marines were having trouble shoving the staff into the rubble. The photographers watched for a moment and then scurried for positions to shoot the action.

Rosenthal frantically piled rocks to get better elevation to make his picture. He focused, and the Speed Graphic's shutter clicked just as the struggling Marines hoisted the new flag. He had preset the exposure at one four-hundredths of a second at between f/8 and f/11.

Genaust caught the action with his Bell & Howell Filmo, and was standing shoulder-to-shoulder with the AP man, shooting the identical and unforgettable scene in color on the few feet of color movie film that remained in his camera. As the second flag was raised, the first was simultaneously lowered. Campbell snapped his shutter at that instant, his photo showing both flags.

Rosenthal made two more pictures; one showing three Marines grasping the pipe after the large flag was raised; the other a group shot of the jubilant platoon with the Stars and Stripes snapping in the wind. He went down off the volcano and continued working until late afternoon, when he hitched a ride to the *Eldorado* for his nightly chores.

In his captions covering the day's shooting, the one for the flag-raising said: "Atop 550-foot Suribachi Yama, the volcano at the southwest tip of Iwo Jima, Marines of the Second Battalion, 28th Regiment,

Fifth Marine Division, hoist the Stars and Stripes, signaling the capture of this key position."

When the press pouch arrived at Guam, and Rosenthal's negatives
were processed, darkroom technicians knew immediately that the Suribachi photo was something very special. It didn't fit the pattern of a
conventional news picture; the face of only one man was clearly visible,
the rest were either hidden by hands and arms raising the flag, or
their heads were turned.

But it was a masterpiece of instantaneous composition and lighting
that captured the mood of the unfolding drama on Iwo Jima. Its stage-
like setting and the powerful position of the men gave it the graven
look of a posed statue; so much so, in fact, that cynics and critics of
the Marine Corps later suggested the photo was staged.

Anyone on the island, friend and foe, could plainly see the second
flag. It touched off new waves of cheers on the beaches, where un-
shaven and weary shore parties thumped one another on the back and
shouted. Those on the front, their ranks already decimated by the
hundreds, felt the battle was at last making some headway.

Whistles, horns, and bells rang out aboard the ships surrounding
the island. The next day, when the photo appeared on front pages of
virtually every newspaper in the States, it became an instant symbol
for millions on the homefront—an indelible portrait of patriotism and
determination.

It took days to track down the names of Rosenthal's flag-raisers,
a frantic quest touched off by a clamor at home to identify the men.
They were, from left to right, Private First Class Ira H. Hayes, a Pima
Indian from Arizona; Private First Class Franklin R. Sousley, a Kentucky mountaineer; Sergeant Michael Strank, from central Pennsylvania's coal country; Pharmacist's Mate Second Class John Bradley,
from the farmlands of Wisconsin; Private First Class Rene A. Gagnon,
of French-Canadian descent, from New Hampshire's Green Mountains; and Corporal Harlon Block, from the southernmost tip of Texas.

Sousley, Strank, and Block were killed before ever learning of
their fame. Bradley was wounded and evacuated; only Hayes and
Gagnon left the island physically unhurt, but both would die as al-
coholics—a situation, friends said, brought on by their inabilities to
cope with fame the two felt was undeserved.

Rosenthal became an overnight celebrity of sorts, albeit a confused one. When Associated Press headquarters radioed congratulations on "the war's most memorable photo," he didn't know which one they were talking about; he'd made dozens of shots since D-Day. The picture won the 1945 Pulitzer Prize and was the official symbol of the Seventh War Bond Drive, when $220,000,000 in bonds were sold. It was later reproduced on a postage stamp and was re-created in minute detail in the world's largest bronze statue, at the foot of Arlington National Cemetery, just across the Potomac River from Washington, D.C.

Bill Genaust never saw what he shot; he was killed a few days later making more footage of Marines in battle. But millions saw his film within days in movie theaters across the nation. Decades later it was being viewed by other millions almost daily in television documentaries. That Genaust was never given credit for the footage, and that he died still filming the action at Iwo, were sore spots with those who knew him. Lowery's and Campbell's pictures received scant attention, but they and Rosenthal remained friends.

And what of the forty men of the Third Platoon who first scaled Suribachi's summit? Four made it to the end of the battle; the others were killed or wounded before the island was conquered.

Suribachi's conquest cost the 28th Regiment 510 men in four days of fighting. Since D-Day, its total casualties—including those killed or wounded on the beaches before the assault on the volcano began— were 895, nearly thirty percent—and the battle for the island had just begun. The regiment stayed on and around Suribachi for another week, cleaning out die-hard Japanese, reorganizing and taking on new men, and refitting before swinging north.

Years later an official Marine Corps monograph summed up the capture of the fortress. "The Japanese had conducted an effective defense," it said. "Making maximum use of their artillery, mortars, and automatic weapons, they did not waste themselves in costly all-out counterattacks. Forcing the Marines to come to them, the enemy inflicted heavy casualties before being blasted or burned out of their fortifications."

Men who had been on the mountain thought the forty-seven words weren't enough to tell the story.

3

Correspondents, those on the beachhead and those on the *Eldorado*, filed a flood of copy daily, a graphic word picture of a battle mounting in intensity and casualties. Photographs of the wreckage-strewn beaches and of Marines struggling up the deep black sand of the terraces took over the front pages of newspapers from coast to coast.

From the time Marines landed on D-Day, Navy censors blue-penciled all mention of specific losses. Reports said only that "no estimate of casualties is yet available." But on February 22, Admiral Nimitz's communiqué shocked the nation. "At 1800, as of February 21, our casualties on Iwo Jima were estimated at 644 killed, 4,108 wounded and 560 missing." The invasion was just fifty-one hours under way.

This was worse than anything the Americans had suffered any-where in World War II; worse than Tarawa, worse than Normandy, worse than on the beachhead at Anzio. There was no doubt that Marines were in the bloodiest battle since Gettysburg.

An anxious homefront bought newspaper extras by the thousands and listened for radio bulletins about the battle's progress. Theaters showed newsreels of the assault, sometimes updating them daily as new footage arrived. For the first time live broadcasts were beamed to the States from a beachhead under fire. As the fighting roared on and casualties skyrocketed, editorials began to appear to question Marine tactics and to demand "Howlin' Mad" Smith's scalp.

As the European war thundered to an end, more and more cor-respondents moved to the Pacific for the final chapter in the global conflict. More than a hundred were scattered among the Iwo invasion fleet on D-Day, turning out an unprecedented flow of copy.

Except for Marine combat correspondents, it was strictly a per-sonal matter whether or not reporters went ashore or covered the action from the relative safety and comfort of the transports and com-mand ships; no one had authority to order the civilians to land. Those who went to the beachhead shared the same dangers and hardships as the troops, but with one glaring difference—they could go back to a ship whenever they wanted to hitch a ride. Those who stayed afloat covered the action through binoculars, monitored radio reports from the island, interviewed men returning from the beaches, and had regular press briefings.

Only a few of the bravest and most dedicated reporters went ashore on D-Day, or—as Bob Sherrod, who landed early that afternoon, put it—"the most foolhardy or stupid." The Associated Press's James S. Lindsley was the first civilian ashore. He scrambled across Yellow Beach I shortly after 1:30 P.M. with Captain John W. Thomason III, the Fourth Division's public relations officer.

Scattered in the maelstrom were some fifteen Marine writers and photographers, mostly sergeants who had been newsmen in civilian life and who had landed with their units in the earlier assault waves.

Lindsley and Thomason were told at the Line of Departure that "the beach had been stabilized." Seconds after they had bolted from a Higgins boat and plunged into a shell hole, artillery blew a following landing craft out of the water. The next round killed several Marines yards away.

"Doesn't look like it's stabilized to me!" Thomason yelled over the din.

They worked up the terrace, darting from hole to hole as machine gun bullets kicked up the black sand around them. The rest of the day they were pinned down most of the time. At sunset, Thomason left Lindsley in a foxhole they'd dug along the edge of the airstrip, and helped carry wounded to the beach.

Lindsley wondered "what in the hell am I doing here?" He spent the night amid the dangers and fears of thirty thousand other Americans on the beachhead.

Somewhere in the confusion were Keith Wheeler, the *Chicago Daily Times* man, and John Lardner, a sports writer-humorist-columnist turned correspondent for *Newsweek* and the *New Yorker*. They were neck deep in a crater, and having the same troubles as Lindsley and Thomason. Within hours, Wheeler would be seriously wounded by a sniper's bullet that struck his jaw.

Sherrod tried all morning to get ashore. Finally, as he descended the gangway of the *Eldorado* to head for the beach, he met a filthy and exhausted Marine debarking from the Higgins boat. "I wouldn't go in there if I were you," he said. "There's more hell in there than I've ever seen in the rest of the war put together."

Once ashore, the *Time-Life* man remembered that Al Crocker of the *St. Paul Dispatch* had decided not to land until the next morning. "Smart man that Crocker, smart man," Sherrod mused.

Washington's new policy of "more aggressive" news coverage was one of the few things going according to plan at Iwo. Five specially designated landing craft, with the word PRESS painted in four-foot letters on their sides, shuttled newsmen to and from the *Eldorado*, picking up copy and film.

Once aboard the command ship, dispatches were passed through censors and sent by high-speed radioteletypes to Guam for instant relay by powerful short-wave transmitters to the mainland. Each day at sunset, a Navy Catalina flying boat ferried still negatives and news-reel footage, radio recordings, and other copy from civilian and Marine correspondents to CinCPac headquarters for processing and trans-mittal to the States.

In all invasions before Iwo, beachhead news copy had been flown to Honolulu on hospital planes evacuating wounded. It was a hap-hazard system; newsmen first had to wait until an airstrip could take the aircraft. Then they had to see that their dispatches were aboard a plane and hope they would reach Navy press headquarters once the aircraft landed at Pearl Harbor. It was a time-consuming process to get anything through censorship and radioed or cabled to the mainland for publication. The time lag created a worrisome vacuum of hard news for the homefront, especially when the action was heavy and costly.

Sometimes days went by before eyewitness stories were in print to put flesh on the bare bones of information released in scrimpy official communiqués. Tarawa's bloody three-day battle was over before the first on-the-spot account of the savage fighting reached the mainland. Civilian newsmen were disgruntled and angry that the first beachhead copy was from Technical Sergeant Jim G. Lucas, an enterprising Ma-rine combat correspondent, who landed in the first waves with the assault forces. The delay was even worse for pictures. It was eight days after the Saipan invasion that the first of them reached San Fran-cisco.

Kelly Turner thought the new system worked too well, and that correspondents were being pampered. Twelve hours after H-Hour on Iwo, more than eighty thousand words of copy had passed through censors on the *Eldorado*, been radioed or flown to Guam, and on to the States for use in newspapers the next morning. During the first twelve days 1,168,875 words were filed from the command ship—no one ever knew who took the word count or why it was made.

In some respects, the admiral *was* right and the coverage *was* too good.

Much of the writing, composed in the heat of battle within sight of blood and smell of death, upset millions of readers. Many stories carried graphic comparisons to Tarawa, Saipan, Peleliu—at that time the most costly of Marine campaigns—and some brought up the carnage of Soissons and the Marne in World War I, where Marine casualties had been staggering.

Secretary Forrestal added to the wave of concern in a live broadcast from Guam after he had flown there from Iwo. He described "the terrible Japanese guns set on that grim and barren island so that there were streams of coverging fire at the beachhead over which the Marines had come scrambling from the sea."

While Joe Rosenthal's photo gave the homefront a mighty surge of pride, it also fanned the flames of tension and anxiety. To millions it mirrored, as nothing before had done so dramatically, the courage and heroism of *all* American fighting men—soldiers, sailors, airmen, and Marines. But to publishers Hearst and McCormick, it symbolized a tragic and needless waste of Marine lives, and gave them added fuel to stroke their editorial fires seeking to make General MacArthur the Supreme Commander, Pacific.

In addition to the chain of twenty-two Hearst newspapers and those controlled by the volatile colonel—*The Tribune* in Chicago and *The Daily News* in New York—the howling, well-orchestrated chant was taken up by powerful supporters in Washington led by *The Times-Herald*, owned and edited by McCormick's niece, the flamboyant Eleanor "Cissy" Patterson.

But the scathing editorials of the Hearst-McCormick-Patterson press failed to recognize, or attempt to explain, the shrewdness of General Kuribayashi and the do-or-die determination of his troops to defend the doorstep to the Japanese homeland. Nor did they face up to the fact that the Marines were taking Iwo Jima in the only way it could be conquered—by an amphibious landing and direct, head-on frontal assault. The incredible logic of the press lords and their lady boiled down to a position of "to hell with everything else, we want MacArthur." The raging battle, ten thousand miles away in the Pacific, hadn't reached its climax, and Marines were being killed or wounded at the rate of more than a thousand a day, when the bombastic controversy exploded in headlines.

On February 27, Hearst's San Francisco *Examiner* printed a front-page editorial with a heavy black border. It said Marines certainly would capture Iwo Jima, but "there is awesome evidence in the situation that the attacking American forces are paying heavily for the island, perhaps too heavily."

Hearst himself had written the words in his crisp, inimitable style from his sprawling multimillion-dollar mountaintop castle at San Simeon, south of San Francisco. It smacked of a scene from Orson Welles's movie *Citizen Kane*, which Hearst abhorred.

In an unmistakable attack on the leadership of Admiral Nimitz and General Smith, the tirade continued: "It is the same thing that happened at Tarawa and Saipan. If it continues the American forces are in danger of being worn out before they ever reach the really critical Japanese areas." In Tokyo, and on Iwo, there was no doubt that the island was "really critical" to the Japanese, that it would be defended to the last man, and that many more thousands of Americans would fall in the fighting.

Hearst had tight-fisted claim to the barony of a press lord. Not only did he own the nation's largest chain of newspapers, he also was absolute master of International News Service, the sole wire service news source for more than four hundred newspapers and radio stations in all parts of the country. Hearst Metrotone News turned out three newsreels every week, and they were seen by millions in more than two thousand theaters. Seven high-powered radio stations were under the Hearst banner, as well as a complex of highly profitable mass-circulation magazines.

But the *Examiner* was his personal voice, his pride and joy, the first newspaper he ever owned—a gift from his doting father, a tycoon United States Senator who had made millions in mining gold. The paper was the nerve center from which the sprawling communications domain took unequivocal direction. When "The Chief"—the name by which overworked and underpaid staffers knew him—wrote for *The Mighty Monarch of the Western Slope*, as the paper called itself on its masthead, he expected all his editors to get the signal and follow the lead.

On February 28, Hearst unleashed the next salvo. It was written

in his unmistakable style—short sentences and paragraphs, key words
in capital letters, pithy and searing prose throughout—and was the
lead editorial in the *Examiner*. It read:

"GENERAL MacARTHUR is our best strategist.

"He is our most SUCCESSFUL strategist.

"He wins all his objectives.

"He outwits and outmaneuvers and outguesses and outthinks
the Japanese.

"HE SAVES THE LIVES OF OUR OWN MEN, not only for the future
and vital operations that must be fought before Japan is defeated, but for their own safe return to their families and
loved ones in the American homeland after the peace is won.

"It is our good fortune to have such a strategist as General
MacArthur in the Pacific war.

"Why do we not use him more, and indeed, why do we not
give him supreme command in the Pacific war, and utilize
to the utmost his rare military genius of winning important
battles without excessive loss of precious American lives?"

Hearst, with the combined power of his millions and his communications empire, not only printed news; he created it. The editorial
blazed from the pages of his mass-circulation dailies in New York,
Chicago, Los Angeles, San Francisco, Boston, and Detroit. It snapped
out in the smaller ones in Albany and Syracuse, New York; in Omaha,
Nebraska; San Antonio, Texas; and Milwaukee, Wisconsin. His wire
service carried it verbatim, and many client papers printed it. Associated Press and United Press found its torrid contents legitimate
news, and their teletypes clattered it out in newsrooms from coast to
coast.

William C. Wren, the *Examiner* managing editor, expected a
wave of excitement, to put it mildly, when the paper hit the streets—
although he wasn't prepared for what came. But he'd taken heat many
times before because of his chief's scathing editorials. Wren was hard-
boiled, a trademark of all Hearst executives who kept their jobs, and
he was cool and imperturbable when pressure was the heaviest. He
was sitting at his desk, chewing an unlit cigar and working on copy,
when he heard a rumbling commotion in the dingy city room.

It was shortly after 10:00 P.M. and the next edition was on deadline. Nearly a hundred Marines stormed toward the editor's cluttered, glassed-in office. Their eyes blazed, and they pushed aside anyone blocking their advance. A frightened staffer turned in a riot call as Marines surrounded Wren.

"Look," he said, "I take orders from my commanding officer, just like you do, and they came from Mr. Hearst at San Simeon. He said to run the editorial as he wrote it, and I did."

Furious Marines demanded that Hearst be called, and Wren got on the direct line. "Mr. Hearst is too busy to be disturbed," he was told. The Chief had spoken, and would have nothing more to say— at least for the moment. Wren calmed the Marines by promising they would have their say in the next day's paper, and the explosive episode was defused.

When San Francisco police and the Navy Shore Patrol tramped up the stairs to the confused scene, the sullen and bitter Marines left. Asked if legal action would be taken against the men, a Marine officer said: "Probably not. They were off duty and acting as individuals. Apparently they read the editorial and didn't like it." He was a man of rare understatement.

Deeply concerned citizens wrote congressmen and senators— and Secretary Forrestal—about the heavy and still mounting casualties at Iwo. The secretary's office released a letter from one woman, who was not identified, nor was it known if she had a son or close relative in the battle. It read:

"Please, for God's sake, stop sending our finest youth to be murdered on places like Iwo Jima. It is too much for boys to stand, too much for mothers to take. It is driving some mothers crazy. Why can't objectives be accomplished in some other way? It is almost inhuman— stop, stop!"

Forrestal answered: "On December 7, 1941, the Axis confronted us with a simple choice: fight or be overrun. There was then, and is now, no other possibility. Having chosen to fight, we had then, and we have now, no final means of winning battles except through the valor of the Marine or Army soldier who, with rifle and grenade, storms enemy positions, takes them, and holds them. There is no shortcut or easy way. I wish there were."

Next day's *Examiner* mentioned the near-riot in a three-paragraph story buried in the paper's back pages: there was no rebuttal from the Marines on the editorial page—or elsewhere. It was a different story

in the *San Francisco Chronicle*, whose offices were a few blocks away.
The lead editorial in the competing morning paper said:

> "The recapture of the Philippines remains competent,
> energetic and immensely heartening to the American people.
> We are proud of that job.
> "To slur the United States Marines in one type of op-
> eration, however, to draw odious comparisons between theirs
> and the type of operations conducted by General MacArthur,
> is to raise a sinister fantasy. To hint that the Marine and
> Naval leadership in that assault is incompetent is an attempt
> at a damnable swindle of the American people.
> "The *Chronicle* does not propose to engage in a contro-
> versy over the relative merits of our fighting forces in the
> various theaters of war. But neither does the *Chronicle* pro-
> pose to remain mute when the United States Marines, or
> any force on the world battle line, is butchered at home to
> make a Roman holiday."

The paper was owned by four sisters. One was Mrs. Phyllis de
Young Tucker. She had been informed three days earlier that First
Lieutenant Nion R. Tucker, Jr., her only son, had been cut down on
D-Day while assaulting Green Beach with the Fifth Division, and had
died of his wounds.

Admiral Nimitz and General Smith were keenly aware of the
furor raging stateside; but there was nothing they could do to stop it.
Marines in the raging battle knew nothing of the blazing controversy—
they knew only that they wanted to win the battle, to leave Iwo alive
and unhurt.

Marine cameraman Private Robert R. Campbell (*left*) and Sergeant William Genaust filmed the flag-raising; Campbell in black-and-white still photographs, Genaust in color motion picture footage. Genaust was killed in action days later. (*Louis R. Lowery*)

Sergeant Louis R. Lowery made pictures of the first flag-raising and covered the battle until its end. (*U.S. Marine Corps*)

Associated Press photographer Joe Rosenthal atop Suribachi with the Speed Graphic camera used in his immortal photograph. (*Robert R. Campbell*)

Sergeant Louis R. Lowery's photograph of the first Stars and Stripes on Suribachi was overshadowed by the shot of the second flag-raising. (*Louis R. Lowery*)

Only four of the forty-man platoon that scaled the volcano, fifteen of whom are in Joe Rosenthal's picture, made it alive and unwounded through the battle. (*Joe Rosenthal*)

Platoon Sergeant Ernest Thomas, one of the original flag-raisers, was congratulated by General Smith on the *Eldorado*, and was killed six days later. (*Arthur Kiely, Jr.*)

Joe Rosenthal's memorable shot of the second flag-raising, the best-known photograph of World War II, inspired the official poster of a war bond drive that raised $220,000,000 and was reproduced on a commemorative stamp that had the largest sale in history. (*Joe Rosenthal*)

The official poster

Stamps

PART FIVE

Brave Men
in
Navy Blue

1

"Howlin' Mad" Smith and his Marines would forever believe that Navy brass was to blame for not softening up Iwo enough before the first waves hit the beaches.

But they would never have a quarrel with naval officers and sailors who landed them on the beaches, protected them from enemy air attacks and bombardment from the sea, treated their wounded, supplied them with what was needed to wage the battle.

Nor would they ever forget that Navy men died just off Iwo's shores before the first Marines set foot on the beach. All were part of a gigantic fighting machine, and the Marines knew it.

Marines were taking the headlines, but nearly ten thousand Navy men were ashore in the thick of the action. As many as 150,000 more were in the ring of warships, transports, and support vessels—all vulnerable to enemy coastal defense batteries and heavy artillery, and facing the threat of kamikaze air attacks.

As long ago as November, Iwo had come under thundering bombardment during seven hit-and-run raids by the cruisers *Pensacola*, *Chester*, and *Salt Lake City*. Each time they had taken near misses from Kuribayashi's twelve-inch guns. Carrier planes slammed the island twenty-two different times before D-Day, encountering enemy interceptors each time.

Tight security kept these actions from the homefront. Even the tragic losses to the gunboat flotilla on D-Day minus one were kept secret, as was the dangerous work of the frogmen. To Americans at home it appeared the Marines were doing all the fighting and taking all the losses, while sailors were little more than bystanders and minor participants watching the butchery from offshore.

But this was not fact—as the public was later to learn. Early on the afternoon of D-Day plus two, fifty Zeke fighters and Betty bombers took off from Katori Naval Airbase at the tip of Kyushu, the southernmost of Japan's home islands, and headed for Iwo. At Hachijo Jima, an island smaller than Iwo and 125 miles nearer the battle, they topped off fuel tanks and were armed with torpedoes and hundred-pound bombs.

It was a suicide mission, pure and simple; even with the additional gasoline, the kamikazes carried just enough fuel for ten to twenty minutes over the target area—and none to get back to Japan.

First warning of the attack came just before sundown. The dimly lighted Combat Intelligence Center aboard the venerable *Saratoga* sprang to life; radar had spotted a swarm of blips closing at 250 miles an hour from due north. A squadron of the carrier's Corsairs and Hellcats was still in the air; it might be they, returning from the final sunset sweep of the sea between Iwo and Japan. Six Corsairs, warmed up and waiting for take-off, were aloft within ninety seconds to check.

Twenty minutes later an excited voice overrode crackling static on the combat radio circuit: "They're bogies!" Then a jubilant: "Scratch two Zekes!" Radar still showed a mass of menacing blips closing rapidly on the carrier. Condition Red was flashed to the rest of the fleet, and a curtain of antiaircraft fire laced the low-hanging clouds.

Minutes later, six Japanese planes broke through the overcast, engines roaring at full throttle, and dove toward the ocean. Skimming the savage swell at less than thirty feet, they aimed straight at the *Saratoga*. Four zoomed and twisted low across the flight deck and disappeared. But the other two, flaming like dying comets from anti-aircraft hits, exploded against the ship on its starboard side near the water line. The blast smashed through the hull and touched off roaring fires and blasts from fuel storage tanks and ammunition lockers.

Damage control teams struggled to halt the spread of destruction. Flames seemed to engulf the thirteen-year-old carrier—the "Gallant Old Lady of the Fleet"—but within forty-five minutes, firefighters had the situation under control. The engine room was undamaged, and the oldest carrier in the Pacific was still able to maneuver.

Just when it appeared the worst was over, another kamikaze wave penetrated the antiaircraft screen. Four planes were bracketed in screaming dives and crashed flaming into the sea some five hundred yards short of the target. The fifth didn't miss. Blazing and twisting like a corkscrew, it pancaked across the flight deck and plunged in a ball of fire into the water, leaving a gaping hole about a hundred feet from the bow.

But by 8:15 P.M., the ship, battered and still smoldering, was ready to recover planes. Twenty-four Hellcats and Corsairs were aloft on patrol when the first wave of enemy planes struck. Pilots were helpless as they circled out of range of antiaircraft fire and watched as the *Saratoga* was hit. Seventeen landed on the escort carriers *Wake Island* and *Natoma Bay*, some twenty miles to the southeast. Seven Corsairs flew patterns ten thousand feet above the *Saratoga* until she could take them in.

Scattered fires still burned and a giant pall of smoke, invisible in the dark night, billowed thousands of feet skyward as the carrier moved from the scene and, with its destroyer screen, headed for Pearl Harbor.

The *Saratoga* had been in action for the last time; it took months to repair her ravaged hull and flight deck, and by then the war was over. She left the waters thirty-five miles southeast of Iwo Jima with a proud fighting tradition. She and her valiant crew had been in the thick of seven Pacific invasions, had steamed a million miles on combat patrol in Japanese waters, had launched more than two hundred hit-and-run air strikes against enemy-held islands. But in her last violent engagement, the battle for Iwo Jima had taken the lives of 123 of her crew and wounded another 192 in three frantic hours.

While the men of the *Saratoga* fought to save her, other kamikazes found other targets. At 6:30, the radar on the escort carrier *Bismarck Sea* picked up an unidentified flight of approaching planes. It was assumed they were from the *Saratoga*, then virtually helpless, and that they were looking for a place to land on one of the baby flattops. But fifteen minutes later, a lone Betty bomber streaked out of nowhere across the stern, picked up speed in a roaring turn, and plowed into the *Bismarck Sea*'s hull.

It struck squarely amidship, and its exploding hundred-pound bombs loosed four torpedoes that detonated like a volcano. The heavy steel aircraft elevator connecting flight and hangar decks was obliterated, crashing to the bottom of its shaft deep within the carrier's bowels. Planes taken aboard minutes earlier, and others ready for take-off, were loaded with gasoline, ammunition, and bombs. They exploded in a giant chain reaction, adding to the inferno.

With water lines severed and pumps sputtering from lack of power to fight the rampant flames, the ship was doomed. Ten minutes later the *Bismarck Sea* was dead in the water. More explosions sent shattered planes and giant hunks of the steel and teakwood deck skyward every few seconds. By now the weather was terrible. A twenty-knot gale blew out of the northeast; cold sleet mixed with snow fell on the dying ship and on the angry black waters.

At seven o'clock, Captain John L. Pratt used the battery-powered emergency public address system to give his final order: "Abandon ship! Abandon ship!" Men who could went over the side into the turbulent, icy ocean. The last sailor hadn't cleared the deck when a gigantic blast lifted the stricken carrier's stern almost out of the water. Then the broken hulk rolled over and sank to the bottom, four miles down in one of the Pacific's deepest troughs.

In its death plunge *Bismarck Sea* took with her 218 of its crew of 812. The *Natoma Bay, Wake Island,* and three destroyers moved in to rescue the survivors. Lieutenant Eugene R. Shannon, of Freeport, Illinois, was pulled mortally wounded from the water. He was the *Bismarck Sea*'s chaplain, and the night before D-Day all hands heard his prayer over the ship's loudspeakers: "Almighty God, may we have ears to hear the call of battle, eyes to see the enemy wherever he lurks, and the skill to save our ships, our planes, and ourselves from the hand of evil, that finally we may glorify in Thee, giver of all victory, through Jesus Christ, our Lord, Amen."

Three more American ships were hit before the last kamikaze was shot down or vanished in the night to splash down hundreds of miles from help when fuel ran out. The escort carrier *Lunga Point* was luckier; she took only minor damage and suffered no casualties when four Japanese bombers were blown to bits in the antiaircraft curtain and when a cascade of their debris landed on her flight deck.

It was tragically different with the *Keokuk*. A flaming enemy fighter smashed into the top deck of the minesweeper tender, a converted train ferry from San Francisco Bay, killing seventeen sailors and wounding forty-four others. The LST 477, loaded with Third Division tanks, took the glancing impact of a lone plane. But the next day it was able to put the tanks ashore. No one had been wounded, and the ship was towed back to Saipan.

It was three hours before the all-clear sounded. None of the enemy planes made it back to Japan; they hadn't expected to. But the kamikazes had done what they'd set out to do: they had sunk one carrier, put another out of action for the rest of the war, damaged another, and hit three other ships. More important, the raid had killed or wounded 717 sailors. The toll of Navy casualties now was 1,126, when the losses of the furious D-minus one action were included. The invasion was less than three days old.

It was never learned how the suicide planes knew the location of the rendezvous area of the carriers, thirty-five miles off Iwo. The best guess of intelligence officers was that a scout submarine had found them and radioed the location to Imperial General Headquarters in Tokyo. The Americans wondered, too, why the enemy struck in force only once. Perhaps the Supreme War Council was hoarding its planes for a final defense of the homeland when the invasion came. Perhaps the massive sweep of Task Force 58 against Tokyo Bay had the enemy off balance, and the warlords feared more heavy attacks from Admiral Mitscher's battleships and carriers. But the fact remains: If kamikazes had been more heavily committed against the Navy, the conquest of Iwo Jima would have been even more costly.

During the raid, there was grave concern for the hospital ships *Samaritan* and *Solace*, at anchor for the night twenty miles southeast of the island. The *Solace* was to lift anchor for Saipan at dawn, loaded with casualties. Six hundred twenty-three wounded Marines occupied every bunk and cot aboard, some even on mattresses in passageways.

Each morning at dawn, one of the mercy ships, and sometimes both, moved to within two miles of shore to take on and treat casualties. From first light until sundown, landing craft shuttled back and forth to the beachhead, each time returning with more wounded and then racing shoreward for new loads. The auxiliary hospital ship *Pinckney*, an attack transport converted solely for medical duty, was nearby with four LSTs equipped for surgery, and many of the attack transports also had hospital facilities.

For the first time in combat, refrigerated whole blood was available to treat the wounded. Medical men said it was far superior to plasma in pulling casualties through heavy shock when their bodies were almost drained of blood.

Battle medicine performed miracles on Iwo's beachhead, but under pressure of savage combat, its life-saving mechanism sometimes broke down, particularly during the first days of the invasion.

The system was designed to work as a swiftly moving chain whose first link was a Navy corpsman in the front lines—a pharmacist's mate who lived and trained with his Marine outfit—and went into battle with it. He was with the troops wherever and whenever they moved in action, and whenever a man was hit it was the corpsman's job to be at his side as quickly as possible. In the first crucial minutes fast control of hemorrhaging and the use of plasma and sulfa could mean life or death; a shot of morphine could dull the pain.

Then the fallen man moved along the chain through a front-line battalion aid station for whatever diagnosis and speedy treatment a surgeon could give; then to a regimental clearing point where more doctors and better facilities were available; then to a division hospital where emergency surgery could be performed; and finally to a hospital ship where specialized operations and highly trained medical teams worked to save those with the most serious wounds.

But until D-Day plus four, conditions were so bad on the beachhead that hundreds of wounded were unattended for hours and waited in agony for help. In many outfits more than half the corpsmen were casualties themselves. Those still unhurt were exhausted and often short of supplies as they fought impossible odds to treat ten times more wounded than had been expected.

Litter bearers were in the lines night and day to rescue men from where they fell and to get them to the beaches. Those wounded who could, limped, shuffled, even crawled to aid stations, where they were treated, then taken to evacuation points. And all this, when everyone was under fire or expecting it.

Once a man made it to a ship with hospital facilities, his chance of survival was greater than ninety-five percent. The *Samaritan* and *Solace* were as long as two football fields, each equipped with every lifesaving tool available to stateside hospitals. Medical staffs on each ship numbered twenty doctors, some forty male and female nurses, and two hundred corpsmen.

Lights were never out in operating rooms. Some surgeons were specialists in brain and chest wounds. Others performed unending miracles in patching up shattered limbs and saving the eyesight of the grievously hurt. Still others had the skills to stem the ravages of horrible burns and start the long and painful process of skin grafts and plastic surgery. Red-eyed from lack of sleep and reeling from exhaustion from dealing with the raw results of combat violence, the doctors and aides worked wonders as a routine matter.

Unarmed and classified as noncombatant vessels under the "rules of war" adopted by the Geneva Convention of 1906, hospital ships were, nonetheless, always in danger. Lying close to shore as they did, and surrounded by constantly firing warships and transports loaded with explosives and other supplies, they took their chances against enemy air attacks and artillery bombardment. In the stark realities of battle, they could expect little or no special consideration.

Thus, the *Comfort*, a sister ship of *Samaritan* and *Solace*, would be hit within a month with a loss of 28 lives, including six nurses, by a kamikaze during the invasion of Okinawa. Whether the attack was deliberate was never determined; most probably it was not. The mercy ship lay at the center of a ring of fighting ships of greater military value, and the enemy plane was flaming out of control when it plummeted into the vessel.

Each day at sunset, the *Samaritan* and *Solace* moved twenty miles to sea where, with all lights blazing like luxury cruise liners loaded with happy vacationers, they anchored for the night. But each dawn they were back within easy range of Kuribayashi's gunners, taking aboard a new and seemingly endless flood of casualties. When their six hundred beds were full, they steamed at twenty-knot speed to Saipan and Guam, where wounded were transferred to base hospitals or flown on to Honolulu or the States. Then it was back to Iwo. Each made four round trips before the mercy shuttle was taken over, near battle's end, by air transport.

Marines were keenly aware that medical teams aboard the hospital ships and transports and LSTs were to be admired and respected for their skills and dedication. But the feeling was much deeper for the Navy medics ashore—the doctors and corpsmen who directly faced the misery and dangers of combat. They were dues-paying members in good standing in the special breed and brotherhood of the Marine Corps. They shared the foxholes, the sights and sounds and smells of battle, the fears and bloodletting, together.

Iwo's cemeteries would have 195 crosses bearing the names of corpsmen. Another 529 were wounded while ministering to Marine comrades. And seven doctors would be killed and twelve wounded before the fighting ended.

2

At Iwo Jima, too, were the Naval Construction Battalions—the Sea-bees.

Ultimately there would be seven thousand of them ashore: four battalions whose job was to land on a beach under fire with the big machines of their myriad trades, and the tons of supplies needed to transform the island, once it was captured, into a powerful forward base 650 miles from Tokyo.

But first there was other work for them to do—work like fighting the Japanese alongside Marines; like opening roads from the beach-head so that tanks and artillery could get into action; like clearing the ravaged beaches of their choking clutter, and clearing minefields and filling bomb and shell craters so the airstrips, when they were captured, could take planes.

About the only thing they wouldn't have to do was build bridges, usually a high-priority task. There wasn't even a foot-wide creek on the island. What water there was couldn't be used without treatment, and wells had to be dug to get to it—so they brought along water distillation and boring equipment.

They brought bulldozers and heavy cranes, road scrapers and rollers, air compressors and jackhammers, large trucks and earth movers, asphalt and concrete mixers. They brought unassembled Quonset huts, lumber and nails, nuts and bolts, roofing materials and paint, electric generators big enough to light a small city, and welding equipment and even mobile machine shops.

"Protect the Seabees," was an axiom common to Marines. "One of them could be your dad." It was an adage rooted in fact; an enlisted Marine older than the mid-twenties was rare. Many had never been away from home before boot camp. But Seabees in their thirties were considered young and knew much of life. In peacetime, most had been skilled construction workers with well-paying jobs. Many had families and were proud to have volunteered.

Now the young breed of Marines and the old breed of blue-collar men were side by side in combat they hoped to survive.

Navy Captain Robert C. Johnson commanded the Ninth Construction Brigade. Beneath the tall, soft-talking, gray-haired fifty-year-old Annapolis career man were three rough and ready peacetime building company ramrods with reserve commissions. They were now temporary lieutenant commanders for the duration of the war—officers with jobs far different from erecting million-dollar industrial plants and skyscrapers, or building bridges or laying concrete highways.

Dominick J. Ermilio was CO of the 31st Battalion; Frank B. Campbell had the 62nd; and Ray R. Murphy, the 133rd. Commander H. W. Heuer, who was regular Navy, led the 23rd, which had the job of stevedoring the Seabee equipment and supplies off the beachhead after it was secured.

Murphy's men were as much a part of the Fourth Division as an assault battalion of infantry. They had lived in tents and trained with the troops on the hills of Maui, and for the first time in the Pacific war were in waves scheduled to land before the beachhead was secure. The one-thousand-man battalion was ashore by early afternoon, when the beaches were the most chaotic, and they paid a bitter price: their casualties were the heaviest suffered by any Seabee unit in the war.

One forty-man unit lost seventeen men by nightfall of D-Day. Seven were killed by a mortar barrage before moving twenty yards from their landing craft. For the next three days, Murphy's battalion functioned more as Marine shock troops than as men whose mission was neither to kill nor to be killed.

Carpenter's Mate Third Class Delmer Rodabaugh and Steward's Mate First Class Cleveland Washington were in an early wave. Rodabaugh had five bulky notebooks to check off supplies as they were landed and to see that everything got to proper supply dumps. Washington, a one-time Pullman dining car chef, was perhaps the first black man to ever set foot on Iwo. He'd hoped to have stoves fired up and hot chow ready by nightfall. But for the next three days, he and Rodabaugh had time for nothing except the dangerous job of manhandling ammunition to the Marines at the front—and trying to stay alive.

Rodabaugh was thirty-four. "Two damned old to be doing this," he thought, bending under the weight of ammo on the first trip up the terraces. Straining for breath and hunkered low under enemy small arms fire, he made it to the edge of the airstrip. A Japanese, in a neat fully buttoned uniform, stared at him blankly from the bottom of a foxhole. He was dead and looked very small and very foreign.

Rodabaugh scampered around the fallen foe and left his wooden case of bandoleers with waiting Marines. He felt even more ancient when, on the trip down the slope, he lunged for cover in a crater occupied by a seventeen-year-old infantryman—a Marine half the Seabee's age.

Washington remembered his first hectic minutes on the beach, where he had knelt briefly to pray. Not only was he devoutly religious but he was a dedicated crap-shooter as well, and had mailed his church fifty dollars from shipboard winnings. A Marine major bolted by, shouting: "You goddamned Seabees, get the hell up that goddamned terrace!" "And that's what we did," Washington said.

Chief Machinist's Mate Douglas Davis was on Yellow Beach shortly after 9:30. Moments later, Motor Machinist's Mate Second Class Nelson Day and Carpenter's Mate First Class Robert Pirie died in the surf behind him. They were killed when a heavy artillery piece tumbled from the ramp of a Higgins boat and crushed them.

Thirty-year-old Seaman First Class Frank Riefle had been a Yellow Cab driver in St. Louis. He found himself on Iwo with a Browning automatic rifle he'd picked up near the body of a dead Marine, and was using the weapon against a Japanese position near the airfield. He wondered if he would ever again see his wife and six children, and had heavy doubts that he would when a sliver of hot fragments from a mortar blast sliced the wedding ring off his finger, hardly piercing the skin.

For a time he kept moving forward because, he said, "the firing seemed always right behind." Then, during a lull between mortar barrages and machine gun fire, he rolled and slid down the terrace. All things considered, since he hardly knew how to use the BAR, there surely was something else he could do to help win the battle—and stay alive.

Machinist's Mate First Class Alphenix J. Benard was a bulldozer operator, and he was trying to open a path to get Shermans off the beach. Behind him were another bulldozer, two tanks and two tank retrievers. Directly in front was a cluster of bodies—mostly Marines, some Seabees—covered with ponchos on the black sand a few yards inland from the surf. "I had no choice," he told himself as he closed his eyes and the steel treads of the heavy machine clanked over the dead men.

Commander Ermilio's battalion had lived with the Fifth Division in the tent camps of Hawaii and trained with them in the mountainous terrain. But only a small contingent of the 31st Seabees, according to the invasion plan, were landed on D-Day. Those who came ashore were mainly demolitions men and bulldozer operators to help clear the beaches and carve roadways inland. The rest of the men would follow with their equipment when the beachhead traffic jam was cleared.

Chief Carpenter's Mate James L. Price and his five-man crew of explosives experts found plenty of messy work when they landed with the shock troops on Yellow Beach II. The powder man from West Monroe, Louisiana, had worked for Gulf Oil on a seismograph team in civilian life, and was a whiz with dynamite and nitroglycerin. He and his men started blasting within minutes, blowing wrecked boats and debris from the landing zones and clearing the beach of smashed equipment and supplies.

Seaman First Class Ben Massey, of Plainview, Texas, brought his bulldozer through the surf with the first wave of the 31st Battalion. Minutes later, shortly after noon, he was hit in the neck by rifle fire. Machinist's Mate First Class Hollis R. Cash Jr., of Calera, Alabama, took his exposed place on the ten-ton machine and moved off the beach to cut an exit for incoming tanks and artillery.

Shipfitter Third Class John C. Butts Jr. was twenty-four, a youngster among his comrades. When he landed he immediately began carrying heavy boxes of hand grenades up the terraces, making five trips before a sniper's bullet killed him. He had a wife and a child back home in Salt Lake City, Utah.

Seaman First Class Giovanni Jannacone and Shipfitter Third Class Terry Terwelleger were buddies who learned fast how to operate a Higgins boat. Just offshore they saw one crewless and about to founder, and swam to it without thinking why; they hadn't the foggiest notion about how to make it run. It was a sinking time bomb loaded with ammunition, but they managed to get it in gear and roared through the surf. Mortar fire bracketed them as the cargo was unloaded by a human conveyor line. Once empty, the derelict was swept back to sea where it was broken up by the heavy waves, adding more wreckage to the flotsam.

According to the invasion plan, the 62nd Battalion would land on D-Day afternoon. It was an outfit of experts at patching bombed airstrips and putting them in shape to take planes. But it was three days

before they could start work on Chidori Airfield, now called Motoyama
Number One by the Americans, and even then enemy mortars and
artillery made the job decidedly dangerous. Two weeks after D-Day,
Commander Murphy and a bulldozer crew were pinned down for
more than two hours as Japanese snipers pinged away at Seabees filling
bomb craters on Motoyama Number Two, the second airstrip.

Commander Heuer's stevedores couldn't land their cranes and
conveyors for five days. When they finally got ashore, the beaches
were still taking periodic fire. But as the "fighter-builders" were able
to put their know-how and heavy equipment to work, order began to
replace chaos and supplies started to flow ashore in an endless flood
and move inland with systematic order.

From H-Hour on D-Day until Iwo was conquered, Seabees were
with the Marines at the front—or not far behind. In the early fighting,
they were combat troops. As the battle roared on, they continued to
brave enemy fire to keep the beaches clear, to build roads and defuse
minefields, to fill shell craters and surface airstrip runways, and to
transform rear areas into a working military base, albeit a crude tent
city within easy range of enemy rockets, artillery, and mortars.

Before the battle was half over, Seabees built distillation facilities
so that drinking water, still with a slight taste of sulphur but potable,
was available on shore, and underground wells were tapped to provide
hot showers. With jackhammers and dynamite, the 31st Battalion
hacked out a road to Suribachi's summit and paved it with asphalt.
Some stayed on after the Marines left; stayed on to erect Quonset
huts and permanent wooden and cinder-block buildings, even a movie
theater and chapel, and to pave the road network and airstrip runways
and bring a measure of American-style civilization to an outpost half
a world from the United States mainland.

Seabees were justifiably and extremely proud of their units and
the jobs they did. "The Army makes some of the landings, and the
Marines make others, but the Seabees make them all," was their oft-
repeated unofficial motto. They boasted that they were "soldiers in
sailors' uniforms"; that they trained as Marines, and did civilian jobs
at a pay scale that would send union men out on strike. And they
could poke fun at their military status. The initials "C.B." (for Construction Battalions, their official designations) actually meant "Confused Bastards"—or so they insisted.

Captain Johnson's battalions paid a heavy cost at Iwo. Seabee casualties were 269, of whom fifty-one were killed or missing in action. "We've paid our dues again," their skipper said the morning the last of his fallen men were buried in the Fourth Division cemetery.

3

Hard-working Navy beachmasters were vital to the success of every Marine invasion in the Pacific. And while the last shouted warning to assault troops before they landed was to "get the goddamned hell off the beach as fast as you can if you don't want to die there," beachmasters had different orders. "Stay on the beach," they were told, "and keep it open!" Given the best of surf conditions and even minor enemy resistance, it was a difficult and dangerous job. At Iwo, for the first four days, it was a murderous and all but impossible one.

In previous campaigns, shore parties were held offshore until the beachhead perimeter had been established—usually a few hours after H-Hour—and the attack had started to move inland. At Iwo, for the first time, beachmasters were in the assault waves with Marines; Makalapa's Monks wanted to battle-test new techniques and equipment they hoped to use in landings on the Japanese home islands.

By 10:30, Lieutenant Commander John J. McDevitt Jr. was ashore on Green Beach with his ten-man team of experts in the tricky business of seeing that landing craft hit the right beaches. By noon, seventy-seven beachmasters had made it and were in action with thousands of Marines on the "hottest" ribbon of sand any of them had ever seen.

Colored banners were lashed to twelve-foot poles marking the limits of the seven landing zones stretching two miles from Suribachi to the northern cliffs below the quarry at the East Boat Landing. Gasoline-powered generators, powerful amplifiers, and loudspeakers were dragged through the surf and set up in and around sand-bagged shell holes to direct landing craft traffic.

From a crater near the base of the volcano, McDevitt radioed orders to the Control Boat at the Line of Departure of what was needed to hold the beachhead: more troops, tanks, artillery, water, gasoline, ammunition, medical supplies; and in what order to dispatch landing craft carrying them. Semaphore signal flags and bullhorns steered amtracs, DUWK amphibious trucks, and Higgins boats to specific beaches once they were a few hundred yards from shore. The system was in place earlier than it had ever been in an invasion, but it would be almost a week, after Suribachi fell and the fighting had moved to Motoyama Number Two airstrip, before it would be working as planned.

Captain Carl E. Anderson, called to active duty from his fish cannery in Alaska, commanded the shore parties—and made it clear he was *the* beachmaster. He constantly barked orders through loudspeakers in a thick Swedish accent, and men on the beaches wondered if he ever slept. Night and day his strident voice was heard everywhere on the roaring perimeter—even when Japanese shelling was at its heaviest.

Troops called Anderson "Squeaky," although his voice was gruff and coarse. When a correspondent asked him how he was able to keep things moving, the husky Swede replied in the tones of his ancestors: "I get so much hell from the admiral I yust pass it on. Then, by God, ve get tings done!"

By D-Day plus six, he had ten thousand men unloading cargo and manhandling it to supply dumps. They were from replacement drafts—confused and frightened men in combat for the first time. They were cooks and bakers and musicians. They were Seabees and shore parties from Marine Pioneer Battalions. They were company clerks and motor transport men whose vehicles had been destroyed or were not yet ashore. It was backbreaking work and death surrounded them, but men and machines and supplies were landed and thrown into battle.

Twenty of Anderson's beachmasters were killed or wounded before the fighting ended, a surprisingly low number in view of the thousands of rounds of Japanese mortars and artillery that fell on the beaches; it was impossible to tally casualties among the thousands of Marines who worked in shore parties. But those who were killed or wounded certainly numbered several hundred, listed as either "dead or missing in action" by their respective divisions.

While General Julian Smith had his point when he scolded Navy brass about coming in "to about one thousand yards" from shore during an invasion, and reminded them of the Marines' armor of khaki shirts when they crossed the beaches, he wasn't talking about the sailors who landed and fought alongside the assault troops.

Nor was he talking about the Navy coxswains and gunners who crewed the landing craft and gunboats—or the Seabees and the corpsmen and doctors and beachmasters. When these men faced the enemy on Iwo's beaches, their armor was the same as that of the Marines—khaki shirts.

Japanese dead in foxhole near base of Suribachi, Nambu light machine gun still within reach. (*Arthur J. Kiely, Jr.*)

Enemy troops killed in pre-dawn attack on Third Division positions near the airstrip. (*Joseph Heiberger*)

LEFT - Navy Secretary James Forrestal (*left*) and General "Howlin' Mad" Smith observe action from Eldorado. (*Arthur J. Kiely, Jr.*)

RIGHT - D-plus five: Order replaces chaos on the beachhead as LSTs, seen from Suribachi's summit, unload supplies. (*Louis R. Lowery*)

Marine gives a Japanese, buried in the explosion of a naval shell, a drag on a cigarette. (*Louis R. Lowery*)

Fourth Division doctors and corpsmen treat wounded at beachhead aid station on D-Day. (*Arthur J. Kiely, Jr.*)

Stretcher-bearers brave heavy enemy fire to carry Marine from edge of Motoyama Number One. (*Charles O. Jones*)

Marine hit by mortar fragments will fight no more on Iwo. (*Arthur J. Kiely, Jr.*)

LEFT - Walking wounded, with tags showing preliminary treatment, head toward the rear. (*Eugene S. Jones*)

RIGHT - Two Fifth Division infantrymen help wounded buddy from the front lines to a battalion aid station. (*Charles O. Jones*)

Hospital ship *Samaritan* ready to take aboard Marines wounded on D-Day. (*Mark Kaufman*)

After Motoyama Number One was secured, and fighting moved into final phase, air evacuation took over movement of wounded from Iwo to hospitals in the Marianas. (*Louis R. Lowery*)

Marine dead are buried in graves dug by a bulldozer. (*Arthur J. Kiely, Jr.*)

D-plus two: Dead Fourth Division Marines are sprayed with disinfectant as their bodies await interment or burial at sea. (*Steven Impenachio*)

PART SIX

Five Days
of
Carnage

1

General Kuribayashi knew from the beginning why the Americans had brought their mighty force to Iwo Jima and why they wanted the island. When it was conquered—if it was conquered—the ugly and barren rock would become a powerful forward base from which to mount all-out air attacks against the Japanese homeland, and a gigantic staging area for the certain-to-come invasion.

He had expected Colonel Atsuchi and his troops to hold out longer than they had on Suribachi. But the shrewd samurai general had known all along that the volcano fortress would fall unless he was able to bleed the Marines to death on the beaches, and drive them back into the sea.

That failing, Kuribayashi planned to slaughter the invaders as they drove up the high ground in the center of the island. It was here that he had placed his main line of resistance, the deep and hard core of defenses.

It was an eerie moonscape of jagged escarpments and ragged chasms that sprawled about completely without pattern. In this macabre setting, twenty thousand Japanese troops waited in reinforced positions so far untouched by naval bombardment or air strikes. From blockhouses, bunkers, caves, and buried tanks, Kuribayashi's forces would make their do-or-die stand for Hirohito.

Frontal assault was the only way to overrun the Japanese positions: every approach was covered by rockets, artillery, and mortars; by dug-in enemy riflemen, machine gunners, and snipers. And while the 28th Marines slammed against Suribachi, in what amounted to an independent battle, the main thrust of the assault had pivoted northward into five days of carnage unmatched in Marine Corps history.

At dawn of D-Day plus one, seven thousand Leathernecks held the thin line of the flaming beachhead. It stretched four thousand yards southward from the quarry, curved inland to the eastern edge of Motoyama Number One, across its southern tip of the western shoreline, and back to Green Beach at Suribachi's base. Less than one-tenth of Iwo was in American hands, miserably short of what the Monks of Makalapa had expected.

Throughout the night, Marines again girded for an all-out banzai; instead they were ravaged by virtually nonstop artillery and mortar barrages that slaughtered the Americans without loss to the enemy. Periodic but heavy fire still fell at 7:30 A.M., when a large mortar landed on the 25th Regiment's Second Battalion command post. It wounded the outfit's skipper, Lieutenant Colonel Lewis C. Hudson Jr., its executive officer Lieutenant Colonel William P. Kaempfer, Major Donald K. Ellis, the operations officer, and eleven enlisted men.

"Dutch" Hermle, the only general on the beachhead, watched from a sandbagged shell hole as Navy bombardment opened up on Motoyama Number One's runways and the plateau north of it. Twenty minutes later, the fire lifted and fifty carrier planes swept in on low-level strafing and bombing runs. The few batteries of Marine artillery that had been able to land joined in the action—a powerful show of force that would become an almost daily pattern before each morning's attack.

At 8:30 A.M., everything was suddenly quiet. It was time for assault troops to jump off into D-plus one action, as Hermle had ordered.

This wasn't the Hollywood version of men going into battle. Filmmakers striving for wide-screen impact invariably show hundreds of shouting men surging forward in an unbroken wave toward fiercely resisting enemy positions. In reality, something entirely different happens: troops take advantage of every bit of protection they can find.

They move in small units; fire teams scamper, one man at a time, in a low, running crouch from one hole to another, from one ravine to another, from one burned-out bunker to another. Live troops win battles, and cover is the key to survival. When a man has no cover, he doesn't stand; he crawls. Only when it is thought an area is secure and cleared of the enemy will men move in anything like a Hollywood-style formation. Even then, they are vigilant, wary, and keep distance between each other.

Most often a push begins in an orchestrated crescendo as firepower builds up a base. The sound of bullets, either from rifles or machine guns, makes a sharp crack or pop—not the ricochet heard in most movies.

"Whenever you're in the assault," one of the men said, "you feel that every shot is aimed at you, and you alone. Machine gun tracers arch like Roman candles fired straight ahead instead of skyward. Near an enemy mortar pit you can hear 'thunks' as shells are dropped into firing tubes, and sometimes you can see their up-and-down trajectories and hear their in-flight whirring sound before the deadly 'whomps' of explosion.

"Artillery and rocket fire are worse, but somehow less personal. You can hear the incoming whine of shells, but you can't hear the lanyard pulled or see the missiles coming. Seldom on Iwo, from D-Day until the battle was over, did you see the enemy—just the sights and sounds of deadly fire from his weapons. You could see comrades moving and hear the shouted commands of officers and noncoms. And, once the attack began, you soon would hear those terrible cries of 'Corpsman! Corpsman!'"

Assault units moved out with limited objectives: "Take as much ground as you can. Consolidate positions. Then move out again." Until the beaches were cleared, and system replaced the confusion of landing men and supplies to meet only the most urgent priorities, it was impossible to do anything else.

In the Fifth Division sector, pointed north from the southwestern tip of the airstrip, two battalions jumped off: Dan Pollock's First of the 26th Regiment, and Donn Robertson's Third from the 27th. Both outfits had taken heavy D-Day casualties in slashing across Iwo's narrow neck at Suribachi's base. Now, as some fifteen hundred men moved into the fresh attack, they could glance backward and see naval shellfire hitting the volcano.

From the start, it was tough going. Every cluster of boulders seemed to hide another bunker or pillbox, and these erupted with machine gun and rifle fire at any sign of movement. But with the help of tanks and artillery, the attack was pushed. By noon, the front had advanced about two hundred yards against resistance more furious than on D-Day.

Seventeen-year-old Private First Class Jacklyn H. Lucas was caught in the melee. He showed no signs of wanting to be anywhere else. From the time he was fourteen, when he had lied about his age and enlisted, his life's desire was to be a combat Marine. It was easy for him to pass as being older; he was all muscle and carried one hundred and eighty pounds on a battering-ram five-foot eight-inch frame.

The burly, loud-talking, usually smiling youth made it through boot camp and infantry training with flying colors. He had been a Marine for nearly three years before his actual age came to light. By then, the enlistment was legal and Lucas shipped overseas to the Sixth Base Depot, a rear-echelon supply outfit in Hawaii. This wasn't the North Carolinian's idea of being a *real* Marine, and he was often in trouble.

First, it was for fighting to settle a grudge. The matter was more serious the second time: stealing a case of beer, and assault and battery on Military Police who arrested him for his peccadilloes. Lucas did thirty days in the brig on each charge, and seemed to flourish on prison fare of bread and water and hard labor. MPs were looking for him again on Hawaii when he landed on Iwo; now he was wanted for being absent without leave.

On the five-thousand-mile journey to the beachhead, men from Pollock's outfit, in which Lucas had a cousin from his home town of Bellhaven in North Carolina's scrub-pine country, had hidden him among their combat gear and provided him chow and water during the six-week trip. In the confusion of D-Day, it was easy to board a landing craft without being found out. Once on the beach, it was a simple matter to pick up a weapon from a dead Marine.

Now, in the early-afternoon tumult of the second day of Iwo, Lucas fought like a demon. He and three other riflemen had worked up a small rocky ravine when the Japanese sprang an ambush. It snorted with machine gun and small arms fire and then with hand grenades. Several sputtered, hissed, and exploded a few yards from the group—then one landed in its midst. Without a second's hesitation, Lucas vaulted over his comrades to smother the blast just as another grenade landed in front of him.

He pulled it under his body as both exploded almost simultaneously.

Lucas screamed in pain. His buddies thought he must surely be mortally wounded, but they stormed the position and silenced it with withering rifle fire and grenades of their own. When they turned to Lucas, they found he was still alive and carried him to an aid station on Green Beach.

"Maybe he was too damned young and too damned tough to die," said an amazed doctor who performed surgery aboard the *Samaritan*. Seven months later, still recovering from his wounds, Lucas was awarded the Medal of Honor. He was disappointed; by then the war was over and he had hoped to be in on the invasion of Japan.

Pollock's battalion still was in a furious fight in late afternoon, and Captain Robert H. Dunlap's Able Company was taking much of the heat and heavy casualties. Since jumping off, they had been at the point of the attack and had moved through a cluster of reinforced pillboxes guarded by mine fields. It was an area with little natural cover on the western slope of the airstrip and was laced with interlocking fields of fire from hidden bunkers.

Now heavy mortars and artillery pinned down the advance as Dunlap's men moved toward the base of a steep cliff studded with caves. Despite the fierce opposition, they had gained nearly eight hundred yards since the jump-off, but the situation was critical.

"Cover me!" Dunlap yelled as he scrambled forward to pinpoint the source of enemy fire. Marines answered with all the rifles and machine guns they could muster as the young captain zigzagged across the open terrain. Once at the bottom of the cliff, he located half-a-dozen concealed cave entrances armed with heavy weapons and mortar pits. Machine gun bullets kicked up a chain of geysers as he darted back to the lines to call in artillery on the enemy positions.

Without waiting for results, Dunlap took off again; this time with a field telephone and its wires. "What the hell," he told himself, "it's all in a day's work." As it turned out, it was much more than that. Dunlap held his one-man outpost for forty-eight hours, directing Marine howitzer barrages against enemy positions—a lonely vigil that made possible, more than any other single action, the clearing of the western beaches. Five days later, as Able Company again spearheaded still another attack, Dunlap was cut down when rifle fire tore into his hip, and he was out of the war.

Captain Robert H. Dunlap, twenty-six, of Abingdon, Illinois, was aboard the *Samaritan* headed for a hospital on Saipan when he was told that he would receive the Medal of Honor for what he had done "all in a day's work."

Donn Robertson's battalion was on the right of Pollock's men in the assault. For two hours they pushed ahead against increasing resistance. But shortly after 10:30 A.M., they slammed into a network of camouflaged blockhouses and pillboxes and were bogged down. It took three hours for demolitions men and flamethrowers, supported by four tanks, to burn out the positions and consolidate the line.

At 4:30 P.M., the order came to halt for the day, and both battalions dug in for the second night on Iwo. They were six hundred yards in front of the jump-off point.

Across the island, the Fourth Division's 23rd Regiment fought all day to silence the line of bunkers and pillboxes along the eastern edge of the mile-long north-south runway of the airstrip. The 25th Regiment, on the right, faced the automatic weapons, mortars, and artillery emplaced in the cliffs above the East Boat Basin on the northern beaches.

Walt Wensinger's 23rd already had lost more than twenty percent of its men on the beaches and in the nightlong artillery and mortar bombardment. Within minutes after the jump-off, they were suffering even heavier casualties as they lunged ahead in the face of crossfire coming from a cordon of machine gun nests whose apertures were hardly visible aboveground. Whenever there was a letup in the torrent from automatic weapons, mortars and artillery took over, and whenever men moved they encountered mine fields.

By midmorning there was a dangerous gap in the lines: the 23rd had lost contact with Pat Lanigan's 25th Regiment on the right flank. All units were pinned down; for nearly an hour no one could move. Only after six Shermans from Lieutenant Colonel Richard K. Smith's Fourth Tank Battalion churned up the steep terraces to silence the furious resistance was the breach closed.

Keith Wheeler, the *Chicago Daily Times* correspondent, watched the jump-off from a foxhole and was pinned down most of the morning. Shortly before noon, he made his way to Lanigan's command post, ducking and dodging small arms fire as he worked up the slope. As he tumbled into the shell crater, a mortar barrage shook the CP. Smith's tanks clanked and roared almost on top of the position as the armor struggled to cut through the volcanic ash to close the gap in the lines.

Major John H. Jones looked up with a smile of recognition. He and Wheeler had shared a shell hole together in another tight spot on Saipan. "You look like you could use this," Jones said, giving Wheeler his canteen. The newsman gulped and gasped. "Wow! I thought it was water!" Jones chuckled: "Bet it's the first time you ever had Benedictine and brandy in a foxhole." Then he took a heavy pull himself.

"Soft lights and soft music," he said. "It never tasted so good after a steak."

Wheeler stood up to get a better view as the tanks started to move again. Something told him it was a stupid thing to do, but it was too late. As he remembered: "A violence nothing had ever taught me to believe possible smashed against the right side of my face. I was falling and as I fell a hot red freshet spouted before my eyes. I was hit!"

If a man shot in the head can be called lucky, Wheeler was. He fell into the arms of two doctors and some ten feet from a box of plasma. And he had taken only a single bullet from a sniper—who could easily have cut loose with a fatal volley—hiding in the wreckage of an enemy fighter at the edge of the airstrip. Nor was Wheeler far from the beach where a landing craft was being loaded at the time with wounded for evacuation to the *Samaritan*.

It would take months of operations and painful recovery before the last wires were removed from the reporter's shattered jaw, but he survived to continue a distinguished career, after he left the Chicago newspaper, with *Life* magazine and as the author of nonfiction books and novels.

There was now a twenty-four-hour accumulation of wreckage on the beaches, and enemy bombardment continued to pulverize the landing zones.

"One sees amphibian tractors turned upside down like pancakes on a griddle," Sergeant David Dempsey, a combat correspondent, wrote. "Derricks brought ashore to unload cargo are tilted at insane angles where shells blasted them. Antitanks guns are smashed and out of action before they have a chance to fire a shot. Packs, clothing, gas masks, and toilet articles, ripped by shrapnel, are scattered across the sand for two miles. Rifles are blown in half. And there are the aid and evacuation stations. Our battalion aid station has lost eleven of its twenty-six corpsmen in these first two days."

Japanese artillery hit evacuation points mercilessly. Just before Wheeler was wounded, he saw a shell land in the midst of medics and fallen Marines. Thirteen corpsmen were killed or wounded and eleven seriously hurt Marines were hit again.

Late in the afternoon, tragedy struck Pat Lanigan's regiment from an unexpected source. A sortie of twelve Navy carrier planes, answering an urgent call for close air support, swept in from the north-east. They dropped bombs in a screaming low-level attack and zoomed skyward. Marines had laid large yellow signal panels fifty yards in front of their positions, but marking the lines was a futile effort. Five Ma-rines died and six were wounded as the bombs fell short. Moments later, a barrage of naval gunfire slammed into almost the same spot. Friendly fire could wipe out Americans as well as Japanese.

Eighty miles offshore, General Erskine was restless. He won-dered how soon his Third Division would be called ashore. It was apparent they would be needed to plug the holes, to provide the punch to push ahead. During the night, Colonel Hartnoll J. Withers's 21st Regiment had moved to within sight of the battle and at dawn were in landing craft ready for the run to shore.

"Howlin' Mad" Smith had spent the sleepless hours aboard the *Auburn*. He *knew* the Third must be committed, but how soon? Kelly Turner and Harry Schmidt had the final say. They decided to wait until the beaches could handle the traffic. The day was miserable— rain and rough water. For six hours, three thousand men of the 21st circled in Higgins boats near the Line of Departure for the signal to land. Hundreds were seasick, and cold spray from the choppy waves drenched the landing force and its weapons.

Instead of improving, beachhead conditions worsened. By mid-afternoon, a twenty-knot gale was blowing, bringing with it a seven-foot surf that lashed the shoreline junk heap. Shortly after 3:00 P.M. the beaches were closed to all but the most vital traffic and Withers's men were ordered back aboard their transports to spend another anx-ious night. Dozens of them, their backs heavy with battle gear, missed cargo nets as they jumped from landing craft to climb up to the decks. Most were fished from the icy water, but several were lost. And in the turbulence and turmoil, several boats drifted all night in the storm-tossed seas.

In something approaching a miracle, in the face of the raging elements and Japanese shelling, some Fourth Division artillery was landed. It took five hours of herculean effort by the 14th Regiment to get its howitzer-carrying amphibious trucks ashore, but they landed and began firing in the torrential downpour.

But not all of the DUKWs made it. At about 3:30 P.M., eight were launched from the LST 1032 some two thousand yards offshore. Once in the heavy seas, giant swells swamped their engines; this, coupled with the weight of cannon and ammunition, spelled catastrophe. Each DUKW carried a nine-ton howitzer and two men. They went to the bottom within minutes.

At five o'clock, the Fourth's assault battalions dug in for the night. Measured in distance, the day's advance was discouraging; from two hundred to five hundred yards, with casualties heavier than on D-Day. But the gains had real meaning. All of the first airstrip was in Marine hands and the front ran in a nearly straight line a mile and a half across the island at the northern end of Motoyama Number One's longest runway.

Men of the 23rd Regiment's First Battalion, like those in other outfits along the front, looked back on two days of costly fighting. They had lost Ralph Haas, the battalion CO, along with twenty-three other officers and 327 enlisted men—more than one third of the force that had landed on D-Day. Those still fighting were exhausted, heavy with anxiety, nagged by fear, hungry, and heartsick over fallen buddies. But, in the way of Marines, they were proud of themselves and men like Sergeant Darrell S. Cole.

His was a story of bravery and self-sacrifice that took less than fifteen minutes to unfold. When his platoon was pinned down under machine gun fire from five pillboxes halfway up the terraces, he grabbed a half-dozen hand grenades and launched a one-man attack. Firing his Colt .45 with one hand and hurling explosives with the other, he darted from one enemy strongpoint to the next, and silenced them one by one.

Twice he scampered back for more grenades as machine gun bullets peppered his path. On the third trip, an enemy grenade thumped at his feet and exploded; he was killed in the blast. But the valor of the twenty-two-year-old sergeant from Flat River, Missouri, had extinguished the Japanese fire, and the platoon again moved to the assault. Cole's actions earned for him the Medal of Honor. His comrades would remember forever what he did to get it.

Nights on Iwo during the first week fell into a sordid pattern: constant harassing artillery and mortars falling everywhere on the beachhead; answering rockets and shells fired into enemy positions from offshore; fire missions from Marine artillery ashore; star shells piercing the darkness with ghostly, wavering light descending under parachutes; intermittent clattering of machine guns and rifles; exploding hand grenades; cries from the wounded. And the nightlong threat and actuality of Japanese infiltration and counterattack.

Shortly after 10:00 P.M. as D-plus one neared its end, the Japanese hit the 27th Regiment in company strength just west of Motoyama Number One. Waiting until the enemy was almost on top of their positions, Marines quickly reacted with a smothering curtain of machine gun and rifle fire. Flares caught the intruders in blinding light, and the Japanese who weren't slaughtered by the torrent of bullets died under a heavy barrage of howitzer fire from Fifth Division artillery at the base of Suribachi.

Along the northern edge of the airstrip, Pat Lanigan's battalion had a quiet night until an hour before sunrise. Again, it wasn't a banzai but small units of Japanese darting behind boulders and up ravines as they tried to surprise the Marines and pierce the lines. And again the attack met disaster; nearly a hundred enemy bodies were counted in the first streaks of dawn, victims of alert Marine infantry and artillery.

As bad as things were ashore, three men would rather have been in a foxhole, whatever its dangers, than where they spent the night.

Corporal Bruno Laurenti and Privates First Class William Seward and Alex Herbert crewed "Mama's Bathtub," an amtrac evacuating wounded to the *Samaritan*. They made the last of six runs and pulled alongside the hospital ship; six casualties were hoisted aboard. Bright floodlights illuminated the tricky transfer, but when the landing craft churned toward its mother ship two miles away, the night quickly became black as pitch. A heavy sea was running when the amtrac reached the LST, and bow doors couldn't be opened to take it and its drenched and weary crew aboard. A giant wave nearly swamped the hapless craft as it turned again for Iwo and whatever haven the three men could find on the beaches.

Then the engines coughed and died. Laurenti got the bilge pumps working; Seward and Herbert bailed water with canvas buckets to stay afloat. But they only drifted farther from shore. They were eight miles out when a Higgins boat took them in tow; then the line snapped and the rescue craft vanished in the night.

"Well, that's that," the corporal said. "Unless we can make it to Saipan, we've had it." But he was wrong. A destroyer sighted the foundering craft at dawn and rescued its crew. As they staggered

below deck for a meal and sleep—they'd had neither for thirty hours—
"Mama's Bathtub" gave up the gallant fight and sank in two miles of
turbulent sea.

2

Everything that can happen in combat seemed to find its place on D-
Day plus two. As Marines smacked headlong against the outer perimeter of the deep defense belt General Kuribayashi had chosen as his
prime killing ground, the battle reached new heights of savagery.

Terrain was worse than that around Suribachi. One escarpment,
the forbidding Hill 382, was nearly as high as the volcano, its steep
slopes studded on three sides with countless concealed caves and
camouflaged concrete blockhouses and pillboxes. Hundreds of machine guns and mortars infested the approaches to the second airstrip,
whose runways were flat as a bowling alley and gave the enemy an
unobstructed lane of fire. The glut of men and equipment and supplies
still on the beaches made them targets impossible to miss.

At 7:40 A.M., the front erupted in a crashing bedlam of explosives
as close-in battleships, cruisers, and destroyers unleashed their firepower. It was a replay of D-Day, as if the Navy's guns were trying to
atone for not knocking out more positions then, as hundreds of salvos
screamed and exploded in no man's land and behind it. Marine artillery
split its fire between Suribachi and the approaches to Motoyama Number Two, adding hundreds of shells to the thunderous crescendo.

In her last day of action, the *Saratoga* launched thirty dive bombers from the oil-stained flight deck. Twenty-four Marine Corsairs from
Bill Millington's squadron took to the slate-colored skies from the *Wake
Island*. Fourteen rocket-armed Hellcat fighters swept in from the ill-
fated *Bismarck Sea*. Wing-tip to wing-tip in three-plane formations,
they flashed across the island, bombing and strafing with fifty feet
separating them from the ground.

At 8:10, the last of the sixty-eight planes zoomed into the overcast
for the twenty-five-mile flight to the carriers. Naval gunfire and artillery halted. Relative calm came to the front. Again, it was time for
the jump-off. Again, the Japanese were waiting.

As they would throughout the battle, the enemy stayed under

cover in deep tunnels and caves, in thick concrete bunkers and pill-boxes, in fortified ravines and ridges—patiently waiting for the shell-ing and bombing to stop so they could spring their own special brand of hell on the infantry. As an official battle report later said: "As Marines gradually gained yards, Japanese fire gained in intensity. Automatic weapons and rifles spurted accurately from the tiny, well-concealed apertures of pillboxes and caves. Again it was tragically apparent to Marine leaders that human flesh would have to succeed where heavy armament failed."

Iwo's second airstrip was its largest, its two intersecting runways the longest. When the island was conquered, Motoyama Number Two would bristle with American bombers and fighters and become the lifesaving haven for thousands of Superfort crewmen. But before it fell, it would become one of the bloodiest battlegrounds of the cam-paign.

At 8:30, a double-pronged attack began: one on Motoyama Num-ber Two, the other to expand the beachhead above the East Boat Basin. Three battalions were in the assault: the First and Second from the 25th Regiment, and the 24th's First. Two were commanded by lieutenant colonels, Hollis U. Mustain and James Taul; the other, by Major Paul S. Trietel. Lieutenant Colonel Justice M. Chambers's Third Battalion of the 25th Marines was in reserve.

Mustain's men pushed off among the cliffs along the northern end of the line—a quagmire of boulders and ravines arching around the quarry, a deathtrap of machine gun nests and mine fields. It took ninety minutes to move fifty yards. By 9:30, seventy-five of the unit's riflemen were casualties of enemy fire from automatic weapons, mor-tars, and artillery, and the battalion was struggling to survive.

Mustain crawled to the top of a ridge to see what could be done. On D-Day, when the men had been stalled on Blue Beach, he had rallied them up the slope. Screaming orders to "get the goddamned hell moving," and standing upright as if on a training maneuver instead of in a firestorm of mortars and machine gun fire, he had led the way. Now he was trying to do it again.

Chambers watched from his shell-hole command post some sev-enty yards away, then scampered and ducked toward Mustain to see if he could help. "Jumpin' Joe" and "Musty" had been with the Fourth Division since it formed. At Tinian they were together when Mustain climbed a telephone pole to fly the first American flag over that island.

Now rifle and machine gun fire chattered around them as they spotted muzzle-blast flashes from several bunkers just ahead, and Chambers headed back to his CP to call in tanks and artillery support.

As he dodged into a ravine for cover, he saw two Shermans clanking over the ridge where Mustain stood against the skyline directing them toward the enemy strongpoints. Then he heard the roar of an antitank gun and shouted at Mustain: "Hit the deck, you crazy bastard!" Even before the cry, Mustain was dead. Chambers vaulted from the ravine to his fallen comrade and knelt beside him as Major Fenton J. Mee took command of the battalion. "Jumpin' Joe" had tears in his eyes and cussed "the goddamned war and the sonuvabitch Japs" as he went back to his men.

In the strange way that news of tragedy can surmount the clamor of battle, the word swept the line: "The Old Man got it." And in the sublime way that such an event can inspire bravery and spark men to do the unthinkable, the attack started moving again. By noon, Mustain's battalion had gained three hundred yards. Even in death, he was a leader.

Sergeant Ross F. Gray was one of the valiant colonel's men, and that morning his leadership and bravery were indomitable. He was twenty-four, deeply religious, and had taken command of his platoon when its lieutenant was killed minutes after the jump-off.

It was natural for Gray's buddies to call him "Preacher"; he had studied for the ministry, read the Bible daily, and sometimes conducted church services. He hadn't claimed to be a conscientious objector when he joined the Marines, but in deference to his religious training and strong beliefs he was given behind-the-lines duties as a carpenter during his first two years overseas.

All that changed on Saipan when his closest friend was killed. Gray picked up a Browning automatic rifle and went to the front to kill Japanese. Comrades said he reminded them of Army Sergeant Alvin York, a devout pacifist in World War I, who single-handedly had killed twenty Germans with a rifle and pistol and forced 132 others to surrender—and received the Medal of Honor for his exploit.

In short order, Gray became a convert to combat—at least until the war was over, when he planned to resume religious work. But now he was moving to his own personal Gethsemane among the unholy rocks of Iwo Jima.

Gray and his platoon were pinned down not far from Mustain's command post when the sergeant spotted a camouflaged pillbox in a shallow ravine thirty yards ahead. "Stay here and we're all dead," he muttered to the closest of three men crouched with him behind a boulder. "Pray for me," he said, and snatched up a demolitions satchel charge.

Weaving and ducking under the chatter of machine gun fire, and oblivious to a mortar barrage, Gray zigzagged to the foot-wide, ground-level aperture of the fire pit and flung the explosive inside. A smothering blast silenced the position. Gray sprinted back to the ravine under a storm of violence coming from other hidden strongpoints. For the next ten minutes he carried on a frenzied shuttle: grab another satchel, dash to another pillbox, hurl the charge inside, dash for cover, then do the same thing again and hope and pray he lived.

Miraculously, he wasn't hit; but six enemy positions were destroyed and twenty-five Japanese died inside them. Then the platoon began to advance, but immediately found itself in a mine field that, somehow, Gray had failed to set off. "He single-handedly cleared a path through the mines," Gray's Medal of Honor citation would read, and the attack moved ahead again with him at the point. His God was with him—he was still alive.

Others weren't so blessed. The two tanks near Mustain's last CP were disabled when land mines blew off their steel treads: cannon fire finished their destruction. Troops could hear enemy mortars dropping into firing tubes, and seconds later came crunching explosions followed by desperate shouts: "Corpsman! Corpsman!" Machine guns and automatic weapons rattled and hand grenades exploded. Artillery shells fell among the men and made new craters and claimed more casualties. But in the face of it all, the attack continued.

To the right of Mustain's battalion, George Company of the 24th Regiment's Second Battalion was caught up in another complex of bunkers and pillboxes. They had been in reserve when the push began, but were thrown in shortly before 11:00 A.M., and now Captain Joseph J. McCarthy's outfit was being cut to pieces.

McCarthy was thirty-three; overage for a company commander. He was Irish and looked it: husky, red complexioned, pug nose. Superior officers sometimes found his manner abrasive, but unlike many Irishmen, he wasn't talkative. He was, in fact, laconic and tight-lipped. "I don't like malarkey or bullshit," the Chicagoan often said. But Joe McCarthy knew the uncompromising business of battle; he had the

Silver Star for leading his company up a savagely contested hill on Saipan and his men called him "the best damned officer in the Marine Corps."

Shortly after 11:15, he showed again why they felt as they did. Across seventy-five yards of open ground he located the source of enemy fire cutting down his men—several pillboxes raking the stalled advance with deadly accurate machine gun bursts. He grabbed a knapsack of grenades and motioned to a three-man flamethrower-demolitions team of old campaigners from Saipan. "Let's get the bastards before they get us!" he shouted. They charged ahead like open field runners in a football game, and plunged to the ground in front of the first position.

McCarthy yanked the pins from three grenades and flung them inside the narrow vent. He heard muffled shouts from the Japanese, then a loud roar as the grenades exploded in unison. Three screaming survivors darted from a rear trap door; McCarthy cut them down with carbine fire. Then he crawled inside and finished off three other Japanese with another clip. In the next five minutes three more strongpoints were silenced by the intrepid captain under covering fire from the men with him. Now the rest of George Company swarmed forward and another hundred yards of Iwo Jima belonged to the Marines.

A few months later, at a small ceremony at the White House, President Truman slipped over McCarthy's close-cropped head a royal blue ribbon from which hung the Medal of Honor. As he had said in times past, and would say on future occasions, the Commander in Chief—himself an Army artillery captain in World War I—told this captain that "there is nothing in the world I'd rather have than this decoration."

Offshore, the Third Division's 21st Regiment was again boated and circling in the choppy waters at the Line of Departure. The beachhead was still piled up with two miles of equipment and supplies, an obscene tableau of destruction. But as fighting roared for Suribachi and along the approaches to the second airstrip, Kuribayashi's gunners were forced to direct more and more firepower along the front lines, and less on the beaches.

Steel matting, brought ashore by landing craft like giant rolls of carpeting lashed to the sides of LSTs, made it possible to navigate the deep sand in several places. Seabees worked to put in place six 130-

ton pontoon causeways that jutted 170 feet out through the surf. Conditions were getting better and fresh troops were landed to reinforce the decimated Fourth Division. And none too soon; in less than seventy-two hours its combat efficiency had been ground down to less than seventy percent.

Shortly before noon, Colonel Withers was on Yellow Beach looking for a place to land his Third Division troops. He was a short, chunky, high-spirited Naval Academy man who had been decorated for leading a tank battalion in the Guam invasion. Most of the 954 men in each of his three assault battalions had been blooded in earlier campaigns at Bougainville and the Marianas. By 5:20 P.M., all were ashore and dug in along the eastern edge of the first airstrip.

No one was lost in the landing. But even hardened veterans were unnerved by what they saw along the shoreline and up the slopes: headless torsos and shattered bodies of Marines on the sides and tops of shell craters, burned-out tanks and demolished trucks, sunken landing craft, and dozens and dozens of wounded men waiting for evacuation. A husky corporal from Milwaukee took it all in stride. "Hell, man," he told his sergeant, "we didn't expect a picnic." Within hours, the corporal was dead.

General Rockey was ashore by midafternoon and set up Fifth Division headquarters between Suribachi and the southern edge of the airstrip. Brigadier General Franklin A. Hart, the Fourth's assistant commander, also landed and had the division's CP functioning from a sandbagged shell crater two hundred yards up the slopes from Blue Beach.

General Cates hoped to join him before sundown, but that part of the beachhead was still under heavy fire, and Hart advised him to remain on the *Bayfield* until the next day. "No sense in both of us getting killed at the same time," he radioed Cates.

Hart was no stranger to blazing beachheads. He had led the 24th Regiment in the landings at Roi-Namur, Saipan, and Tinian, and had taken German shellfire as an observer with Lord Mountbatten and British commandos in a 1943 hit-and-run raid on the French coast. But he'd never seen such carnage before. Nor had he come closer to being killed than the instant his landing craft grounded in Iwo's surf, when seventy-three men were killed or wounded in an artillery barrage that ripped into an ammunition dump and sent a violent chain reaction up and down the shoreline for three hundred yards.

"Something tells me we're not welcome here," he told a young sergeant who had plunged into a shell hole beside the general. It was another hour before Hart and his staff made their way up the terraces and set up shop.

3

More than sixty thousand Americans were on Iwo Jima when the order went out at five o'clock to consolidate the lines for the night. The Fifth Division, west of the airstrip, had the easiest day it would have during the battle; by sunset it had advanced five hundred yards and taken light casualties by Iwo's harsh standards. But it had been a hard and costly day for the Fourth: nearly five hundred killed and wounded. Its deepest penetration was the scant three hundred yards made by Mustain's men after the colonel was killed.

That night Bob Sherrod made his way to the *Eldorado* to write of the day's events in Mustain's sector. "Every hillside, every ravine, had its camouflaged cave or pillbox; some were so carefully hidden that men stepped on them before they were aware of them," his copy said. "One cave in the Fourth Division area, northeast of the first airfield, had a tunnel eight hundred yards long with fourteen entrances. Each entrance was covered by a series of pillboxes containing machine guns. If the inmates of one pillbox were killed, the Japs could easily send out replacements from another entrance. Japs would pop out of holes in the ground far behind our own lines."

Nightfall again brought parachute flares to light up the front. There was the usual quota of artillery and mortar barrages; of attempts to infiltrate the lines; of sporadic small arms firefights; of hand grenades exploding in and around Marine positions. Shortly after 3:00 A.M. a lone Japanese plane dropped three bombs on Blue Beach. Little damage was done and no one was wounded. It was the only time enemy bombs fell on the island, but until battle's end further aerial attacks were always a possibility.

That night the 21st Regiment moved into rendezvous areas just behind the lines, ready to join the assault the next morning. "Howlin' Mad" Smith still wasn't convinced the time had come to commit the Third Division, despite the staggering losses to the Fourth and Fifth.

"Always keep something in reserve to hit the sonsabitches when you've got 'em off balance," he'd often told Graves Erskine in other battles. "And never forget you might need fresh troops to save your own ass."

Correspondent John Lardner had misgivings about the great number of troops ashore. "Fighting indicates that the Japanese garrison is as strong as an island five miles by two will accommodate," he wrote in a dispatch for the North American Newspaper Alliance and the two hundred-plus dailies it served. "Since two divisions of Marines as well are on it, someone has to give ground. Until now the enemy has done so, but grudgingly."

"Grudgingly" was hardly the word. "Murderously" would have been closer to the mark. Months before D-Day, General Kuribayashi had posted a proclamation exhorting his troops to fight to the death. He called it "The Iwo Jima Courageous Battle Vows," and his men were fanatically following its stern code of Bushido. Marines found copies in the first destroyed bunkers on the beaches, and they would find others in caves, tunnels, pillboxes, and other bunkers—and on the bodies of enemy dead—everywhere on the island. In classic, bold Japanese characters, the proclamation read:

> Above all else we shall dedicate ourselves and our entire strength to the defense of this island.
> We shall grasp bombs, charge the enemy tanks, and destroy them.
> We shall infiltrate into the midst of the enemy and annihilate them.
> With every salvo we will, without fail, kill the enemy.
> Each man will make it his duty to kill ten enemy before dying.
> Until we are destroyed to the last man, we shall harass the enemy by guerilla tactics.

Marines couldn't measure how much the battle vows, which each of Kuribayashi's men had taken a blood oath to uphold, had inspired the enemy. But they knew only too well the Japanese were fighting with skill and determination unmatched in the war. Whether it was because of Kuribayashi's stern discipline or his shrewd plan of battle; whether it was the heavily fortified defenses; whether it was the uncompromising terrain; whether it was a combination of all, it mattered not—the invasion timetable was completely out of kilter and hundreds of men were being killed and thousands wounded each day. And in the three days of struggle, the front lines were still 1,200 yards from where they were expected to be on D-Day.

So on D-Day plus three, the battle again cranked up in all its fury. At 5:00 A.M., as dawn cut through the low cloud ceiling and a cold windswept drizzle began to fall, the fresh troops of the 21st Regiment moved into the lines for the first time.

About two-thirds of the men were combat veterans who knew what to expect; at least, they did to a degree. But the other thousand were about to be hurled into something beyond their wildest nightmare.

Under the best conditions, a regiment relieving another on the front is tricky and dangerous. Mix in bad weather, unfriendly and strange terrain, and heavy enemy fire, and it becomes murderous. As the 21st moved into the lines to replace the battered 23rd, which had lost nearly a thousand men since D-Day, conditions couldn't have been worse.

Confusion bordering on chaos was the result—six hours before the Third Division men were in place and their exhausted, decimated Fourth Division comrades out of the lines. The grim process claimed nearly three hundred more casualties. One was Captain Gerald F. Kirby, commander of Fox Company, who was in the fight less than fifteen minutes when a mortar barrage killed him. Fifty yards away, Lieutenant Colonel Marlowe C. Williams, the First Battalion's CO, was hit by shell fragments that slashed deep into his right arm. But he fought on until dark, when he keeled over from loss of blood and was carried on a litter to the rear. Major Clay M. Murray took over. Within hours he was cut down by a machine gun burst that sent two bullets through his left cheek.

Months later, a usually staid battle report contained unusually graphic words to describe the day's action: "The weather turned even worse during the morning, with the rain falling in torrents and visibility becoming extremely poor. Although air support was desperately needed, planes could not help ground troops when visibility dropped to almost zero. Tanks were further handicapped and virtually useless, since drivers could see but a few yards ahead. On the other hand, the well-entrenched Japanese took full advantage of the situation with prearranged fire that covered the Marine positions. Casualties mounted disproportionately to the few yards that were taken. The advance during the morning netted only fifty to seventy-five yards."

Thus did the men of the Third Division get their first bitter dose of the violence the Fourth and Fifth Divisions had taken since D-Day. No sooner had the 21st moved into the lines when machine gun fire and mortars slammed them from a complex of pillboxes and ridges directly ahead. Even oldtimers, who had fought in the jungles of Bougainville and among the hills and cliffs of Guam, found Iwo's battleground strangely frightening. To battle neophytes, it was sheer terror.

Machine guns and rifles cracked on both sides of the line. Artillery and mortars added to the tumult and the casualties. Hand grenades exploded in almost constant blasts. The combination of withering enemy fire and the jumble of ravines and ridges made flanking movement impossible.

"There's only one direction to move on this narrow island," Sergeant Frederick K. Dashiell, of Chapel Hill, North Carolina, wrote of the action, "and that's directly ahead into the face of what is perhaps the bitterest opposition Americans have met in the Pacific war." The slight, soft-spoken, scholarly, bespectacled combat correspondent knew what he was writing about: he'd been on the lines with the 21st in the Guam campaign.

"Patrols reached the front only to be pinned down by streams of fire," he continued. "Moving a few yards forward of the lines is an open invitation to suicide. A few have done it and returned safely, but even they don't advise the experiment for anyone who wants to live."

On Guam, and in other invasions, Marines had fought an enemy they could see. On Iwo, the hundreds of hidden fortifications concealed their firepower. Again, the words of Dick Dashiell:

"Suddenly three Nip machine guns chew noisily. A score of Marines crumple, a look of bewilderment on their faces. Others dive for the dirt, hitting the ground with their chests almost before their feet have left the earth. In the afternoon, one company begins to shovel into the soft, granular, volcanic soil. A mortar whangs and explodes, catching two Leathernecks in the legs, another in the face. The latter, a lieutenant, is dead."

Try as they might, it was impossible for tanks to be of much help.

The Shermans roared and clanked and churned to gain position to support the attack, but whirling treads cut deep troughs in the ashy goo and the armor barely moved. Even without the driving rain, the terrain was a natural mass of tank traps. And when the machines could maneuver, they had to be within a few yards of the target: only a direct hit could silence most of the enemy fortifications.

And so the 21st quickly learned the hard way what the other regiments had known since D-Day. At the bottom line, Iwo's yard-by-yard conquest was another dirty job for Marine footsloggers and their rifles, machine guns, mortars, demolitions, and flamethrowers. Since D-Day, a Marine was being killed or wounded every two minutes.

4

It seemed to "Jumpin' Joe" Chambers and his outfit that they had been in the middle of every bitter action whenever the Fourth Division made a landing. Their cynical outlook had been put to words in a lugubrious battalion lament.

> We are the ghouls of the Third Battalion,
>> One thousand men and one Italian.
> We waded through swamps;
>> The earth we learned to hug.
> And all we got was a goddamn dizzy bug.
>> But ten thousand dollars went home to the folks.
> But won't they be happy; won't they be surprised,
>> When ten thousand dollars go home to the folks!
> We landed on Kwajalein like a bunch of Spars;
>> When we got back some were issued Silver Stars.
> Our next landing will be a hoax,
>> And ten thousand dollars go home to the folks.
> Happy, happy we will be when we board the LST,
>> Busy little tractors heading for the shore,
> Everybody's looking for a clean gook whore,
>> And ten thousand dollars go home to the folks!

The dirge mirrored the stoic humor of a close-knit band of men who knew the costs of battle and were devoted to one another. The "one Italian" was a well-liked company commander. The ten thousand dollars was the amount of government insurance, for which the men laid out a monthly premium, paid to survivors of the dead. The "bunch of Spars" referred to women serving in the Coast Guard.

Lieutenant Colonel Justice Marion Chambers was six-feet two-inches tall; raw-boned, hoarse-voiced, and, his men proudly said, "as tough as a fifty-cent steak." No one knew precisely why he was called "Jumpin' Joe." Some oldtimers believed the man from Huntington, West Virginia, picked up the nickname because of his loping stride. Others were certain it was his flamboyant, devil-may-care approach to combat going back to his days as a captain in a Raider Battalion in the south Pacific. He carried a razor-sharp bayonet and a polished Western-style .38 revolver in a quick-draw holster on his cartridge belt. Under his left armpit was a government-issue Colt .45 pistol. He was an expert with each weapon.

If the 28th Regiment had a world-class character in Chandler Johnson, the 25th could match him with Chambers. Both were rambunctious and cut of the same cloth—unflinching in battle and possessing unfaltering devotion and confidence from the men they led. Both at times could be, as the troops said, "unmitigated sonsabitches," loud and profane when something went wrong on maneuvers or in combat. But both had smiles that soon soothed the sting of rebukes.

"Jumpin' Joe" had his thirty-eighth birthday en route to Iwo. Fellow officers had given him a party in a sweltering mess compartment aboard ship. Someone came up with a Hallmark card the men had signed with such sentiments as "Grandpa, what long hair you have," and "Too Old for Combat Duty."

Now the party was behind them and the battalion was struggling to take one of Iwo's few ridges that would have a name in the battle's history. It was called "Charlie-Dog"—an escarpment guarding the east-to-west runway of the second airstrip. Shortly after four o'clock, Chambers decided to take one last shot at swarming the crest before nightfall. It would be nice, for a change, to have the high ground and look down on the Japanese in the morning when the attack began again.

"Jumpin' Joe" called for a rocket-launching truck. He hoped its string of five-inch missiles would pin down the enemy long enough for the battalion to take Charlie-Dog in one final push. As the rockets shrieked toward the slopes, he loped forward to lead the men in the attack.

Now came a burst of machine gun fire. Chambers crumpled and fell. Three men pulled him to the cover of a shallow ravine, and he felt someone stuffing gauze into a gaping hole in his left shoulder. Lieutenant Commander Michael Francis Xavier Kelleher, the regimental surgeon, knew instantly that the colonel's days on Iwo were over. A bullet had torn through his left lung and out his back.

Captain James G. Headley was beside the stricken man. They were longtime comrades who had been together in the Solomons and in the battles of the central Pacific. Headley gently kicked the big man's foot. "Get up, you lazy bastard," he said. Chambers grinned. He was lifted to a stretcher, taken to the beach, and evacuated to the *Solace*.

Jim Headley took command of the battalion, and the thirty-three-year-old reserve officer led its men to the end of the campaign. When the "ghouls" went back to Hawaii, they were minus twenty-six of the thirty-six officers, and nearly six hundred of the 918 troops who crossed Blue Beach on D-Day.

Four days later, Chambers was in a hospital on Saipan, and months later he was at the White House with President Truman, a small group of the Marine's family and friends, and members of the press. The Commander in Chief read part of a citation for valor. "Exposing himself repeatedly to enemy fire, Chambers inspired his men by fearless example and aggressive leadership during the first bloody days until, seriously wounded, he was evacuated," it said. And then, with a big smile, the President proudly placed the Medal of Honor around the Marine's neck.

Out on the *Eldorado*, meteorologists didn't like what they saw on the weather maps. Data radioed from special cloud-tracking aircraft and Superforts on missions over Japan showed a front moving in with heavy, cold rain, low-hanging clouds, and thirty- to thirty-five-knot gales for the next twenty-four hours. The sour forecast was flashed ashore to Hermle and Hart, and at five o'clock the generals ordered the troops to dig in for the night on a line barely a hundred yards closer to the second airstrip than it had been at dawn.

Conditions were ideal for the Japanese to try massed infiltration, and the Marines knew it. The first attempt came shortly after sunset on the high ground around the quarry, when some two hundred troops were seen running in close ranks toward Marine lines. It was the largest number of Japanese so far spotted on the island and it was a suicide mission; they were annihilated by machine guns and artillery in the violent rainstorm.

Shortly after midnight, a small band of loin-clad infiltrators swam ashore on the western beaches in a senseless attempt to surprise the 27th Regiment. They were armed with swords and small arms, most of which were waterlogged and wouldn't fire. Within ten minutes they were wiped out. The same fate met another hundred marauders cut down in a vain stab at the lines held by Chambers's battalion near the airstrip. Each attack was organized—not the screaming bedlam of banzais of other invasions, but missions with a purpose. Kuribayashi's troops were adhering to his "courageous battle vows" to harass the Americans "until we are destroyed to the last man."

On the beaches, the situation still was critical. The wounded shivered in the icy downpour and waited for dawn to be evacuated. A six-foot surf pounded the shoreline, but even in the turbulence and darkness some landing craft still operated. And doctors and corpsmen went about their grim tasks of trying to save lives, ministering to the wounded until they could be taken from the island. LST 807 was on the beach, its tank deck an operating room where surgeons worked throughout the night treating more than two hundred casualties. It was a miracle the gallant ship wasn't hit by nightlong artillery fire. Only two Marines died on the operating tables.

5

Iwo Jima's battle was four days old before the Japanese homeland learned that Americans were on the island in large numbers. They had been told earlier that the invasion had been beaten off by Kuribayashi's naval guns and artillery. Since then, there had been total silence about the savage struggle raging 650 miles south of Tokyo Bay. But at 7:00 P.M. on February 22, on the nightly "Home and Empire" news roundup, Radio Tokyo lifted the blackout.

The strangely worded broadcast denounced Kelly Turner and Ray Spruance, and made no mention of "Howlin' Mad" Smith or the Marines. It said only that the Americans were ashore, and that they would be beaten back into the sea. Turner was called "an alligator" whose "true nature is that once he bites something he will not let go." Spruance was described as a man "with a powerful offensive spirit." But the admirals had, the report continued, "led their men to a point where they are indeed close to the mainland, but they find themselves in a dilemma, as they are unable to either advance or retreat."

General Kuribayashi and his defenders were exhorted to make certain that Turner, "who has been responsible for the death of so many of our precious men, shall not return home alive—he must not and will not." When Turner heard of the broadcast, he signaled Spruance on his flagship *Indianapolis*: "Maybe you'd better send a few Marines to protect me." It was one of the few times the dour admiral's staff could remember his joking about anything.

The assault force had a small piece of good news at daybreak of D-Day plus four. The weather forecast had been wrong; easterly winds had blown away the rain, the surf was down, casualties were being evacuated. The beachhead was still a mass of rubble, but conditions were improving and men and supplies were being landed. By noon, the generals would be ashore to control the battle: Harry Schmidt in overall command of the Fifth Amphibious Corps, Clifton Cates with his Fourth Division, and Keller Rockey with the Fifth Division. At last, after five days, the Marine fighting machine was shifting into high gear.

At 7:30 A.M., the attack began. Objectives were unchanged from the previous day: crack the defenses of the second airstrip and seize it; swarm the ridges behind the quarry and drive the line ahead to where it was supposed to be at nightfall of D-Day. Within minutes, the push was in trouble.

Except for the fresh but already bloodied 21st Regiment, the troops were exhausted; the assault battalions teetered on the sharp edge of having suffered all they could take without falling apart. The men had seen too many comrades wounded or killed. It had been more than a hundred hours since they had slept or had a meal. Weapons were misfiring from constant use. In some units ammunition was critically short. Food and water were mounting problems.

Gene Jones, the corporal who thought Iwo looked like a giant pinball machine when he came into the beach on D-Day, was very hungry. "I found a can of beans and strawberry jam and poured them together into my canteen cup," he remembered. "It was the best goddamned meal I ever had in my life." He had found the chow in the pack of a Marine killed beside him and had to wipe off the man's brains before opening the rations.

At the western end of the line it was an evil day for the 26th Regiment from jump-off until nightfall. Chet Graham's outfit was now in the worst terrain it had yet encountered—an open area directly fronting a line of steep cliffs from which came a steady cascade of artillery and mortar fire. Less than half an hour after the attack began, the Second Battalion's CO, Lieutenant Colonel Joseph P. Sayers, was seriously wounded by a shellburst.

Unless things got better soon, all the landing force's original battalion commanders would be gone; Sayers was the seventh to fall. By battle's end, the Second Battalion would suffer the heaviest losses of any outfit in the Fifth Division. It had landed with thirty-seven officers and 917 troops; when the last shot was fired, it had lost forty officers and 911 enlisted men, including replacements.

In the center of the cross-island front, the 21st Regiment started toward a network of bunkers armed with antitank guns aimed straight down the north-south runway of Motoyama Number Two. Before there was any hope of taking the objective, these strongpoints had to be taken out, and the fortified positions were protected by the usual interlocking network of pillboxes that laid down curtains of machine gun fire.

Major Robert H. Houser now had the First Battalion; he'd taken over from Clay Murray as the outfit's third commander in two days, and the battalion was at the point of the assault. Despite savage opposition, limited gains were made by the shot-up unit in the morning—an advance of about seventy-five yards.

Shortly after 1:30 P.M., the Japanese picked up the already furious tempo of the action. Concealed positions bypassed in the morning's push sprouted torrents of machine gun fire. Artillery and mortars from the high ground beyond the airstrip crashed among the Marines with appalling accuracy, and shells from the antitank guns screamed down the unobstructed runway.

There was nothing to do, Houser decided, but to pull back to the edge of the airstrip, regroup where there was some cover, take out the bypassed pillboxes, hope that Marine artillery and air support would silence some of the enemy's bombardment—then start the push again from scratch.

During the next four hours, Houser's battalion—and the entire 21st Regiment—struggled to survive. But, one by one, the pillboxes were overrun by front assault. Twenty-one-year-old Herschel W. Williams, a corporal from Quiet Dell, West Virginia, demolished half a dozen during the frantic afternoon. He was the last of Charlie Company's nine flamethrower operators.

"I figured, what the hell, I might as well join them wherever they were," he said later. He checked the fuel and ignitor, slung the heavy flamer tanks over his back and, covered by four riflemen, went to work. As he charged the first pillbox some twenty yards ahead, the nozzle hissed flame and incinerated its occupants. To the right, a Japanese tried to cut Williams down with rifle fire, but the corporal dropped to one knee and burned him to a crisp. Four more enemy troops lunged from cover and were instantly caught in another tongue of killing flame.

And so it went as the valiant mountaineer darted from one pillbox to the next, thrusting the fire-spitting nozzle into their apertures and burning screaming Japanese to death. It was a major miracle that Williams lived, but he did. He was the first Third Division man on Iwo Jima to get the Medal of Honor for "personal valor above and beyond the call of duty," as his citation read.

As sunset approached, the men consolidated the lines. Many used the same foxholes they had occupied the night before. It was the same story with the Fifth Division on the left, the Third in the center, and the Fourth on the right flank. The Marines might be winning the battle, but at a frightful cost.

"Hell," one begrimed corporal said, "the sonuvabitch Nips still have more of this fuckin' rock than we do." He and his comrades were glad to see the tiny flag atop Suribachi, but they were happier to see the sunset; happier to know that the rain-swept weather front had passed and that they could now at least see the crazy terrain around them, and that their weapons wouldn't clog as they had in the ashy muck from yesterday's downpour.

It was decision time for Harry Schmidt and his generals. The inescapable fact was that the attack on Motoyama Number Two was stalemated, and that the assault battalions were being ground to pieces. In fact, some platoons and companies already were little more than outfits on paper.

Shortly after three o'clock, Cates and Rockey joined Schmidt in his command post, a sandbagged revetment below a cliff at the northern edge of the first airstrip, in a solemn battlefront meeting with a grim purpose. Some way had to be found to get the push moving again; what and how it could be done were the onerous questions facing the brass.

Harry Schmidt, whose family had been plains farmers for two generations, was the man to find the answers and get the job done. At fifty-eight, he had a reputation for pushing and prodding, whether from behind a desk at Marine Corps headquarters in Washington or a battleground CP. He'd left Holdredge, Nebraska, to enlist in 1909. The taciturn but forceful general-to-be had pulled the mandatory duty tours as a shavetail lieutenant on Guam, in China, and the Philippines. He had been a seagoing captain commanding Marines aboard the battleship *Pennsylvania* in World War I, and was decorated for bravery in the "banana wars" of Latin America in the 1920s and '30s.

For two years after Pearl Harbor he'd been top aide to the Marine Corps Commandant, ramrodding through the military bureaucracy the mountains of paperwork to train and field a half-million-man fighting force and screaming every day for a combat command. He got his way in early 1944, and commanded troops on Saipan and Tinian. Since July, he'd been CG of the Fifth Amphibious Corps, the largest body of Marines anyone would ever command in battle—anywhere or any time.

Schmidt carried 160 pounds on a rugged five-foot nine-inch frame. A newsman once said of him: "He looks like a prize fighter who would beat an adversary to a pulp without change of expression or display of emotion." Under heavy, black eyebrows, his eyes were cold and penetrating. Stone-like features concealed a tough, agile mind, and he kept an icy calm in the most serious and difficult situations. The Nebraskan didn't have the devotion of the troops as did "Howlin' Mad" Smith; that wasn't his nature or desire. But he was devoted to his men, and he knew how to get the most from them and their commanders when the chips were down. He rarely smiled; even if he'd been prone to jocularity, there was nothing to smile about now.

In cold reality, the generals—stoic and stolid Schmidt, dapper and determined Cates, courageous and confident Rockey—had few options.

They could pull back most of the Marines from the lines, try to hold the gains they'd made, rest and reorganize and take on replacements, and, after a couple of days, try to get the push going again with the help of the Third Division.

But it was extremely doubtful—almost a foregone conclusion—that General Smith and Admiral Turner would go along with such a scheme; it was completely foreign to how they believed battles were won, and anathema to Marine Corps tradition and doctrine. And Kuribayashi would use the respite to rest his troops and strengthen his defenses.

So the generals decided that the battle would go roaring on just as it had—Marines slashing in frontal assault with all the courage and firepower they could muster. They would hold and attack, and hold and attack again until Kuribayashi's defense line cracked and broke open. It reminded Cates of his second lieutenant days back in France. Pinned down in no man's land and wounded for a third time, he had sent a message to the rear: "I have no one on my left and only a few on my right. I will hold."

Back in his CP he told aides to get ready for another attack. "We'll keep hitting them," he said. "They can't take it forever. We've got to keep pressing until they break." Commander Reuben L. Sharp, the division surgeon, ducked through the canvas flaps of the sandbagged blackout tent while the general was talking. The doctor had the day's casualty reports and nodded wryly, wondering how soon *someone* would break.

So the fighting quieted down for the night, and the word went out for another jump-off in the morning. What Harry Schmidt instinctively knew, and why he opted to keep pressing the enemy, was that the Marine fighting machine *was* starting to shift into high gear. More firepower, crushing firepower, *was* building up behind the lines as more tanks and artillery landed, as the beachhead wreckage was cleared, as the Third Division's Ninth Regiment prepared to join the battle, as the weather continued to improve to permit more naval gunfire and air support, as hundred of tons of ammunition and supplies were fed to shore. All that was needed now was for the infantry to come up with something approaching a minor miracle so the juggernaut could be brought into full play.

That night Larry Tighe, a correspondent for the Blue Network of the National Broadcasting Company, described the battle's progress in a live broadcast from the *Eldorado:* "This is the toughest fight yet faced by the Marines," he told millions of radio listeners.

Aboard the *Auburn,* General Smith told correspondents: "The fight is the toughest we've run across in a hundred and sixty-eight years." A deeply concerned James V. Forrestal agreed.

And Radio Tokyo reported: "The Japanese garrison on Iwo Jima is now fighting heroically, and exacting a heavy toll of enemy forces."

It was perhaps the only time the Americans and the Japanese would speak with a single voice about how the battle was going.

General Schmidt shuttled in darkness back to the *Auburn* to check in with General Smith and set in motion naval firepower to kick off the sixth day of battle.

There was much to do and he wasn't finished until well past midnight: you don't just turn on heavy bombardment and air support like a fire hydrant. He wanted seventy-five minutes of shellfire and as many planes as could get into the air before the jump-off. And he wanted to be sure the Navy knew exactly what it was supposed to do. Both he and "Howlin' Mad" were still bitter about the ships and planes Spruance had taken on the Tokyo raid. "We sure as hell could use 'em," Smith said, "and Marines will die because we haven't got 'em."

Right on schedule, the old battlewagon *Idaho* fired the first salvo at 8:00 A.M. and sent a barrage of fourteen-inch shells screaming from its main battery into preselected targets behind Motoyama Number Two. The cruiser *Pensacola,* on station half a mile off the northeastern shoreline, let go with eight-inch guns. Destroyers and gunboats unloaded ten thousand rounds of rockets in the next half hour. Before the fire lifted for the air strikes, nearly 500,000 pounds of TNT and steel crashed into the island. Acrid gray smoke blotted out the sun.

Then the planes came roaring in: Marine Corsairs with hundred-pound bombs, napalm, and machine guns. Naval Hellcats and Avengers with five-hundred-pounders and rockets. It was a circus of destruction for fifteen minutes as they crisscrossed the center of the island, sometimes as low as a hundred feet off the ground.

When the planes climbed into the overcast and headed for the carriers twenty-five miles offshore, Marine cannoneers began yanking lanyards on every artillery piece on the island. In firepower, the pre-attack concentration, as Harry Schmidt had hoped, was as heavy as on D-Day. But, as he feared, it would prove almost as ineffective.

It wasn't that the bombardment and air strikes didn't help. They certainly killed some Japanese and drove enemy troops to the deepest cover they could find—at least temporarily. But the shrewdness of General Kuribayashi, and the way he had built and placed his forti-fications, made shelling and bombing largely useless. The positions were masterpieces of concealment and construction: walls of many were more than three feet of steel-reinforced concrete and impossible to spot from the natural terrain upheavals that camouflaged them. Some measured ten by twenty feet, had five-foot ceilings, and were made up of three separate rooms with twelve-inch concrete walls, the areas connected by narrow crawlways.

Apertures for cannon were virtually invisible, jutting from rubble of volcanic boulders. Atop many of the installations were pillboxes with heavy machine guns and an artillery rangefinder, and these were covered by eight to ten feet of sand—all but impregnable fortresses that could take a direct hit from naval shellfire or a bomb from planes without suffering much damage. Even when Marine demolitions men could fling a satchel charge into a gun vent, the blast would have little or no effect on the other two rooms.

It was into a complex of these deathtraps that the 21st Regiment found itself as it jumped off. And the attack had only one way to move because of the terrain—straight ahead along the flat, unobstructed north-south runway of Motoyama Number Two.

Eight Shermans from Lieutenant Colonel William R. Collins's Fifth Tank Battalion caught the brunt of the first fury of enemy re-sistance. They had moved less than thirty yards onto the airstrip when one triggered a land mine; the tank's treads were blown off in the deafening explosion. The next clanked ahead another ten yards and was knocked out by a buried five-hundred-pound aerial torpedo. Bunk-ers from the north end of the runway slammed volleys of 47-millimeter antitank rounds into the next three; within seconds they were flaming hulks. In less than five minutes, five tanks were lost and fifteen crew-men killed or wounded. Under a screen of smoke grenades, the sur-viving armor retreated to the reverse side of a ridge on the west side of the runway.

Two companies of Third Division men—units of Wendell H. Duplantis's Third Battalion from the 21st Regiment—crouched just behind the tanks and were now without the support so needed to keep the push alive. The lieutenant colonel, who had led the outfit on Bougainville and Guam, watched from his command post, then darted forward to a shell hole where the commanders of Item and Kate Companies were huddled trying to figure out what to do next.

"We're in one sonuvabitchin' mess," Duplantis said, "but we've got to have the goddamned airstrip today." He could have saved his breath on the first statement, and both he and the young captains knew there was just one way to accomplish the other—with head-on attack and heavy casualties. The colonel said he'd get back to communications to see if he could get more tanks and artillery and try to call in close air support from dive bombers.

Twenty-two-year-old Clayton S. Rockmore was Company I's CO. Rodney L. Heinze, twenty-four, had Company K. Most of their six hundred Marines were even younger, and all were heavy with fear and combat gear. Riflemen, with M-I Garands and carbines at the ready, lugged extra hand grenades hung on web belts and in knapsacks, and bandoleers of 30-caliber ammunition over their hunched shoulders. Mortar men grunted with the backbreaking weight of steel base plates, firing tubes, and shells. Flamethrowers sweated with seventy-two pounds of explosive fuel and oxygen strapped to their backs—walking human fire bombs who could die in a roaring blaze if they made a mistake. Automatic weapons men and machine gunners struggled to find fields of fire to lay down cover for the advance. Demolitions men checked charges and primed unwieldy bangalore torpedoes, and waited for orders to move against a bunker or pillbox.

Their objective was to advance eight hundred yards across completely exposed terrain resembling a rumpled gray pool-table cover and take a fifty-foot ridge at the intersection of Motoyama Number Two's twin mile-long runways.

Rockmore and Heinze seemed to be everywhere: shouting orders, screaming exhortations and warnings, always at the point of the attack, always where the action was the heaviest. And with them were the troops, darting and scrambling ahead—solitary men, some in pairs, others in fire teams and squads.

When they could find a shell crater or a burned-out pillbox, they took momentary cover and then were off again; to stay in one spot was an open invitation to death. Machine guns spat in rat-tat-tat, rat-tat-tat bursts. Sniper fire zinged every time a man left whatever meager protection he had. There was hardly a minute when mortars weren't crumping down along the front. Grenades fell like hailstones whenever Marines neared an enemy position. And with each yard gained came the shout: "Corpsman! Corpsmannnnnn! Over here!" But the charge didn't stop—shades of Antietam and Gettysburg—and shortly after ten o'clock Heinze and some of his men reached the edge of the runway intersection.

Someone yelled: "Grenades! Goddamnit! Grenades!" Then came two explosions, and searing fragments ripped into Heinze. Blood spurted from his thighs as he fell back into a shell hole. It didn't take long to locate the source of the missiles—a hidden spider trap ten yards away. As its metal cover lifted again moments later, a BAR man splattered the head of a peering Japanese about to throw two more explosives. It was two hours until litter bearers could come for the captain and take him to the beach for evacuation. First Lieutenant Daniel Marshall, also in his twenties, took over the company, and they held their ground.

A few yards away, Clay Rockmore and fifteen men made it across the runway. He was a Cornell University dropout; right after Pearl Harbor he had joined the Marines, and had fought and been wounded and decorated for leading an infantry charge on Guam. Minutes after Heinze was cut down, a sniper's bullet found its mark: Rockmore died instantly when the slug ripped through his throat.

After five days of slaughter, Marines now could claim the second airstrip. As historian Frank Hough would write: "They fought and died with the same valorous determination as General Pickett's men in the Confederate charge at Gettysburg." But with one difference: the Marines would carry the day on Iwo Jima.

First Lieutenant Raoul Archambault now led Rockmore's men. It would have been hard to find a better company commander; he'd won the Silver Star leading a bayonet charge up a hill on Guam, and the Bronze Star in beating back an enemy attack during a rainstorm on Bougainville. He covered the captain's body with a poncho and yelled for Dominic Grossi, a first lieutenant platoon commander, who'd started the day with forty men and now had twelve.

"Let's go, Dom!" he shouted above the clamor. Grossi straightened up and relayed the order: "You heard the man! Move out! Move! Move!" Archambault grabbed a submachine gun and a satchel of grenades and started across the runway. Grossi and his dozen men were five seconds behind, darting, zigzagging, ducking as they ran toward the base of the enemy-infested cliff.

Five yards beyond the shell-pocked runway intersection, a beehive of pillboxes came alive with machine gun fire. Connecting the positions were waist-deep trenches, and they swarmed with Japanese whose screaming battle cries were lost in the clatter of their weapons. Marines vaulted the sandbagged pits, flinging hand grenades in the wild charge, and scrambled for a foothold on the fifty-foot hill. They were halfway up the rocks when Marine artillery started falling; Colonel Duplantis had come through with the hoped-for howitzer support.

By then, two hundred Marines—sparked by the dash of Archambault and Grossi and their men—were across the strip and hugged the steep slopes as shells slammed into Japanese positions on top and behind them. Then the barrage began landing among the Marines, and the errant friendly fire was called off before the company took serious losses. After the confusion cleared, it took half an hour for the troops to form a scrimmage line and start again to claw toward the crest of the ridge.

Units of one platoon reached the top and were met with torrents of rifle and machine gun bullets coming from three directions—a system of trenches in the front, and camouflaged pillboxes on the right and left. A cascade of mortars whomped into the men still among the coarse, cutting rocks on the slope. In fifteen minutes the Marine attack was beaten back and the men pulled from the hill to regroup among the Japanese dead in the demolished trenches at the rubble-strewn base.

Archambault was on the walkie-talkie to Duplantis. "We'll have more artillery for you in five minutes, and it'll keep coming for the next fifteen," the colonel told the lieutenant. "Then, goddamnit, go after the sonsabitches again!" Archambault answered: "Will do, Colonel! But tell the bastard artillery to hit the fuckin' Nips and not us!" The word was passed to the company, now down to fewer than a hundred men, and they checked weapons and ammunition and waited for the artillery to come. When it stopped, Archambault and Grossi were the first to lunge ahead.

There was nothing halfhearted about the attack. But the men

were exhausted and still reeling from the firefight, their ranks slashed by more than half in less than an hour. They were twenty-five feet up the hill in the desperate surge when the Japanese counterattacked in greater force and ferocity than before.

From positions higher up the tortuous incline, the enemy swept the faltering line with rifle and automatic weapons fire, with machine guns and grenades. It was a classic enactment of a battlefield scene as old as war itself: too many determined and well-entrenched defenders beating off too few highly vulnerable attackers, and so the charge failed. Archambault again pulled the men off the hill and, this time, across the runway.

It was noon. Since 9:15 when they had jumped off, the Marines had moved eight hundred yards up the pool table that was Motoyama Number Two. They had been atop the ridge that commanded the intersection of its runways. But twice they had been beaten back by determined defenders, whose positions still controlled the airstrip.

In the next ninety minutes the power of the American fighting machine—stifled since D-Day by Kuribayashi's battle plan, his do-or-die troops, Iwo's friendly-to-the-enemy terrain, and the strategic demands of how to win the war in the Pacific—showed its invincibility.

Archambault's men consolidated their thin line. Troops regrouped and picked up more ammunition. Wounded were trundled to aid stations and evacuated. Ships offshore pummeled the obstreperous ridge. Carrier-based planes swarmed in with ground-level bombing and strafing runs. Marine artillery hit the slopes and the ridge. The runway was a tableau of devastation.

Raoul Archambault again shouted the order: "Let's go, Marines!" The men took off in a screaming charge across the runway. Then, feet sideways digging for traction, the troops hit the slope. Hunched bodies were nearly parallel to the sharp incline, and some men crawled as they moved from one shell hole to the next, from boulder to boulder, still yelling like Indians on the warpath, and firing their weapons like cowboys on a drunken spree. In less than two minutes they scaled the hill and plunged over the crest against surprisingly light opposition. Then a swarm of Japanese roared forward with fixed bayonets. They had waited to hit the Marines at the crucial instant, and now they poured from a gully on the reverse side of the ridge.

What followed was a desperate man-against-man struggle for survival. Victory or defeat on the hill wasn't what mattered to friend or foe; it was an explosion of the primitive instinct to kill to keep from being killed. Japanese officers swung ceremonial swords and were impaled on Marine bayonets. Japanese troops lunged at Marines with bayoneted rifles and were clubbed to death with weapon butts, entrenching picks, even rocks. Hand grenades played no favorites, and their blasts maimed and killed attackers and defenders alike. Machine guns and rifles and pistols barked, and all around men fell screaming in pain as they crumpled to the ground.

It was over in ten minutes. Archambault and his men had seized the ridge in action more violent and deadly than Chandler Johnson's troops had found on the slopes and summit of Suribachi. In taking the murderous hill, the capture of Motoyama Number Two had been sealed. But more important: Kuribayashi's main defense line in Iwo's center had been broken. The Marines now had their desperately needed battlefield miracle.

As with any miracle, no one knew exactly how this one came about. Tactics were no different from those used since D-Day: Marines slamming against fanatic Japanese using tortuous terrain and fighting with deadly skill to answer each thrust. "Perhaps it was the sheer impetus born of desperation," Frank Hough, himself a Marine captain who had seen other battles, later speculated, "but for whatever reasons, the fire that had been checking the whole attack failed to stop this particular outfit." Colonel Duplantis called it "the most aggressive and inspiring spectacle I ever witnessed."

K Company had followed Item's surge across the runway and joined Archambault's thin line of survivors to mop up the summit and dig in for an expected counterattack in force.

"Hold at any cost!" was the order from a proud and sanguine Colonel Withers, who was seldom satisfied and was now prodding the rest of his 21st Regiment to exploit the long-sought breakthrough. The ridge might belong to the Americans, but the furious Japanese attempt to hold the airstrip and to kill Marines roared on.

Under heavy artillery and mortar barrages, nearly two thousand Marines and twenty tanks were hurled into the push. This time there were few land mines, so the armor was able to support the attack with its firepower and cannon and machine guns. But it was still rough going for the infantry. They didn't have three inches of steel, as did tank crews, to protect them from enemy shellfire, machine guns, small arms, snipers, and grenades.

Many units were dangerously low on ammunition. Aid stations were backed up with casualties waiting for jeep ambulances to carry them to the rear. With still four more hours of daylight, and despite the sweep up the airstrip and the conquest of the ridge, there was a gnawing prospect that the Marines might not be able to hold the ground already seized. Unless troops could get ammunition—bullets for rifles and machine guns, shells for the tanks and mortars—the outlook of being pushed back by a heavy counterattack was a serious concern.

Calls went out along the beaches, two miles behind the blazing action, for volunteers to carry supplies to the front. Seabees cranked up bulldozers and pulled loaded trailers up the terraces, across the first airstrip, and to within two hundred yards of the line. What became a three-thousand-yard human conveyor belt, with hundreds of men packing crates and backpacks, pushing carts of ammo and water, went to work to refuel the attack.

William J. Middlebrooks, a twenty-two-year-old corporal from Marianna, Florida, was one of the volunteers. He'd been in the thick of the fighting all day. On Guam, he had been a rifleman with the 21st Regiment. Now he was a combat correspondent. But his loyalties and instincts still were more with his old outfit, Item Company, than in finding copy, so he was carrying ammo to his buddies. On his third trip across the airstrip, a sniper's bullet tore into his spine. He died minutes later in the arms of a corpsman in an aid station in a bombed-out culvert. "We couldn't do nothing for him," said the medic, a buddy from the days on Guam, as tears washed down his grimy face.

Resupply went on after dark, even after the emergency had passed and the 21st could look back on the shell-pocked runways behind them. Hours after sunset, Marines were flabbergasted to see two flashlight beams swinging back and forth to point the way for a clanking bulldozer pulling a trailer across the runway.

"In a lotta ways, you gotta be crazy to be in the Marine Corps," a bemused old sergeant of twenty-four said. "But those bastards are fuckin' stupid to boot." He thought differently as he helped unload the cargo of bullets and mortar shells, and steel containers of hot food and coffee.

On the 21st Regiment's right flank, the Fourth Division's 24th Marines waged a daylong struggle against Charlie-Dog ridge, the elevation that had claimed "Jumpin' Joe" Chambers. It was five hundred yards east of Archambault's hill, a formidable escarpment where the Japanese had constructed nearly a hundred concrete bunkers and pillboxes.

Fighting matched the fury of seizing Motoyama Number Two. Within minutes after the jump-off, hopes for taking Charlie-Dog by noon had vanished. It was again a battle for survival, a struggle to hold ground already gained in three days of costly combat. From point-blank range, the Japanese unleashed streams of rifle and machine gun fire. Mortars and artillery fell every few seconds. Land mines stymied any movement of tanks. Antiaircraft guns fired shells timed to explode with deadly airbursts. So many Marines were casualties that eighty white phosphorus smoke shells were laid down to screen litter bearers scrambling to retrieve the wounded. Stretchers were in such short supply that ponchos were often the only way to get fallen men from the battlefield, a Marine on each corner lugging the casualty like a bag of potatoes.

Lieutenant Colonel Alexander A. Vandegrift Jr., CO of the 24th Regiment's Third Battalion, still had hopes that Charlie-Dog might fall by sundown. About 2:30 P.M., he left his command post, some fifty yards behind the point, to see about a final effort to take the hill. He scampered forward, admonishing troops as he ran past foxholes in a low crouch: "Better keep down until things get better," he yelled. "Watch out for mortars and snipers or the bastards'll get you!" It was a needless warning; the battalion had lost nearly a hundred men since jump-off, and those still able to fight were using every bit of cover they could find.

Vandegrift made it to a front-line observation post and plunked down among six Marines in the crater of a shell hole. He raised up to see if he could find a new route up the ridge as a bracket of mortars landed twenty feet away. He was hit in both legs by searing shrapnel and grievously wounded; but he was lucky at that. Four men on the lip of the hole were killed, and another lost both legs.

Vandegrift's combat know-how and leadership would be missed, but the loss of battalion commanders was rapidly becoming an onerous statistic in the battle of Iwo. Back in Washington, when headquarters got the word, at least one person took the news as more than a statistic. The latest of eight battalion COs to fall so far was the thirty-nine-year-old son of the Commandant of the Marine Corps.

Correspondents Lardner and Sherrod had spent several hours with Vandegrift's outfit before he was wounded. They were heading for the beach to write copy and send it to the *Eldorado* to be radioed to the mainland. Moving gingerly along the runway of Motoyama Number One, supposedly a quiet area for the past three days, they counted sixteen dead Marines and saw another nine Japanese bodies.

Sherrod was about ten feet in front of Lardner when, as he later said, "we heard the old familiar whine of Jap sniper bullets, one whine per fifteen steps. There was nothing to do but keep walking and hope we didn't get hit." He heard a thud that "sounded as though an ox had been hit on the head with an axe." Lardner slumped to the ground and crawled a few feet into a shell hole.

There, grimacing with stabbing pain from his groin, the lanky, bespectacled, soft-spoken ex-sportswriter looked for the wound. "That felt like no bullet," he told Sherrod. "It felt like a rock." Which it was—a ricochet from the sniper's bullet, and the correspondent wasn't seriously hurt. "That's what I get for writing the Japs are suckers for a fast curve," he lamented in describing the episode. Months later, while showering in his New York apartment, a small chunk of Iwo's volcanic rock plunked in the bathtub. Lardner told friends that his wife, expressing connubial concern, remarked with real surprise: "And to think that for all this time I could have been shot by a stray Japanese bullet."

General Schmidt was on the field phone to Cates and Rockey at 4:30 P.M., and told them to quit as soon as conditions permitted. The situation map and casualty reports told the story of the day's fighting. In the face of the most bitter resistance yet encountered during the campaign, the men of the Fifth Amphibious Corps had smashed ahead for the biggest gains of the battle so far. The 24th Regiment, on the right flank of the line, was five hundred yards ahead of the morning's jump-off point, and Archie Vandegrift's battalion had seized Charlie-Dog in an inspired, all-out charge after he was hit. In the center, the troops of the 21st had swarmed eight hundred yards up the runways of Motoyama Number Two, and Archambault's men had been reinforced and were in strength atop their bloody ridge. The 26th, west of the airstrip, had battled across five hundred yards of gullies and ravines infested with pillboxes and bunkers.

D-Day plus five had been another one of bloody work for the Marines; bloody work in the rock-strewn crevices, on the formidable ridges, and on the runways of the airstrip. It had been a grinding day of battle for the tanks and artillery, but even more frantic for the infantry with their rifles and machine guns and hand grenades, with their flamethrowers and demolitions charges, with their fixed bayonets and razor-sharp combat knives, with their entrenching tools and picks and rifle butts and fists and rocks—everything and anything that could be used in the business of killing.

But the troops had pulled off the hoped-for miracle. At sunset, after six days of unimagined and unprecedented bloodletting, seven thousand Marines held a strong in-depth line across the island. They had finally reached the D-Day objective.

People at home bought newspaper extras by the thousands for the latest reports about the savage battle for an ugly island they hadn't known existed a week before. Millions turned radio dials to catch live broadcasts from the beachheads; at times the sharp sounds of gunfire could be heard over the crackle of static. Eyewitness copy described the bloody shambles of the wreckage-strewn beachhead, told of the frantic fight for Mount Suribachi, of the carnage from the push for the high ground and the airstrips. A surging wave of pride, unity, and determination to win the war against Japan swept the nation in the wake of Joe Rosenthal's flag-raising photo.

But the surge of patriotism was tempered by the floodtide of casualties. During the first three days of the invasion, no specific figures were released about losses. "No estimate of casualties is yet available," Admiral Nimitz's D-Day communiqué had said. But news stories made it clear that they were worse than Tarawa, worse than D-Day in Europe, worse than the battles Marines had fought in World War I. And on February 21, the nation was shocked and appalled by an official announcement from Nimitz. "At 1800 hours, our casualties on Iwo Jima were estimated at 644 killed, 4,108 wounded, and 560 missing," the grim, headline-producing announcement said. It sent a shock wave of horror across the country.

Under firm orders from the White House, no further mention of American losses was made in communiqués. In the first place, it was a major error to let the enemy know the price the Marines were paying for Iwo, and the Japanese monitored every broadcast statement. It also added fuel to the anti-Nimitz, anti-Smith tirades in the Hearst-

Patterson-McCormick press, and among their coterie of supporters in Congress.

But "Howlin' Mad" Smith and the Monks of Makalapa knew the figures, or at least a close approximation of them. At the end of the sixth day of the invasion, more than nine thousand men had been killed or wounded or were missing in action. Since the first wave of troops had hit the beaches, a Marine had fallen every fifty seconds.

Left to right: Kelly Turner, Harry Schmidt, and "Howlin' Mad" Smith at Fifth Corps command post. (*Arthur J. Kiely, Jr.*)

Left to right: Generals Rocky and Smith and Admiral Hill at "official" flag-raising. (*Arthur J. Kiely, Jr.*)

D-plus four: Third Division command post at northern end of Motoyama Number One. General Graves B. Erskine (without helmet) outlines plan of attack with staff. Author is behind radio gear in jeep to the rear of the Division commander. (*Joseph Heilberger*)

Generals Cate, Smith and Schmidt at Fourth Division CP as battle enters final stage. (*Arthur J. Kiely, Jr.*)

Chandler Johnson, field phone in hand, at his CP with men of Easy Company the morning Suribachi was conquered. (*Louis R. Lowery*)

General Rocky, helmet in lap, at Fifth Division headquarters along edge of Motoyama Number One. (*Arthur J. Kiely, Jr.*)

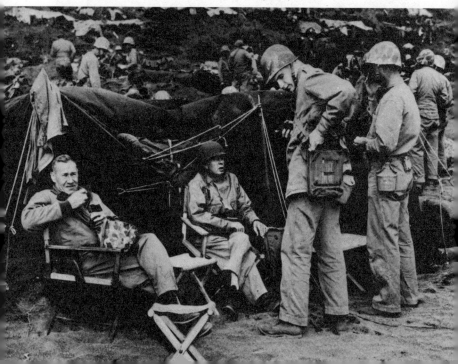

PART SEVEN

Of
the Living . . . and
the Dead

1

Nearly four decades after the battle was over, the surgeons of Iwo Jima still marveled at what they'd been able to do. It wasn't that they were boastful of superior medical skills, or basking in an illusion that other doctors couldn't have done the job. It was simply a sober recognition of the fact that *they* had done it; that in the thirty-six days of monumental mayhem they had performed miracles—not once or twice, but hundreds of times.

Surgeons and corpsmen were on the beaches with the first assault waves. Until the last shot was fired, there was work for them to do. And wherever the pharmacists' mates were, a surgeon was alongside or not far away.

Each battalion had a surgeon, thirteen corpsmen, and twenty stretcher bearers. Their base of operations was an aid station, and to save lives it had to be close to the front; the closer, the better—but never more than two or three hundred yards from the action. For the first three days on Iwo, the distance was measured in feet.

What happened to Lieutenant Charles J. Hely was typical of medical teams in the beachhead inferno. The twenty-seven-year-old doctor from Westfield, New Jersey, landed shortly after 9:30 on D-Day in the deep black sand of Green Beach. Moments later, he and his medics were treating the first casualties, men hit by small arms fire and scattered mortar bursts. Half an hour later, their aid station was functioning in an open shell hole some two hundred yards up the terraces toward the quarry, when General Kuribayashi sprang his ambush. "It was three days before we moved," the young Irishman recalled. "There was no place to go. We couldn't move, and anyway we were right on the front, where men were getting hit."

When a Marine was wounded seriously, his first and best hope for survival was that a corpsman be nearby. It meant life or death, in the first crucial minutes after a bullet or shrapnel tore into a man, that something be done to control hemorrhaging: to start the flow of lifesaving plasma, to douse the wound with sulfa, to inject morphine to dull pain, and to get him to an aid station.

First aid on the front was something like being caught up on a factory assembly line gone amok. A corpsman would get to a wounded Marine as quickly as he could, and do what he could. Then stretcher bearers would try to move forward, usually with sniper fire cracking around them and often under mortar and artillery shelling, to carry him to the aid station, usually a tarpaulin-covered shell crater or burned-out bunker, sometimes a sandbagged culvert or revetment.

Even after a wounded man reached an aid station, it was just the start of a continuing ordeal until he was evacuated and aboard a hospital ship. He was still within yards of the front, where aid stations were favorite targets for enemy shellfire and snipers. And at best, a battalion surgeon could only make a quick diagnosis of the wound and, in life-or-death cases, perform simple patchwork surgery.

After the wounded Marine's fatigue jacket was tagged to show preliminary diagnosis and treatment, he was ready for someone to take him the next step to survival. After the first week, when the fighting had moved beyond Motoyama Number Two, it was a jeep ambulance driver whose vehicle could carry as many as four casualties to a division hospital. During the early fighting, however, it was a painful, slow, and dangerous trek by litter to the beaches and often an agonizing wait for hours before a landing craft made it through the devastation to ferry wounded to hospital ships.

More often than not, jeep ambulances drew sniper and mortar fire as they shuttled to and from the front, and casualties were heavy among drivers. A Marine combat correspondent wrote about the curious but understandable reaction of one of the battleground chauffeurs—eighteen-year-old Private First Class Gerald Gruggen of Minneapolis, Minnesota—to the deadly Japanese harassment:

"Bleary-eyed, dirty and with a faint trace of beard, he stopped his vehicle near an artillery emplacement. The operation was nearing the middle of the third week, and the driver looked as if he had been in action continually since D-Day.

"'Where's the trigger that shoots this cannon?' Gruggen asked the artilleryman, who pointed to the lanyard. 'If it's okay with you fellows, I'd like to pull it the next time you fire. Those Nips have been shooting at me for two weeks now, and I'd like to give them something in return.'

"The gunner nodded his approval; the gun crew grinned, and Gruggen grasped the lanyard with both hands. Came the word to fire and he did, with a mighty pull. Having given the enemy 'something in return' he left without another word and drove off."

If countless Marines survived because of the valor of corpsmen and the skills of combat surgeons, it couldn't have happened without the brawn, bravery, and sacrifice of stretcher bearers. Each assault battalion, when it landed, had twenty men—most of whom were musicians with regimental and division bands when not in combat— assigned as litter men. Many became casualties themselves very early in the battle.

As their ranks were cut down, and with the unending deluge of casualties to be recovered, new men untrained for stretcher duty were constantly thrown into the blood bath: cooks and bakers, motor transport men whose vehicles were twisted wrecks on the beaches, landing craft crewmen whose amtracs and Higgins boats had been sunk or were half submerged hulks in the surf, company clerks whose files and typewriters were useless, buglers without bugles, and frightened replacements fresh from the States and in battle for the first time.

Captain Raymond Henri, the Third Division's public relations officer, told of what happened to one litter detail. The four-man team had picked up a corporal whose legs had been shattered on Archambault's ridge and was carrying him across the runway when an artillery burst landed. The wounded man somehow dived off the stretcher and plunged into a shell hole. The blast caught the stretcher bearers; two were killed and the others badly maimed. The corporal escaped without a new wound, and another team rescued him within minutes.

Henri recalled another instance when a private first class, wounded in the thigh, was being carried away from the lines. A sniper opened up and a bullet grazed his chest. "As the bearers rushed him off," the captain remembered, "the Marine lifted himself up on his elbow and, in perfect choler, shook his fist toward the hidden sniper and yelled: 'Goddamn you! Isn't once enough?'"

Sergeant Francis W. Cockrel, a combat photographer with the Fifth Division, made pictures of stretcher teams from the 28th Regiment under fire on D-Day. "I saw them carrying casualties down the hill to the beach, through small arms fire coming from both sides, through bursts of mortar shells," he later wrote. "They couldn't run very fast carrying a litter. They had to be upright. They had to stop for rest in that sand, and when they did there was rarely a handy hole to fit four men and a litter case. So they made a dandy target."

Even after casualties made it to a division hospital and were
treated there and tagged for evacuation, they still faced a cruel ordeal.
For most of the campaign there were no areas on Iwo where safety
was more than a wish. Beachhead evacuation points were still taking
artillery and mortar barrages two weeks after D-Day. Some men were
wounded a second time—and a few a third—while waiting for a ride
to a hospital ship.

Then there was the surf. The restless sea rarely quieted down,
and constantly shifting winds made the pounding waves unpredictable
and sometimes impossible to surmount. Even when the surf was down,
swells tossed evacuation craft with such force that strong men had to
grasp handrails to stay on their feet during the turbulent half-hour
run from shore.

The toughest stage of the evacuation came last: getting the
wounded safely aboard ship from boats that bobbed like huge slabs of
cork, rising and falling as much as ten feet with each wave. It was a
dangerous and delicate maneuver that demanded split-second timing
even when special cranes were used to hoist stretchers straight up. If
a litter was hooked to the cable an instant too soon, or too late, a
sudden swell would smash it against the hull.

Once on the hospital ship's deck, the odds for survival were on
the side of the wounded. Better than ninety-five percent would live
and most would completely recover. But there were others—some
with missing limbs, some sightless, some without voices, some without
faces, some paraplegics—who would endure the mental and physical
pain of shattered bodies for the rest of their lives.

Admiral Nimitz and the Monks of Makalapa had expected, when
the invasion was planned, that the Fourth and Fifth Division hospitals
would be in operation by the afternoon of D-Day plus two. But it was
five days before the first one—the Fourth's—would begin treating
the wounded.

Commander Richard Silvis, the outfit's ruddy and raw-boned chief
surgeon, landed in an early wave on D-Day. His Fifth Division counterpart, Lieutenant Commander William W. Ayres, also was ashore
before ten o'clock.

Battalion and regimental surgeons hit the beaches with the troops,
and immediately were swamped with casualties. Working in shell
holes, they did everything possible for the flood of early wounded.
But it was very little. It was impossible to operate in the chaos of the

beachhead, and there were so many casualties that all the doctors could do was to try to stop bleeding, infection, and pain—and tag the wounded for evacuation and hope they would make it to the operating rooms on the *Samaritan* or *Solace* or to transports and LSTs with hospital facilities.

By noon of D-Day, there was little doubt that at least some Third Division troops would be called in from the floating reserve, and Commander Anthony E. Reymont, the Third's chief surgeon, landed while the 21st Regiment was still aboard its transports. "We need all the help we can get to save the lives of my Marines," General Smith said. So Reymont was on the beachhead with most of his doctors.

By midmorning of D-day plus four, when a semblance of order had begun to emerge along the shoreline, the Fourth Division's hospital took its first wounded through the tent flaps of a makeshift facility in the revetment of a highly vulnerable site along the eastern edge of Motoyama Number One. Bulldozers had carved an embankment in a cliff to provide protection from shelling, but artillery and mortar bombardment still crashed into the area with disconcerting regularity.

Two long dark-green tents and six smaller ones formed the nerve center of the crude complex. One of the big tents was part receiving ward and part operating room for less critical cases. Eight operating tables, lighted by large nonshadow electric lamps, were at one end of the receiving tent along with an x-ray machine and a refrigerator for drugs, plasma, and whole blood. Generators would often sputter and quit for a time, especially when shells exploded nearby, and emergency battery-powered lights would take over. The other tent was the recovery ward, with eighty cots where wounded were taken after surgery to await transfer to hospital ships or, later, when ambulance planes could land, to be airlifted to base hospitals on Saipan, Guam, and the Hawaiian Islands.

Two rain-catching cisterns became operating rooms for chest wounds, amputations, and brain and eye surgery. Their roofs were waterproofed canvas from a truck mired on the beach. But the walls and floors were thick concrete, and gave solid protection from shellfire, except for the always present danger of a down-the-hatch direct hit. Until the island was finally conquered, the lights in the operating rooms were never out.

In a farfetched fashion, the scene would later become familiar to millions of Americans in the 1970s and '80s watching the M*A*S*H television series. Dedicated and skilled doctors operating endless hours under impossible conditions; the sights and sounds of combat; the constant presence of danger and death.

But the reality of Iwo Jima and the television version of an operating room had little in common; there were no bosomy nurses, no steady stream of comedic, if cynical, repartee on Iwo. And the M*A*S*H facilities could only be described as safe, antiseptic, and well-equipped compared with Iwo's blood-stained cisterns and tents without floors.

Receiving and recovery wards were eerie scenes of grimy, smelly, grievously hurt Marines who hadn't washed since landing, much less changed clothes. The air was always heavy with stale cigarette smoke, and reeked with the putrid odor of ether, ruptured intestines, and lost limbs. It seemed remarkable that in the midst of so much pain there was so much calm as the wounded waited with stoic resignation for whatever would come next.

"Many men come in here with a sense of relief," said Lieutenant Commander Howard Johnson, a surgeon from Uniontown, Pennsylvania. "The battle is over for them and they figure they're lucky to get out alive." Lieutenant Commander Paul Giddings, from Augusta, Maine, who had operated under fire at Roi-Namur and Saipan, had never seen "such wounds as they bring into the hospital here."

Surgical teams, three doctors to a team, worked in each cistern. Chain-smoking Commander Reuben Sharp, from Camden, New Jersey, was an expert at treating stomach wounds, and, despite the primitive conditions, was justifiably proud of the results his team achieved. "The mortality rate in belly cases is generally seventy percent, but we ought to save half of those we've operated on today," he told a newsman. A month after the battle, eleven of the forty-five had died of their wounds.

Many Marines lived because of transfusions of whole blood, now available for the first time in the Pacific war. It was in the veins of critically wounded men within a week after being given by donors on the West Coast and flown six thousand miles to the battle in special ice-packed containers. "This whole blood is wonderful stuff," Doctor Silvis said, "much better than plasma when there is severe hemorrhaging." In some instances, donors had added a personal touch to their gifts of life: they had scrawled their names on the pint bottle of precious fluid.

While the fighting raged for the second airstrip, a jeep ambulance brought seven cases of whole blood to an aid station on the front. "Break it out on the double," Lieutenant Commander Leo Theilen, a battalion surgeon, shouted to corpsmen, and minutes later the scarlet fluid was going into the arms of Marines on stretchers in the sandbagged, canvas-covered shell crater. After the invasion began, it had been drawn in donor centers in Los Angeles, San Francisco, San Diego, and Portland. "Bless it," said Captain C. P. Archambeault, a Third Division surgeon from Brooklyn.

Whole blood also had a heartening cosmetic value. When Marines could take time from battle to visit wounded comrades, they'd expected to find them looking like paraffin mummies, as they had appeared in earlier campaigns. Instead, the visitors saw faces and lips with a more normal glow. "You docs sure as hell know what you're doing," said a husky Fifth Division gunnery sergeant. "Oh, we just put make-up and lipstick on them," was the tongue-in-cheek explanation.

It was nearly two weeks before the Third and Fifth Division hospitals were in full operation, but meanwhile their teams of medics worked around the clock in sandbagged revetments near Motoyama Number One, and in front-line aid stations, waiting for the fighting to move forward so there was space for their wards and operating tents; the need was always there.

On D-Day plus fifteen, the Navy set up the first operation of its kind in the Pacific war, a beachhead evacuation station. It was on Purple Beach, not used in the assault landing, on the western shore near the base of Suribachi, and by nightfall its two hundred cots were full of Marines who earlier had had surgery performed in division hospitals and were recovering.

Major Samuel S. Kirkland and twenty-two officers and 182 enlisted medics soon set up the Army's 38th Field Hospital. They would remain as Iwo's permanent medical unit after the invasion force left; but there was plenty for its six surgeons to do before then—by the time the battle was over, they had operated on 592 Marines, 360 for major surgery.

Up on the lines, the Japanese constantly were making certain hospitals didn't want for patients. But with skilled doctors ashore, and with more and more facilities to work with, the chances of survival for the wounded was always on the upswing. Maybe, after all, the last Marines wouldn't die "knocking out the last Japanese gunner," as General Erskine feared.

2

Since primitive man first took up crude arms against one another, disposing of the dead has been a military fact of life. On Iwo Jima, it was an especially cruel business.

During the first two days, most dead Marines were left where they fell. There was no place to bury them, and Japanese bombardment was so heavy, the machine gun and small arms fire so intense everywhere on the slim beachhead, that Marines still alive and unhurt were fully occupied with trying to survive. But unburied dead on Iwo, as on all battlegrounds, posed a serious health—and morale—problem. And late in the afternoon of D-Day plus one, the Graves Registration Officer on the Fourth Division landed on Yellow Beach with the first working parties to begin the ugly assignment of burying the dead as soon as possible. Their Fifth Division counterparts followed the next morning on Red Beach.

It was two hundred yards inland from Red Beach—where the coarse, black sandy terraces sloped up from the surf and across the narrow neck of the island and down the western shoreline—that the battle planners at Makalapa had decided to locate the burial grounds on Iwo Jima.

There ultimately would be three crowded cemeteries: the Fifth Division's, closest to Suribachi, and the Third and Fourth Divisions', side by side on the incline leading up to the north-south runway of Motoyama Number One. The sites were in an area infested with land mines, some as big as garbage cans, and duds from Japanese artillery and American naval bombardment and air strikes. These had to be defused or detonated before burials could begin, and the ticklish operations brought down heavy enemy cannon and mortar fire. It still fell spasmodically, but with deadly results, among the gravediggers two weeks after D-Day.

By the time the push to take Motoyama Number Two was at its climax, collecting the dead was a methodical part of Iwo's daily routine.

Service troops, unaccustomed to the ghoulish work but pressed into it by necessity, retrieved bodies and, in many cases, parts of bodies from where the men had been killed—sometimes on the front, sometimes in no man's land, sometimes behind the lines where the fighting had already passed by. "Jap snipers seemed to take a special delight in trying to kill Marines trying to recover bodies of Marines already dead," Francis Cockrel remembered.

Bodies were placed on litters or ponchos, along with the dead man's rifle, and carried to collection points. There they were picked up, four to six at a time, on a twice-daily schedule by Graves Registration teams, and taken to the cemeteries.

Then began the slow, painstaking, sometimes futile process of establishing positive identification. Nothing was left to chance and the grim task was performed by experts. Dog tags, wallets, names stenciled on dungarees and rubber-stamped on shirts and underwear, ID bracelets, engraved watches, rifle numbers—all were checked and double-checked. Fingerprints were pulled and dental charts made. Personal belongings—letters, photographs, Bibles, notebooks, rings, watches; anything found on the body—were tagged and boxed for the long voyage home.

Most of the handwritten letters were poignant chronicles of the latest doings from friends and loved ones. Not so, the typewritten ones. In the breast pocket of a private was found a no-nonsense communication from a loan company. "Unless we receive immediate payment," it said, "you can find yourself in serious trouble." The young draftee's wife and two small children were living with her parents in California. Seven months earlier, the dead man had been working at a Lockheed aircraft plant in Burbank.

Interment was, of necessity, a mass and impersonal affair; there were too many bodies to do otherwise. Bulldozers cut trenches in the volcanic ash—eight feet deep and about thirty yards long—that were the graves. Shrouds were green GI blankets or ponchos. Bodies were placed in the ground in accordance with Marine Corps regulations: "Three feet from center line of body to center line of body, fifty bodies to a row, three feet between rows." Each grave was listed on a master location chart with the dead man's name, rank, serial number, and unit. Prepainted wooden crosses and slab-like markers, cut to specifications by a lumber contractor in the States, came bundled for efficient handling and were put together and stenciled with the dead man's name. In cases where parts of bodies and those so mutilated that positive identification was impossible, the graves were stenciled "UNKNOWN."

For 146 Marines who were hit on the beaches on D-Day and died aboard transports after being evacuated, burial was at sea "in water at least a hundred fathoms deep," as directed by Naval regulations. Later, when the beachhead was less hectic, those who died aboard ships were taken back to the island for interment.

Two weeks after D-Day, with the front nearly three miles to the north from the beaches, Private First Class Gordon E. Diggs, of Paris, Texas, was walking near the Fourth Division cemetery. He'd come down from the lines to look for the grave of a buddy when he stepped on a land mine. The explosion ripped off one of his feet at the ankle, badly mangled his other leg, his hands and arms were badly torn and burned black by the blast. "Jesus Christ, Doc, I musta gone forty feet high when I stepped on the goddamned thing," he told the surgeon who operated on him.

Even as the battle was reaching its peak in the highlands of the north, and while hundreds of Marines were being buried daily, the cemeteries already had the look of hallowed ground.

Winds carried the sound of bombardment back from the front, but each day the ashy, wind-blown soil was carefully raked between the rows of white crosses. Seabee carpenters used the wood from empty mortar cases to build picket fences, which were painted white, around each burial ground, and stonemasons from their ranks laid entrance arches from Iwo's ample supply of boulders. In time, grave keepers managed to coax growths of scrub grass and small beds of flowers to bring splashes of color to the otherwise barren landscape. But months after battle's end, Army garrison troops still found land mines and unexploded shells in the area.

What to do with Japanese dead was a constant concern. Left unburied, they, too, posed disease problems, and the stench and sight of their bloated bodies were repugnant even to hard-bitten and blood-ied Marine infantrymen. When enemy bodies were found in a cluster, bulldozers heaped a mound of earth over them, but this seldom happened—part of General Kuribayashi's strategy was to conceal his losses from the Americans.

When they could, the enemy sneaked out at night to recover bodies and hide them in caves. While there were no cemeteries for the Japanese on Iwo, Marines entombed thousands whose bodies would rot underground in emplacements sealed by demolitions charges. Other thousands died of wounds in catacombs extending hundreds of yards into the sides of Iwo's countless cliffs and ridges. Uncounted others killed themselves by holding grenades to their stomachs and pulling the pins in a final act of Bushido.

Twenty-three-year-old Charles M. Blodgett, a first lieutenant from Des Moines, Iowa, led a patrol of scouts and snipers into one cave among the craggy ledges of the Fourth Division zone on Iwo's eastern shore. Like dozens of other charnel houses discovered by Marines, it had been used as a fortification, then as a makeshift hospital, and finally as a place to dispose of the dead.

A captured Japanese medic led the way as the Marines warily started down one of the cave's six entrances. He was followed by Sergeant Howard B. Inman, a war dog handler from South Amboy, New Jersey, and his Doberman pinscher that had first sniffed out the installation; the rest of the patrol followed—all with weapons at the ready. Dave Dempsey, the Marine correspondent, was with them as they moved down the twisting, dungeon-like passageway.

"Narrow, tunnel-like veins led off each side and we approached them stealthily," he wrote of the eerie episode. "The most amazing thing about this miniature city is that it was no natural cavern, but was made entirely by hand. Chisel marks on the walls testified to the infinite patience that had gone into the making of this bomb-proof haven. The entrances were flanked by 47-millimeter guns, but the gunners had been killed by our shelling and lay sprawled grotesquely behind their weapons."

As the Marines went deeper into the catacomb, they saw dead enemy troops lining the passage. Many bodies were partially cremated; others were bloated and the stench was overpowering. Empty cases of medical supplies spoke silently of vain attempts by the Japanese to save their wounded. The Marines were some sixty feet underground and perhaps a hundred yards from the cave's mouth when their prisoner made contact with one of his comrades.

"He went ahead to talk with his people," Dempsey said, "and we waited tensely in the gloom. In a few minutes, he returned to tell our interpreter that an officer and eleven men were still alive. They wanted two hours to talk among themselves about surrendering. At the end of that time, they would either commit mass suicide or come out."

Lieutenant Blodgett sent word back that they could have an hour, and the patrol eased cautiously toward the mouth of the cave, where Marines had been posted and demolitions men were standing by. Dempsey described the scene:

"It was a long, suspense-ridden sixty minutes. We waited expectantly, for a dull thud of hand grenades, or the appearance of the Japanese. Finally, they came. The officer had been shot in both legs and was carried on a stretcher by four of his men. Six others, also wounded, hobbled behind in the strange procession. The officer sat upright on his stretcher and bowed. Resignation mingled with pride in his awkward gesture. He asked that he be allowed to keep his saber. Our lieutenant granted permission."

The demolitions men sealed the entrance of this cave, along with five others, entombing forever more than two hundred of Iwo's defenders in an unmarked grave some 650 miles from the Japanese homeland.

Ten years later, the body of each Marine buried in the division cemeteries would be exhumed and returned to American soil. The Punch Bowl, Hawaii's National Cemetery in the extinct volcano where Ernie Pyle was buried, would be the final resting place for many.

Others would be consecrated in the national shrine at Arlington, Virginia, across the Potomac River from Washington, D.C., near where a remembering nation would later erect a giant bronze replica of Joe Rosenthal's picture of the second flag-raising on Suribachi. National cemeteries scattered across the country would hold the remains of other Iwo dead. And family plots in home cities and towns would be the last grave sites of many. Where Iwo's fallen would finally rest was a decision made by next of kin.

And now over each grave, taps would be sounded. There hadn't been time for this on Iwo.

3

Wherever Marines fought in the Pacific, they went into battle knowing the fortunes of war had to be on their side if they were to come through *any* invasion alive and unwounded. From the first frightening, confusing day in boot camp, the deadly nature and cost of the war, of invading Japanese-held islands defended by fanatical troops ready to fight to the death, were drummed into recruits every waking hour and carried into their troubled dreams.

That was the purpose of boot camp: to mold the broadest mix of young Americans into skilled tradesmen in a kill-or-be-killed business, and to keep intact and untarnished the glory and traditions of the United States Marine Corps.

Gene Jones remembered his rude awakening, his brusque post-midnight introduction to recruit training in early 1943 soon after he turned eighteen: "The moment I got off the train at Parris Island with a bunch of tough older Philadelphia dockworkers, a hard little corporal, who was about nineteen and had a Purple Heart and two battle stars, looked us in the eye and the first thing he said was 'I promise that sixty percent of you will be casualties within the year, and most of you will be killed.'"

Since November 10th, 1775, when saloonkeeper Robert Mullen recruited—some cynical historians claim "shanghaied" is the better word—the first company of Marines at his Tun Tavern on King Street in Philadelphia, the men of the Corps have gone to the nation's wars as first-to-fight shock troops.

Of the 140 Marines with Captain John Paul Jones on his tiny ship *Bonhomme Richard* in their first battle with the British in the Revolutionary War, sixty-seven were killed or wounded. But in three hours of deadly hand-to-hand combat, fighting with muskets and cutlery, they carried the day and captured the *Serapis*, a much larger and better-armed man-of-war.

At one time during the struggle, the British commander called on Jones and his Marines to surrender. Jones's answer—"I have not yet begun to fight!"—became a gallant battle cry of the yet-to-be-born United States. That day the fighting Leatherneck tradition was born.

Since then, in big wars and minor scrimmages in all parts of the world—from, as the Marine Corps hymn proudly proclaims, "the halls of Montezuma to the shores of Tripoli"—theirs has been a heritage born of training, discipline, and esprit de corps that has set them apart from all other armed forces.

Two boot camps, officially called Marine Corps Recruit Depots, were the high-pressure cauldrons from which came every enlisted Leatherneck and many officers who fought in World War II, Korea, and Vietnam. When the Japanese struck Pearl Harbor, the *entire* Marine Corps—70,425 officers and enlisted men—could have fitted into the Rose Bowl with 30,000 seats to spare. By V-J Day, nearly 500,000 men had passed through one or the other of the recruit depots—remote Parris Island in the pine country of South Carolina, or San Diego's base on a sand spit reclaimed from the Pacific Ocean five minutes from the center of the bustling city with a permanent population of 334,387.

Both had year-round moderate temperatures, but they were worlds apart in physical appearance and natural surroundings. San Diego's boot camp was typically Southern California—a complex of airy, two-decked hacienda-style brick and stucco barracks connected by arched walkways fronting on a half-mile-long, quarter-mile-wide paved drill ground that blistered with heat during the day. As the war in the Pacific gained momentum and sweep, hundreds of pyramidal tents and dozens of Quonset huts crowded the sandy soil beyond the drill grounds as thousands of boots arrived in a never-ending flood to become Marines.

Architectural centerpiece of the installation—whose next-door neighbors were the San Diego Municipal Airport, known as Lindbergh Field, and the Ryan Aircraft plant where the flier's *Spirit of St. Louis* had been designed and built—was a 3,000-seat, air-conditioned theater painted in weird camouflage stripes of dull green and brown. It was off limits to recruits except to watch training films about how to avoid venereal disease, detect Japanese booby traps, or why the war was being fought—a gamut of productions that it was hoped would inspire or inform young Americans about what they would face in the war against Japan.

Weary recruits struggled to stay awake in the cool, peaceful surroundings of the pleasantly dark movie palace. Once a week after the fledgling troops were well into the dawn-to-dark ten-week training schedule, if their drill instructor thought the platoon had performed exceedingly well and he wanted to be a nice guy for a change, boots were marched in formation to see a Hollywood feature and the latest newsreels—and more training films.

Three times a week, in Southern California's nightly chill, recruits learned water-survival techniques: how to swim below the surface with full packs and to do at least two lengths of the Olympic-sized pool while fully clothed. Those who couldn't make it didn't get leave at the end of the recruit training.

Parris Island also had its permanent barracks, Southern-style brick buildings dating back to World War I mingled with others of the same design put up since Pearl Harbor. As at San Diego, these were augmented by Quonset huts and tents to handle the booming influx of thousands of Marines-in-the-making.

The sprawling base was 7,819 acres of towering moss-draped oak trees and stubby palmettos infested with thousands of long diamond-back rattlesnakes. It was surrounded by smelly and treacherous marshes, bottomless quicksand pits, putrid streams swarming with alligators—a frightening moat around the dismal and primeval island that was connected to the mainland by a single narrow causeway. On its drill ground the stomp and cadence of troops marching in close order, along with the shouted commands of DIs, sounded through the humid air from daybreak to dusk, and often far into the night.

Parris Island also had its theater, but most training films were shown at night out of doors. It also had a huge swim tank used mainly for the same purpose as San Diego's pool. Both camps had monster combat courses where men learned to climb ropes, cross gullies on rope bridges, vault over trenches and other obstacles, and to develop physical stamina in a hundred different ways.

Boots spent two weeks on the rifle range mastering M-I Garand rifles and carbines, firing Colt .45 pistols and high-powered BARs— World War I vintage Browning automatic rifles. They picked up a nodding acquaintance with Thompson submachine guns, learned to use deadly hand grenades, and spent time in a sealed chamber where tear gas introduced them to the terrors of chemical warfare.

While the bases were a continent apart, the harsh discipline and the strenuous physical ordeal of training were carbon copies designed to mold radical new mental attitudes, to build bodily endurance and test it to the limit, to teach and sharpen deadly skills to kill the enemy and survive. Everything had a methodical purpose. It was by plan that sleepy and confused boots got their first taste of recruit life in postmidnight darkness following cross-country trips in converted box-cars with wooden bunks, or ancient Pullmans resurrected from railroad junk yards to carry troops.

Recruits from west of the Mississippi River went to San Diego. Parris Island got those from east of the dividing line. Regardless of when they arrived, even if it was an hour before daybreak, their first day in bootcamp began at dawn. The first morning, few ate breakfast from steel trays in crowded mess halls, but by noon the befuddled newcomers were ravenously hungry.

First order of business was a final medical check. Then the recruits drew from the quartermaster a canvas seabag where they stowed their gear throughout boot camp, and in which they carried personal be-longings whenever they traveled aboard ship and headed for combat. It was stuffed with two sets of dungarees, a dress uniform, socks, and underwear. A galvanized scrub bucket, two bars of Ivory soap, and a heavy-duty brush were handed out for daily laundry chores. It, too, went into the seabag.

The men were issued a rifle, two knapsacks, two canteens, a first-aid kit, a web cartridge belt, and two pairs of shoes, one for dress, the other, "boondockers," leather reversed with smooth surface in, for regular wear. Then they were assigned to training platoons and marched, usually for the first time, in ragged formations to the bar-bershop where heads were clipped to the skull by civilians. Boots paid twenty-five cents in chits—they weren't allowed to have cash—to look like frightened and shorn sheep.

Thus began seventy days, eighteen hours a day, of near-constant bedlam, of unremitting prodding and harassment, of muscle-building physical conditioning, of training under live ammunition, of method-ically becoming integral cogs in the Marine Corps' fighting machine. It was a pivotal time for young men, many of whom had never been away from home before leaving for boot camp, and they would never forget it. Reveille sounded in a cold predawn darkness, and woe unto the man who hadn't shaved, relieved himself, made up his bunk, and dressed in the prescribed uniform of the day within ten minutes. Then came a fast-paced run to a mess hall where twenty minutes were allotted for breakfast.

Everything was on a demanding schedule. After chow, ten minutes were given to square away tents and barracks for inspection and to muster for roll call, followed by forty-five minutes of rigorous calisthenics. Then came four hours of close-order drill, always strenuous put particularly painful during the first days before medical inoculations had lost their sting. And then a fast mile run to chow hall for the noon meal. If the men had performed to the harsh demands of hard-nosed DIs, they were given a thirty-minute break. Otherwise it was double-time back to the drill ground for a penalty session of nonstop close-order marching.

The afternoon routine brought no letup. It was crammed with bayonet drill, judo, and hand-to-hand combat scuffling—the more strenuous and savage, the better. Each platoon had three drill instructors—usually a sergeant and two corporals—who barked, yelled, and cursed at the sweating, tired, often frightened-out-of-their-wits recruits, and threatened them with dire consequences if they didn't slug each other with greater violence. Then came trade school, as troops learned to strip down their rifles and reassemble them until they could do it blindfolded. And they crawled under barbed wire with machine gun fire cracking inches above their heads. And they learned something about bazookas, flamethrowers, demolitions charges, and enemy booby traps.

Things quieted down toward evening, when the trainees were lectured about military courtesy, tactics in combat, the history and traditions of the Marine Corps—a litany of what was not only expected but demanded of every man who finished boot camp. Before supper there was time for a shower, policing the platoon's area, and again the march to the mess hall. There was still much to do before "lights out" at ten o'clock: rifles to be cleaned, clothes to be washed; writing short letters home, and studying the *Guidebook*, a thick manual with blood-red cover that contained pertinent official regulations including eleven always-in-force General Orders governing conduct and chain of command, highlights of Marine Corps history, and the deeds of its legendary heroes. The *Guidebook* was the Bible of Marine Corps life as far as boots were concerned. And like shaving cream and soap, it was purchased by chit from the Post Exchange. But recruits weren't allowed to buy candy—it was called "pogey bait" for some unknown reason—or gum. Sweets might be all right for sailors and soldiers, DIs made it clear, but not for someone who wanted to be a Marine.

Sleep came quickly to the exhausted men, but not before most wondered if life in the Marine Corps would always be this bad. Or would it, could it, get worse? Rare was the boot who didn't flirt with the idea of "going over the hill" and running away from the whole thing. Very few tried. Parris Island's formidable moat, and San Diego's twelve-foot brick and chain-link fence saw to that.

Regardless of season, and contrary to Chamber of Commerce boosters in San Diego, boots found the climate miserable most of the time at both camps. Nights could be bone-chilling during winter months and daytime temperatures could soar to hundred-degree-plus readings. Days of heavy rain meant next to nothing to the rigid schedule. Twenty-mile hikes with full combat gear were routine in blazing sun and in driving nighttime downpours.

Postmidnight "bugout" evacuation drills were commonplace as shouting DIs stormed among the bunks and rousted the men, exhausted, undressed and shivering, into the cold darkness. Sometimes it was punishment for a goof-up by the platoon. Sometimes it was merely a show of power, of absolute authority, that drill instructors wielded.

"Just think what could happen to you stupid bastards if I really wanted to get tough," recruits were told as they braced in formation and shook with a combination of fear and cold. Hardly a day passed that some boot wasn't ordered to smoke a pack of cigarettes, whether he was a smoker or not, while standing at attention with a bucket of sand on his head. It was standard treatment for not reacting to an order in a split second, or for daring to talk back to a DI. The routine penalty for having a dirty rifle—and dirt meant a few smudges of dust in a barrel—was for a recruit to sleep, or attempt to, with the weapon under his back or buttocks in the narrow bunk.

Thus did the young men become Marines and learn the stern code of the Corps. They learned it in an atmosphere of constant apprehension and fear, of constant challenge to physical capabilities and mental stress. It was not uncommon for a boot to be physically beaten by an especially hard-nosed drill instructor, and both San Diego and Parris Island had several cases of suicide by recruits who couldn't comprehend or endure the mind-boggling physical and mental pressures.

It was all right for boots to bitch to each other about horrible treatment and miserable conditions. But carrying it further, either in complaints to officers or in letters home, verged on treason. Those who did, and were discovered, were ostracized by comrades going through the same thing."Hell, Cry Baby, if you can't take the shit, why the hell did you join the fuckin' Marines?" was the blunt reaction. More often than not, the recalcitrant would "shape up" and make it through training. A few were mustered out as unfit for Marine Corps duty.

Once a recruit passed through the front gates of boot camp, he was there until he graduated or was discharged as unfit; if he was given an emergency furlough, it was a rare occurrence usually involving serious illness or death in the immediate family. Overnight or weekend liberty passes were unheard of, and recreation was strictly limited and doled out to platoons when DIs felt so inclined—and this was seldom.

Some platoons put on boxing matches, but these were roughhouse melees with many fighters purposely mismatched to test the mettle of the underdog. Newspapers were seldom seen, and these were usually outdated editions. The only radio in the platoon's area was in the drill instructors' Quonset duty hut, and it was for their ears only.

Sunday brought a welcome break in the grueling routine, but it was hardly a holiday. Reveille was late—it sounded at six o'clock instead of the usual 5:00 A.M. But the firehouse stampede to shave, shower, suit up, and fall out for inspection was missing; on Sundays the men had an hour to get it all done and march to a steak-and-eggs breakfast.

Church call came at 9:00 and base chapels usually overflowed, as much to get away from the platoon area as for religious reasons. The rest of the day, after noon chow, was spent washing clothes, cleaning rifles, writing letters, shining dress shoes that wouldn't be worn until graduation, boning up on General Orders and studying Marine Corps regulations in the *Guidebook*, hashing over the hectic happenings of the week, talking about civilian life, speculating over the future, and visiting hometown buddies in other platoons if DIs permitted such indulgences.

Boots could sit on bunks, but cat naps, "crapping out" in Marine parlance, were forbidden. A card game, with matches for chips, might be in progress with players coming and going, but only if the DIs thought learning to gamble was part of the making of good Marines. Most did. But they made it clear they didn't want to catch men with money on the table. By now the men had drawn their first Marine

Corps pay and DIs had a knowing wink when they declared that any form of gambling for cash was against regulations.

For some, Sunday brought a touch of home and civilian life. Recruits could have visitors for two hours in the afternoon, and the special area was jammed with family and friends, many of whom had brought picnic baskets. Many traveled hundreds of miles to be with "their Marines" and boost their sagging spirits.

So went boot camp at Parris Island and San Diego. In less than three months, raw recruits became fledgling Marines in the only way the Corps wanted to do the job. It had taken young men, little different from counterparts in the Army and Navy, and molded them by Marine Corps methods into indomitable fighters. They had been driven to the limits of their physical stamina, browbeaten and cajoled, worried over and encouraged, understood and misunderstood. But they were learning their new trade: what it meant to be a "fighting Marine."

When they marched in review on graduation day, they were in the best physical condition of their lives. And they marched with the pride that only a Marine can know. On the way to learning the basic rudiments of the uncompromising kill-or-be-killed business of war, they had been imbued with the élan and *raison d'être* of the Marine Corps. They had passed the first test—ultimate testing would come later in battle—and were full-fledged members of a very special breed of fighting men. For the rest of their lives—and for many this would be a tragically short time—they would glory in the words: "Once a Marine, always a Marine."

Drew Middleton, military correspondent for *The New York Times*, wrote in late 1983 about "an indefinable inner strength" of the Marine Corps. He traced much of it to boot camp: "Graduates never forget the experience; indeed, a certain type of fraternity is forged during those weeks. In 1958, when the Marines landed in Beirut for the first time, an American ambassador visiting a Marine assault ship asked a sergeant when he had graduated from Parris Island. The Marine said he had been in the Class of 1948. 'Ah,' the ambassador replied, 'I was a bit ahead of you, Class of 1912.'"

A few outstanding graduates left San Diego and Parris Island with the single stripe of privates first class. After two weeks' leave—for many the only time they would be home until war's end, and for many the last time ever—the new Marines were assigned to combat units. Most went to infantry outfits to become riflemen, machine gunners, flamethrowers, demolitions men, company clerks, buglers, cooks and bakers, and truck and jeep drivers. Others became members of tank battalions. Some learned to operate amtracs. A very few got coveted sea duty and served aboard battleships, cruisers, and aircraft carriers. Some with strong aptitudes for electronics and aircraft engines went to aviation units as gunners, communications men, and ground crewmen.

But regardless of duty, or where they served, they would remember boot camp and their crusty instructors who had shown them giant pictorial blowups of dead Marines floating face down in the blood-red lagoon at Tarawa and of headless torsos at Peleliu. "Look at this!" they had been told. "This is what you'll face in a few months!"

Eight out of every ten Marines *would* see comrades wounded or killed in battle. But there was hardly a man who didn't think he would be lucky—that fate would spare him. "Hell, I made it through the hell of boot camp," was the common thread of confidence and optimism of the cocky, self-assured new Marine. "And I can make it the rest of the way," It was the visionary hope for the thousands who would fall at Iwo...just as it had been for thousands before them in earlier Pacific campaigns.

4

Fear is a recurring soul mate of front-line troops in battle.

General Kuribayashi's fortifications, the determined defenders, the grinding terrain, the thunder of battle, the sights and cries of wounded and dying comrades, constantly stoked the fires of fear among the Marines who fought on Iwo. It is the enduring mark of their courage that they overcame it.

"It's difficult to imagine battle without thinking of heroics and dramatics, of dashing figures and climactic spectacles," Francis Cockrel said. Iwo had more than enough of these, he remembered, but more often it was "dangerous drudgery—mean, exhausting work at which men got shot and blown apart." The main feelings were of frustration and tiredness and anger, but when a mission was handled with a minimum of loss, there was grim satisfaction.

How Marines appeared on Iwo was a savage mirror of the in-

humanity of battle. You could see it in their eyes and on their faces
and in the ragged uniforms they wore. They had, as Gene Jones
remembered, "the look of the hawk." Their eyes were hard and cruel,
and encrusted dirt ringed the deep sockets. Their skin was pallid;
pimples and blemishes and freckles stood out like big nailheads on
the faces of the young warriors.

Stubbles of beards marked the older men, those in their early
twenties. Some had heavy mustaches that took months to grow and
they were the adornments of rank and combat experience of corporals
and sergeants. Everyone spoke in the muttered cadence and hoarse
tones of men with sore and parched throats. Their talk might be
studded with stoic humor about what was happening, but there was
seldom laughter—maybe a few tight grins about their malefic plight.
More often than not, they'd been next to a close buddy when he was
hit. They had known nauseating fear, and many had vomited at what
they saw; had shaken with the clutching realization that they could
be the next to fall.

Their clothes were those described in an irreverent but honest
World War I marching song about "raggedy-assed Marines on parade."
Sergeant Gilbert Bailey, another Marine correspondent, put it this
way: "He looks like a sandhog who has long gone without a shave or
a bath. His tired eyes are the mark of an inner struggle between dread
and courage. He carries his souvenirs with him: a bullet hole in his
helmet, a crease in his canteen, a bayonet cut in his dungaree jacket,
a slight wound that 'doesn't amount to anything.'"

More words from Bailey, who had seen the early dark days of
Guadalcanal, and had been in the bloody struggle with the Fourth
Division on Saipan: "These men would be legendary characters if
history could absorb them—unnoticed people who, for the first time
in their lives, heard the call of greatness and glory, and recognized it
when it came." He wrote of the corporal who was wounded three
times but always talked his way back into the lines "to get back to my
outfit." Said Bailey: "Stories will never be written about most of them.
There are too many, and what they do has come to be taken for
granted."

What drove the men of Iwo Jima and those in all the other savage
Marine campaigns in the war against Japan? What set them apart from

others who might have faltered and broken in the constant nightmare of slaughter? Where did they muster the courage and conquer their fears in a seeming indifference to suffering and death as comrades crumpled around them? Were the Marines braver, more valorous than millions of Americans who fought other battles in a global war unforgiving of human frailties? Were they more patriotic and dedicated, with a deeper hard-core pride in themselves, their outfits, and in devotion and self-sacrifice to flag and country? Were discipline and leadership stronger, and were they bound together by an unfathomable understanding of purpose and unity? Were they better trained than other fighting men to endure the inhuman struggle where every day brought new, inhuman battle? What creates and sparks and sustains such men who will accept nothing less than victory or death?

Even the most resolute Marine Corps hardliners have found it all but impossible through the years to divine and explain why its men stand alone as a special breed of warrior. General Paul X. Kelley, the Commandant in 1983 when hundreds of Marines were dying in Lebanon, tried to define what it meant to be a Marine.

"It's like trying to describe your feeling for your country, your wife, and your children," Kelley told Drew Middleton. "It's there, but words are insufficient." *The New York Times* reporter elaborated: "The Corps is at once a home and a profession. It is set apart from the other fighting services, removed from the people it serves by an almost mystic belief on the part of the Marines that the Corps is unique, that it can do anything." While he wrote of Marines in Lebanon in 1983 and 1984, it was a solid reflection of the Marines on Iwo Jima—and in all other battles fought by the Corps since its creation in 1775.

In 1950, an official manual sought to explain the complex, indefinable inner psyche of Marines. "The Corps," it said, "emphasizes the rugged outlet for men's energies and never permits its members to forget that the example of courage is their most precious heritage." Frank Hough, the historian, felt the answer was almost entirely the result of esprit; the virtual blood oath that one Marine would never let another down in combat; that failure to live up to that code was treason and a betrayal of faith in everything worthwhile. "Observing this mode of thought carried into action," he wrote in 1947, "had led more than one outsider to remark that these men seemed to be fighting less for the United States than for the United States Marine Corps."

Thousands of Marines were on Iwo because they *wanted* to be; not that they would have selected the island as a battleground if they'd had any choice in the matter, but because they wanted to be Marines. And because they were ready to go without question wherever, whenever the Corps' Globe and Anchor battle flags took them. Membership in the *corps d'élite* was to them the highest possible calling as rugged individuals whose first duty was to the Marine Corps... then to God and country.

These were the "old salts," the "old breed" of noncommissioned and commissioned officers—the John Basilones and the Chandler Johnsons—whose home, career, and life were, by choice, the Marine Corps. They were the "old pros," most in their midtwenties or early thirties, who had met and defeated the Japanese in earlier campaigns, some as many as four times, beginning at Guadalcanal. It was a rarity for any of them to have escaped being wounded at least once by the time they landed on Iwo Jima.

Immediately after Pearl Harbor, thousands of eighteen- and nineteen-year-olds had joined the Marine Corps to fight the Japanese, and to be part of the best, until the war was won. Now they were in their early twenties, motivated by élan and with battles behind them, and fighting on Iwo Jima. It was a spirit being voiced by other young men in 1983. Peter S. Paine III, a junior in Princeton University's Platoon Leader Course, told Middleton: "I'm in the Marines, quite simply, because they're the best. When the Marines have a job to do, they don't compromise."

Many of the senior noncoms on Iwo—the platoon, gunnery, and first sergeants—had joined up in the tag-end days of the Great Depression when jobs were impossible to find. Now they knew no other life than the Marine Corps, and were devoted to it; to the sense of belonging it gave, to its traditions and comradeship.

Almost without exception, battalion and regimental commanders on Iwo were career officers: majors, lieutenant colonels, and colonels whose thick service records showed they'd graduated from the Naval Academy at Annapolis, or such private schools as historic Virginia Military Institute that, for more than a century, had turned out an imposing number of commanders for all armed forces of the United States.

Others were graduates of colleges and universities across the country, and had earned commissions from the Marine Corps' "trade school" at Quantico, Virginia. Some were "mustangs" who had enlisted fresh out of high school, and had advanced, promotion by promotion, through the ranks with years of exemplary service before becoming officers. Many had been corporals and sergeants in the Philippines and China, and had fought the "bandits" in Latin America's minor upheavals in the 1920s and '30s. All three division generals—Erskine, Cates, and Rockey—had been second lieutenants in France in World War I, and had been wounded and decorated for valor and leadership.

A seemingly large number of Marines, officers and enlisted, were Southerners, or from small towns in other parts of the country. John Lardner once said, "if the Marine Corps has a battle cry, it is the rebel yell." But Leathernecks at Iwo, and in the other Pacific battles, were not just a fraternity of Confederate descendants or an assemblage of warriors from hamlets and farms. Men who came from the streets of big cities, and from metropolitan suburbs, in reality probably out-numbered their rural-area counterparts. All were equally dedicated to the values and traditions of the Corps.

There was a broad ethnic mix of second-generation Americans, except for blacks. Like the rest of the armed forces in World War II, the Marine Corps was segregated. In boot camp, blacks had separate platoons and, after recruit training, they were assigned to Pioneer Battalions or Field Depots where they were service and supply troops. A scattered few became cooks and bakers, and some served as mess-men to senior officers.

Despite their second-class status, blacks were vital to victory in many campaigns and were often under fire on the beaches and in the lines. Frank Hough remembered one valiant outfit on bloody Peleliu: "The Negro Marines of the 16th Field Depot," he recalled, "had dis-tinguished themselves throughout the operation as stretcher bearers, working under the heaviest fire and most difficult conditions with courage, cheerfulness, and patience notable in the hardened First Division. About sunset of any afternoon, small knots of them could be seen trudging forward from their rear area behind a sergeant or corporal to do their bit in the lines. Volunteers, all of them; by now this outfit had the reputation of being the 'volunteeringest' in the Marine Corps. One officer was embarrassed on one occasion when, calling for volunteers, he saw his entire unit step forward before he had time to explain that this was not a dangerous mission but a mere burial detail. Altogether, the men of the 16th wrote a bright chapter at Peleliu in their race's contribution to the history of the war." The same could be said of black Marines at Iwo Jima.

Iwo Jima's remorseless chamber of horrors claimed its toll of men who broke under the strain. Most of the 1,897 cases of combat fatigue were temporary—individuals who had taken, for the moment, all they could and were pulled off the lines. Some were so seriously in shock that they were evacuated, and some spent the rest of the campaign on noncombatant duties. But most returned to their outfits within days, many to fight valiantly from then on and many to be wounded or killed as the battle roared. Through all the fighting, not one group panicked under fire or deserted its post.

Captain George K. Dike, a twenty-six-year-old farmer from Grafton, North Dakota, whose battalion was the first artillery outfit ashore, found two men cowering in a deep foxhole and shaking with fear— "such an overpowering fear that their legs wouldn't move," Dike said. "I know I'm useless," one of them told the captain. "Shoot me and get it over with!" Both men were evacuated as serious battle-fatigue cases and, after treatment, were assigned to rear areas. But, according to Dike, "neither was shot or court-martialed as far as I know."

Even some men decorated for bravery in previous campaigns broke under the strain of massive enemy bombardment, of withering machine guns, of cascades of exploding hand grenades, of the torture of trying to advance in the man-killing terrain, of seeing comrades blown to pieces. "There is fear in every man," General Erskine said, "and every man has his breaking point." It was the measure of the men of Iwo Jima, the general was certain, "that most beat back their fears, as they did the Japanese; and, in so doing, did not break."

Mrs. Rose Stein, the Yugoslavian mother of Medal of Honor winner Tony Stein, said her son was like this. "Tony always had to do things, hard things. That's why he just had to be in the Marines. He wanted to see if he could do it." Newspapers across the country carried her statement. It was made December 15, 1945, when his body was brought home for final burial nine months after he was killed on Iwo.

General Alexander A. Vandegrift Sr., who had led the First Division on Guadalcanal and now was the Corps' four-star commander, had his version of how Iwo Jima and the other Pacific islands were conquered. The battles were won, he said, "by the individual fighting man operating as a member of a squad, a platoon, a company." He'd found in the two World Wars, and in nasty little campaigns in the Caribbean and Central America, that esprit de corps must be there. But he'd also found that "in the heat of battle, a man cannot stop to think about the larger ideal; he must fight with courage and resourcefulness because his own life and his self-respect, without which few men can live, depend upon association with, and the respect of, his comrades."

At the other end of the military totem pole was Wilson D. Watson. He was a Third Division private from the Ozark mountains of northwest Arkansas, and he had definite ideas about what courage meant and how the Marines won on Iwo Jima.

"Hell, man, we had to forget about being afraid, and do what we had to do, and that was kill the goddamned Japs and win the goddamned battle." His words were spoken, but not reported at the time, to a Marine correspondent who talked to the slight, soft-spoken, drawling BAR man after he had been awarded the Medal of Honor.

5

Wherever Marines fought in the Pacific, black humor was part of the beachhead lifestyle. Iwo Jima was no exception. Fifty yards up the narrow roadway that had been bulldozed in the slopes of Suribachi was a hand-lettered gem:

SURIBACHI HEIGHTS REALTY COMPANY
Ocean View
Cool Breezes
Free Fireworks Nightly!

Another was emblazoned in fire-engine red paint, brought ashore by the sign's author, a Fifth Division corporal, whose handiwork was over the entrance of a burned-out cave:

ICHIMOTO'S INN
Under New Management
Soon Available to Personnel
Of the U. S. Army (We Hope)

A Fourth Division man, whose temporary living space was near Charlie-Dog ridge, used a cardboard ration box and a heavy crayon to post his statement of ownership in crude letters:

NOTICE!!!
This Foxhole is Privately Owned
And Was Not Constructed With The
Help of the Federal Housing Administration
Not built for Comfort but for Speed.

Atop a thirty-foot cliff just north of Motoyama Number One, half-a-dozen Marine correspondents and photographers were temporary occupants of a blockhouse that had been an enemy communications center. After a day at the front, they would return to write copy and captions, and to sleep. Each morning, when they went back into the lines, a sign was hung above the fortification's entrance to ward off squatters. Its six-inch letters said: DANGER! MINED AND BOOBY-TRAPPED! The ruse worked just two days.

"We had all the comforts of home," said Sergeant Harold A. Breard, of Monroe, Louisiana, one of the lucky occupants, "but it didn't last long." On the third day, conscientious demolitions men took the warning at face value and blew the place to smithereens. "Easy come, easy go," was Breard's reaction. "For the rest of the time on Iwo, we lived in foxholes."

Behind the lines up front, where troops were in reserve, they talked among themselves in the brief twilight after digging positions for the night. Dick Dashiell wrote of what they said before darkness came.

"My wife's birthday comes this month," one said. "She's eighteen."

A platoon sergeant spoke. "If there's any justice, it won't rain tonight so those Nips can't get fresh water."

A husky man walked up to his lieutenant and said: "Here's a letter they found in Mike's pocket right after he died."

A tired-looking Marine approached. Someone shouted, "My God! There's Smitty! Hey, Smitty, I heard you was dead. Damn you! I was feeling sorry for you!"

A man who had been on outpost duty said, "You shoulda heard those Nips yelling last night. When we sealed up that cave, they hollered and squealed all night."

A plaintive voice: "Say, Sarge, you think we can secure this rock in a few more days? Boy, the Army's welcome to this place. I'd go nuts if I had to stay here long."

A corporal grinned. "Had some coffee today. Feel like a million now."

Sitting near a cluster of men, a lieutenant spoke, almost to himself: "All the officers I came overseas with are gone now—all killed or wounded."

One of the men answered quietly. "I know how you feel. Trinkler and I are the only ones left out of our tent."

Another Marine said: "Mind if I hole in with you fellows tonight? My buddy hasn't come back."

Another voice: "Any you guys get any souvenirs? Me, I'm through souvenir hunting. The other day I reach out for a Jap rifle and a sonuvabitch sniper almost takes my hand off!"

A languid voice breaks in. "Anybody know of a good abandoned pillbox? I'm tired of foxhole life."

"Comb that hair, boy! Comb that hair! There's nothing that will help win the war like combing your hair." A few men smiled.

"When the hell is Sunday? I lost track. Meant to go to church, too."

"Where's the guy who said we'd take this island in five days? I hope he's on the front lines right now."

"Oh, oh! Looks like that Jap mortar hit some guys over yonder."

Then, sudden quiet. A mortar shell whipped overhead. And an exclamation: "Look at this, Charlie! Wonder when that bullet landed here? I'm moving. You guys can stay here and get picked off by a sniper if you want to. Me, I gotta get back to the CP."

"Those rats stomped around our pillbox last night. They musta been wearing horseshoes."

Silence; then: "There are only two kinds of Marines on this island—the lucky and the unlucky. Let's hit the sack. It's seven o'clock."

Marines welcomed twilight. And while it meant that they faced another night of harassment fire, and possibly infiltrators, they were glad they'd lived through another day. As darkness came, artillery and mortars fell with less frequency. Small arms fire petered out. The stillness was eerie: something akin to Times Square without traffic, to a steel mill without roaring blast furnaces. The lines would erupt again in sectors when Marine outposts spotted enemy attempts at infiltration, or when the Japanese unloaded mortars and artillery; otherwise the lull would continue until total darkness came. "It's like a change in shifts at the Chrysler plant back in Highland Park," a black Marine from the Fourth Pioneer Battalion said, "but I sure wish I was back workin' on the assembly line in Detroit instead of bein' here."

After D-Day plus five, sunset brought new sights and sounds to the island. One must have triggered a shock wave of fear among the Japanese that the Americans had begun using poison gas. What they saw, and what the Marines had been told to look for, were two carrier-based torpedo bombers laying down clouds of DDT from shoreline to shoreline across the front.

Rigged with five-hundred-gallon tanks of the chemical, they made low-level sweeps like crop-duster planes over an Alabama cotton field to ward off the chance of an epidemic caused by black swarms of giant flies swollen from feasting on bloated, unburied Japanese and parts of bodies that littered no man's land.

At battalion CPs just behind the front, the sounds of American dance music became a sundown ritual that must have convinced the Japanese the Marines were, indeed, crazy.

With battle transmission at a low ebb, radio receivers on communications jeeps were tuned to powerful signals from Guam and Pearl Harbor, some to Tokyo Rose's records and latest reports of the Japanese version of what was happening on Iwo and elsewhere in the Pacific. The music of Glenn Miller, Benny Goodman, Tommy and Jimmy Dorsey, the Andrews Sisters, the Ink Spots—all the tunes on the Lucky Strike Hit Parade—wafted loud and clear among the ravines and cliffs.

Nearly four decades later Gene Jones would remember it all even after he had been wounded three times as a civilian correspondent making documentary films of Marines fighting in Korea and Vietnam and had become a highly successful writer, director, and producer of feature motion pictures.

"I'll never forget how sweet and beautiful that music was," he said, "how marvelous and comforting. Out across the shattered landscape, across the bodies of dead Marines, we heard swing music, dance music; languorous and poignant. We had won so little ground and lost so many men and were so tired, but we all listened to the music. It meant so much to hear these tender sounds on that awful island amid the killing."

Bullet-pocked sign in Japanese and English, posted in 1937, was found by Marines on D-Day. (*Obbie Newcomb*)

While fighting still rages in the northern part of the island, Marines and Seabees ready Motoyama Number One for aircraft. (*Louis R. Lowery*)

Not quite the comforts of home, but Third Division Marine enjoys a helmet bath nonetheless. (*Joseph Heilberger*)

First B-29 bomber to land on Iwo, the *Dinah Might*, was crippled on a raid over Japan. Marine watches from Japanese anti-aircraft gun position at northern end of Motoyama Number One. (*Mark Kaufman*)

A steaming flow of sulphur water doubles as a stove for Marines heating C-rations. (*Joseph Heiberger*)

Ensign Gwendelin Jensen of Oakland, California, was one of the Navy nurses who flew aboard air evacuation flights to carry wounded from Iwo to rear area hospitals. (*U.S. Marine Corps*)

Weapons of dead Marines were repaired and reissued as battle roared into its third week. (*Arthur J. Kiely, Jr.*)

D-plus ten: Beachhead, a junkyard of devastation on D-Day, is crammed with men and equipment as the battle reaches a crescendo in the northern highlands. (*Louis Lowery*)

Communications jeep is link between Fifth Corps headquarters and the division command posts near the front. (*Robert Wilton*)

Marine artillery spotter pilots study chessboard while awaiting their next mission. (*Bill D. Ross*)

PART EIGHT

Halfway
to
Victory

1

D-Day plus six was the first Sunday on Iwo for the Americans, and the end of the first week. Offshore, mess compartments of warships and transports were jammed as men answered church call and prayed for a swift and victorious end to the fighting.

On Iwo itself, there still wasn't time, and too little space not under almost constant enemy fire, to hold many rituals. Marines knew divine intercession would not end the bloody conflict; it must run its own course.

But where conditions permitted—in shell holes along the front and in revetments and craters behind the lines—chaplains held interfaith services as small groups of men, their weapons at the ready, knelt to seek surcease from the killing, and whatever inspiration they could find. Services were purposely brief: a cluster of Marines in one place for more than a few minutes invariably drew heavy enemy mortar and artillery fire.

Japanese forces still held more than half of Iwo, and resistance was as fierce as ever. But as the invasion roared into its second week, the battle's ultimate outcome was no longer in doubt. Marines now outnumbered Kuribayashi's troops, and any hope the enemy had of driving the Americans into the sea had disappeared. But when the fighting would end, and what the final cost in dead and wounded would be, remained dark questions. Every yard of ground was in easy range of enemy cannon, heavy mortars, and rockets. But despite harassing bombardment and the ferocity of front-line fighting, Iwo Jima was taking on the look of an American forward base—albeit an embattled one.

Beaches no longer were chaotic junk yards. Although the two-and-a-half miles of shoreline still were littered for hundreds of yards at a stretch, the mess had been sufficiently cleared so that manpower, supplies, and equipment could land in a steady stream.

Marine and Seabee crane operators and demolitions teams worked night and day to hoist or blast grotesque hulks of demolished landing craft and mired trucks, tanks, and artillery from the deep sand and constant surf. Thousands of men, working as snaking human conveyor belts, manhandled thousands of tons of necessities to supply dumps—the "beans, bullets, and bandages" vital to feed the gulping appetite of battle.

Bulldozers clanked and churned around the clock as they carved more roads inland from the beaches for what was rapidly becoming a busy network connecting all of Iwo in American hands. Others scraped the shell-pocked runways of Motoyama Number One to get the airstrip ready for land-based Marine artillery spotter planes, for Army Mustang fighters, for Navy transports soon to airlift casualties to the Marianas, and for disabled B-29 Superforts frantically seeking a place to land. Operators dove for cover when frequent artillery and mortar fire targeted them—land mines and unexploded shells also were constant dangers—but when fire lifted, they were back at work.

Hundreds of telephone wires, strung on poles cut from faraway forests in Oregon, hummed with battle communications from battalion to regimental command posts that were connected with division CPs, and these with Fifth Corps headquarters. Beachhead hospitals functioned with amazing efficiency, and now the wounded could be evacuated without agonizing waits. A Fleet Post Office aboard an attack transport sent eleven sacks of mail to Yellow Beach—letters from Hawaii for Marines whose families didn't know, but fearfully suspected, that their men were in the fight for Iwo.

Piece by piece, everything was falling into place to mount the climactic big push to take the island. General Erskine was now ashore with nine thousand more troops. Colonel Howard M. Kenyon's 9th Regiment of crack, well-trained infantry, Colonel Raymond F. Crist's 12th Regiment with its cannoneers and howitzers, and Major Holly M. Evans's Third Tank Battalion added armor to the massive firepower already in the battle.

But it would take two more weeks of close-in butchery before the back of enemy resistance was broken; two terrible weeks that would claim twelve thousand Marine casualties—a man wounded or killed every ninety seconds. And then, for another two weeks, the battle, like a stubborn forest fire, would rage in isolated spots as General Kuribayashi and his troops fought on in suicidal determination.

Assault outfits took on replacements to prop up depleted ranks with any manpower available. A tragic number of these were frightened, undertrained very young men—almost boys—who often became casualties within minutes after their first exposure to combat. A battle neophyte was blessed with fabulous good fortune if he escaped being wounded or killed.

Richard Newcomb described what happened to eighteen-year-old Private John Lane of Brooklyn, New York, who was sent into the lines as a raw replacement in the 25th Regiment. "The sergeant's instructions for battle were a brief statement of military wisdom," Newcomb wrote. "He said: 'This here is G Company. We're going to move out this morning. This won't be no straight line, so when you see a Jap, shoot him! You know what a Jap looks like. Don't shoot any Marines!' The sergeant was gone. What more could a guy need to know?"

Lane was lucky beyond belief. The line didn't move, and he crouched alone in a foxhole all day, waiting and clutching his rifle. He never saw a live Japanese and never fired a shot. That night he was assigned as a battalion runner and most of his missions from then on were to carry messages to the rear.

Things were far different for Craig Leman. He was older—twenty-four. He was far better-trained; he'd graduated as a second lieutenant from Platoon Leaders School at Quantico, and had a nodding acquaintance with what combat was all about. But Leman, a premed student from the University of Chicago, was a replacement too, and shavetail officers had an extremely short life expectancy. After several days on the beach helping to unload landing craft, he went into the lines for the first time. "I joined H Company, 26th Marines, replacing a platoon leader who had been killed," he wrote a friend. "The platoon was down to twenty-two men then; when I left with a head wound five days later, we were down to about a dozen."

Forty years later, Leman still remembered: "I lost most of my best friends on that island; most of us didn't really expect to live through it. My father saw a picture in a newspaper of a dead Marine on the beach and he thought it looked like me; he kept it from my mother for two weeks before he learned I was wounded and not dead." After V-J Day, he continued medical studies at Harvard and later became what he called a "working sawbones"—in reality, a distinguished surgeon—in Corvallis, Oregon.

General Schmidt revamped the plan of attack for the D-Day plus six assault. The revised scheme was classically simple in concept, but making it work was another matter. Iwo's volcanic terrain, General Kuribayashi's devilish fortifications, and his do-or-die defenders made sure of that.

Since being thrown into the blood bath to seize Motoyama Number Two, the 21st Regiment had fought as part of the Fourth Division. But with the decision to commit more of General Erskine's troops, the Third Division lost its "floating reserve" status, although its battle-tested, combat-ready 3rd Regiment was still aboard transports twenty miles at sea.

Under the hard-driving Big E, the division would now fight under its own colors and take over from the other divisions the assault up the center of the island. It would hammer Kuribayashi's main defense belt centered around the second airstrip and crush it, then push through the flat Motoyama Plateau to the north and drive the enemy from unfinished Motoyama Number Three, finally breaking through to Iwo's northern shoreline.

On its right, the Fourth would move northward and, at the same time, pivot east into the rugged cliffs along the east coast—a sector of convoluted hills and defiles stripped naked of cover by bombardment and infested with hundreds of heavily armed camouflaged emplacements. The Fifth Division, on the left flank, would strike straight ahead on the western front in a two-square-mile area that was a natural deathtrap for tanks and infantry, a zone of winding ridges and deep canyons where Kuribayashi had laid his most insidious system of connecting caves and would ultimately make his last stand.

Back home, Iwo Jima was front-page news as Americans anguished over the casualties and wondered when the slaughter would end. But the struggle was rapidly becoming "sidebar" copy—a story of diminishing impact and importance as Allied forces drove deeper into Germany and the day of victory in Europe neared. Fewer than twenty civilian reporters and photographers remained on the scene: representatives of the press services, radio networks, the weekly news magazines, and a few mass-circulation dailies. Most of the restless brigade of newsmen on hand on D-Day had left for Guam, along with Secretary Forrestal and Admiral Spruance, to join the gathering armada for the invasion of Okinawa.

Some of Iwo's worst fighting would receive little more than fleeting mention in news stories as the battle ground on toward its finish. It was left to Marine combat correspondents to write most eyewitness reports of what happened, and many of these would be delayed in military channels before publication in the States.

Now and then, stories of some especially spectacular or heroic action would be written by civilian reporters and sent stateside by high-speed radioteletypes at their disposal; now and then came a live broadcast from the *Eldorado*. But in the main, scant attention was given to the unfolding battle in an Armageddon of strange and faraway names—Hills Peter and Oboe, Turkey Knob, The Amphitheater, Hill 382, Motoyama Village, Nishi Ridge, Kita, Cushman's Pocket, and the countless other objectives without name that took a merciless toll of Marines during the next month.

After the first week, more and more of the spot news about the campaign was written from Admiral Nimitz's daily communiqué. Even as the battle roared toward its climax, it was becoming a "meanwhile" story in roundups of what was happening in the "other war." After reporting latest developments in General Eisenhower's "Crusade in Europe," front-page news generally would read: "Meanwhile, the Marines on Iwo Jima..."

Censorship was part of the reason for not reporting the battle in daily detail. The Monks of Makalapa wanted to keep secret from the Japanese the extent of the frightful Marine losses and to keep them from the home front as well. Nothing was to be gained, or so the brass felt, by an official yard-by-yard, day-by-day account of what was happening on the island.

General Kuribayashi, and the warlords in Tokyo as well, knew the Americans now were on Iwo Jima to stay—that it was only a matter of time and lives before the island fell. Shortly after midnight of D-Day plus six, Admiral Ichimaru, Kuribayashi's second in command, said as much in a message to Imperial General Headquarters. He asked Emperor Hirohito's forgiveness for not pushing the Marines back into the sea on D-Day, but vowed to fight to the death. "Real battles are to come from now on. Every man of my outfit fully realizes the importance of this battle for the future of the nation and is determined to defend this island at any cost, fulfilling this honorable duty."

Skies were cloudless at dawn as the second week of battle came to life. Beginning at eight o'clock, Japanese positions were blasted for fifty minutes with thousands of tons of shells from the big guns of battleships and cruisers and Marine heavy artillery, followed by sixty carrier planes, unleashing five-hundred-pound bombs and screaming five-inch rockets along the front.

It was the first time Colonel Kenyon's 9th Regiment had witnessed, close up, the mighty show of American firepower as they awaited the signal to move to the attack. He was "Red" Kenyon to every man in the outfit; a tough and stern disciplinarian who knew his way around in combat; an acknowledged character with close-cropped red hair and a luxuriant copper-hued waxed mustache that curved upward at the ends. His five-foot-ten frame carried the look of a fighting Marine, and his men were proud to serve in his outfit. "He can be seven kinds of a bastard when he wants to be," said one hard-bitten gunnery sergeant, "but he's our sonuvabitch and we'll go wherever he says to go."

That morning the objective was Hill Peter, a 360-foot jumble of blasted stubble and rocks bristling with Japanese defenses, the last major obstacle to securing Motoyama Number Two and the formidable terrain around it. H-Hour was 9:30. The attack began on schedule with two battalions in the assault: the First and Second, commanded by Carey A. Randall and Robert E. Cushman, both lieutenant colonels and decorated veterans of the campaigns on Bougainville and Guam.

Within minutes the push sputtered and all but collapsed; the 9th Marines rapidly learned that everything they'd heard about the ferocity and accuracy of enemy fire was all too true—and most of it was coming from the caves and summit of Hill Peter. Six of Holly Evans's Shermans moved onto the edge of the airstrip in a desperate attempt to silence enough of the Japanese fury to get the stalled attack moving again.

Even before they were in a position to fire, armor-piercing shells crashed into the three leading tanks. "Angel" and "Agony" took direct salvos and were enveloped in flame and smoke. Crewmen frantically opened hatches and scrambled out to escape the inferno. "Ateball" was damaged, but its 75-millimeter cannon and machine guns could still fire; they laid down nonstop cover as the Marines darted for any protection they could find.

Twenty-two-year-old William R. Adamson plunged to earth alongside Agony's motionless treads and was immediately hit in the leg by a burst of machine gun fire. The corporal saw blood spurting from the wound but was amazed that he felt so little pain. He dragged himself ten yards to the front of Ateball, where he made a tourniquet from his bloody pants leg. For several minutes he sat there in a crouch, wondering what to do next.

He was certain he'd never again see his folks in San Jose, California, but he'd decided to die fighting. "What the hell else can I do?" he thought, muttering to himself at the instant he spotted the flash of the antitank gun that had knocked out the Shermans and was still firing.

Adamson half crawled, half hobbled a few steps forward and, waving wildly and yelling as loud as he could, the gutsy Marine pointed toward the weapon, hoping Ateball's crew would see his signal. They did. The tank's cannon silenced the position with a single round. Now crouched in a shell hole, the corporal saw four machine gun pits and again alerted Ateball, whose hatch was open for a better view of the action. An arcing series of machine gun bursts wiped out the enemy positions and their twelve gunners.

But the furious firefight wasn't over. A lone Japanese, clutching a satchel of demolitions, broke for the tank and was cut down in the clatter of fire. As he slumped screaming to the ground, thirty enemy troops charged the Sherman from a ravine thirty yards away, firing bayoneted rifles as they came. The tank's cannon and machine guns slaughtered them in their tracks.

Suddenly there was a lull, but only for seconds. Adamson crawled under Ateball and was pulled through its bottom escape hatch. Within minutes, a tank retriever pulled the battered monster to cover. Other tanks took the point and clanked out across the airstrip two hundred yards ahead of the infantry. Adamson survived and was awarded the Navy Cross. He had been wrong about not seeing home again, and he hadn't died fighting. "But it was a goddamned close call," he said.

In all, twenty-six tanks and two thousand Marines were caught up in the melee, and except for the suicide charge by the Japanese who tried to reach Ateball, they hadn't seen more than a dozen enemy troops since the jump-off. Antitank weapons, machine guns and rifles firing from hidden emplacements, and heavy mortars and artillery from the back of Hill Peter had all but stopped the attack.

At 2:30 P.M., after five hours of brutal combat, the gain in the center was less than one hundred yards. One platoon managed to punch its way to the base of the hill but was forced back. Its losses were so heavy, and ammunition so short, that it couldn't hold—fourteen men remained of the forty who had started the push.

At 3:30, there was no forward movement anywhere and the situation had passed from grim to desperate. A dangerous gap opened up in the lines between the battalions, and a frantic attempt to close the breach with reinforcements only added to the deadly confusion. It was nearly dark before the lines were consolidated when Lieutenant Colonel Harold C. Boehm's Third Battalion was able to come to the aid of Bob Cushman's shot-to-pieces outfit and link up with Carey Randall's men.

Nearly four hundred Marines had fallen during the 9th Regiment's first day on Iwo, and Hill Peter's defenders still wracked the front with murderous fire. Nine of Holly Evans's twenty-six tanks were knocked out, and seventeen crewmen had been killed or wounded in the daylong struggle.

On the Fourth Division front, the battle raged in fury to match, possible exceed, that which seared "Red" Kenyon's men. General Cates, dapper even in combat and chain-smoking Chesterfield cigarettes in an ebony holder, had shaved before dawn. During the night, his tarpaulin-covered shell-hole command post had been shaken several times by heavy mortar blasts. Now the University of Tennessee law graduate, who never hung out his shingle but joined the Marines instead, was on a raspy field phone to Walt Wensinger, whose 23rd Regiment would spearhead the day's attack. "See if you can find a weak spot in the bastard's front," Cates told his commander, "and keep slugging the sonuvabitch until you do!" Walt Jordan had the same orders for his 24th Marines, but in slightly different words.

What their four assault battalions, some 3,800 troops, faced was an unknown number of Japanese, strongly entrenched in a maze of terrain unbelievable even for Iwo Jima—a complex of fortifications that Marines quickly dubbed, and with supreme cause, "the Meat Grinder." It was a defensive masterpiece of concealment and construction, and it would be seven terrible days before it was silenced— a week before it stopped chewing up Marines who daily slammed into a quartet of natural strongpoints made almost impregnable by the Japanese, who had dug connecting tunnels and reinforced every key position with concrete and steel.

Components of the defense network were Hill 382; the rubble of what once was Minami Village; a bowl-shaped and boulder-strewn area called "the Amphitheater"; and a craggy escarpment the Marines would remember as "Turkey Knob." Individually, each was formidable. Collectively, they were a killing ground.

Hill 382 stood 250 yards northeast of where the Third Division still fought to drive the last Japanese from Motoyama Number Two. Across the crest of 382 was the crumpled skeleton of a Japanese radar tower. Twisted steel girders lay among the rubble of a cinder-block building, below which was a two-story concrete blockhouse bristling with artillery and antitank weapons. The stronghold was ringed by camouflaged machine gun pits, concealed spider traps with steel covers to protect lurking snipers. Each position covered the other with lanes of crossfire.

An elaborate tunnel system honeycombed the hill—nearly a thousand yards of caves for ammunition supply and for troops to reinforce threatened positions or escape when one was overrun. Light and medium tanks were dug in turret deep among the labyrinth of chasms and ridges in the immediate area, and their cannon covered every approach to the escarpment.

Turkey Knob was an ugly outcropping of volcanic rock shaped like a lopsided football. It was six hundred yards south of Hill 382 and Iwo's second highest elevation—only Suribachi was higher.

At ground level, 382 looked barren and harmless. But its sloping summit was a massive observation post, equipped with high-powered binoculars and primitive electronic artillery-detection gear that covered every yard of the southern end of the island. Deep within the bowels of the hill was a thirty-by-forty-foot communications center with concrete walls four feet thick and a steel-reinforced roof able to withstand heavy naval bombardment and direct hits from five-hundred-pound bombs without serious damage.

Two hundred yards west of Turkey Knob the ground fell sharply away to form a tiered natural bowl resembling a stadium without seats—the Amphitheater. On its three terraces the Japanese had built concrete blockhouses along the south side of the depression. These were linked by seven hundred yards of tunnels with walls lined with communications and electric light cables. Antitank guns and machine guns covered all approaches to the area from the south.

Minami had been one of Iwo's five villages. Now it was a rubble of debris, but in the devastation of its half-dozen concrete buildings was a concentration of machine gun positions, mortar pits, and sniper-infested spider traps. The landscape was a jumble of torn scrub trees, of sharp rocks, and of dug-in Japanese waiting for Marines to attack.

Hill 382, with its commanding elevation and heavy fortifications, was the keystone of the Meat Grinder's awesome defense system. Before there was any hope of silencing the other objectives, 382 had to be seized. And as long as it was in Japanese hands, it also hampered the Third Division's push up the center of the island.

So shortly after eight o'clock on D-Day plus six, the Marines went to work on the hill. The attack was preceded by the customary naval bombardment and air strikes. When Major James L. Scales' outfit, the Third Battalion of the 23rd Marines, jumped off, it was immediately hit with the customary violent reaction; the Japanese again had waited for the shelling and bombing to lift before opening up.

Six tanks clanked forward in a futile attempt to spearhead the assault. Four were knocked out within minutes: two struck land mines and two took direct hits from antitank guns. The two survivors made little headway; they simply roared and churned as treads dug deep tracks in the volcanic ash. Machine guns, rifle fire, hand grenades, and mortars ripped into the infantry. Bringing up flamethrowers and demolitions men was impossible, but scattered squads and individual Marines moved ahead.

A platoon from the company commanded by Captain Stanley G. McDaniel, of Duncan, Oklahoma, managed to claw its way to the summit, but was immediately cut off by a savage counterattack. Fire from bypassed positions was merciless, and enemy artillery and mortars made it impossible for the rest of the company to get through.

It took two hours of sometimes screaming hand-to-hand combat before the isolated platoon could pull back under a smoke screen. The situation was so desperate that ten wounded had to be left on the hill until after dark, when they were rescued by volunteer stretcher teams. One Marine, cut off from the rest of the company, lay throughout the night and part of the next day suffering from a broken leg and sharing a shell hole with a dead buddy. Japanese swarmed around the outpost all night, but somehow he wasn't discovered—or the enemy thought him dead—and he was rescued shortly after 10 A.M., when Marines regained the ground.

By midafternoon, it was obvious that the attack was going no

place until something was done to lessen the resistance—something
Marine infantry and tanks so far hadn't been able to do. Orders went
out at four o'clock to prepare for heavy shelling and air strikes against
the hill.

Howitzers unleashed the first of thirty minutes of nonstop bombardment at 4:30 P.M., a rolling barrage that fell two hundreds yards
into no man's land and lifted a hundred yards deeper into enemy-held
ground every five minutes. Then for fifteen minutes Marine Corsairs
and Navy Hellcats crisscrossed the front in pulverizing low-level
bombing and rocket attacks. The blistering combination of firepower
did what it was supposed to do; it put a damper on the torrent of
Japanese artillery and mortar fire, and drove enemy machine gunners
from their pillboxes to the safety of the hill's deep caves. It was nearly
sunset, too late to mount a fresh attack before nightfall, but now the
Marines could collect their wounded and set up a solid defense perimeter for the night.

Nearly five hundred men were lost during the first day in the
Meat Grinder, a sickening cost to pay for a gain of a hundred yards—
and Hill 382 was still firmly in Japanese hands. Heavy firefights developed several times during the night as the enemy tried to infiltrate
Marine positions.

Thirty Japanese marauders, many of them wielding sabers, hit
Captain Donald S. Callaham's company shortly before midnight. "Some
of them spoke English," he said the next morning. "They jumped into
empty foxholes around us and yelled like Marines, but their English
was pretty phony and we spotted them." Some twenty enemy bodies
surrounded the positions the next morning. There were no Marine
casualties from the ill-advised stab at infiltration, but Callaham's outfit
had lost sixty men in the day's futile push to take the hill.

"Find a weak spot in the bastard's front," General Cates had
ordered. There were no weak spots. "And keep slugging the sonuvabitch until you do!" Slugging was all the Marines *could* do.

Jim Lucas, the Marine correspondent whose eyewitness report
of the blood bath of Tarawa had been the first to reach the States,
had been under fire on the front all day. Now a breveted and decorated
first lieutenant for his work at Tarawa, he wrote: "It was bad there,
but it was all over in seventy-two hours. This bastardly battle just goes
on and on from one ridge to another. When will it end? And will
anybody be alive when it does?"

*

"Harry the Horse" Liversedge's 28th Regiment finished the mop-up around Suribachi, left a security platoon to guard the observation post on the summit, which now could be reached by a narrow road, and moved north to join the battle of the Fifth Division front.

There was no Marine attack along the 1,200-yard western sector on D-Day plus six. Exhausted troops rested, refitted, and took on replacements—and stayed on the alert for Japanese infiltrators or a counterattack. In other campaigns the day probably would be remembered as one of heavy action—but not on Iwo. Enemy shells fell regularly among Marine positions and claimed 163 casualties. And shortly after 3:30 P.M., part of the front erupted in fifteen minutes of heavy Marine artillery bombardment when Japanese were spotted trying to trundle 75-millimeter cannon and antitank guns to new positions.

It was a foolish maneuver, and the only time the enemy attempted it in daylight during the battle. More than a hundred Japanese were wiped out in the shelling, and Kuribayashi lost nine sorely needed artillery pieces, several trucks, and a cache of his dwindling supply of ammunition.

About an hour after dark, General Erskine sent a runner for Colonel Kenyon. "Red, we've got to do something different to break through," he said. "Something we haven't tried anywhere against the Nips." The general read the colonel's quizzical look and anticipated his unasked question. "You think your men could pull off a night attack?" he asked. Kenyon said they'd do their damndest, but they were dead tired and the battalions riddled with casualties. Erskine studied the sector map, thought about some of the night attacks he'd led against German lines in France in World War I, and decided to shelve the scheme—for the time being.

Aboard *Eldorado*, Kelly Turner went over the entire day's radioteletype transmissions from Harry Schmidt's headquarters on the beachhead, and scanned copies made by harried yeomen of all other traffic, be it an urgent dispatch from Admiral Nimitz on Guam or a simple request for a late weather forecast. It was an inviolable order of the admiral that he see every message received or sent by his flagship, sometimes as many as hundreds a day. It was one of his ways, "Howlin' Mad" Smith suspected, "of keeping his finger in the Marine pie, another case of an admiral wanting to be a general, whether or not it was any of his damned business."

Aboard *Auburn*, General Smith had little to do but play a nightly game of cribbage with Admiral Hill; conduct of the battle was in the hands of others, and the cantankerous old warrior knew it. He fumed over Nimitz's explicit order to go ashore "for inspection purposes only," and lamented to a newsman who had been with him at Tarawa: "I guess they brought me along in case something happens to Harry Schmidt."

Marines on the lines kept a sharp lookout for infiltrators, and still expected a banzai as they took turns at trying to sleep under the nightly display of pyrotechnics and between barrages of harassing fire from mortars and artillery. Behind the lines, down on the beaches and around Motoyama Number One, the inexorable build-up of American military might continued around the clock. The first signs of creature comfort began to appear as Marine cooks and bakers found propane stoves and pots and pans in regimental supply dumps, set them up, and went to work.

Corporal Wilbur L. Houston, of Taylorville, Illinois, was a cook who had his problems. He spent the night brewing coffee—"Joe" to the Marines—to be carried to the front by jeeps in twenty-gallon Thermos containers. He'd planned to send along donuts and pastries, but mortars hit a nearby ammunition dump and his batter became a casualty of the explosions. "Those bastard Japs'll do anything to make things rough for a guy," he lamented.

2

Dawn of D-Day plus seven broke under cloudless skies. It gave every sign of being warm by Iwo's standards, but the Marines still found it chilly. Hill Peter again was the objective of the 9th Regiment as it jumped off following now-routine naval bombardment, artillery fire, and air strikes against Japanese positions along and behind the front.

Holly Evans's tanks were at the spearhead of the two-battalion assault. With a flamethrower at the point, its blazing tongue imme-diately lit a line of pillboxes and bunkers in front of the hill. Six more Shermans, their cannon spewing fire as fast as sweating crewman loaded more shells into breeches, blasted everything that looked like an enemy bunker. Thirty Marine artillery pieces fired timed barrages that screamed into no man's land only two hundred yards in front of the push.

Infantrymen scampered from hole to hole, rock to rock, crevice to crevice in the face of savage eruptions of mortars and a bedlam of grenades and small arms fire. It was another day of gains measured in feet, not yards.

"All day long, the 9th Marines battled to gain the high ground that blocked its way, but by nightfall there had been no significant gains," was the way the regimental daybook summed up the action. That night, Erskine and Kenyon met again in the general's blackout tent. Erskine had decided to go ahead with the night attack, and told the colonel to start getting his men ready.

After a day of rest, and with new weapons to replace burned-out rifles and machine guns, the Fifth Division jumped off with fresh determination. A feeling of "let's get it over with and get the hell off this goddamned rock" gave urgency to the attack. But the surge of resolution was quickly snuffed out by reality as Chet Graham's 26th Regiment moved into the deep chasms and craggy hills of Iwo's western front.

Major Amedeo Rea's Second Battalion was at the point and took the brunt of the enemy reaction—a murderous cascade of artillery and mortars, and nonstop streams of machine gun and small arms fire. By 10:30 A.M., it had gained fifty yards and lost thirty-four men. Three tanks moved up to help out, but they were unable to maneuver, and by noon, when a chilly rain put a final damper on the bogged-down attack, the battalion had clawed ahead another fifty yards—and taken another twenty-three casualties.

A recurring phenomenon of Iwo was that, many times, a series of mini-battles was raging simultaneously, but cut off from one another by a hill or ravine. Often, while one outfit was fighting for its life in one area, another unit a short distance away on the other side of a ridge was having a relatively easy time.

This was the case with the Second Battalion of the 27th Marines. Major John Antonelli's troops were some two hundred yards to the left of Rea's men; the terrain was less rugged and provided scant cover for the enemy. Instead of taking heavy losses from hidden and well-fortified positions, Antonelli's force met light opposition from Japanese they could see—about a hundred riflemen in shallow open trenches and foxholes. The Marines made quick work of them and scrambled ahead four hundred yards in less than forty-five minutes.

Soon after four o'clock, with sheets of rain turning Iwo's ashy soil into a quagmire of mushy goo, the Fifth Division's attack sloshed to a halt and the men established their line for the night.

Hill 382 still was the defiant obstacle to the Fourth Division advance, but General Cates was determined to have it by nightfall. Its defenders were just as determined to hold out as long as they could and to kill Marines until the last man fell.

Jim Scales' Third Battalion of the 23rd Regiment was the first to move out, this time with Lieutenant Colonel Louis B. Blissard's First Battalion. It was immediately obvious that the Meat Grinder had lost none of its ferocity. Both 382 and Turkey Knob came violently alive with the first sign of the Marine attack. The torrent of fire ambushed the First Battalion's Charlie Company. Within thirty minutes, seventeen men were killed and twenty-six others wounded. Smoke grenades covered stretcher teams as they carried casualties to the rear and the rest of the men scurried forward. Miraculously, the push carried to the base of Hill 382.

One of the reasons was a nineteen-year-old rifleman from Rochester, New York. Private First Class Douglas T. Jacobson had lied about his age to enlist, but he already had been part of the bloody conquest of Saipan, and now was putting his combat know-how to work on Iwo. When a bazooka man was cut down by machine guns, he snatched up the fallen man's weapon and a satchel of explosives. For the next thirty minutes he was a one-man machine of destruction.

Grunting under the burden of the bazooka and the load of demolitions, his ragged dungarees drenched with the sweat of exertion and anxiety, Jacobson sprinted in a running and weaving crouch to the embrasure of a pillbox spouting fire from a clattering machine gun. It was knocked out in a loud explosion, and he could hear the screams of its burning occupants as he vaulted over a boulder in front of another bullet-spitting firepit. In a single blast from the bazooka it went silent.

A concrete blockhouse was next; then another and another and another until there was no more ammunition, and Jacobson was forced to halt his rampage. The real miracle of it all was that to use a bazooka usually required two men; somehow Jacobson had done it single-handedly. Marines later counted sixteen Japanese positions destroyed and seventy-five men dead in the young warrior's charge.

Like most displays of heroism on Iwo, Jacobson's was witnessed by only a few men in his platoon; most of the company was fighting to hang on to its tenuous foothold on the obstreperous hill, and too occupied trying to survive to watch. But his onslaught opened a gap in 382's defenses, and in the acrid smoke and pelting rain, Item Company clawed up the southwestern slopes to the summit, only to be pushed off by entrenched enemy troops late in the afternoon.

"We hit Hill 382 the hard way; by sending men in a frontal assault against the Japanese," Dave Dempsey wrote. "Our tanks couldn't operate on the rocky hillside. It was impossible to bring up flame-throwers and demolitions experts. Our men had to fight their way through terrain flanked by enemy guns. Bazookas proved to be the invaluable weapon, firing pointblank into enemy positions. But after four-and-a-half hours, Item Company had to pull off the most expensive hill on this island."

At 4:30 P.M., General Cates called a halt for the day; further assault was senseless, and it was after nine o'clock before the line was consolidated in the downpour. The Fourth Division had dented, but certainly not broken, General Kuribayashi's ring of steel around the Meat Grinder. The Marines had gained about two hundred yards at a tragic cost: 512 fallen Marines, of whom 119 would be buried in the division's burgeoning cemetery. And Doug Jacobson had survived the most hectic day of his young life to earn the Medal of Honor.

That night, in the slanting downpour made a ghastly white by parachute flares, Marines heard the muffled movement of Japanese troops reinforcing Turkey Knob and the reverse slope of Hill 382; they would be ready and waiting for the morning attack. Replacement Marines moving into the lines, and others bringing bandoleers and machine gun belts to replenish exhausted supplies, had a more open and dangerous route to travel to get to the front; the only way was across the same area of the day's fighting, and it was raked throughout the night with machine guns and mortars.

Where did the invasion stand after eight days of battle? "In spite of the strength of our established beachhead, the enemy still holds three-fifths of the island," Lieutenant Colonel Gooderham L. McCormick wrote that night in the Fourth Division's intelligence summary. "The best area for cover and concealment, with many excellent observation post sites, still remain in his hands. With U. S. forces in control of air and sea, ultimate defeat must be obvious to the enemy. Balancing these factors, it would appear most likely that the enemy will endeavor to conserve his strength and continue his stubborn underground defense to make our securing of this airbase as slow and costly as possible." General Kuribayashi, had he known of Mc-Cormick's analysis, would have agreed.

Back on Motoyama Number One and on the beaches the overpowering build-up was becoming a floodtide of men, machines, and supplies. It was reaching its high mark on D-Day plus seven as thousands of men—replacements and service troops—worked cargo on the still cluttered but now organized beachhead. At the base of Suribachi, amtracs unloaded artillery shells on the western beaches—unused in the assault landings—from the ammunition ship *Columbia Victory*, anchored two miles offshore, and carried some cargoes right to battery firing positions. The cannon were hungry; the previous day they had fired 5,652 rounds of high explosives at enemy targets.

Supply dumps mushroomed wherever space could be found. Bulldozers gouged roads from the western beaches to relieve the glut along the eastern shoreline. One led to a cluster of sandbagged tents—a two-hundred-bed evacuation hospital ready for the first hospital planes to land on Motoyama Number One. Food was getting better for all hands. Seabees and service troops now were fed at least one hot meal a day.

A beached LST converted its tank deck into a cavernous mess hall and served 611 hot meals to Marines the first twenty-four hours it operated. The place smelled of fuel oil, but the men didn't mind. "It was just like Thanksgiving or the Marine Corps' birthday when we always eat well," one of them said. Early birds in the chow line, which snaked up the beach from the vessel's gaping bow, got small servings of mushy ice cream. All signed a mimeographed form with name, rank, serial number, and outfit. "We'll take it out of your pay," grinning messmen told them. Now that the complexion of the battle was changing, the Navy was doing things "by the book" and wanted something for the record to show where the rations went.

While he was on an errand on the beach, a Fourth Division corporal, Franklin C. Robbins, picked up two cases of "ten-in-one" rations, so named because each corrugated box held food for one meal for each of ten men. Back on the front, he explained to buddies how he'd been able to get the chow from the supply dump. Robbins said he'd found paper and pencil and written: "Issue two cases of 10-in-1 rations to the undersigned," and scribbled his name. The MP guard took the chit without question; he, too, wanted something for the record.

Captain Emmet E. Hardin, a forty-two-year-old former postal inspector from New York, could easily have won a popularity contest that day. He opened the Fourth Division's post office in a cistern near Motoyama Number One, handed out ten canvas bags of letters from the Fleet Post Office anchored offshore, and passed the word that the first mail plane, a Navy Catalina flying boat, would take off for Saipan at sundown with letters for the States.

Fifth Division engineers drilled seven wells near the base of Suribachi to supply a distillation system for drinking water. It bubbled to the surface at scalding temperature through the thin seam of Iwo's volcanic crust. Ingenious Marines tapped the pipes before the water entered the equipment and bathed with gusto, feeling clean for the first time since leaving shipboard—despite the ugly yellow water and its evil stench of sulphur.

When word reached the front, Marines didn't begrudge comrades their slice of better living, but they couldn't help being envious. "Lucky bastards!" was the common reaction. "I wish I was one of 'em." Understanding commanders of troops in reserve looked the other way when a few men at a time made their way to the rear to luxuriate in the makeshift spa.

Major General James E. Chaney, commander of Army Garrison Forces, landed with the vanguard of his outfit, the 147th Regiment, which would take over defense of the island after Marines conquered it. Two Army antiaircraft and coastal defense artillery units landed, trundled their weapons across the beaches and up the terraces to the edge of the Motoyama Number One, and readied them for firing. A communications jeep started monitoring aircraft radio frequencies from a revetment near the airstrip.

Advance elements of two Army Air Corps fighter squadrons— the 47th and the 78th—were ashore and getting ready for what would become a force of nearly three hundred P-51 Mustangs to protect B-29s on the last leg of their massive strikes against Japan's home islands. And there were a smattering of men from the 545th Night Fighter Group of P-61 Black Widows—deadly radar-equipped twin-engined fighter-bombers mounting 20-millimeter cannon—that would fly nightly patrol missions from the island.

Shortly after noon, while the weather was still good but low clouds brought the first hint of rain, two slow, low-powered Marine planes appeared from the southeast. Careful not to fly over the front, they circled around Suribachi and landed within six hundred feet from their touchdown on Motoyama Number One's runway. The unarmed, fabric-covered craft were the vanguard of ten other artillery spotters—modified Stinson two-seaters popular with private civilian pilots—that the Marines called "Maytag Messerschmitts" or "flying grasshoppers."

From now on, the olive green planes would replace Navy carrier-based observers on spotting missions: the first two were on the ground just a few minutes before taking off and heading for the Meat Grinder.

Marines on the front were glad to see them. Because their pilots lived and trained with the troops, and because the planes could fly lower and more slowly over the targets than the big high-powered Navy craft, they knew more about pinpointing targets and calling in close artillery support. Most of the tiny grasshopper fleet were ferried to Iwo aboard carriers, but five made the trip on the weatherdeck of LST 776 and were catapulted into the air by a giant slingshot called a Brodie gear to get ashore. First Lieutenant Roy G. Miller, one of the pilots, said it had to be named after "that stupid bastard who first jumped off the Brooklyn Bridge."

Within days, ingenious ground crews and weapons experts armed the Maytag Messerschmitts with bazookas, rockets, and small bombs. When the planes spotted an inviting target, they not only called in artillery fire, but marked the position with explosive calling cards. Each division had four planes and five pilots. They logged 623 hours darting and zooming over the blazing front. Three pilots were killed during the battle; Second Lieutenant Mort Adamson flew twenty missions without a scratch, only to die of multiple sclerosis before the war was over.

In the wardroom of the *Auburn* half a dozen correspondents were briefed by General Smith on where the battle stood at the end of D-Day plus seven. "We expect to take this island in a few more days," the Old Man said. He wouldn't be pinned down about how many more days it would take. There would be more heavy fighting and more heavy losses, he confided, but he couldn't be quoted, and any reference to his statement would be censored.

"But you can say the Japanese are getting jittery, and are low on water and ammunition and can no longer take care of their wounded," he told the newsmen. Then he excused himself and left to play a few hands of cribbage with Harry Hill and to read his Bible and pray. He knew the battle would take longer—and claim many more lives— than he had dared to indicate to the reporters.

General Kuribayashi, at about the same time, sent another long message to Imperial Headquarters in Tokyo. Japanese troops, he said, still held most of the island and were "inflicting demoralizing casualties on the Americans." He hadn't yet informed the high command of the loss of Mount Suribachi, nor did he mention the critical shortage of water and ammunition, and the extent of his own terrible troop losses. But he did ask again for reinforcements and help: "I can still hold the island for the Emperor and the homeland," he assured the warlords, "if the Imperial Navy would strike the American fleet with mighty blows from our steadfast submarines, battleships, and aircraft." Intelligence officers aboard the *Eldorado* decoded the radio transmission almost as soon as it was sent, and monitored the frequency all night for a response. None came.

3

If any man on Iwo was cast in the mold of Lieutenant General Holland M. Smith, it was Major General Graves B. Erskine. Before taking command of the Third Division after the conquest of Guam, Erskine had been Smith's chief of staff since the desperate days after Pearl Harbor. The two men had a deep, genuine fondness for each other, nurtured by the mutual respect of an old warrior—the oldest three-star fighting general in all of America's armed forces—and an up-and-coming younger professional fighting man, the Marine's youngest two-star general.

A generation separated them in years, but there was no gap in their ingrained beliefs in how men should be trained for combat and how battles must be fought and won. Working as a team, they had directed the training of thousands upon thousands of men in the States when the Marine Corps exploded in size in 1942 and 1943, and they had commanded them in the campaigns from the frigid cold of Iceland and the Aleutians to the tropic climes of Tarawa, Roi-Namur, Kwajelein, Saipan, Tinian, and Guam.

In all of the Corps' six divisions, a large percentage of its platoon, company and battalion officers, and senior noncoms carried the indelible imprint of having trained for combat and fought the Japanese under their knowing leadership. The Smith-Erskine breed of Marines knew the full meaning and importance of stern discipline, aggressiveness, and total dedication to everything that esprit de corps entailed.

Following one of the rough-and-tumble preinvasion planning conferences at Makalapa, Smith called Erskine aside. "Bobbie, if we'd tried to put seventy-five thousand people ashore in early 1942, as we're going to do at Iwo, we'd have to use every damned person in the Marine Corps from newest recruit to Commandant," he said. "Now there's six divisions in the Pacific, and we had a helluva lot to do with whipping every one of them in shape to fight."

"Howlin' Mad" reminded Erskine of their conversation the first time they met on Iwo. "Christ, Bobbie," the general had said, "I wish to hell I could stay ashore." But Nimitz had decreed otherwise, and as D-Day plus eight began, the old war horse was under tight rein aboard ship while Erskine was ashore, and about to send his troops into another attack.

Hill Peter, with its two-hundred-foot elevation, was still the defiant fortress blocking the advance. At 8:00 A.M., two battalions of the 9th Marines—again Carey Randall's First and Bob Cushman's Second—pushed off toward its savage slopes and those of Hill Oboe, two hundred yards northeast, whose summit was one foot lower and whose sides were as strongly fortified.

One of Holly Evans's flamethrower tanks was at the point, spewing streams of hissing fire. Artillery crashed into the sides and crests of both hills. The Japanese reacted as expected—with heavy machine gun fire and mortars—whenever the fire lifted for even a minute. But the Marine armor drove a small wedge in the line, and Randall's men surged halfway up Hill Peter. Shortly before eleven o'clock, one platoon reached the summit. It was immediately pinned down and cut off by a firestorm from bypassed strongpoints and from Hill Oboe. The men dug in and waited for help.

Two hours of bedlam passed before it came. At 12:50 P.M., after ten minutes of artillery shelling by two dozen howitzers, both battalions broke the deadlock and moved forward. Randall's men overran Hill Peter, swarmed down its reverse slope, and up to the crest of Hill Oboe. Cushman's outfit drove ahead on the boulder-strewn but level ground on the left to bring its lines abreast of the other battalion.

Wilson D. Watson, a twenty-three-year-old private from Earle, Arkansas, was the first man atop Hill Oboe. It wasn't planned that way, and several times he didn't expect to make it. But when the artillery barrage lifted, he took off in a running crouch, firing his BAR at a Japanese bunker that had come to life. The only way to go was straight ahead. He sprayed the aperture of the ground-level strongpoint and tossed in two hand grenades. The muffled explosions were followed by the shrill screams of dying Japanese inside, and Watson plunged into a ravine beside two dead Marines.

Just ahead, a pillbox chattered with machine gun fire. Watson vaulted from his shallow cover and silenced it with the same technique—a rapid burst of bullets from his weapon and two grenades. Slamming a fresh clip of ammo into the BAR, he took off again up the ragged slope. Over his shoulder he could see other Marines dart forward in a yelling charge.

In ten minutes Watson and another man clawed to the crest, only to find themselves alone when they reached the top; a fountain of grenades and machine guns fire had pinned down the rest of the troops on the rocky hillside. It was thirty minutes before the thin line of Leathernecks broke through and lunged over the summit. None too soon, Watson thought. His weapon held two rounds of ammunition.

Hill Oboe was far from secure as more men of Cushman's battalion swept up and over the top and down the other side. Time and again the fighting exploded as bypassed positions opened up with machine guns and tried to stop the Marine surge.

Watson always seemed to be in the vortex of the heaviest action. He stalked another pillbox, his BAR firing from the hip, and killed its two occupants. Then he went after another position that had pinned down four Marines with machine gun fire, and wiped it out. He was leading a squad against another bunker when a mortar crumped down twenty yards away. Searing fragments grazed his shoulder, but he wasn't seriously hurt and continued to fight for another half hour until a captain ordered him off the hill to have the wound treated at the division hospital. Forty-eight hours later the wiry five-foot-eight, 140-pound Arkansas farmer was back at the front.

In his first two days on Iwo, he single-handedly had killed ninety Japanese in the battle for Hill Oboe, and he would fight on with his decimated outfit until it left the island. Months later, back on Guam, Watson learned his one-man display of valor and combat know-how had earned him the Medal of Honor.

After three days of seemingly endless struggle against Kuribayashi's main-line defenses, the Third Division had seized Motoyama Number Two and driven the enemy from the commanding high ground to the north. Now General Erskine could again put his scheme for a night attack on the back burner—but he was certain there would be another time to use it.

In the Fifth Division's sector, signs of the enemy's acute shortage of water were increasing. Shortly after midnight a large group was spotted winding down a shallow ravine toward a well near the shoreline, and Marines called in artillery and naval gunfire. In the bright moonlight, the foragers made excellent targets and were obliterated. Otherwise, things were quiet except for the predawn movement by Colonel Wornham's 27th Regiment into the lines to relieve Colonel Graham's 26th Marines.

Troops were in place by 7:30 A.M. for the eight o'clock jump-off against Hill 362A, another volcanic eyesore the Japanese had armed to the teeth. Its boulder-strewn dome held six rapid-fire antiaircraft guns with barrels cranked down for pointblank fire. They were connected to four elaborate tunnel systems—one burrowed through a thousand feet of rock, with seven entrances on three sides of the hill—that supplied the emplacements with ammunition and troops.

Tom Wornham's 27th Marines moved out in three-battalion strength as naval gunfire and carrier planes finished plastering the hill, some five hundred yards ahead, in a push-off prelude. Donn Robertson's Third Battalion was on the right; John Butler's First in the center; and John Antonelli's Second was nearest the western shoreline. For ninety minutes the advance made rapid progress against light opposition—sporadic artillery and mortar fire. By 11:30 A.M., the line was about two hundred yards closer to the base of 362A. Then the attack faltered for a combination of reasons.

Robertson's men lost contact with Third Division troops on the right, and their push was halted until the gap in the lines was closed. When it started up again two hours later, the Marines were in a web of camouflaged pillboxes and a sprawling mine field. Butler's troops were snagged in a concentration of machine guns and mortars in a weird jumble of ravines. Antonelli's battalion was ensnared in a quilt of mine fields ringed by snipers.

Tanks were called up to neutralize the fierce enemy reaction but had trouble maneuvering. A flamethrowing Sherman was disabled by mortars, but other thirty-ton monsters silenced enough of the opposition, including a dug-in Japanese tank whose high-velocity cannon was the core of enemy firepower, to spring the advance.

Gains were steady through the rest of the afternoon; steady, but slow and costly. Savage artillery exchanges thundered along the front, with the Japanese sending white phosphorous shells among the Marines—shelling that spread fears of a poison-gas attack. But the murky smoke clouds lifted harmlessly, and the fight continued.

After Robertson's battalion finally was able to link up solidly with the Third Division, the line slugged ahead another two hundred yards toward 362A. But each stab brought a torrent of resistance from strong concentrations of machine gun nests and rifle pits hidden in a series of undulating ridges guarding the frontal approaches to the hill's slopes. About 4:00 P.M., the colonel called for ten minutes of artillery fire to be followed by a final push.

Twenty-two-year-old William G. Walsh, a gunnery sergeant from Roxbury, Massachusetts, was ready with his platoon when the barrage lifted. He'd already passed the word about the objective: a ridge fifty yards dead ahead. "Let's move! Move out!" he yelled, and vaulted from his cover in a combat man's scampering slouch toward the rise. Right behind, in a clatter of small arms fire from enemy troops momentarily stunned by the artillery, came the charging Marines.

In a nonstop surge, they made the ridge before the Japanese knew what was happening. But before Walsh's platoon could take cover, it was hit from three directions. Japanese survivors of the roaring shellfire had shaken off its effects and opened up with a fusilade of machine guns directly in front of the Marines, and on their left and right.

It was suicide to stay in the exposed positions, and the charge drew back to a line of shallow trenches where heavy fire still laced Walsh and his men. "Hell, we can't stay here! Let's hit the sonsabitches again!" the sergeant shouted. They checked weapons, gulped for breath, and followed the "gunny" back into the maelstrom.

This time only half a dozen men reached the crest. Gasping for air, they hit the ground and crawled to the protection of a shell hole. "Grenade! Grenade!" someone yelled as the hissing missile bounced on the crater's lip and rolled into their midst. Without a word, without an instant's hesitation, Walsh smothered the blast with his body. The valiant sergeant died instantly. If there was a last scream of pain, it was lost in the din of battle as his unwounded comrades fought on to hold their perilous position on the ridge: a lonely battle for two hours until help came.

It was twilight when the line was stabilized five hundred yards ahead of where it had been at jump-off time. But the 27th Marines again had paid heavily for another small advance. That night Walsh's poncho-shrouded body was carried to the rear and buried the next morning in the Fifth Division cemetery. A Marine major notified his parents a week later of their son's death, told them how he gave his life to save his comrades, and of his award of the Medal of Honor.

Hill 382's capture remained the key to defanging the Meat Grinder on the Fourth Division front, and Walt Wensinger's 23rd Regiment still had the unfinished job. Two battalions—Lou Blissard's First and Jim Scales's Third—were again the shock troops as the third day's attack began in the Meat Grinder. They moved out simultaneously with the other divisions in a cross-island push when naval bombardment, artillery, and air strikes lifted. But enemy opposition was more intense, if that were possible, than on D-Day plus seven.

Pat Lanigan's 25th Marines, attacking three battalions abreast, took on obstreperous Turkey Knob. It was another daylong struggle with nearly four thousand Fourth Division troops in frontal assault against strong emplacements dug in along the slopes.

As Shermans moved to cover the push, they came under heavy fire from 47-millimeter antitank guns and were bogged down in volcanic rocks and deep sand. Within half an hour, two were knocked out. Another was hit, but was able to make the protection of a nearby ridge, limping back under a murderous mortar barrage.

Six rocket-launcher trucks sped forward, rooster tails of dust marking their path, and unleashed 432 rounds of 4.5-inch missiles into the western slopes and summit of 382. It took just five minutes to unload the screaming firepower; then the trucks roared away in a cascade of mortars. All the bombardment seemed to do was further whip into fury the hornet's nest of Japanese reaction. Jim Lucas called it "another day at the factory, another day when dead and wounded Marines poured from the Meat Grinder's deadly conveyor belt."

Time and again Scales's battalion smashed against the side of the hill, only to be rolled back like spent surf. Part of one platoon from Don Callaham's company fought to the crest in a deluge of small arms fire and hand grenades. There, in the ruins of the crumpled radar tower and the rubble of its building, they held out for two hours in hand-to-hand combat against counterattacks; wave after wave of superior numbers of Japanese were beaten off until Marines exhausted their ammunition and had to fall back down the hill.

Blissard's battalion met resistance just as violent when it tried to drive around the base of 382, a maneuver designed to isolate the hill and enable the Marines to assault it from all sides. Every hummock seemed to hide an enemy machine gun nest; every ravine, another line of dug-in riflemen; every boulder, an outpost for a sniper. But the positions were overrun, one by one, and by 2:00 P.M. a thin line surrounded the hill.

Each yard of advance claimed more casualties. Fritz C. Truan, a professional rodeo rider from Cody, Wyoming, was one. Back in Hawaii, seven months earlier, he'd won the All-Servicemen's Bronco Busting Championship, a rip-roaring contest with heated interservice rivalries. Some riders claimed he had the edge; before enlisting in 1940, he'd taken top honors at the annual Madison Square Garden rodeo as the world's champion all-around cowboy.

Shortly after eleven o'clock, Truan was leading his platoon, as he'd done since taking them across Green Beach on D-Day, when a burst of machine gun fire caught him in the chest and he was killed. Four months later, at the next servicemen's rodeo in Honolulu, six thousand soldiers, sailors, and Marines stood in silent tribute as the brave cowpoke's riderless horse pranced slowly around the darkened arena. Private First Class Robert L. Mather, a buddy from Clinton, New York, who was with the sergeant when he died, played taps.

Things were no easier for Lanigan's battalion fighting to quench the firestorm on and around Turkey Knob. Tactics of his 25th Regiment were the same as Wensinger's 23rd Marines on Hill 382: keep slugging to scale the slopes and swarm the summit while, at the same time, driving to surround the cave-infested fortress.

By midafternoon, Major Fenton Mee's First Battalion had carved a narrow, bitterly contested line about halfway around the base of the hill from the southwest. At jump-off, Shermans spearheaded the attack, but rugged terrain and fierce fire from high-velocity antitank guns forced them to pull back. A pack howitzer was manhandled into the line and unloaded eighty-five rounds of pointblank shelling into Japanese positions.

"It did wonders for morale," Mee later recalled, "but little more except to bring down even heavier Nip artillery and mortars." It was another exercise in futility—enemy emplacements were so strong that many could take direct hits from the Navy's sixteen-inch guns without being knocked out. "What chance did a 75-millimeter pack howitzer have?" Mee wondered.

So again every yard of advance came down to a dirty and costly job for the infantry—for riflemen, flamethrowers, demolitions squads, and bazooka men who overran the positions, one at a time, in head-on attack.

Lieutenant Colonel James Taul's Second Battalion made virtually no headway trying to link up with Mee's men in a push around the northwest side of the Knob. Its route was even more exposed to small arms and machine gun fire from concealed cave mouths on the hill. After five hours, the batallion gained less than a hundred yards and was forced to pull back to its original line.

Captain Jim Headley, who'd taken over when "Jumpin' Joe" Chambers was hit, made even less progress in the Third Battalion's attempt to scale the hill. From concrete bunkers up the slopes, the Japanese swamped it with a rain of grenades, satchel charges, and machine guns. Tanks and artillery were stymied in efforts to spring the advance; again the impossible terrain and the concealed, reinforced positions were solid allies of the Japanese.

General Cates was annoyed at Pat Lanigan; not because he didn't know why the attack had done so little to knock out the Meat Grinder's teeth, but because he'd been unable, for nearly an hour, to reach the colonel on the field phone to tell him to quit for the day. The reason was simple. Lanigan had been in the thick of the fighting in front of Hill 382 for a close-up look at what was happening and what could be done to break the deadlock—to find, as Cates had ordered, "a weak

spot in the bastard's front, and keep slugging the sonuvabitch until
you do!"

All that could be done at the end of the ninth day on Iwo, the
general and colonel both knew, was to dig in, mount another attack
in the morning—and hope. Neither commander doubted that Kuribayashi's defenses had suffered heavily in the day's fighting; that
hundreds of his troops had been killed; that countless positions had
been destroyed. But how many? And was there "a weak spot in the
bastard's front"? Both men were certain there was none—for the time
being. But they were equally certain that there ultimately would be
a breakthrough; relentless pressure by the Marines and air and naval
might would see to that.

During the day, American airpower at Iwo had begun taking on
new dimensions. Seven twin-engined transports from the Marianas
dropped five tons of medical supplies in brilliant red and green parachutes on Motoyama Number One and the western beaches. Six
Navy Catalina flying boats, long-range search planes that could stay
aloft for twelve hours, flew in from Saipan to take up station with
three tenders anchored two hundred yards off Suribachi.

From now on, whenever B-29s were aloft on missions against the
enemy homeland, at least three of the big twin-engined "dumbos"
would be in the skies at all times flying set courses over bomber flight
paths to and from targets, monitoring radio frequencies from disabled
Superforts. Until these could land on Iwo, hardly a day passed when
at least one crew of a ditched bomber wasn't rescued by the wide-
ranging Catalinas.

Marine intelligence officers were convinced that at least half of
Iwo's defenders had been killed since D-Day. As of 6:00 P.M., February 27, an official summary placed known enemy dead at 5,483. "Of
course this figure is only an estimate," the report said, "as it cannot
accurately account for the large number of Japanese sealed in caves."

General Kuribayashi certainly didn't know how many men he'd
lost as more and more of his positions were overrun or bypassed. In
most cases, communication with his front-line commanders was possible now only by orders carried by runners, many of whom were cut
down by Marines as they moved along the roaring line. If Kuribayashi
harbored any hope of help, it was dashed when Tokyo finally answered

his urgent pleas for more men and for heavy air and naval attacks against the invaders.

"I regret that except for full submarine support and some air support, we cannot send reinforcements to Iwo," the message from Admiral Soemu Toyoda, Commander in Chief of the Japanese Navy, said. "However, in view of the overall requirements, I earnestly hope you will maintain calm and fight staunchly by all means." Kuribayashi had no other option, and he knew it. He knew, too, that it was inevitable the island would be conquered by the Marines, and that most of the Japanese—certainly he—would perish in its last-ditch defense.

Admiral Toyoda kept his word—to a degree.

That night he sent a token flight of planes from Honshu Island to drop ammunition and medical supplies on the Fourth Division front. Radar tracked the intruders from sixty miles at sea, and three planes were shot down by carrier-based night fighters before reaching the drop zone. Planes penetrating the screen of interceptors dropped a single string of a dozen parachutes that were immediately spotted in the brilliant light of flares. Japanese scurrying to recover the sorely needed cargo, five hundred yards to the rear of their front lines, were easy targets for naval bombardment and artillery. It was the enemy's only attempt at an air drop during the battle.

Toyoda's promise of "full submarine support" was feeble at best, and as futile as the faint-hearted stab at air supply. During the next two days, planes from the escort carrier *Anzio* sank two large submarines: the I-368, twenty miles west of Iwo, and the RO-34, about the same distance west of Chichi Jima. The escort destroyer *Finnegan*, on patrol sixty miles south of Iwo, found the I-370 and sent it to the bottom with depth charges. It was never learned if other submarines were in the area. If so, they went undetected, posed no real threat to American ships, and returned to home waters without firing a torpedo or floating a mine.

As far as Imperial Headquarters was concerned, it had written off Iwo Jima and its defenders. The warlords now would gird for the invasion of other islands nearer Japan—and inevitably the homeland—and hope that General Kuribayashi, the valiant samurai, and his troops could delay the timetable by killing Marines.

4

On February 28, D-Day plus nine, the Third Division's two regiments ashore had new orders from General Schmidt. "Take the rest of the high ground in front of you and drive to the northern shoreline," he told General Erskine. The job fell to Colonel Withers's 21st Regiment, rested and refitted after two days in reserve while Colonel Kenyon's 9th Marines had slammed against Hills Peter and Oboe to smother the last resistance around Motoyama Number Two.

A flurry of firefights with enemy snipers and machine gunners flared as the 21st passed through the 9th's lines, but troops were in place for the 8:15 A.M. jump-off. For once, thirty minutes of naval bombardment and air attacks had the hoped-for results and the push gained four hundred yards by 9:30.

Japanese troops, stunned by the shelling and bombs, now came alive with a vengeance. By 11:30, the advance was stalled along the entire front. It was a stand-off until shortly after one o'clock, when another pulverizing artillery barrage broke the impasse.

Colonel Duplantis's battalion then mounted a wild charge through the cluster of rocks and pillboxes that once had been Motoyama Village. In earlier days, it had been the scrubby metropolis of Iwo Jima, the largest of its five dismal settlements—the others were Nishi, Kita, Higashi, and Minami—where a polyglot population of some one thousand Japanese and semi-indentured Korean laborers eked out a hard-scrabble existence in a dilapidated sugar mill and by exporting sulphur fertilizer to the home islands.

Motoyama's dusty main street had been the center of a loud and daylong welcoming celebration the day after General Kuribayashi's arrival on Iwo. Its beer hall, general store, school, geisha house, government offices, and fifty single-story houses were bedecked with banners. An island-wide holiday was declared as the general, with an honor guard of two hundred troops, marched through the village as brightly dressed, freshly scrubbed children clutching tiny Rising Sun flags cheered wildly.

Roofs of every building were catch basins for rainwater, with pipes draining to cisterns to capture every drop. Tuft grass and bean vines fought to survive among patches of vegetables in stone-walled garden plots. Hot springs of water bubbled to the surface throughout the village, but they reeked with the sickening smell of rotten eggs and were useless. Now the civilians were long gone, evacuated to Chichi Jima and Japan months before D-Day. All that remained were the rubble of sun-baked buildings bristling with Japanese machine gunners and snipers.

Duplantis's men took the positions in hand-to-hand fighting and surged on to seize the high ground overlooking the unfinished third airstrip, the last of the main objectives of the invasion. By nightfall, as the official battle report said, "it appeared that the Third Division had finally burned and blasted through the enemy's main line."

"There was nothing spectacular about the day's action," a Marine correspondent wrote, "but death was everywhere and heroism was commonplace."

Technical Sergeant Nolle T. Roberts told how a corpsman saved the life of a Marine by slitting his throat with a pocket knife: "Pharmacist's Mate Second Class Floyd L. Garrett of Gadsen, Alabama, saw that the corporal was bleeding to death from a severed jugular vein and that it would all be over very soon unless something was done quickly. Grabbing the end of the vein in one hand, Garrett slit the skin of the throat so that he could reach enough of the vein to apply a hemostat."

Lieutenant Cloyd L. Arford, Garrett's battalion surgeon, remembered the corpsman's action as "the most amazing presence of mind I ever saw under fire." The surgery wasn't especially complicated, the doctor said, "but Garrett had no assistance, poor light, and was under fire from enemy mortars at the time. Besides, it takes a lot of guts for a nonprofessional man to start cutting on a man, even to save his life."

Shortly after noon, a young Marine found his way to one of the battalion aid stations. "He was hardly out of boyhood," a corpsman recalled, "and he stumbled in, shaking and sweating." He wasn't visibly wounded, but racked with uncontrollable fear. "In other times, he'd probably have been sent to the rear as a case of combat fatigue," the medic said, "but everyone was too busy trying to save the lives of the wounded, and the kid was told to return to his outfit on the line."

The young Marine began to cry as he shuffled away. About forty feet to the rear, he slumped down and sat with his back to a boulder. Half an hour later, he was still sobbing softly and quivering with fright when a mortar exploded at his feet and he died in the blast.

While Duplantis's men swept through the rubble of Motoyama Village and pressed its attack, the rest of the 21st Marines—Randall's First Battalion and Cushman's Second—hammered strong enemy defenses on the flanks.

Nearly three thousand men were in the push along the curving 1,500-yard front. Duplantis's steamroller advance, six hundred yards ahead of the other units, bypassed countless heavily armed positions on the right and left, and created a wide gap in the lines. It was an afternoon of savage firefights before infantry, flamethrowers, and demolitions squads closed the breach and the three battalions linked up for the night.

Shortly after sundown, Colonel Withers was on the field phone to General Erskine. "Shall we keep going?" he asked. "Go ahead! We'll send a Higgins boat to the north shore so you won't have to walk back!" was Erskine's answer. Both wished it could be that easy. It would, in fact, take another six days of costly close-in fighting before the Third Division reached Iwo's northern coast.

Hill 362A was still six hundred yards ahead of the Fifth Division's front lines, a Gibraltar-like fortress whose flat top bristled with heavy artillery, rapid-firing antitank guns, and heavy mortars. Its tortuous slopes and sheer cliffs concealed nearly fifty cave entrances leading to tunnels connecting all sides of the escarpment, where 1,500 of Kuribayashi's best troops were in place. And among the ravines and hummocks around its base was a deep line of camouflaged pillboxes and bunkers, all armed to the hilt.

Two battalions of the 27th Marines—John Butler's First and Donn Robertson's Third—pushed off at 8:15 A.M. in the D-plus nine attack and moved toward the hill. Robertson's men, supported by six tanks, were at the point and met an immediate nonstop screen of small arms fire in the sharpest resistance they'd faced in ten days of battle.

Time after time the assault bogged down. Then, with riflemen braving the torrent of fire from hidden firepits, the Shermans ground through the coarse sand to blast bunkers and pillboxes into temporary silence, their cannon firing as rapidly as crewmen could load. Demolitions squads followed with flamethrowers, bangalore torpedoes, and satchel charges to finish the job.

By noon, the tanks were out of shells. A Japanese suicide squad rushed one tank with hand grenades that exploded in roars of green smoke. The Sherman was undamaged, but in moving to safety it plunged into a ravine and threw a tread. Three crewmen tumbled from the turret of the trackless machine and scrambled to the shelter of another tank.

Three more Shermans clanked forward; their fire blasted a path for the battalion to dash past a cordon of Japanese positions and gain a shaky toehold at the base of the hill. Now the men were taking heavy fire from caves high up the slopes and from both flanks and bypassed strongpoints.

Two companies, trapped in the crossfire, battled until 4:30 P.M. to hold out against the resistance. A twenty-man patrol from Item Company managed to push up the southwest side to the crest. But it was a case of too few Marines with too little firepower to hold out against superior numbers of Japanese hitting them in wave after wave of counterattacks. The advance not only had been halted, but runners went out to call back the troops from the slopes and thinly held positions at the bottom of the hill to a line about one hundred yards from its base.

Some units didn't get the word. Others couldn't move, surrounded by strongpoints infilading them with fierce machine gun and rifle fire.

John H. Willis, of Columbia, Tennessee, was with one of the cutoff outfits halfway up the southwest slope. The twenty-three-year-old corpsman, a Pharmacist's Mate First Class, had been with Robertson's men all day, scrambling from one wounded Marine to another with his satchel of drugs, plasma, and bandages. Shortly after two o'clock he caught a chunk of hot shrapnel and was ordered off the hill. He made his way back to the battalion aid station, where the wound was treated and dressed.

Thirty minutes later the corpsman was back in action, ducking and darting under machine gun bullets as he clambered up the incline. Halfway to the crest, he lunged into a shallow hole beside a Marine hemorrhaging with deep wounds.

There was just time to plunge a rifle, bayonet-first, into the ground and rig a bottle of plasma to its stock. Before he could do anything more, the first of a string of grenades landed beside them and Willis hurled it back toward the enemy. Seven more came in rapid succession. He did the same with them. The next one exploded in one hand while the other hand grappled to see that plasma was still flowing into the arm of the wounded man.

Lieutenant Charles J. Hely, Willis's battalion surgeon, wept when the corpsman's body was carried off the hill. Four decades later, still in practice in Westfield, New Jersey, the doctor remembered: "He was the bravest young man and the best damned corpsman I ever saw. He'd have made one helluva fine doctor." When Willis's family, back in Tennessee, was told of his death, they couldn't escape the grief—or the pride his Medal of Honor brought them.

Butler's battalion fared better in the day's push along the western shoreline. It met strong opposition, but the terrain wasn't as bad and the men skirted the hill instead of hitting headlong against it. They were some three hundred yards ahead of the jump-off point at twilight. But 362A was still firmly in Japanese hands, and the dent the 27th Marines had made in the fortress had claimed nearly two hundred more casualties.

Chet Graham's 26th Regiment spent most of the day in reserve. It used the time to salvage and replace weapons and to take on replacements—and to clean out several clusters of bypassed pillboxes and sniper nests. "Harry the Horse" Liversedge's 28th Marines had moved off Suribachi to add muscle and firepower to the push in the days ahead.

That night the Fifth Division front was a weird combination of uneasy quiet and thundering violence. Early on, except for the occasional chatter of harassing machine gun fire and scattered mortar shelling, there was little activity along the lines—so little, in fact, that handlers on outpost duty had trouble keeping their war dogs alert. Their usually vigilant German shepherds and Doberman pinschers, full of food and bored by the strange stillness, were kept awake only by constant prodding.

Soon after 2:00 A.M., things began to change. At first, what seemed to be random enemy artillery shells started falling in a helter-skelter pattern along the western edge of Motoyama Number One. The area was jammed with supply and ammunition dumps, crowded with artillery positions, cluttered with trucks and jeeps parked almost hub to hub, with thousands of Marines and Seabees sleeping in foxholes, and a hodgepodge of hospital tents, tarpaulin-covered revetments housing kitchens, communications centers, various rear-area command posts—even the division post office.

Mass bedlam erupted when a shell hit the main ammunition dump, touching off a chain reaction that sent explosives hundreds of feet skyward. A giant mushroom cloud of acrid smoke blanketed the southern third of the island, laced by crazy trajectories of multicolored signal flares, rockets, and phosphorous shells and grenades. Artillery and mortar rounds detonated in a rolling thunderclap that roared on and on. Machine gun and rifle bullets crackled like thousands of giant firecrackers exploding in an endless string.

Marine Gunner Paul White, a combat photographer from New York, saw the spectacle of pyrotechnics from the *Eldorado*, where he was working on a packet of press negatives and copy bound for Guam. "It looked like a Coney Island Fourth of July celebration set off by a gang of lunatics," he said. For a befuddled sergeant on shore, it was something different. It was, he said, what he'd always imagined a Chinese New Year would be like—"totally fucked up like one of their fire drills, only a fucking lot louder and a helluva lot more deadly."

With the cacophony still mounting, hundreds of stunned Marines and Seabees formed fire brigades to smother what flames they could with sand. It was, Private Charles J. Brown of Des Moines, Iowa, said, "like charging the gates of hell with a leaky bucket of water." Singly and in small groups, men darted into the fringes of the inferno to carry out shells and ammunition cases. Startled bulldozer operators cranked up their machines and ignored the danger to push mounds of dirt over the flaming debris.

A Condition Red air-raid alert sounded just before 2:30 A.M.. At three o'clock, when the conflagration was greatest, someone thought exploding white phosphorous artillery shells signaled a poison-gas attack. Sirens screeched the alarm across the island as thousand of scurrying men cursed the fact that they'd abandoned gas masks on the beaches or left aboard ship.

Ten minutes later the alarm was canceled, but the air alert remained in force for good reason. At 2:45, a lone twin-engined Japanese bomber, probably from Chichi Jima, roared out of the offshore darkness and unleashed a torpedo toward the destroyer *Terry*, on station three miles from Kitano Point at the northwestern tip of the island. It passed fifty feet astern the ship without damage; the plane zoomed into the night and didn't return. But tragedy struck the *Terry* just after dawn, when a battery of General Kuribayashi's six-inch coastal guns sent a barrage of shells crashing into her deck and forward engine room.

This touched off a fierce counterbattery exchange, with the battleship *Nevada* and the cruiser *Pensacola* closing on the shoreline to silence three enemy emplacements in fifteen minutes of nonstop firing. Eleven of the destroyer's crew were killed and nineteen others wounded. That afternoon the dead were buried at sea, the wounded were ferried to the *Samaritan*, and the *Terry* limped back on one engine to Pearl Harbor.

When the pandemonium was at its peak, Japanese gunners launched a rocket attack on Suribachi—a nightly occurrence since the Marines had captured the volcano. As usual, most of the giant missiles missed the mark. But the screeching sound and long trails of sparks that marked their erratic flight paths were spectacular and frightening, and when one landed on the slopes, it exploded in a deafening roar.

"Then the mountain would shake like a bowl of jelly," Lieutenant Keith Wells, CO of the observation post on the summit, said. The five-feet-long buzz-bombs, fired from crude wooden chutes hidden in the hills beyond Motoyama Number Two, were more a loud nuisance than anything else. "I would see little streaks of fire at the other end of the island three or four miles away," Wells remembered, "and I'd light a cigarette and take several puffs before the bomb screamed overhead and into the sea." But that night, nervous Marines feared that, with the rest of the thousands of tons of exploding shells, the slumbering volcano might erupt and the whole island disappear.

Shortly after 4:00 A.M., when it seemed that most of the fire was under control, near catastrophe struck when still another explosion sent a cascade of 105-millimeter artillery shells skyward. One landed a few yards from the communications center, which handled fire missions for Fifth Corps howitzers. There were no casualties, but the blast knocked out telephone lines and put out of action most of the 105s on the island until new wires were strung to the front. And for the next twenty-four hours the Fifth Division was faced with the threat of ammunition shortages; more than twenty percent of its stockpile had been destroyed.

At the front, Marines wondered what was happening as the din of explosions carried to the lines and billowing fires lit up the night. Some speculated that hundreds of Japanese had used a secret tunnel to attack the rear in the long-expected banzai. But by dawn, the only evidence of the inferno were a few harmless and smoldering fires, a fresh quilt of shell craters, and thousands of Marines and Seabees bleary-eyed and exhausted from a night of hard, dangerous work.

And, miracle of miracles, not a man was killed; only a handful had received minor wounds during the raucous, roaring spectacle.

When Lieutenant E. Graham Evans, one of the division's surgeons, awoke the next morning he was amazed at the destruction. "When all hell broke loose," he said, "I decided to stay in my cot regardless of what happened." After eighteen hours of operating, he was "just too damned tired to move or give a damn about anything." He found his tent riddled with shell fragments and the ground littered with spent steel, but he had slept through it all without a scratch.

On the Fourth Division front, on D-Day plus nine, the Meat Grinder's appetite was still unsatisfied. Six thousand Marines jumped off at 8:15 A.M. in yet another assault against Hill 382 and Turkey Knob. As usual, naval bombardment and air strikes preceded the attack, but when the push began it was quickly snared in an avalanche of enemy resistance. It came not only from the two hills, but from the Amphitheater and Minami Village, and it was devastating.

Gains were again measured in feet and each forward movement claimed more casualties. Yet through it all, headway was made; by late afternoon both escarpments were surrounded, but their slopes and summits were still held firmly by the Japanese. It was obvious there was no weak spot in the eastern sector's defenses and that only more savage fighting—straight-ahead assault—could hammer through them.

Colonel Pat Lanigan's 25th Regiment was again the hammerhead of the attack, moving in the fresh attempt to take the Meat Grinder. Several times during the day the situation became critical because of withering heavy mortar fire and hand grenades coming from a maze of positions on the high ground. Tanks were of little help; again, they couldn't move because of terrain, and one was quickly disabled by a

land mine. Two others managed to fire on a large concrete communications bunker atop the Knob, but the 75-millimeter shells had no
visible effect on the thick walls.

Major Arthur B. Hanson, the 24th Marines' intelligence officer,
could easily understand one of the reasons the resistance was so effective. "You know how big their damn mortars are?" he asked William
Hipple, a *Newsweek* correspondent, and answered his own question.
"We've found some as big as 220-millimeters, and there are others
like the goddamned 'spigot mortar' that is five feet long and twelve
inches in diameter," Hanson said. "You can see the bastard arching
through the air like a flying ash can, and when one of these big babies
land they can kill people twenty yards in all directions."

At 4:45 P.M., General Cates ordered the lines consolidated. It
took another two hours for some units to disengage, and artillery had
to lay down a smoke screen for some to pull back. It was dark before
all the men were in place for the night—some in the same foxholes
they'd left that morning.

Colonel Edwin A. Pollock, Cate's shrewd intelligence officer, wasn't
puzzled by the pace of the advance—nor was he surprised by the frightful casualties. He had expected both. But he also knew that the Japanese
were inexorably being beaten back; that hundreds of enemy troops were
also being slaughtered every day in the Meat Grinder; that shortages of
ammunition, water, and medical supplies were mounting without hope
of resupply. All this was confirmed by questioning of the small bag of
Japanese prisoners taken in recent days.

That night in his daily battle summary, Pollock told Cates he also
was sure that Kuribayashi's communications were being hacked to
pieces; that for this reason it wouldn't be possible for the enemy to
mount a massed counterattack against the Fourth Division. But he
warned of nightly attempts at infiltration. "Although gains have been
small," his report said, "the division has finally cracked the central
defensive core of resistance before Hill 382 and Turkey Knob. The
division is prepared to continue the attack."

Pollock was right about infiltrators hitting the lines. Shortly after
ten o'clock, and again about 2:30 A.M., bands of marauders snaked
down the ravines in front of Jim Headley's battalion. Alert Marines
caught them in the light of parachute flares and wiped out the force,
estimated at some two hundred well-armed troops, with artillery,
mortars, and machine guns.

5

General Erskine was up an hour before dawn of D-Day plus ten, the first day of March. As the early streaks of light cut through a low overcast, he was in a Higgins boat bouncing through choppy waves to General Smith's flagship two miles offshore. It was to be a stormy meeting, one that was to cloud relations between the two men the rest of their lives.

Erskine wanted to land his 3rd Regiment, the last force of uncommitted troops still afloat, to give the Third Division nine thousand fresh men—many of whom were experienced combat veterans of the Bougainville and Guam campaigns—to add manpower and armor for the final push to Iwo's northern shore. But Smith had replied to what Erskine believed a logical and routine matter with a terse radioteletype message: "Request denied."

The Big E was adamant that the troops were needed; not desperately, but needed nonetheless to roll on to victory with the fewest possible losses. After all, his argument went, he was fighting with two regiments while the Fourth and Fifth Divisions had three—and the Third Division was expected to take an area larger than those assigned to either Cates or Rockey.

General Schmidt agreed with Erskine, but this didn't sway "Howlin' Mad." And it was one of the rare times when he and Admiral Turner saw eye to eye on anything. Both were steadfast in the belief that there wasn't room on the front for another regiment to maneuver—or enough area behind the lines for nine thousand more men to be a land-based reserve. "It was a table-pounding session," Erskine later said, "and I knew the Old Man well enough to know I couldn't win. General Smith always wanted an uncommitted force in reserve, just in case. Maybe he was right, but I didn't think so and I spoke my mind in no uncertain terms."

Erskine left the *Auburn* with orders to "fight the battle with the troops you have—at least, for the time being." Smith walked with him to the ship's gangway where he sought to soothe his angry protégé. "We'll keep the 3rd Marines in floating reserve until we see what

happens without it," he said. There was no response from the rankled
Third Division commander as he descended, two steps at a time, and
jumped into a landing craft for the thirty-minute return to shore.

The Big E was in his CP by seven o'clock, had briefed Colonels
Withers and Kenyon about his futile mission, and ordered the new
attack to begin at 8:30. Three battalions jumped off without naval
bombardment or air support, but with fifteen minutes of heavy pre-
push artillery shelling. The Second and Third Battalions from the 21st
Regiment, and the Third from the 9th, were the assault troops.

Their objective was to exploit the breakthrough at Motoyama
Village and seize the third airstrip. Resistance was amazingly light.
No one knew why. It was possible the Japanese were surprised by
the absence of shelling and bombing and didn't expect the attack when
it came. And there was the possibility that the enemy simply had
pulled back to a new, more tenable line after the defenses around the
village were crushed. For whatever reason, the advance gained five
hundred yards by noon and most of the airfield was controlled by the
Marines.

To keep the steamroller moving, Marine artillery opened up again
at 12:30 P.M. and tanks joined the attack as it plowed ahead. Another
three hundred yards fell by midafternoon, but by then resistance was
stiffening from bypassed positions and concealed bunkers. At four
o'clock, General Erskine called it a day.

In ground gained, it had been the best so far for the Third Division. By Iwo's yardstick, it was a day of unspectacular battle, but it
was grinding combat that claimed nearly two hundred new casualties.
And the push had carried to a point where opposition was certain to
be more fierce as Marines dug in near the base of Hills 362B and
362C, counterparts in elevation and defenses to Hill 362A.

Colonel Liversedge's 28th Regiment moved into the lines at dawn
to spearhead the Fifth Division attack. Jump-off was at 8:30 and it was
preceded by forty-five minutes of massed artillery shelling and naval
fire. Hundreds of rounds from the *Nevada, Pensacola,* and *Indianapolis* pounded the steep sides and flat top of 362A and raised a grayish
black curtain of smoke and dust hundreds of feet into the sky. The
bombardment touched off daylong counterbattery fire that damaged
two supply ships, the *Calhoun* and *Stembel.*

Nearly three thousand troops were in the assault. Jackson Butterfield's First Battalion and Chandler Johnson's Second headed abreast up Hill 362A against moderate resistance. Charley Shepard's Third moved across the rock-strewn ravine that skirted around the western side of its sheer eighty-foot cliffs. Lessons learned on Suribachi paid off against 362A. By midmorning, Marines pushed to the crest and across its top with remarkable ease and light casualties, and the base of the escarpment was surrounded.

Most of its defenders had escaped through the hill's network of tunnels to take up new positions on Nishi Ridge, some three hundred yards to the west. The ridge was virtually the same elevation as 362A and was fortified with dug-in concentrations of firepower that ripped into Marines on the summit and the perimeter below. There was just one way to continue the attack: leave enough Marines on 362A to hold it, pull the other troops back down the slopes, and point the thrust toward Nishi Ridge.

"If we didn't need the fuckin' hill, why the goddamned hell did we take it in the first place?" a bitter sergeant wondered as his squad stumbled and slid toward the base under heavy fire. But 362A in Marine control was the key to the capture of Nishi Ridge and to cracking the major defense belt in the western sector.

Automatic weapons and sniper fire came from caves in the northern face of the hill and from camouflaged emplacements in the looming ridge. The ravine at the front and around the sides of 362A was honeycombed with hidden bunkers, and a deep tank trap was cut down its middle. The ground leveled off beyond the draw to a jagged landscape of rocks and boulders for about two hundred yards, then erupted sharply to form Nishi Ridge.

Tanks worked all day to support the attack; flamethrowers incinerated bypassed positions and other Shermans fired pointblank when targets were spotted. But even with armor, the advance was slow and costly. Artillery and mortars constantly bracketed the tanks, and when one was disabled in the tank trap its crew poured from the turret and escape hatch and fought alongside the infantry to clear the immediate area.

Captain Aaron G. Wilkins thought his men of Able Company could fight through the mess by pushing along the eastern edge of the ravine. The outfit, first to slash across Iwo at Suribachi's base on D-Day, followed the twenty-five-year-old commander but made little headway. Every movement brought down fire from the caves up the slopes of 362A, from firepits along the ravine, and from positions on Nishi Ridge.

Tony Stein, cradling his ubiquitous "stinger," volunteered to take a patrol and see what could be done to relieve the pressure. Nineteen men went ahead with the hell-for-leather corporal, scampering and ducking from hole to hole in the ravine as small arms fire and mortars tore into them. Stein wasn't among the nine who made it back; a sniper's bullet killed him within minutes without his ever learning of the Medal of Honor citation for his wild, barefoot, helmetless rampage on D-Day.

Wilkins, the last of the battalion's original company commanders, was dead within the hour, killed with three other men in a mortar blast. Captain Russell J. Parsons took over the battered company and the fight went on.

Captain Robert A. Wilson tried to push around the hill's base from the other direction against another wall of resistance, but the attempt was snuffed out by enfilading fire from the sides of the ravine and from the high ground. After thirty minutes, the fury suddenly diminished and the worst seemed over. But then mortars and hand grenades started falling among the Marines like giant hailstones.

Fragments from one blast tore into Wilson. He fell with serious wounds, the second of Butterfield's company commanders lost in less than an hour, and was carried to the rear under the withering fire. First Lieutenant Charles A. Weaver now was Baker Company's CO. It was the second time; he'd taken over on D-Day when Captain Dwayne E. Mears was killed storming a beachhead bunker.

D-plus ten was as costly for Chandler Johnson's men as any day in the battle for Suribachi as they struggled among the boulders of a steep slope west of 362A in front of Nishi Ridge. Terrain was not as wicked as on the volcano, but the enemy's violent resistance claimed frightful casualties for each yard of advance. Before day's end, three of the men in Joe Rosenthal's photo were dead—and two who had helped raise the first small flag on Suribachi's summit were cut down with near-fatal wounds.

Sergeant Michael Strank, third from the left in Rosenthal's picture, was leading Easy Company's push with four other men when they were isolated by Japanese machine gunners and mortars. For four hours they fought a desperate holding action. "We'd better send someone to tell the company where we are," Strank told Corporal Joe

Rodriquez as he sketched their position in the sand. No one heard the incoming mortar until it exploded. Strank was killed in its whomping blast, blown backward with arms above his head.

Corporal Harlon Block was on the far right in Rosenthal's photo. He died in the same explosion. Like Strank, he never knew of his fame as a Suribachi flag-raiser. Nor did Sergeant Henry Hansen, whose life had been saved by the incorrigible Private Ruhl who died to save the sergeant. Hansen was moving toward the ridge when someone yelled a warning that their position was under heavy small arms fire. "You worry too much," was Hansen's shouted answer as he skirted around a boulder and was killed by a machine gun burst.

Corporal Charles Lindberg, still carrying his flamethrower, took a bullet through the forearm and chest. The Notre Dame professor-to-be, Corporal Robert Leader, was hit in the stomach by small arms fire. By nightfall, both were aboard the *Samaritan* and would fight the Japanese no more.

At sunset, the Fifth Division was solidly on the crest of Hill 362A and had surrounded its base. The front stretched one thousand yards in front of Nishi Ridge and was three hundred yards closer to the objective than it had been at the jump-off. But casualties were the heaviest yet suffered by the 28th Regiment. Men new to battle would be thrown into the ravaged ranks, but it would be impossible to replace the likes of Tony Stein, Aaron Wilkins, Robert Wilson, Harlon Block, Michael Strank, Henry Hansen, and the hundreds of others from the outfit who had fallen since D-Day.

Across the island on the Fourth Division front, the 24th Regiment made yet another attempt to take Hill 382 and silence the Meat Grinder. Paul Trietel's First Battalion and Dick Rothwell's Second began the push at 8:30 A.M. after forty-five minutes of preparation shelling. But the attack was another replay of what had happened so often before: it stalled almost immediately when the spearhead companies came under heavy Japanese artillery and mortar fire. It was nearly three hours before the bombardment was quieted by naval shellfire, carrier planes unloading napalm bombs, and barrages from Marine 155-millimeter howitzers.

Even then, fierce resistance flared from positions on the hill and Turkey Knob. By midafternoon, Fox Company had gained a scant 150 yards and George Company was pinned down on the slopes of 382.

There was little cover for the Marines from intense small arms and machine gun fire from the high ground and bypassed caves. Headway came only from close-in combat as individuals and small units worked forward to carve out yard-by-yard, position-by-position gains.

Late in the afternoon, part of one company from the Second Battalion made it up 382 and started to dig in along the western edge of the two-ridge crest. Scarcely a hundred yards to the east, Japanese troops manned a strong complex of reinforced positions spouting heavy machine gun fire from the other ridge. When Colonel Rothwell moved up with a reconnaissance patrol to scout Marine positions for the night, they found the no man's land a blazing scene of give-no-quarter action.

In a melee of hand-to-hand combat, Marines struggled to push tenacious Japanese from the crest, and the enemy sought to drive the attackers from their flimsy toehold. At sunset, it was a stand-off. But an important piece of Hill 382 now belonged to the Marines; whether they could hold it was another matter. Rothwell left Captain Roland E. Carey's Easy Company with the job and scrambled down the rocky slope to plan the next day's attack.

Major Trietel's battalion fought with limited success throughout the day in its thrust to strengthen the lines around the base of the hill, and to move up Turkey Knob. Heavy machine gun and mortar fire came from strongpoints hidden in a patch of boulders and scrub trees—positions so well concealed that they couldn't be seen from low-flying "grasshopper" spotters or by forward artillery observers.

Opposition was so severe, casualties so heavy, that the troops were ordered to pull back to the jump-off point. This triggered even heavier enemy small arms and mortar fire, and artillery barrages from north of the Meat Grinder. Only after a smoke screen was laid down could the wounded be evacuated and the line consolidated.

Fourth Division losses for D-Day plus ten were 374 killed and wounded. In eleven days, it had suffered 5,595 casualties and slightly less than one half of Iwo was in American hands. But General Cates had at least one consolation from the day's action: his Marines were now atop Hill 382 and in position to swarm the rest of it from all directions.

Cates knew, too, that General Kuribayashi's defenses in the sector had to crack soon. There was simply no way the Japanese could much longer take the constant pounding from the Navy's big guns, the night-and-day battering from artillery, the bombing and strafing from carrier planes, the relentless attacks by Marine infantry. Ammunition, water, and medical supplies certainly were running low. Communications between the general and the front, and between his combat units, had to be a serious problem as the battleground began to lose a small measure of its violence.

6

General Erskine was still chafing over the refusal of General Smith and Admiral Turner to release the 3rd Regiment for the drive to crush Japanese defenses in the center of Iwo and drive to the northern coast. He was confident the 9th and 21st Marines could break through the line, but he remained resolute that the job could be done faster, and with proportionately fewer casualties, with the firepower of three thousand more troops.

But orders were orders. So at 8:00 A.M. of D-plus eleven, the Third Division attack began again, with the men and arms already on the front.

Erskine was inwardly proud—not satisfied, for he seldom was, but proud of the grinding headway of the division. His men hadn't stormed the beaches on D-Day, but since landing they had seized Motoyama Number Two and hammered through Kuribayashi's strongest defenses to steamroller through Motoyama Village, overrun part of the strongly defended third airstrip, and now were less than fifteen hundred yards from splitting Iwo in two parts by driving to its north shoreline.

Thirty minutes of artillery fire preceded the push. Nothing spectacular, but as a sergeant from the 9th Marines said, "it meant the butcher shop was open for another day's business." Nearly four thousand men were in the double-pronged, five-battalion attack, with one thrust pointed due north toward Hill 362B, and the other aimed eastward to clear the rest of the third airstrip.

Strong opposition flared immediately from enemy positions along the hump-shaped thousand-yard front. Violent enfilading machine gun and mortar fire came from a cluster of emplacements atop the hill and in hidden cave mouths on its slopes where the 21st Regiment pushed the assault. Several Shermans moved out across the flatness of Motoyama Number Three ahead of the 9th Marines, but were stopped by high velocity 75-millimeter guns barking from hidden concrete bunkers and Japanese tanks buried to turret depth.

Lieutenant Colonel Lowell English's Second Battalion was the spearhead of the 21st's bogged-down movement. Less than thirty minutes after jump-off he was hit by mortar fragments, but refused to go to the rear. "Just a nick," he said of the wound, and fought on at the front until shortly before 5:30 P.M., when more shrapnel ripped into his shoulder. This time he was carried off the line, still giving orders as he was placed on a litter.

Major George A. Percy took over the hard-hit outfit. At forty-seven, he was the battalion's executive officer, the oldest battle front commander in the Marine Corps. Hardly anyone could understand why he was even in the armed forces, much less fighting on Iwo Jima. But Percy had his private reasons. "We've got to win this war. I'm going to do my part, and I'm going to be a Marine to do it," he told family and friends when he had enlisted two years earlier.

Percy had been a successful Wall Street broker, overweight and overage, hardly fit material for the Marine Corps. But he wangled a commission as a paymaster and talked his way overseas. When he applied for combat duty, flabbergasted superiors turned him down with the flat statement that he was too old and physically unfit to lead troops in battle, possibly even a little off his rocker to suggest such a billet.

"He used all the salesmanship he'd learned in selling stocks and bonds," English recalled, "and he got what he wanted." In training, Percy had trudged along with the men in backbreaking field exercises on the steep semi-mountains of Guam, and it didn't take long for troops to learn he was a born leader, an opinion confirmed when the 21st Regiment launched its push up the rugged backbone of Iwo Jima.

"The Old Guy seemed to be everywhere," a bewildered gunnery sergeant said, "and especially when the going was roughest." In nine days of combat, the intrepid major had been wounded twice by mortar fragments. Both were serious enough to warrant evacuation, but he was off the front just long enough to have them dressed and then returned to the fight. He was still leading the battalion when the island was conquered. "He'd still be going if the outfit hadn't run out of Japs," Ray Henri said of the battling broker.

Tanks and artillery tried three times during the day to spring the attack. Shells screamed over the heads of Marines as barrages roared into 362B and defenses just beyond the eastern fringe of the airstrip. But when the fire lifted, heavy Japanese resistance flared again and kept the advance pinned down. At sunset, the line showed little change; the enemy still held part of the airfield, a three-hundred-yard patch of mine fields and clusters of machine gun pits, and artillery and antitank gun positions. Hill 362B was a cauldron of defiance.

Fifth Division men later learned why Nishi Ridge was so hard to take. But when the D-plus eleven attack began, they knew only that it was still a Japanese stronghold blocking the push on the western front. Its stark two-hundred-foot elevation was a formidable obstacle by itself, a fortress held by a thousand of Kuribayashi's best troops. It was only after it fell that Marines found the ridge was probably Iwo's most intricate and strongest fortification.

Its steep slope extended almost to the western shoreline, and held nearly a hundred camouflaged cave entrances armed with machine guns and mortars. Like other Japanese defenses, these were connected by an elaborate system of tunnels, one more than a thousand feet long with numerous offshoots that burrowed through the ugly escarpment. The network was lighted by electricity, and where the tunnels merged, two shafts led to the flat summit and provided ventilation and a quick way to move troops from one position to another and to supply ammunition to the bunkered artillery on the mesa's crest.

Marines were on the summit of bypassed Hill 362A, but its sides were infested with pockets of resistance with a clear field of fire on the troops attacking the ridge, behind which was the flattened rubble of Nishi Village's tiny cluster of a half-dozen adobe buildings. It was a strange battle, even for Iwo. When the assault jumped off, Marines were advancing while answering Japanese fire from two directions—ahead toward Nishi Ridge and backward on 362A.

Forty-five hundred men were in the push—three battalions from Chet Graham's 26th Regiment and two from Harry Liversedge's 28th Marines. There was the usual preassault bombardment: thirty minutes of artillery, some heavy naval fire and air strikes. As usual, the Japanese were stunned. But not for long; as soon as the Marines moved out, the enemy answered with devastating firepower.

Tanks spearheaded the thrust of Graham's men, carving out meager gains in the rocky ground in front of the hill. Liversedge's troops, with Chandler Johnson's battalion at the point, advanced in a hail of mortars and small arms fire; it was Suribachi all over again as each yard of headway claimed more casualties. But yard-by-yard gains were made by grinding frontal assault.

Jackson Butterfield's battalion fared better. It was in reserve, mopping up stubborn bypassed positions in the ravines in front of Nishi Ridge, but taking strong crossfire from the elevation and 362-A's caves behind it. Three heavy machine guns were trundled forward to spray the honeycombed face of the ridge, but whenever positions were silenced, more came to life.

Other Shermans made repeated and futile stabs at smothering the firestorm but were bogged down by tank traps and the terrain. Headway was made only after an armored bulldozer and a Sherman with a scraping blade carved a narrow path through the obstacles. As they rumbled forward, Japanese sappers darted from bypassed spider traps with sputtering demolitions charges hurled against the tanks. They detonated in roaring blasts but did little damage; three-inch wooden planks protected the steel hulls and absorbed the impact. Only after a flamethrowing Sherman joined the melee with its tongue of fire was the opposition to the mop-up wiped out.

It was panic-button time for Chandler Johnson's battalion twice during the morning, when mortars crumped down and exploded in heavy clouds of green smoke. Acrid fumes hugged the ground and vomiting men were everywhere along the front. But except for heavy nausea and burning, tear-filled eyes, no harm was done. The mystery gas, probably picric acid, soon dissipated and the fighting went on.

Despite everything, the advance punched forward yard by yard, position by position, until the line was cracked. In early afternoon, 150 well-disciplined Japanese hit the Marines in a desperate counterattack. The charge was beaten back and the assault hammered across the last ravine in front of Nishi Ridge.

Captain Dave Severance's Easy Company, the first outfit atop Suribachi, scrambled to the base and began to dig in. Chandler Johnson wasn't far behind. Throughout the fight he'd moved with the men as he had on D-Day and in the battle for the volcano—oblivious to enemy fire, in tattered fatigue cap with upturned bill, Colt pistol wrapped in a handkerchief and jammed in his hip pocket.

Shortly after two o'clock a spell of quiet had settled on the front as the chunky colonel, grinning like a vacationing tourist, sauntered among the weary men. Some were propped up, backs against boulders, opening C rations. Others cleaned rifles and checked ammunition, grateful to be alive.

One man merrily rode a Japanese bicycle, circling around his amazed buddies and dinging a bell on its handlebars like an ice cream peddler in a park. He had found it in a nearby cave whose steel door had been blasted open half an hour earlier by a bazooka. "Plenty more wheels where this came from," he grinned, "if you guys would like to join the parade." Several men watched a grunting gun crew pulling and pushing a 37-millimeter antitank weapon into firing position.

One grimy, bleary-eyed corporal, his dungarees tattered and stained with sweat and volcanic ash, chuckled loudly as he saw his jaunty, rambunctious colonel approach a shell hole. He was sure Johnson expected to find Marines there: instead, Japanese dead were sprawled in the crater. In that instant, a shell exploded at Chandler Johnson's feet and he was blown to bits.

"One second he was striding along in all his vigor; the next he was in pieces scattered all over the place," said Sergeant Richard Wheeler of the bizarre scene made more bizarre and tragic by the fact that Johnson was probably killed by friendly fire. "The biggest piece we could find was his rib cage," Private First Class Rolla A. Perry told comrades. Private Arthur J. Stanton found the colonel's shirt collar without a drop of blood on it and cut off at the neck as with a pair of sharp scissors. Yards away was a hand and a wrist with a ticking, unscratched watch.

Tears were shed without shame by the men; if they talked, it was with heavy lumps in parched throats. "Sonuvabitch! Fuckin' no good war! He's gone!" one of them managed to mutter. "I can't believe it— the colonel's gone."

Years later, whenever aging survivors of the battalion would meet at Fifth Division reunions, talk invariably would turn to the exploits of Chandler Johnson—the rough-talking, stern but often gentle, always indomitable warrior who had yelled and cursed and led his men across Iwo's strange, blood-stained beaches; who with certainty and pride had sent "his" platoon to Suribachi's summit to raise the first flag; who had sent the second one up the slopes because "some sonuvabitch is going to want that flag, but he's not going to get it." But most of all, these men of Iwo Jima would recall how the colonel died. They still lament his loss.

Major Thomas B. Pearce, the executive officer, took over the stunned outfit, a shadow of its D-Day strength. He wasn't of Johnson's mercurial temperament or flashy flamboyance, but his three medals for valor on New Georgia and Bougainville were solid credentials of fearless and knowledgeable leadership under fire. The men knew "the new Old Man knew his stuff" and were reassured he could handle whatever they might face during the rest of the battle.

They set the perimeter that night knowing the struggle for Nishi Ridge wasn't over, but that Hill 362A was behind them and silenced. Chandler Johnson and the others who were cut down in the day's push were but part of the 212 troops from the Fifth Division who fell that day on Iwo's western front. No one ever knew Japanese losses, but sixty-eight caves were closed and hundreds of enemy bodies were sprawled among the rocks and ravines along the front when darkness came.

Lieutenant Colonel George A. Roll, the Fifth Division's intelligence officer, was especially interested in the body count. "It appears the enemy's losses have become so heavy that he no longer can retrieve his dead and pull them back to caves behind the lines," he wrote in the day's battle journal.

In the fury of D-plus eleven there was no letup in the pressure to shut down the Meat Grinder on the Fourth Division front. But for the first time, General Cates ordered the attack to move in a probing action ninety minutes before the main assault. So at 6:30 A.M. the 25th Regiment's First Battalion jumped off. "Maybe the Nips forgot to set the alarm clock," a sergeant said as the muffled push began to envelop Turkey Knob.

He was wrong; the Japanese weren't duped. For twenty minutes the action appeared to be going well. But instead of surprising the enemy, Fenton Mee's nine hundred men moved into a murderous ambush. From countless hidden positions on the elevation's slopes and crest the Japanese unleashed a thunderstorm of rockets and mortars to pin down the advance. Withering machine gun fire and a hail of grenades clobbered startled Marines as they lunged for cover.

It was the start of the fifth day of combat in an area little larger than three city blocks, dawn-to-dusk slaughter of friend and foe in the ravines in front of the knob, on its devilish slopes, and around the big concrete blockhouse on the summit. Artillery and air support were impossible; bogged-down Marines and enemy positions were too close to one another. Tanks were morale boosters for the attackers, but couldn't uncork the advance until midafternoon.

Eight Shermans, engines roaring and treads grinding foot-deep tracks in the volcanic ash, struggled repeatedly to rekindle the push. They took spasmodic heavy fire from mortars and antitank guns, making scant headway until armored bulldozers carved narrow paths through the rubble. Then, paced by two flamethrowers, the line was dented around the base of Turkey Knob. More than a thousand gallons of jellied fuel incinerated enemy emplacements, and the tanks poured more than two hundred rounds of 75-millimeter cannon fire into the blockhouse.

For a frantic half hour in late afternoon, patrols trying to close a pincers around the knob from opposite directions were less than fifty yards apart. This time tanks couldn't help; the terrain was impassible and heavy artillery was making the area a deathtrap. Riflemen and demolitions teams were caught in merciless machine gun fire as the enemy beat back every attempt to close the narrow gap and seal off the malevolent objective. At 4:30 P.M., a pullback was ordered. Turkey Knob was still not surrounded, and its top was still in Japanese hands.

While the 25th Regiment battered the ring of steel around and on Turkey Knob, Walt Jordan's 24th again hit Hill 382 in a three-battalion attack to drive the last Japanese from the tenacious defenses on the eastern ridge of the fortress. With heavy action already raging six hundred yards to the south in the assault to take the knob, naval bombardment, artillery, and a thirty-plane air strike ripped enemy positions for nearly forty-five minutes before H-Hour at eight o'clock.

The western ridge was held by Roland Carey's Easy Company, an exhausted, hard-hit, half-strength outfit that had worried through strong machine gun, mortar, and grenade harassment in its nightlong vigil on the embattled hilltop. Now the Japanese were counterattacking again across the no man's land separating the two ridges. The Marines hadn't a chance of holding against the superior force without help from men and firepower all but trapped and immobile on the slopes.

Second Lieutenant Richard Reich managed to make the summit

with part of his platoon after thirty minutes of desperate clawing up the sharp rocks and boulders in a sizzling, nonstop firefight. Two platoons of Walter Ridlon's Fox Company were doing their best to follow. Machine guns and mortars were cutting them to pieces, but a few men lunged over the lip of the hill under a curtain of bullets and a hailstorm of grenades.

Carey crawled down a shallow ravine to a shell hole where Reich had taken cover. Ridlon joined them moments later as small arms fire zinged overhead and raised small sand geysers a few feet away. After a three-minute parley, they agreed that their best bet—probably the only way to hold the feeble line—was for Carey to rally the troops stymied on the slopes. Halfway down the hill, in a violent stumblng and sliding descent, he was cut down by a machine gun burst. A corpsman scrambled to his side within minutes, but it was nearly an hour before it was quiet enough for stretcher bearers to drag him from the scene.

Captain Patrick Donlan became Easy Company's CO. But before most men knew he was their commanding officer, Donlan was hit by mortar fire. First Lieutenant Stanley Osborne ignored the continuing barrage to dash to Donlan's side as another mortar dropped in their midst. Osborne was killed in the blast, Donlan's leg was blown off just below the knee, and two other men were wounded, one mortally. Twenty-two-year-old Reich now commanded Easy Company; he was the only officer left.

Most of Fox Company still hugged the incline, pinned down in the frenetic fight for survival. "The sonsabitchin' Nips are doing their goddamned best to make this the worst day of my life," twenty-five-year-old Ridlon told James Bedingfield, his twenty-year-old platoon sergeant, as the men struggled against a concentration of pillboxes blocking their route to the summit.

Nothing less than superhuman individual drive finally sprung the Marines from a torn clump of stunted banyan trees and the rubble of boulders just below the crest. Shortly after 3:30 P.M., when the push was six hours old, Ridlon sent a message to the battalion CP at the foot of the slope: "Almost to the high ground!" For the next half hour the walkie-talkie was silent, then it crackled: "Fox Company on top of radar hill!" Nearly two hundred Marines were now on the summit of 382. But they couldn't claim that the violent fortress had been conquered; only that they were atop it with more men and arms and that, as one said, "you can bet your sweet ass we intend to stay."

It was a nervous, noisy night along the thin line on 382's western ridge. First Lieutenant William Crecink, a platoon leader from Fox Company, now commanded Easy Company, its fifth CO in ten hours. He was certain the men would hold. "We haven't exactly got it made," he told Thomas Cottick, his inherited platoon sergeant, "but after the hell on the hill, we can take anything the bastard Nips can throw at us." The scene was again nightmarish as parachute flares lit up the violent front and cast eerie shadows from the toppled, twisted girders of the radar tower.

Tracer bullets laced the skyline as enemy machine guns clattered spasmodically and were answered by Marine bursts. Artillery, mortars, and grenades fell throughout the night on both sides of the lines. At times Marines could hear the muffled sounds of Japanese moving through the maze of tunnels under the fortress to reinforce and resupply positions to meet the next inevitable attack. And so it went for the ten hours of darkness.

Kuribayashi and his staff were busy during the night moving the general's headquarters from its deep concrete blockhouse east of the third airstrip to a vast cave near Kitano Point, where he would make his last stand. And Marine stretcher bearers and jeep ambulances carried the last of the day's 610 Fourth Division casualties from the front—207 to the cemetery in the shadow of Mount Suribachi.

7

General Schmidt ordered a change in the battle plan on D-plus twelve. He directed that the Fifth Division relieve the Third Division troops in the attack on Hill 362B. It wasn't that the Fifth Corps commander was upset with the Third's headway against the position; rather, he wanted General Erskine's firepower for a steamroller offensive to drive to Iwo's northern shore. This would split the island in the central highlands once and for all, and cut off Kuribayashi's remaining forces from each other: one isolated on the western front and the other on the eastern.

Flying in crisscross patterns from five hundred to a thousand feet over the front, Marine spotters in Maytag Messerschmitts watched the attack come to life in brilliant, chilly sunlight. Theirs was a familiar spectacle on Iwo, but totally foreign to anything else in military history. Below them was a battlefield where one army fought above ground, and the other fought almost totally beneath it; where thousands of troops moved in the same area at the same time, Marines maneuvering on the surface in the attack, the Japanese moving in tunnels from one underground strongpoint to another whenever the tide of combat called for more firepower or reinforcements.

Clearly visible were battalions of Marines crouching in foxholes and waiting for the signal to attack. When it came, they could be seen moving out in small units—fire teams and squads darting forward from cover to cover, from shell hole to shell hole, from boulder to boulder as increasingly heavy barrages of Japanese artillery and mortars landed among them.

Everything beyond the line was completely barren and devoid of any sign of enemy troops—a rugged, uninhabited landscape as mysterious as a solar planet.

There were thirty minutes of preattack naval and artillery shelling; "just enough to wake up the Nips and let 'em know we were coming again," a sergeant said with undisguised sarcasm as the push began, pointed toward yet another forbidding hill some five hundred yards east of 362B—an ugly elevation carried on the sector map as Hill 375. It was the last high ground astride the Third Division route to the north coast and, according to intelligence reports based on a captured map, bristled with at least a thousand troops waiting in yet another maze of fortifications and tunnels.

Colonel Withers's 21st Regiment learned within minutes that intelligence was correct. With two battalions, George Flood's First and George Percy's Second, in the assault, it became what the ex-stockbroker called a "gigantic back-fence cat fight, only the cats were snarling and deadly tigers." From dawn to dusk, the Marines battled in the vicious complex of caves, bunkers, pillboxes, and dug-in tanks concealed in a chaotic jumble of torn rocks in front of and on the precipitous hill.

To make matters stickier, Percy's men were taking heavy machine gun and small arms fire from Hill 362B in the adjacent Fifth Division sector. But enemy artillery and mortar shelling weren't as fierce as in the past; probably, intelligence officers speculated, Kuribayashi was hoarding precious, rapidly diminishing ammunition for a massive last-ditch counterattack.

Tanks, when they could churn through the rocky defiles, knocked out some strongpoints in the early going, but were unable to break through to spark the advance. So, in Iwo's constant pattern, it was another infantry slugging match every yard of the way as enemy positions were overrun in costly head-on assault.

Thus, by eleven o'clock, after four hours of close-in combat, Percy's determined skirmishers hacked out four hundred yards to the base of Hill 357. By noon, a patrol clawed to the crest, a signal for a screaming surge up the slope by the rest of the battalion. The hill was captured.

"Although deadly battle was still in progress," the official combat report said, "it now appeared that no important enemy resistance remained to block the Third Division's path to the sea." Like most projections of Japanese staying power on Iwo, this one missed the mark as still-to-come bitter fighting and heavy casualties would prove.

That night Kuribayashi's troops mounted a final charge to drive Percy's men from the crest of Hill 357. Shortly after 1:30 A.M., two hundred infiltrators struck in a well-organized raid. It began as a probing action with suicide squads hitting outposts in front of the line, and quickly exploded into a string of full-scale counterattacks.

Bleary-eyed but alert Marines opened fire when they heard muffled sounds of movement and spotted shadowy forms darting among the boulders. Within minutes, the firefight roared with all the firepower the Marines could muster cutting into the screaming swarm of Japanese. For the next hour and a half, wave after wave of enemy troops were beaten back with bayonets, knives, and entrenching tools in hand-to-hand combat fought in the glare of star shells and in the stinking sulphur fumes that hugged the ground in nauseating patches.

At dawn, Marines counted 163 Japanese bodies strewn along the lines. "I must confess I thought it was a grand sight," Percy said, "but the bastards killed or wounded nineteen of our people and I sure as hell didn't like that."

March 3, D-plus twelve, was a day of incredible violence and unbelievable heroism for the Fifth Division. It became, in General Rockey's words, "a legacy of valor." Five men received the Medal of Honor, and 519 fell in the maelstrom as Marines finally took Nishi

Ridge, blasted through the flattened rubble of the village, and hammered two hundred yards beyond.

Twenty-two-year-old William G. Harrell, a sergeant from Mercedes, Texas, was on outpost duty twenty yards in front of the lines before Nishi Ridge with Private First Class Andrew J. Carter, nineteen, a lanky Kentuckian from Paducah. They'd shared a foxhole every night since D-Day and were dug in, bone tired from the day's action and shivering from Iwo's cutting chill. If trouble came from infiltrators, and they expected it would, they'd catch it first.

Carter, called "the Duke" by buddies, was on watch shortly after midnight when he spotted silhouettes darting among the boulders in the half-light of a parachute flare. He nudged the slumbering Harrell. "They're coming out of the ravine," he whispered, and opened fire as Harrell rolled to his knees. "Got four of 'em," Carter said, still speaking in hushed tones.

Harrell fired twice at two forms vaulting forward from the shadow of a ravine, and saw the figures crumple. The Duke jammed a fresh clip of ammunition into his weapon and squeezed off three shots before it jammed. "Sonuvabitch," he muttered. "The fuckin' sand fucks up everything!" He jumped to his feet. "Be right back! I'll get another rifle and more ammo," he said, disappearing in the darkness.

Moments later, a hand grenade rolled over the lip of the foxhole and exploded. Harrell was covered with dirt and felt the warm ooze of blood soaking through his dungarees. His left leg buckled as he tried to get up; he couldn't move his left arm. Falling backward, he felt an unseen body slip into the hole. "Bill, I'm back" came the Duke's hushed voice. "What's wrong?" "I'm hit! Grenade! Bad, I guess!"

Harrell was trying to reload his carbine with one hand when two Japanese sprang from the ravine. One was swinging a long saber with both hands, and the other was hurling grenades as the Duke triggered his borrowed weapon. It misfired. Split-second instinct took over. He grabbed an enemy rifle, a prized souvenir he'd carried since D-Day, and lunged to his feet to meet the sword-wielding intruder who impaled himself in a screeching yell on the bayonet. He died with the saber still in its violent down swing. It sliced deep into Carter's left knuckles from thumb to little finger.

Harrell, now firing his Colt .45, saw geysers of blood explode from the second man's head as he was cut down in midstride. Neither Marine spoke for a few seconds. Carter was wounded and without a weapon; Harrell was certain he was dying. The valiant Texan broke the wordless spell. "Duke, you still alive?" he asked. "Yeah, Sarge. I'm alive but the bastard almost cut off my hand." Carter responded. "What the hell do we do now?"

A full-fledged firefight roared around them as the entire line came to life. Machine gun tracers cut amber arches through the night and the sharp crack of rifles added to the action. Mortars seemed to be falling everywhere and artillery joined the crescendo. Grenades exploded every few seconds.

"Duke, I don't think I'll make it," Harrell, the senior man, said. "There's no use in both of us dying here. Get your ass back to the CP and stay there," he ordered.

"You're the boss. But I'll be back with help." Carter clasped the bleeding hand to his chest, eased over the lip of the foxhole, and crawled back to the perimeter.

Never in his life had Harrell felt so completely alone. He was in awful pain, bleeding profusely from more wounds than he could count, and he could see in the fading glare of a star shell that his left hand hung like a lifeless claw from tendons at the wrist. He didn't expect Carter to return. He'd be lucky to make it alive back to the lines. But it was lonely as hell, propped up like a stringless puppet, waiting to die. He hoped the enemy would just forget about him.

It was not to be. He hardly had time to think about his fate when a Japanese plummeted into the hole, the two men's heads scarcely a yard apart. Another intruder crouched on the rim as his comrade slammed a grenade against his helmet to activate it, dropped the missile at the Marine's feet, and vaulted from the deathtrap. He had taken one stride toward the ravine when Harrell's pistol cracked and the Japanese dropped with an agonizing scream. The Marine grabbed the hissing grenade and dropped it on the lip of the hole. The blast killed the other Japanese, obliterated Harrell's Colt .45, and blew off his right hand.

No more Japanese came. As daylight cut through dawn's dull sky, the Duke returned with stretcher bearers and they carried the semiconscious, half-alive sergeant back to the lines for evacuation. The saber of one of the Japanese, later identified as a captain, was beside him on the litter.

Marines that morning tallied twelve enemy bodies within yards of the outpost in front of Nishi Ridge where Harrell earned his Medal of Honor. With mechanical hooks for hands, he later returned to Texas A & M College, where he had studied for two years before enlisting, to get his degree and later to run cattle on a ranch with another Texan, Private First Class Louis Boling, from a tiny town called Donna.

Pharmacist's Mate Third Class Jack Williams was a corpsman with the 28th Regiment's Third Battalion. The slight, slow-talking twenty-year-old was from Harrison, Arkansas, a sleepy town in the Ozark mountains in the state's northwest corner, a harsh land of hardscrabble farming and timber logging. He'd joined the Navy two years earlier with no thought of ending up as a combat medic with the Marines. "I'm just a hillbilly who wants to get away from the hills, maybe fight a few Japs, and see the world," he told friends the day he boarded a bus for Little Rock on the first leg of the long trip that ultimately would lead to Iwo Jima.

Williams had lost count of how many wounded men he'd treated since D-Day. Sometimes he believed it must have been most of the battalion—a thought not far from fact, since nearly four hundred of its original 954 men had been killed or wounded since hitting Green Beach. Now he was at it again with his satchel of bandages, sulfa, plasma, and morphine as the D-plus twelve attack pushed north from Nishi Ridge.

Of all of Iwo's terrain, this was the most fiendish in its natural defenses and had been made all but impregnable by man-made fortifications. Upheavals in the island's thin volcanic crust littered the zone with hundreds of large sandstone boulders surrounded by carpets of loose rock where the Japanese had dug countless caves with concealed entrances connected by tunnels extending several hundred yards in all directions.

A complex of eroded gorges, whose steep sides bristled with machine gun nests and sniper pits, covered the area. Fields of fire were usually less than twenty-five yards, and Marines had little cover from enemy fire unless they piled loose rocks on the surface.

Hill 362B, which had stymied the Third Division's attack for two days, was now the roadblock to the Fifth Division advance. Its slopes and crest still bristled despite the tons of artillery and naval bombardment. The battleground was made to order for Kuribayashi's forces and they were making the most of it.

Since the jump-off at 7:45 A.M., Williams had braved stifling enemy fire to do what he could to save fourteen Marines. Five others were dead by the time he reached them. The corpsmen was crouched in a shallow hole treating yet another man shortly before noon when a sniper opened up at short range. Three bullets tore into Williams's abdomen and groin. But he finished bandaging his comrade before trying to halt the gushing hemorrhage from his own belly wounds. Then, ignoring searing pain and fighting to keep from blacking out, Williams patched up another Marine.

Sniper fire ricocheted among the rocks of the exposed position as he weighed the odds against survival for himself and the other wounded men. There was only one chance and it was a long shot. He had to get back to the lines somehow and send out stretcher bearers. Otherwise, all three certainly would bleed to death or die in a storm of sniper bullets.

Clasping both arms around his stomach, Williams struggled to his feet and, in an agonizing lurch, headed for help. He'd taken two steps when a single rifle shot ripped through his chest and he fell dead. It was nearly sundown before a patrol reached the scene. Miraculously, the other two Marines were still alive. Volcanic ash had helped coagulate their bleeding and they survived to recount the gallantry and self-sacrifice that brought Williams a posthumous Medal of Honor.

Another Fifth Division corpsman, Pharmacist's Mate Second Class George Wahlen of Ogden, Utah, also earned the nation's highest decoration that day. By all rights, the twenty-year-old shouldn't have been at the front; he'd been wounded twice by mortar fragments, each time seriously enough to be evacuated. Instead, he'd talked his way back to the lines after being treated at the division hospital. "Christ, Doc, I'm not hurt that bad and I'm a damned good corpsman," he told a surgeon. "And besides, my outfit needs men; there's just three medics left in the battalion."

So here he was with the 26th Regiment's Second Battalion in the fight for Hill 362B, and it was a very busy day. When the attack began, it quickly moved three hundred yards across relatively undefended flat terrain. But then the Marines found themselves in the same mishmash of rugged gorges and jutting outcrops of rocks that bedeviled the assault of the 28th Marines, a zone where Japanese reaction was bitter and close-in.

Wahlen was in the vortex of the struggle. "Fierce hand-to-hand combat raged and flamethrowers, bazookas, and hand grenades were the principal weapons used in this jungle of stone," the day's battle report said. Time after time, Wahlen answered the urgent call for help from a fallen Marine: "Corpsman! Corpsman! Over here!" Wahlen's dungarees were in tatters, his satchel of dressings and drugs nearly empty when he was cut down by a fusilade of small arms fire from pointblank range. He continued to crawl forward toward another wounded Marine. But it was a futile gesture. Wahlen collapsed in a pool of his own blood and moved no more.

There was no logical explanation for Wahlen's survival. Perhaps it was a will to live, an indomitable and bottomless well of determination and faith. Considering the extent of his wounds, there were no other answers. The valorous medic still was conscious when comrades managed to reach him half an hour later.

"I was beginning to think you guys had missed the train," he said with a feeble smile as they placed him on a litter and headed for the rear under a heavy mortar barrage. Wahlen was in a hilltop hospital on Guam when, three months later, he learned of his Medal of Honor. "Ain't that something," he said to the doctor who brought the news.

Less than five hundred yards from where Wahlen was hit, a corporal from Quincy, Massachusetts, had been pinned down with his outfit for most of three hours in the same fight. William R. Caddy was nineteen, a well-regarded, somewhat boisterous youth who was proud of a recent promotion to assistant squad leader and liked Marine Corps life most of the time, but was still undecided about becoming a career Leatherneck. He had all the qualifications: expert rifleman, solid but wiry physique; a strong sense of discipline; ingrained qualities of leadership; and above all, a complete dedication to his comrades—a devotion that would earn for him the Medal of Honor and claim his life.

Shortly after 4:00 P.M., Caddy was slouched with two other men in a shell hole near the base of the hill. His back was against one of the sandy sides of the crater. He was gasping for breath, shaking with a combination of fear and exhaustion, and wondering what would happen next.

Small arms fire snorted overhead, and mortars and grenades exploded yards away in no man's land. One Marine had squirmed to the lip of the hole, trying to spot an especially bothersome sniper's nest and the other sat shivering and bleary-eyed at the bottom.

Only Caddy saw the Japanese hand grenade arch through the air and fall in their midst. Without a word, he lunged on top of the hissing missile and took its full blast in the chest and stomach. "He smothered the explosion with his body, protecting his comrades from serious injury," the corporal's Medal of Honor citation would read, and it would be framed and hung alongside the coveted posthumous decoration in his parents' home.

Corporal Charles J. Berry was a slender, blue-eyed, high-voiced twenty-one-year-old fire team leader from Lorain, Ohio, a bustling blue-collar industrial suburb of Cleveland. As a teen-ager, he had worked at catch-as-catch-can jobs before joining the Marines. He'd looked forward to combat duty since boot camp days, and was known to his buddies as "one gung-ho Gyrene."

Since the 8:30 A.M. jump-off, Berry's outfit—the First Battalion of the 28th Regiment—had experienced nothing but misery in the convoluted gorges north and west of the rubble of Nishi Ridge. Expected air support was scrubbed at the last minute by a sudden deluge of rain and low-hanging clouds. Tanks couldn't operate in the quagmire, and artillery spotters couldn't find targets because of poor visibility. Rifles clogged and wouldn't fire because of the muck, but dug-in Japanese were protected from the elements and methodically cut down more Marines each time they ventured from cover. By late afternoon, the advance was less than one hundred yards and claimed more than a hundred casualties. Darkness came quickly, and patches of ground-hugging fog mixed with steaming sulphur mists to make the night perfect for enemy infiltration.

Berry and two other riflemen dug a foxhole atop the edge of one of the gorges that crisscrossed the sector, and settled in for their thirteenth night on Iwo. Two men could try to sleep while the third stood watch. But sleep was impossible in the intermittent clatter of small arms and machine gun fire and the occasional salvos from friendly and enemy artillery. When there was a lull, Berry and his comrades could hear Japanese troops moving from one position to another and see figures scooting among the rocks when an exploding star shell penetrated the overcast.

Just after 2:00 A.M., one of the Marines nudged Berry and whispered: "Here come the fuckin' Nips." An instant later a fusillade of bullets ripped into the backside of the foxhole. Then came a hailstorm of grenades and one rolled over the parapet.

Berry reacted without a thought of survival, covered it with his body, and died in its explosion. The Japanese didn't bother the foxhole for the rest of the night as the firefight ebbed and flowed. Just after daybreak, litter bearers removed the wounded Marines and Berry's body from the blood-spattered outpost. There were few survivors among the one-hundred-plus infiltrators who had hit the zone; ninety-seven enemy bodies were counted the next morning. Chuck Berry's buddies didn't think this evened the score for his loss—but his posthumous Medal of Honor would help.

Another of the men who had scaled Suribachi to raise the first flag, Platoon Sergeant Ernest Thomas, was killed that day. His folks in Tallahassee, Florida, knew he'd become part of a new Marine Corps legend when they heard his voice on a live NBC broadcast from the *Estes* a few hours after the historic event. "Howlin' Mad" Smith had arranged it; he wanted to personally commend the twenty-year-old warrior and pass along a grateful "well done" to all hands. The young man soft-pedaled his own heroism, but had words of highest praise for the platoon and all of Easy Company. "They're the best outfit in the Marine Corps," he told the nationwide audience.

Before returning to the beach, Thomas availed himself of a slice of life he'd all but forgotten existed—a hot fresh-water shower and a full meal, including two heaping slabs of ice cream. Once ashore, he trudged back to the lines, somewhat embarrassed by sudden fame.

Now, nine days later, Easy Company was battling to take an unnamed ridge north of Nishi Village, and Thomas and his platoon were pinned down. He'd just picked up a field phone to call for tank support when a bullet tore through his head. Corporal Harold Keller, the farmer from Brooklyn, Iowa, who had been on Suribachi with the sergeant, was crouched at his side. "As was so often the case, there was no telling where the shot came from," Keller said. On Iwo Jima death came from all directions.

When maps were updated that night under the glare of a hissing Coleman lantern in General Rockey's blacked-out CP tent, front lines in the Fifth Division sector showed gains of from one hundred and fifty to six hundred yards. "Not much to brag about," the general remarked to aides in his characteristically laconic manner, "but the men did one hell of a job." He paused for several seconds, closed his eyes, massaged them with right thumb and forefinger, and spoke again. "I don't know how they can do it day after day," he said. "I guess it's because they're Marines."

Rockey was deeply troubled and compassionately concerned about the suffering of his troops and their mushrooming casualties. Time and again he had lamented "the tragic losses of these fine, brave young men," and wondered when it would end. He was especially distressed about the plight of Chet Graham's 26th Regiment—it had lost more than half of the 3,256 officers and men who had landed on D-Day.

But the first glimmer of hope was beginning to emerge: a vague indication that the worst *might* be coming to an end on the Fifth Division front. Despite the intensity of the day's fighting, the minor advances, and the heavy toll of fallen Marines, there had been a discernible shift in Japanese reaction: no signs that the enemy was about to quit, but torrents of artillery and mortars hadn't hammered assault troops with the previous ferocity.

This didn't mean that frontal attack against Japanese positions would be any less violent for the Marines, or claim fewer casualties in still-to-come fighting. It meant only that the enemy was cutting back on his use of artillery and mortars in the Fifth Division front, and shifting to more desperate close-in, position-by-position, man-to-man combat—if that were possible in light of the savagery of what had come before.

Rockey's determined attackers, it now appeared, had at last torn the seam of Kuribayashi's fanatic defenses on Iwo's western front, and Erskine's hard-hit Third Division had breached the line in the center of the island. But it was a different story with Cates's Fourth Division. For the sixth day it was locked in the continuing butchery of the Meat Grinder.

At 6:30 A.M., shortly after dawn, Walt Jordan's 24th Marines moved out again; to complete, it was hoped, the conquest of Hill 382. Walt Wensinger's 23rd Regiment once more tackled Turkey Knob with the same expectation. The attack jumped off without bombardment or air strikes in an attempt to catch the enemy off guard.

Some men of Walt Ridlon's Fox Company were atop Hill 382 and others were still on the slopes sealing off bypassed caves and pillboxes with flamethrowers and demolitions. The captain and about twenty men on the crest were on an innocent-looking mound and taking small arms fire and mortars when the knoll began to rumble and shake like an earthquake. They were on the roof of a camouflaged bunker and its cannon now was roaring as rapidly as it could be fed 75-millimeter shells. The Japanese weren't firing at the Marines trying to take the hill, but at the cluttered beachhead two miles away. Startled Marines demolished the position with satchel charges and grenades tossed through its narrow aperture.

At first the push made gratifying headway, both on the summit and the sides of the hill. But then the fighting ground down to Iwo's conventional style of combat. "As had been true throughout the operation," the day's battle report said, "only through the slow and tedious maneuver of infantry teams employing demolitions, flamethrowers, bazookas, and hand grenades could such a stronghold be reduced. This type of fighting required able and aggressive leadership at the small-unit level, and the high casualty rate among junior officers and noncommissioned officers seriously retarded this progress."

Bill Crecink, the young lieutenant who had taken over the remnants of Easy Company, was a case in point. He was wounded and evacuated under heavy fire shortly before 9:00 A.M. There were countless other examples of the losses cutting down front-line officers. Dick Reich, the twenty-three-year-old "Johnny-on-the-spot," shavetail lieutenant, took over the company until Captain Charles Ireland arrived. Ireland was shot in the left leg ninety minutes later and was carried to the rear.

Reich took over again until Captain Robert M. O'Mealia, a regimental bandmaster, came forward. He was killed by a mortar blast within minutes. Now there was no reason for Reich to take command another time. Easy Company, Second Battalion, 24th Regiment, Fourth Marine Division no longer existed. The Meat Grinder had chewed it to pieces and its twelve surviving, exhausted, bewildered, stupefied, dirty, bleary-eyed men were merged into Fox Company.

Turkey Knob, the Amphitheater, and Minami Village continued to take their toll of the 25th Regiment in fighting that was relentless. A four-room blockhouse, with thick walls and roof of reinforced concrete, still sprouted defiance after almost a week of close-in combat. Mines were strewn in every approach to the structure and made tank operation almost impossible until the way was cleared by demolitions teams. The inverted bowl of the Amphitheater held a network of blockhouses, pillboxes, and caves that had to be demolished one at a time. The leveled cluster of huts of Minami still contained deadly sniper nests and mortar pits.

By noon the attack had become another slugging match. Throughout the afternoon demolitions men and bazooka teams worked over caves and bypassed bunkers and pillboxes. Shermans braved narrow, twisting, mine-infested paths to support the push. An almost constant stream of artillery blasted enemy positions barely a hundred yards in front of Marine lines. But riflemen again were the hammerhead and gains came at heavy cost.

When the Marines took up final positions for the night, the deepest penetration in the Amphitheater was some three hundred yards. Minami remained defiant, and the blockhouse atop Turkey Knob still was held by the Japanese. But Walt Ridlon's men on Hill 382 had pushed across the no man's land on the summit and moved down its eastern slopes.

"We'll close the Meat Grinder for good tomorrow," General Cates told aides that night as he took a final look at the sector map. Then he shaved with an heirloom straight razor and quickly went to sleep in his sandbagged revetment command post, oblivious of occasional enemy artillery and mortars falling nearby.

8

Dawn came slowly to Iwo on March 4, D-Day plus thirteen. Clouds hung low over the island and a chilly rain was falling. Poor visibility canceled air strikes from the carriers and artillery spotting missions by the Maytag Messerschmitts. For the same reason there was very little naval gunfire for fear of its landing on Marine lines. But the morning's attack was mounted nonetheless. It began at 7:30 A.M..

Three hours earlier seventy-three Army B-29 Superforts, taking off at thirty-second intervals, had roared down the three-mile-long coral-surfaced runways on Saipan and Guam. In close formations at 35,000 feet, the bombers flew directly over Iwo Jima for another high-altitude raid on the Tokyo area, now almost a daily occurrence. Crewmen could make out the island through breaks in the sodden clouds and see the flash and smoke from occasional artillery shells exploding behind enemy lines.

Raymond Fred Malo, a first lieutenant from Danville, Illinois, was at the controls of the lead bomber in an early wave. This was the third mission over the Japanese homeland for the twenty-four-old aircraft commander and the ten-man crew of *Dinah Might*. They had flown to Saipan from the States five weeks earlier after completing combat training to become part of the Army Air Corps' ever-increasing attacks against Japan's heartland.

Just after 11:30 the B-29s began their bomb runs. It was more than thirty degrees below zero at the six-mile altitude. Heavy anti-aircraft fire laced the formations, but only a few Japanese interceptors could reach the attackers. So far the Superforts were having an easy time of it.

"Bombs away!" Second Lieutenant Lee R. Escham of Warren, Ohio, shouted over the plane's intercom as its ten tons of explosives fell earthward, tumbling end over end toward the target area, an aircraft plant southwest of Tokyo. "I think we hit the bastards good," he added as an afterthought.

"That takes care of that," Malo said to Second Lieutenant Edwin Mockler, his copilot from Park Falls, Wisconsin. "Now let's get the hell out of here and head for home." A near miss from antiaircraft fire rocked the bomber as Malo put it into a steep turn and headed south toward the Marianas.

Then from bombardier Eschman: "The goddamned bomb bay doors won't close!" He slammed the control lever again. Still no movement. Squirming to the rear of his cramped quarters in the plexiglass nose of the plane, Eschman peered through a heavily frosted porthole into the cavernous bomb bay. "I can't see any damage from ack-ack," he reported. "I think the fuckin' doors are frozen open!"

Now Malo's voice crackled over the intercom. "No sweat," he assured the crew. "As long as we can hold this altitude, we won't have to worry about Nip fighters, and the antiaircraft fire already is behind us." His eyes scanned the fuel gauges. "It'll be a long, slow trip back to Saipan, and we've got enough gas to make it." But Malo knew, despite his confident words, something the crew suspected—luck would have to fly with *Dinah Might* for nearly fourteen hundred miles if they were to survive.

Malo immediately throttled back to conserve fuel. This and strong headwinds cut the bomber's speed to under two hundred miles an hour and it was soon a lonely speck in the sky, far behind faster formations on a course that would take it just east of Iwo. Three hours from Japan, and twenty minutes north of the island, a red light flashed above the gauges to the main wing gasoline tanks.

Malo said nothing to the crew. Still no sweat, he told himself, but it was time to switch to the thousand-gallon reserve tank. When he flipped the transfer valve, nothing happened. Copilot Mockler watched what went on and saw the anxious look on the plane commander's face. "Now it's time to sweat," Malo said. *Dinah Might* had fuel to stay aloft less than half an hour.

Malo had two options. He could ditch at sea and hope he and his crew would be picked up by a Catalina flying boat, or maybe a destroyer or submarine on picket duty. Or he could try a landing on Iwo Jima. Neither was inviting. As B-29 crewmen were prone to put it: "Once you ditch you have two chances to survive: 'Slim' and none at all and 'Slim' just left town." Malo knew the battle still raged on Iwo and that no disabled Superforts had yet landed on the island.

"Let's give Iwo a call anyway," he told the radioman, Sergeant James C. Cox. "Maybe if we're luckier than hell we can get in there." Cox switched on his transmitter and called "Gatepost," the code word for air-sea rescue operations.

Aboard the *Auburn*, Radioman Second Class J. William Welsh heard the signal. It so far had been an uneventful Sunday for him. Rain and heavy mist had canceled all carrier missions, the purpose for monitoring the emergency channel, and he had just finished the crossword puzzle in the ship's mimeographed daily newspaper. Now Welsh was about to set in motion a chain reaction that would continue until the war's end. The real purpose of Iwo's bloody battle, what the invasion and fighting were all about, was about to unfold for the first time—the saving of American lives instead of taking them.

"This is Gatepost," Welsh responded. "Who are you? What's your problem? Can we help?" Cox's answer: "We're a B-29 low on fuel. Can you give us a bearing for Iwo and can we land there?"

"Roger," Welsh answered. "We'll get a fix on your position and see if the airstrip can take you." The *Auburn*'s radar and direction finder pinpointed the Superfort in less than a minute. Major J. B. Bertelling, the duty communications officer, alerted all hands aboard ship and the radio room was jammed almost immediately. A Catalina flying boat took off from near the eastern base of Suribachi into the overcast but clearing skies to be ready to rescue survivors if the bomber ditched.

Auburn's transmitter crackled with Welsh's calm words: "You are thirty miles north of Iwo Jima. You should be able to see Kita Jima."

"We have it in sight, Gatepost! We see it!"

"Roger. Your course for Iwo is 167 degrees. Do you want to ditch offshore or try a landing?"

Malo cut in: "We'd prefer to land, thank you."

"Roger, we'll clear bulldozers off the strip for you. But watch out for enemy antiaircraft and mortar fire."

Ten minutes later on the *Auburn*'s crowded bridge, anxious eyes spotted the slow-flying B-29 through binoculars approaching Iwo from the northwest below the scudding overcast at seven hundred feet. *Dinah Might* buzzed the island in two low-level passes while Malo scanned cockpit instruments and studied his final approach. There was no letup in the battlefront action. But Marines and Seabees on the fringe of the airstrip followed the plane's sweeping circle as it swung around, banked steeply west of Suribachi's summit, and lined up on the north-south runway of Motoyama Number One.

Less than a hundred feet from the ground Malo lowered flaps and landing gear. Then the B-29 slammed hard onto the packed volcanic earth, bounced twice, and stayed on the runway as Malo jammed the brakes and reversed thrust of the four-bladed propellers to slow the skidding plane. A cloud of dust billowed behind *Dinah Might*, careening along the airstrip and screeching to a stop at the northern tip—but not before its left wing crumpled a telephone pole.

As Malo swung the plane into a fast turn and taxied toward Suribachi at near take-off speed, Japanese gunners from beyond Motoyama Number Two hit the runway with a barrage of ineffective mortar fire. Hundreds of Marines and Seabees watched the plane come to a halt with propellers still turning. They swarmed around the sixty-ton giant, cheering and waving as the crew tumbled from escape hatches.

"One hatch opened and four or five men jumped and fell to their hands and knees," Private First Class Frank L. Crowe of Cambridge, Massachusetts, recalled. "What a contrast! Here were men so glad to be on the island that they were kissing it. A mile or two to the north were three Marine divisions who thought the place was hell on earth, its ground not even good enough to spit on."

Half an hour later, the faulty transfer valve had been repaired and gas again flowed to the engines. Bomb bay doors had closed in flight, the mechanism unfrozen once the aircraft descended to lower altitude. With grateful smiles and hearty handshakes, the Army fliers declined a chorus of Marine invitations to "spend the night on lovely Iwo Jima" and swung aboard the aircraft. It was midafternoon and they wanted to be on Saipan before sundown.

Malo started the engines, taxied onto the runway, and the bomber started to move, slowly at first, then faster and faster with dust churning in its wake. The Japanese opened up with antiaircraft fire as *Dinah Might* became airborne, banked steeply to the right, and disappeared into a cloud bank.

Dinah Might was back on Iwo again on April 12, heavily damaged in a low-level fire-bomb raid on Tokyo. A quick fix was impossible and Sergeant Robert W. Bracket was left with the aircraft until major repairs could be made. Malo, Mockler, Eschman, Cox, and the rest of the crew were flown back to the Marianas and assigned to other Superforts. All were dead within six weeks, shot down in flames over Honshu Island or killed in a blazing take-off crash on Tinian. Bracket survived the war and *Dinah Might* ended its days on a warplane scrap heap in Arizona.

"To the Marines, Iwo looked like the ugliest place on earth," Bob Sherrod wrote, "but B-29 pilots who made emergency landings there called it the most beautiful." One crew flew eleven missions against Japan in three months following the battle's end, and found a haven on Iwo five times. "Whenever I land on the island, I thank God and the Marines who fought for it," the plane's commander said. During early summer of 1945, when the B-29 offensive against the enemy home islands was at its peak, an average of twenty Superforts made emergency landings daily on Motoyama Number One.

Within a week after *Dinah Might*'s in-and-out visit, the airstrip was handling a dawn-to-dusk flow of air evacuation flights—sometimes as many as twenty-five a day. While most casualties still were going to the Marianas aboard the *Samaritan* or *Solace*, air evacuation to many seriously wounded was, in the words of Valentine Hollingsworth, "a godsend and a miracle."

Hollingsworth was a front-line artillery observer, a strapping second lieutenant from York, Maine, who had been hit twice by sniper fire that shattered his left leg. Within minutes a jeep ambulance had him at the Third Division hospital for surgery, plasma, and morphine. An hour later he was flying to Guam. Five hours after being cut down near Motoyama Village, he was recovering in a Navy hospital nearly seven hundred miles from the battleground. Prospects for survival of the wounded had changed decidedly for the better since the early fighting.

Commander Clarence A. Keller piloted the first hospital plane to land on Iwo. He brought in his twin-engined Douglas transport *Peg O' My Heart* shortly after dawn on March 3.

He was skittish about setting down among the bulldozers and trucks scraping and patching the runway and had trouble seeing the strip through the clouds of dust they churned up. The landing was bumpy and jostled the cargo of drugs, plasma, a ton of mail, a doctor, a corpsman, and a civilian passenger.

A communications jeep, with a windsock flapping on a pole wired to its rear bumper, led the plane to the shelter of a revetment below a cliff at the northern end of Motoyama Number One's north-south runway where Keller shut down the motors near the Third Division hospital.

Marines were flabbergasted when they saw the first person to jump from the plane. It was Barbara Finch, a correspondent for Reuters, the British news service, who somehow had wangled a bucket seat among the litters and cargo. She was dressed in a nurse's khaki uniform of slacks and blouse—a petite blonde; an aggressive, smooth-talking, competent Australian who had written about the Marines since the early south Pacific days with husband Percy, who later would co-author "Howlin' Mad" Smith's autobiography.

Corporal Joe Purcell, a *Leatherneck* correspondent from Boston, was among the gaggle of curious Marines. He was a long-time friend of the Finches and didn't know whether to embrace or upbraid Barbara for being on Iwo while Japanese shells continued to drop with regularity on the airstrip.

"What the hell are you doing here?" he yelled just as mortar fire started to pepper the area. They ducked through the flaps of a tent where casualties were awaiting evacuation. An unappreciative surgeon unceremoniously shoved them outside and into a sandbagged foxhole. "Goddamnit, woman, get down on your face and stay there!" he ordered. "And you, Corporal, make goddamned sure she does!" The doctor had enough problems without having to worry about having a female civilian around who could get wounded or killed.

Thirty minutes later twelve Marine casualties had been strapped into the plane's litters and *Peg O' My Heart* was airborne with its unwelcome passenger, headed for the Marianas. When Nimitz heard of the episode back on Guam, Navy public relations men, who had given approval for Mrs. Finch's adventure, were dressed down in no uncertain terms in a display of anger seldom shown by the admiral. A few days later he had all but forgotten the matter, but was concerned by the fact that by then other women were making regular in-and-out flying trips to the battleground.

Most were Navy nurses, but one was Dickey Chappelle, a photographer and writer on assignment from the Red Cross to do pictures and stories on the use of whole blood to treat casualties. On Iwo, she was to begin a reciprocated love affair with the Marines that would endure until she was killed in Vietnam. She triggered a land mine while covering that war in 1965, the only American woman correspondent ever to die in battle.

Ensign Jane Kendleigh of Oberlin, Ohio, was the first of some twenty Navy flight nurses who made the 1,500 mile round trips between the Marianas and Iwo.

Another was Lieutenant Dorothy Barrows from Portland, Oregon. One seriously wounded Marine remembered her as "a slender, charming girl in GI pants and shirt, hair wrapped in a red bandana," who moved constantly among the stretchers hung four deep from ceiling to deck in webbed slings along the starboard side of the plane's fuselage. "She was always bringing water, fruit juice, sleep shots, and a smile and cheerful words," the sergeant said. "She did much to change our minds about women being in combat zones."

Lieutenant Colonel Malcolm S. Mackay flew seven supply missions, beginning a few hours after *Peg 'O My Heart*'s first landing. His big Curtiss Commando was one of fifteen from Marine Transport Squadron 592 assigned to the airlift. On the first trip, he asked for landing instructions five miles from touchdown and was advised to come in downwind.

"Why not an upwind approach?" Mackay asked the ground control communications jeep. "Better not try it. That's over the front," was the no-nonsense answer. "The Japs'll shoot the shit out of you."

Mackay touched down with the wind at his tail, roared past the flight line of Maytag Messerschmitts and a disabled Navy fighter-bomber, and swung around a sandbagged revetment at the northern end of the runway. He gunned the engines and kicked up a cloud of dust, taxiing at high speed to the south edge of the strip where Marines immediately began unloading the priority cargo.

"It ain't safe anywhere on this fuckin' island," one of the men told the pilot as his litter was lifted aboard. "The bastard Nips got artillery a couple of miles north and they dropped three rounds down here just before you landed." Twenty minutes later, the plane lifted off and disappeared into a bank of clouds. "Worst looking island I ever saw," Mackay said to his copilot. It was an observation made with knowledge: a few months earlier Mackay's transport had been the first to land on Peleliu while fighting still raged there.

From March 3 to March 26 an average of 124 casualties were airlifted daily from Iwo. In all, 2,449 wounded were flown to the Marianas without a man dying in flight. Two hospital planes were hit by antiaircraft fire while taking off, but both returned safely to Motoyama Number One and the wounded were taken out on other planes.

"Leaving Iwo by air was first class all the way," said a Third Division sergeant who had lost both legs in the push beyond Motoyama Village.

No one will ever know precisely when the Fourth Division's battle for the Meat Grinder started losing its fury. But it was sometime between dawn and dusk of D-plus thirteen, the eighth day of combat in the sector. When the 23rd and 24th Regiments began the attack at 7:30 A.M., nothing indicated that the worst might be coming to an end. Only minor gains were made in the morning as the assault battalions moved against heavy resistance still coming from Turkey Knob, the Amphitheater, and Minami Village. But with Hill 382 now firmly in Marine hands, patrols pushed cautiously ahead from its rugged eastern slopes toward the coast, where the terrain would no longer be as much an ally of the Japanese.

Every yard of advance continued to take its toll. "The battle that surged back and forth over the Meat Grinder's rocky crags and cliffs, in and out of the labyrinth of caves, in the chambers of hidden gun emplacements and in the bowels of its buried tanks, cost as much as any single engagement on Iwo Jima," Jim Lucas wrote of the struggle. (After V-J Day Lucas would become a Pulitzer Prize correspondent for the Scripps-Howard newspaper chain and cover other wars from the frozen hills of Korea to the deserts of the Middle East and the rice paddies and jungles of Vietnam. He died in 1973 from complications of elephantiasis, a tropical disease that first struck him as a Marine sergeant in the Solomon Islands of the south Pacific in 1942.)

Flamethrower tanks and rocket-launching trucks supported the attack wherever and whenever possible. But many Japanese positions were too well hidden to be discovered until Marine infantrymen were so near that heavy weapons couldn't be used to dislodge the enemy. By midafternoon there was no forward movement. At 5:00 P.M., following a fifteen-minute artillery bombardment of Turkey Knob and the Amphitheater, another attack was mounted. It gained less than two hundred yards, and General Cates ordered the lines secured for the night.

Throughout the day fighting had been intense and costly. But since shortly after the jump-off, Marines sensed a shift in Japanese tactics as the Fifth Division had found on the western front the previous day: noticeably less heavy enemy artillery and mortar bombardment, and more close-in small arms and machine gun fire.

Cates realized his hope for closing down the Meat Grinder on D-plus thirteen hadn't become a *fait accompli*, and that many more Marines would fall before the enemy bastion was silenced for good. Nonetheless, the general was sure that the Fourth Division's troops at last had penetrated Kuribayashi's main defense belt on the eastern front. Henceforth it would be a matter of exploiting the tear in the enemy lines; of taking out bypassed positions and demolishing what remained of the strongpoints atop Turkey Knob and among the rubble of the Amphitheater and Minami Village.

"Find a weak spot in the bastard's front and keep probing and slugging the sonuvabitch until you do!" Cates had ordered. Marine casualties were grim evidence that there had been no weak spot: 2,880 Marines had been killed or wounded in the slaughterhouse.

Third Division troops were alerted to begin their attack at 7:30 A.M. in the center of the cross-island front. But it was nearly noon before the 21st Regiment was able to move through the rain squalls. George Percy's hard-hit Second Battalion and Wendell Duplantis's cut-to-pieces Third were the assault forces trying to slog through the muck beyond Motoyama Village and across the last high ground overlooking Iwo's northernmost beaches.

Infantrymen were totally spent from the day-after-day attacks, drenched and shivering from the rain despite a seventy-five-degree temperature. Resistance was heavy from concealed weapons spewing small arms and machine gun fire. Visibility was less than fifty yards in any direction among the craggy ravines. Clouds of steam hugged the ground in patches, and sulphur fumes gagged men whenever they took a deep breath. "It was like a scene from a Frankenstein movie," a bedraggled Fox Company sergeant said.

Whenever winds cleared the front for a few minutes, Marines moved ahead until they were pelted by more rain and pinned down by enemy fire. A twenty-minute artillery barrage, and naval gunfire from destroyers five hundred yards off the north shore, failed to spring the advance. At five o'clock the word went out to the troops: "Hold your ground and dig in for the night." Percy's men had moved a scant hundred yards, and Duplantis's battalion had gained a like distance.

Just before twilight, Marines were amazed to see a rainbow in the northeast as a brisk breeze pushed away sodden clouds and Iwo was bathed in fading sunlight. "Give us some rest and replacements and a day of good weather and we'll be able to wade in the ocean," General Erskine said, watching the sunset from his command post. "Then maybe we can start thinking about getting off this goddamned island and turning it over to the Army."

Fifth Division troops battled all day of D-plus thirteen among unnamed ravines and ridges northeast of Nishi. Terrain was more rugged and resistance more stubborn than that faced by the Third and Fourth Divisions in their futile pushes in the center and eastern end of the line stretching two and a half miles across the island.

Because of poor visibility and the closeness of enemy lines, neither artillery nor naval gunfire could be used to support the attack. Tanks were stymied by mine fields systematically laid in the narrow corridors of the contorted landscape, and Marines came under constant small arms and machine gun fire from dozens of hidden caves and pillboxes. Shermans could move only after armored bulldozers had carved roadways for them to maneuver and demolition squads had taken out bypassed strongpoints.

"This was a slow and laborious process," according to the day's action report, "but any attempt by infantrymen to continue the advance before the destruction of enemy positions resulted in excessive casualties." It was, in other words, a typical Iwo-style struggle where Japanese were rarely seen until they were dead.

"Occasionally the tanks flushed out enemy personnel who would be killed by the infantry," the battle summary said, "and this always raised the morale of the Mariens. Although the division made only minor gains, the fighting was bitter and costly, and units were shifted from company to company, and often between battalions, to strengthen weakened outfits, most of which were fighting at half strength or less."

Numbers told the story more forcefully. Colonel Chet Graham's 26th Regiment landed on D-Day with 3,256 officers and men. Since then it had lost fifty percent of them: 1,644 killed or wounded. Colonel Tom Wornham's 27th Marines had fared better, but not much. Its losses were 1,319, almost exactly forty percent. Colonel Harry Liversedge's 28th had suffered worst of all: 1,952 casualties, nearly sixty percent of its landing force.

Alarming and tragic as the numbers were, the cold mathematics didn't reflect the seriousness of the situation—or its impact on the ability of the Marine fighting machine to continue the battle. Not only had eleven battalion commanders been killed or wounded since D-Day, but the loss of junior officers and senior noncoms at the company, platoon, and squad levels had been devastating—not to mention the thousands of seasoned, battle-tested troops who had fallen.

More than two thousand replacements—mostly second lieutenants new to combat and men fresh from the States—had been thrown into the struggle. Even when these men were well trained, which most often was not the case, they were not yet members of the team. They had to be told and shown what to do to survive—too often, not enough.

*

General Kuribayashi now was powerless to control the ebb and flow of the battle: he could only react to the constant pressure of the Marine assault. But Harry Schmidt—as Fifth Corps commander his was the direct responsibility for winning the battle, notwithstanding the offshore presence of "Howlin' Mad" Smith and Kelly Turner— was acutely aware that something must be done.

Shortly before 5:00 P.M., two weeks after D-Day, teletypes in the command posts of Erskine, Cates, and Rockey clattered with orders: "There will be no general attack tomorrow. Except for limited adjustment of positions, each division will utilize the day for rest, refitting, and reorganization in preparation for resumption of action on 6 March." In fourteen days of battle and bloodshed unmatched in Leatherneck history, Marines now held a solid line stretching across Iwo Jima approximately where the invasion plan had expected it to be on the evening of D-Day plus one.

Sergeant William Genaust, the motion picture cameraman who had filmed the second flag-raising side by side with Joe Rosenthal, was killed March 4. He had spent most of the morning with Tom Pearce's battalion, Chandler Johnson's valiant outfit, in the bogged-down attack among the ridges and crevices overlooking the western shoreline on the Fifth Division front. Because of low visibility and poor light, he'd shot little footage. But he had been with the troops at the point of the advance each time it was able to move, doubling as a rifleman and hoping conditions would improve enough so he could film some of the action.

Just before noon, when a rain squall was at its heaviest, Genaust and a comrade spotted the entrance of a bypassed cave. They approached it cautiously, entered its hidden mouth, and were face to face with a squad of Japanese defenders. As the two surprised Marines turned to escape the deathtrap, they were cut down by small arms fire. Both died instantly, shot in the back in the fusilade before they could scamper to safety.

Neither body was recovered. Within minutes, Marine demolitions men flamed the entrance and sealed the cave for all time.

Like most of the Marines who were first on the summit of Suribachi to raise the flags, Genaust never learned of the impact on the home front of those epic moments in history.

Genaust's name is unknown except to a handful of his comrades who remember the valor and dedication of a man who so wanted to be a Marine that he enlisted when he was thirty-six, had been wounded at Saipan, had been recommended for the Navy Cross, had been awarded the Purple Heart and Bronze Star medals, and who died at thirty-eight as a Marine sergeant upholding the traditions of the Corps.

Lone Marine moves through Dante-like scene among the crags and ridges at the northern end of Iwo, near where General Kuribayashi had his last headquarters. (*Louis R. Lowery*)

Team of flamethrowers burn cave in Fifth Division sector in battle's final phase. (*Robert R. Campbell*)

Mortarmen of the 27th Regiment lob shells at the enemy from a front-line position. (*Robert R. Campbell*)

Third Division troops await signal to jump off into new assault against Japanese holding out in Cushman's Pocket. (*Arthur J. Kiely, Jr.*)

Covered by riflemen, a Marine flamethrower torches an enemy cave as breakthrough is achieved. (*Mark Kaufman*)

Third Division Marines at the point of assault hug the sides of a ravine as tank bulldozer clanks forward to clear obstacles holding up the advance. (*Henry Rohland*)

TOP - Marine rocket-firing trucks played a vital role in blasting the enemy from emplacements. (*Stewart Robbins*)

MIDDLE - While a Marine tank burns from a direct hit by enemy fire, Fifth Division Infantry lay down cover for crew to make escape. (*Charles O. Jones*)

BOTTOM - Dug-in at the end of a day of heavy fighting, Fifth Division Marines await another night on Iwo. (*Bill D. Ross*)

PART NINE

Stalemate
and
Breakthrough

1

Daybreak of Monday, March 4, D-Day plus fourteen.

Two miles behind the front, hard-working cooks and bakers had been at stoves and ovens most of the night, preparing hundreds of gallons of hot coffee, huge trays of fresh donuts and pastries, and enough sandwiches for nearly 15,000 Marines on the lines.

Artillery and mortar fire from friend and foe fell across the island to signal the start of another day of battle, albeit one when there would be no Marine attack, as jeeps and trucks hauled their loads of chow to within a few hundred yards from where shells were dropping. "Not exactly what you'd call room service at the Waldorf-Astoria," a Third Division sergeant observed, "but it sure as hell beats cold C-rations."

Regimental and battalion commanders had spent part of the past twelve hours merging shot-up units to bring them as near as possible to full strength for the renewed offensive. Replacements, confused and nervous, found their way to bivouac areas and were assigned to undermanned platoons and companies where they soon would face combat for the first time—and for a tragic number, the last. For some of the oldtimers in grimy and ragged dungarees they'd worn for two weeks, there were new uniforms.

Runners scampered among command posts with mail from home. Ordnance men fitted new barrels to overworked machine guns. Riflemen, whose weapons were inaccurate and constantly misfiring from a combination of Iwo's sand, muck, and excessive use, were issued new M-1 Garands and BARs. Supplies of cartridges and hand grenades were replenished. Corpsmen got fresh knapsacks of medical supplies.

Bullet-pocked flamethrowers were patched up, and demolition squads assembled new satchel charges of explosives. Artillery men cleaned and repaired their howitzers. Tank crews labored on their Shermans: tuning the engines, fixing damaged treads, adjusting communications gear, and replacing worn-out cannon and machine guns.

Back on Motoyama Number One, bulldozers and heavy tractors pulling giant earth rollers worked on the runway, interrupting activities frequently for an increasing stream of air traffic from the Marianas. Every half hour, from early morning until sunset, a hospital plane landed or took off. And the first of nearly two hundred more Army P-51 Mustang fighters arrived to fly cover for B-29 missions over Japan and help out with close air support along the front.

Wreckage still littered the beachhead in places, but now beached LSTs and other large landing craft had replaced amtracs and Higgins boats in putting troops, equipment, and supplies ashore. A few men went swimming on the western beaches near the base of Suribachi. A mimeographed daily newspaper appeared for the first time, and copies were passed from man to man until the stapled eight-page *Iwo Gazette* came apart.

Some men broke out galvanized buckets from the bottom of sea-bags and scrubbed clothes. Volunteer barbers clipped the heads of buddies sitting on wooden ammunition boxes. A movie projector was set up in one hospital recovery tent where Marines awaiting evacuation viewed a Gary Cooper film, a selection of short subjects, and a recent newsreel highlighting the war in Europe.

Shortly after 8:30 A.M., "Howlin' Mad" Smith was ashore for an inspection of front-line positions and a stormy session with Harry Schmidt and his division commanders. During the night, Schmidt and Erskine had made another urgent request to land the 3rd Regiment to provide new muscle for the final phase of the campaign—but again to no avail.

General Erskine was silent throughout the meeting; he'd already had his say in his personal confrontation with the Old Man. But Generals Rockey and Cates joined Schmidt in the verbal melee. All three were outspoken in their contention that 3,000 fresh men in the lines would bring the battle to a speedier end and save hundreds, if not thousands, of lives.

But "Howlin' Mad" remained steadfast in his—and Kelley Turner's—position: there wasn't room enough on the island for another regiment to maneuver. Marines ashore could take the island, he said, and Admiral Turner would not release the regiment from floating reserve unless General Smith would certify that Iwo Jima couldn't be conquered without it. And this, "Howlin' Mad" refused to do.

Weighing heavily on Smith's decision was a fact unknown to the other generals: Erskine's Third Division was scheduled to spearhead the invasion of Japan on Honshu Island, and "Howlin' Mad" wanted to make certain it had one regiment of combat veterans to lead the assault—an outfit that hadn't been shot to pieces on Iwo. Without a hint of this, the meeting broke up at nine o'clock.

"Let's go to the front, Bobbie," Smith said to Erskine, "and see what's happening." The longtime comrades-in-arms spent the rest of the day together, moving along the lines across the island from one command post to another. Several times they were forced to take cover when enemy mortars exploded yards away.

"It's like old times, General," Erskine remarked during one barrage. "Howlin' Mad" didn't answer. But his eyes were misty as he nodded, smiled, and chomped hard on the omnipresent unlit cigar stub. It was the last time the two men would be side by side in combat.

What the generals saw during their inspection of the front on Iwo's "day of rest" would have been considered a major dawn-to-dusk engagement in most other battles. While there was no attack as such, units of the Fourth Division were, in the words of the day's action report, "still involved in the considerable task of containing and cleaning up resistance along the southern edge of the Amphitheater-Turkey Knob complex."

In the Third Division sector, artillery duels flared intermittently throughout the day as patrols from four battalions of the 9th and 21st Regiments demolished bypassed strongpoints north of the third airstrip and Motoyama Village. Air strikes and naval gunfire were called in several times to pound known and suspected Japanese artillery emplacements on and around Hill 362C overlooking the route to the northern shoreline.

Infantry action on the Fifth Division front was restricted to the straightening of lines among the ravines and ridges along the west coast. There was little reaction from Japanese troops, but artillery and mortars harassed Marines resting in bivouac and those reducing bypassed bunkers and caves. Two Shermans were disabled in supporting the mop-up operations, one by a land mine, the other to antitank fire.

General Kuribayashi, whose headquarters now were believed by Marine intelligence officers to be in the area, must have been mystified and concerned by what the Leathernecks were doing—or not doing.

But he kept up artillery and mortar fire from dawn until sunset, and his high-velocity antitank guns were especially active and effective in the afternoon.

Shortly before 2:30 P.M., Lieutenant Colonel John Butler, CO of the 27th Regiment's First Battalion, was in a jeep with three men moving slowly down a bumpy road, hardly more than a rock-strewn trail, inspecting the lines and mentally plotting what his outfit would do when the attack cranked up again the next morning.

"Stop a minute," he told the driver as they approached a hardly visible intersection in the road. "I want to take a better look at that ridge over there," he said, pointing dead ahead at the ruins of Iwo's primitive sugar mill. The jeep hardly had come to a halt when an antitank shell decapitated Butler and wounded two other men. The tall, dark, intense, well-liked officer was the twelfth battalion commander to fall since D-Day.

Lieutenant Colonel Justin G. Duryea, the regimental operations officer, took command of Butler's outfit. He was no stranger to the battalion; he'd been its CO at Camp Pendleton, back in California, and had trained it before the Fifth Division shipped out for combat. Duryea would have his command four days. On March 9, he was maimed by a land mine while moving forward with his men in the push toward Kitano Point.

And so the "day of rest" came to an end.

An hour before sundown, Erskine had gone to the beachhead at the East Boat Basin with General Smith. With firm handshakes and snappy salutes, the protégé and mentor parted company as "Howlin' Mad," four officers, and three enlisted men—armed with Thompson machine guns—waded through the gentle surf to the open ramp of a Higgins boat for the two-mile trip to the general's quarters on the *Auburn*.

Missing from the armada that still surrounded Iwo was the cruiser *Indianapolis*, Admiral Spruance's flagship. During the afternoon, it had weighed anchor to speed Admiral Nimitz's man-on-the-spot back to Guam to mount the invasion of Okinawa.

Gone, too, were the attack transports of the 3rd Regiment. Even as General Smith had held his meeting with the Iwo battle commanders earlier in the day, the 3,000 Third Division troops were headed back to the Marianas for garrison duty and to start training for the invasion of Japan.

mortar attack and machine gun and rifle fire in a pattern of mayhem that continued far into the night.

It was an especially bad day for Easy Company of the 23rd Marines' Second Battalion. Its company commander and nearly a dozen men were wounded by mortars less than fifteen minutes after the push began. Understandably, the attack sputtered and came to a halt after a gain of fifty yards. Late in the day, another mortar barrage hit the hapless company's CP. The new CO—a twenty-three-year-old lieutenant—was wounded, his executive officer killed, and twenty-two enlisted men were casualties. When the battalion intelligence officer took over the company, he became its third commander in twelve hours and its seventh since D-Day.

Major Doyle Stout's Third Battalion of the 24th was more fortunate, benefited by terrain where tanks could support the infantry. With four flamethrower Shermans at the point, the outfit moved 350 yards with moderate losses.

Even with a day of rest, reorganization, replacements, and new weapons, the cumulative effects of two weeks of bloodletting and sheer physical toil cut deeply into the ability of the Fourth Division to carry on the battle. That night Colonel Edwin A. Pollock, the division's personnel officer, estimated the outfit's combat efficiency at forty percent. "The results of fatigue and lack of experienced leaders are very evident in the manner in which the units now fight," he noted in the day's action report. The same could have been said about the plight of the Third and Fifth Divisions.

Inescapable was the fact that all replacements on Iwo had been thrown into the battle. And with the 3rd Regiment's three thousand men now steaming for Guam and already two hundred miles at sea, no more trained troops were available. Rear echelon noncombatants—clerks, cooks, bakers, truck drivers, carpenters, mechanics, musicians, anyone who could carry a rifle—now must be used to fill the ranks of front-line units.

Out on the *Auburn*, General Smith was aware of the situation but there was nothing he could do about it. "I knew many of our best men had been lost," he said years later, "and that there was no way they could be replaced."

So far, 2,777 Marines had been killed, another 8,051 had been wounded, and 1,102 were out of the battle because of combat fatigue:

Gone, too, were nearly four hundred men of the Third, Fourth, and Fifth Divisions. They had been killed or wounded during the "day of rest."

While General Kuribayashi may have found some initial solace in the absence of an all-out Marine ground assault on D-plus fourteen, it is unlikely that it lasted for long—he was too shrewd, too much the complete professional soldier not to realize what the Americans were doing. And he certainly had to welcome the day of respite from constant attack on his own troops, who now were on a starvation diet of battle necessities from food and water to medical supplies and ammunition.

General Schmidt—stolid, methodical, pragmatic—now could see the battle's victorious end. How long it would take, and how many more Marines would fall, were still deeply troubling concerns to the laconic Nebraskan. But he was determined to finish the campaign as quickly as possible and with the fewest possible losses. To this end, he'd spent most of the day planning the next phase of the push.

There would be no basic change in strategy or tactics. The battle for Iwo Jima was being waged in the only possible way it could be fought—with infantry in head-on assault, position by position, until the last Japanese defender was wiped out or surrendered. But now that the beachhead was bulging with everything needed to win, with transports and fighters using Motoyama Number One, with the treatment and evacuation of casualties a smoothly functioning machine, with the enemy being bled to death with no hope of resupply or reinforcements, Schmidt was set to close the pincers.

The process began at 7:00 A.M. of March 6, D-Day plus fifteen, in thundering barrages of artillery, naval gunfire, and wave after wave of carrier planes dropping clusters of napalm bombs as their machine guns and rockets ripped into enemy lines in low-level passes across the island. In tons of steel and explosives, the firepower approached that unleashed on D-Day in the final hour before Marines hit the beaches.

Virtually every Marine howitzer on Iwo—132 75- and 155-millimeter guns from eleven artillery battalions—was in action. They first fired for thirty-one minutes on the western half of the island, and then rocked the eastern sector for the next thirty-six minutes. In sixty-seven minutes, 22,500 shells slammed down along the front, often as close as a hundred yards in front of the Marines waiting to jump off.

From less than half a mile offshore, a battleship and three cruisers unloaded 450 rounds of eight- and fourteen-inch high explosives. Three destroyers and two landing craft moved close in along the western shoreline to plaster the cliffs and caves with mortars and rockets. High explosives fell along the front every ten seconds.

"It seemed impossible that any defense could withstand such a pounding," an action report said. But Marines found differently when the infantry attack began shortly after eight o'clock.

Tom Wornham's 27th Regiment and Hartnoll Withers's 21st moved out first at the western end of the line. Walt Wensinger's 23rd Marines and Walt Jordan's 24th Regiment were the assault troops on the eastern front. Japanese reaction was immediate and deadly across the island. Incredibly, the pulverizing pre-attack bombardment and air strikes seemed not to have affected the enemy at all.

As soon as the shells stopped falling and the carrier planes zoomed skyward and left the scene, the Japanese were alert and full of fight. "It was apparent that all the blasting by artillery, naval gunfire, and planes had accomplished little to reduce the enemy's ability and will to resist, but a progressive diminution of enemy artillery had been noticed for several days," an official action report said. "It was the mortar and automatic weapons fire that now made every yard of advance so costly."

Patrick Capelletti, a twenty-five-year-old Fifth Division corporal from New Brunswick, New Jersey, put it more succinctly: "All the bombardment did was let the Nips know we were coming at them again. It stirred them up like a hornet's nest, and the sonsabitches were waiting in their caves and bunkers to kill more Marines just as they had every goddamned day since we landed."

At 5:00 A.M., the Second Battalion of the 27th Regiment, Major John Antonelli's outfit, had taken positions in pre-dawn darkness to spearhead the assault. But even before the jump-off, a torrent of mortars laced Easy Company's staging area, claiming thirty-five casualties. "A helluva way to start the day," Antonelli observed, as corpsmen and stretcher bearers went about their disheartening and dangerous jobs.

Heavy machine gun and mortar fire, as well as snipers and land mines, stopped the Fifth Division push before it was barely underway.

Pillboxes and ever-present caves concealed in the jumble of ridges and crevices took their constant toll. Only after flamethrower tanks and demolitions squads were able to incinerate strongpoints could minor gains be made—gains measured in meager and bloody yards.

Along the Third Division front, to the right of where the Fifth was waging its futile daylong battle, the attack had some momentum—briefly.

Two platoons from George Company of the 21st Regiment's Second Battalion, commanded by a soft-spoken twenty-three-year-old lieutenant, William H. Mulvey, managed to claw to the crest of a ridge less than a quarter-mile from Iwo's northern coastline. "There it was," he said later. "We could see the shore and it was an inspiring sight." But enemy small arms and mortar fire were so intense and accurate that the outfit could move neither forward nor backward.

Mulvey sent Corporal Jerome J. Radke and another man for help to hold the precarious line. Radke made it back to the command post where he quickly found a dozen volunteers—flamethrowers and demolitions men—to move to the aid of their embattled buddies; he could have had twice that number. Within minutes, as they darted and ducked through a nonstop storm of bullets and mortars, six of the rescue squad were killed and two others wounded in the vain attempt to bolster the outpost.

For the remainder of the day, in the incredible jumble of rocks and broken ground in the sector where General Kuribayashi now had his headquarters, the Marines fought to survive. In this part of Iwo, the island literally gurgled with heat from underground volcanic fissures and crevices, making it all but impossible to dig foxholes because of blistering temperatures and sulphur fumes.

Late in the afternoon, under cover of smoke grenades and an artillery barrage, Mulvey's battered survivors brought back their dead and wounded to positions beyond Motoyama Village. Many men spent the night in foxholes they had used two days earlier. Third Division gains were negligible—from fifty to two hundred yards. Casualties weren't. Two hundred Marines, virtually a man for every yard of advance, had been killed or wounded.

Two battalions from Walt Wensinger's 23rd Regiment and two from Walt Jordan's 24th were the Fourth Division's assault force on D-plus fifteen. Spearhead companies immediately came under heavy a total of 11,930 casualties. Little wonder that news stories were using Antietam and Gettysburg as historic yardsticks with which to compare what was happening at Iwo Jima. And while the end of the campaign might be in sight, it was far from over.

Motoyama Number One was taking on the look of a busy battle-zone airfield-in-being. During the day, Brigadier General Ernest C. Moore flew in with more of the first echelon of the Army's 7th Fighter Command—twenty-eight Mustangs and a dozen Black Widow night fighters. Ten Marine Curtiss Commando transports landed with cargoes of mortar and artillery shells, plasma and whole blood, and thirty pouches of mail.

Offshore, the *Samaritan* lifted anchor with its last complement of casualties and headed for Guam; henceforth, most of the seriously wounded would be evacuated by air. Landings and departures were interrupted several times by artillery and mortar shelling that caused much excitement but little damage. Minutes after the fire lifted, another plane was touching down or lifting off.

On Suribachi, Seabees labored with bulldozers, jackhammers, dynamite, and earth movers to widen the road to the top of the volcano. When they finished, it would be a two-lane route, thirty-five feet wide and nearly a mile long, with none of the incline steeper than ten percent. "From now on," Richard Newcomb wrote, "those too lazy to climb up could ride." Atop the crest now were radar, weather, and navigational equipment to aid B-29s and Mustangs in their strikes against the Japanese home islands.

A few Japanese were still in Suribachi's labyrinth of tunnels and caves. "But there was no fight left in them," Newcomb recalled. "They came out only at night, searching for food and water. Every day there were fewer left."

In his command post at the foot of the cliffs at the northern end of Motoyama Number One, General Erskine called a meeting of his staff and combat commanders. The Big E had decided now was the time to spring the pre-dawn attack on the Japanese. What he had in mind was not a small-scale foray before an assault in force, but a major push made in darkness—a surprise thrust that he hoped would catch the Japanese asleep, or at least catnapping and off guard.

Such a tactic hadn't been used on Iwo, and seldom had Marines employed it in earlier Pacific campaigns. It might work now, Erskine felt, as it had in France against the Germans in World War I. Maybe this could be the key to open the way for a breakthrough sweep, without heavy American casualties, that would carry to the island's northern shoreline.

Lieutenant Colonel Howard J. Turton, the Third Division's dour and shrewd intelligence officer, wasn't keen on the idea for a number of reasons. "Got its points," he said, "but it's risky as hell. We've already been shot to pieces, and we're at the bottom of the barrel of experienced people—officers and men." Besides, he continued, the troops weren't trained in the demanding skills of night fighting, the terrain was an open invitation to ambush, heavy bombardment had leveled so many landmarks that maps were next to impossible to decipher, and there was no assurance the enemy wouldn't be alerted by the first movement of Marines and be ready and waiting when they came.

Captain Oscar Salgo, the six-foot-four burly and gung-ho commander of the division's reconnaissance company, had some misgivings about the outcome of the venture. "I don't know what the hell will happen, General," Salgo said, "but we'll do our goddamndest, you can be sure of that."

Rain was beginning to fall as Erskine was on the field phone with General Schmidt for authority to attack at five o'clock instead of 7:30 as ordered. It didn't take long for the Third Division commander to outline his scheme. "Permission granted," Schmidt said, and Erskine was in business.

2

Two companies from Colonel Boehm's Third Battalion of the 9th Marines began moving into the lines at 3:20 A.M. to spearhead the attack. The objective, Hill 362C: 250 yards to the southeast. Its capture would remove the last strongpoint between the Marines and Iwo's north shore.

Company commanders tried to orient themselves in the light of parachute flares, but the steady downpour and black night practically obliterated the landscape. Radio silence was in force all along the line, and Marines moved as quietly as possible to launch the attack. At 4:50 A.M., all illumination of the front stopped as ordered, but at five o'clock an errant Navy star shell, fired from a destroyer, burst over the lines.

Apprehension swept Erskine's command post as the hushed, drenched troops froze in their tracks, fearful they would be slaughtered before the assault began. But the brightly burning flare was almost immediately extinguished in the pelting squall; once again the front was in total darkness.

Five minutes later Marine artillery fired a barrage of smoke shells to further screen the movement of the attackers, who began crawling forward again. They moved without detection for half an hour until a Japanese machine gun opened fire and gave the alarm. The position was silenced in seconds by a flamethrower. Now the enemy was aroused, but not before Marines had passed through the lines without being discovered and without suffering a casualty.

Dawn's light was cutting through the overcast, and the rain had stopped when Erskine began getting early reports. "I had a hunch it would work," he beamed at Turton, the doubting intelligence officer. "We caught the bastards asleep just as I thought we would."

Now radio silence was broken and circuits crackled with news, all of it good—or so it appeared. Assault troops still were meeting only scattered resistance, but the enemy was coming to life. Many Japanese had been killed in their foxholes and pillboxes. Colonel Boehm reported that K Company was atop Hill 362C. But euphoria was brief. At about 6:30 A.M., after a check of the terrain against maps and aerial photographs, Boehm found that the Marines were on Hill 331—not 362C. It was another 250 yards ahead.

The explanation was simple. Given ideal conditions of terrain and weather, and with experienced troops and commanders, a night attack is warfare's most difficult maneuver. On Iwo, with its jumble of escarpments nearly the same elevation, it was difficult in broad daylight to distinguish one hill from another, to determine one ridge from the next. In the darkness and rain, the wrong objective had been pointed out and taken.

Fortunately, the thrust was in the right direction. At 7:15, after ten minutes of heavy artillery fire against Hill 362C, Marines resumed the attack. But by then, the Japanese were fully awake and resistance was fierce. Not only were the attackers being hit from the front, but from positions bypassed in the silent sweep through the lines. It was late afternoon before 362C was finally in American hands.

Boehm's outfit wasn't alone in slipping through scores of slumbering Japanese before being detected. Lieutenant Colonel Robert E. Cushman's Second Battalion and Major William T. Glass's First gained several hundred yards before heavy fighting erupted around them at 7:30 A.M.. One instant everything was quiet; the next, the attack was in an enemy ambush. From directly in front, and from bypassed bunkers and pillboxes only yards away, Marines were caught in a hailstorm of bullets and mortars. Within five minutes, the assault was not only pinned down but both battalions were cut off from Marine lines.

Two of Cushman's companies—Easy and Fox—now were surrounded and in a roaring struggle for survival in an area that would quickly become known as Cushman's Pocket. Tanks and infantry from the 21st Regiment tried repeatedly throughout the day to extricate the embattled Marines, but without success. Fighting as fierce as any during the campaign would rage for six days in the narrow maze of ravines and ridges before the last Japanese gunner and his weapon was silenced.

Baker Company's commander, Second Lieutenant John H. Leims, had serious doubts that he or any of his men would make it through the first day. The outfit from Glass's battalion had lost twenty-three killed and twenty wounded by midafternoon in holding its position four hundred yards in front of the lines, and had lost contact with the rest of the bogged-down attack. Iwo was the first combat for the twenty-two-year-old Chicagoan, but he'd become battle-wise since D-Day and knew something drastic must be done if anyone in the company was to live.

"If we spend the night here by ourselves, we'll all be wiped out," Leims told his platoon sergeant. "I'm going for help." With that, the lieutenant sprang from behind the cover of a boulder and was spotted immediately by the Japanese. Sometimes crawling flat on the ground, other times ducking and darting in a scampering crouch, always under heavy fire from small arms and mortars, he zigzagged toward the rear. "I knew that every time I moved, it could be the last and that I'd probably die out there," he said later. "But what the hell else could I do? I was a Marine."

Fate was with the gallant shavetail on his perilous ten-minute trip across no man's land to the CP. He made it unharmed.

Minutes later, after showing Glass on an aerial photograph where the company was being systematically slaughtered, Leims headed back

Gone, too, were nearly four hundred men of the Third, Fourth, and Fifth Divisions. They had been killed or wounded during the "day of rest."

While General Kuribayashi may have found some initial solace in the absence of an all-out Marine ground assault on D-plus fourteen, it is unlikely that it lasted for long—he was too shrewd, too much the complete professional soldier not to realize what the Americans were doing. And he certainly had to welcome the day of respite from constant attack on his own troops, who now were on a starvation diet of battle necessities from food and water to medical supplies and ammunition.

General Schmidt—stolid, methodical, pragmatic—now could see the battle's victorious end. How long it would take, and how many more Marines would fall, were still deeply troubling concerns to the laconic Nebraskan. But he was determined to finish the campaign as quickly as possible and with the fewest possible losses. To this end, he'd spent most of the day planning the next phase of the push.

There would be no basic change in strategy or tactics. The battle for Iwo Jima was being waged in the only possible way it could be fought—with infantry in head-on assault, position by position, until the last Japanese defender was wiped out or surrendered. But now that the beachhead was bulging with everything needed to win, with transports and fighters using Motoyama Number One, with the treatment and evacuation of casualties a smoothly functioning machine, with the enemy being bled to death with no hope of resupply or reinforcements, Schmidt was set to close the pincers.

The process began at 7:00 A.M. of March 6, D-Day plus fifteen, in thundering barrages of artillery, naval gunfire, and wave after wave of carrier planes dropping clusters of napalm bombs as their machine guns and rockets ripped into enemy lines in low-level passes across the island. In tons of steel and explosives, the firepower approached that unleashed on D-Day in the final hour before Marines hit the beaches.

Virtually every Marine howitzer on Iwo—132 75- and 155-millimeter guns from eleven artillery battalions—was in action. They first fired for thirty-one minutes on the western half of the island, and then rocked the eastern sector for the next thirty-six minutes. In sixty-seven minutes, 22,500 shells slammed down along the front, often as close as a hundred yards in front of the Marines waiting to jump off.

From less than half a mile offshore, a battleship and three cruisers unloaded 450 rounds of eight- and fourteen-inch high explosives. Three destroyers and two landing craft moved close in along the western shoreline to plaster the cliffs and caves with mortars and rockets. High explosives fell along the front every ten seconds.

"It seemed impossible that any defense could withstand such a pounding," an action report said. But Marines found differently when the infantry attack began shortly after eight o'clock.

Tom Wornham's 27th Regiment and Hartnoll Withers's 21st moved out first at the western end of the line. Walt Wensinger's 23rd Marines and Walt Jordan's 24th Regiment were the assault troops on the eastern front. Japanese reaction was immediate and deadly across the island. Incredibly, the pulverizing pre-attack bombardment and air strikes seemed not to have affected the enemy at all.

As soon as the shells stopped falling and the carrier planes zoomed skyward and left the scene, the Japanese were alert and full of fight. "It was apparent that all the blasting by artillery, naval gunfire, and planes had accomplished little to reduce the enemy's ability and will to resist, but a progressive diminution of enemy artillery had been noticed for several days," an official action report said. "It was the mortar and automatic weapons fire that now made every yard of advance so costly."

Patrick Capelletti, a twenty-five-year-old Fifth Division corporal from New Brunswick, New Jersey, put it more succinctly: "All the bombardment did was let the Nips know we were coming at them again. It stirred them up like a hornet's nest, and the sonsabitches were waiting in their caves and bunkers to kill more Marines just as they had every goddamned day since we landed."

At 5:00 A.M., the Second Battalion of the 27th Regiment, Major John Antonelli's outfit, had taken positions in pre-dawn darkness to spearhead the assault. But even before the jump-off, a torrent of mortars laced Easy Company's staging area, claiming thirty-five casualties. "A helluva way to start the day," Antonelli observed, as corpsmen and stretcher bearers went about their disheartening and dangerous jobs.

Heavy machine gun and mortar fire, as well as snipers and land mines, stopped the Fifth Division push before it was barely underway.

Pillboxes and ever-present caves concealed in the jumble of ridges and crevices took their constant toll. Only after flamethrower tanks and demolitions squads were able to incinerate strongpoints could minor gains be made—gains measured in meager and bloody yards.

Along the Third Division front, to the right of where the Fifth was waging its futile daylong battle, the attack had some momentum—briefly.

Two platoons from George Company of the 21st Regiment's Second Battalion, commanded by a soft-spoken twenty-three-year-old lieutenant, William H. Mulvey, managed to claw to the crest of a ridge less than a quarter-mile from Iwo's northern coastline. "There it was," he said later. "We could see the shore and it was an inspiring sight." But enemy small arms and mortar fire were so intense and accurate that the outfit could move neither forward nor backward.

Mulvey sent Corporal Jerome J. Radke and another man for help to hold the precarious line. Radke made it back to the command post where he quickly found a dozen volunteers—flamethrowers and demolitions men—to move to the aid of their embattled buddies; he could have had twice that number. Within minutes, as they darted and ducked through a nonstop storm of bullets and mortars, six of the rescue squad were killed and two others wounded in the vain attempt to bolster the outpost.

For the remainder of the day, in the incredible jumble of rocks and broken ground in the sector where General Kuribayashi now had his headquarters, the Marines fought to survive. In this part of Iwo, the island literally gurgled with heat from underground volcanic fissures and crevices, making it all but impossible to dig foxholes because of blistering temperatures and sulphur fumes.

Late in the afternoon, under cover of smoke grenades and an artillery barrage, Mulvey's battered survivors brought back their dead and wounded to positions beyond Motoyama Village. Many men spent the night in foxholes they had used two days earlier. Third Division gains were negligible—from fifty to two hundred yards. Casualties weren't. Two hundred Marines, virtually a man for every yard of advance, had been killed or wounded.

Two battalions from Walt Wensinger's 23rd Regiment and two from Walt Jordan's 24th were the Fourth Division's assault force on D-plus fifteen. Spearhead companies immediately came under heavy mortar attack and machine gun and rifle fire in a pattern of mayhem that continued far into the night.

It was an especially bad day for Easy Company of the 23rd Marines' Second Battalion. Its company commander and nearly a dozen men were wounded by mortars less than fifteen minutes after the push began. Understandably, the attack sputtered and came to a halt after a gain of fifty yards. Late in the day, another mortar barrage hit the hapless company's CP. The new CO—a twenty-three-year-old lieutenant—was wounded, his executive officer killed, and twenty-two enlisted men were casualties. When the battalion intelligence officer took over the company, he became its third commander in twelve hours and its seventh since D-Day.

Major Doyle Stout's Third Battalion of the 24th was more fortunate, benefited by terrain where tanks could support the infantry. With four flamethrower Shermans at the point, the outfit moved 350 yards with moderate losses.

Even with a day of rest, reorganization, replacements, and new weapons, the cumulative effects of two weeks of bloodletting and sheer physical toil cut deeply into the ability of the Fourth Division to carry on the battle. That night Colonel Edwin A. Pollock, the division's personnel officer, estimated the outfit's combat efficiency at forty percent. "The results of fatigue and lack of experienced leaders are very evident in the manner in which the units now fight," he noted in the day's action report. The same could have been said about the plight of the Third and Fifth Divisions.

Inescapable was the fact that all replacements on Iwo had been thrown into the battle. And with the 3rd Regiment's three thousand men now steaming for Guam and already two hundred miles at sea, no more trained troops were available. Rear echelon noncombatants— clerks, cooks, bakers, truck drivers, carpenters, mechanics, musicians, anyone who could carry a rifle—now must be used to fill the ranks of front-line units.

Out on the *Auburn*, General Smith was aware of the situation but there was nothing he could do about it. "I knew many of our best men had been lost," he said years later, "and that there was no way they could be replaced."

So far, 2,777 Marines had been killed, another 8,051 had been wounded, and 1,102 were out of the battle because of combat fatigue:

a total of 11,930 casualties. Little wonder that news stories were using Antietam and Gettysburg as historic yardsticks with which to compare what was happening at Iwo Jima. And while the end of the campaign might be in sight, it was far from over.

Motoyama Number One was taking on the look of a busy battle-zone airfield-in-being. During the day, Brigadier General Ernest C. Moore flew in with more of the first echelon of the Army's 7th Fighter Command—twenty-eight Mustangs and a dozen Black Widow night fighters. Ten Marine Curtiss Commando transports landed with cargoes of mortar and artillery shells, plasma and whole blood, and thirty pouches of mail.

Offshore, the *Samaritan* lifted anchor with its last complement of casualties and headed for Guam; henceforth, most of the seriously wounded would be evacuated by air. Landings and departures were interrupted several times by artillery and mortar shelling that caused much excitement but little damage. Minutes after the fire lifted, another plane was touching down or lifting off.

On Suribachi, Seabees labored with bulldozers, jackhammers, dynamite, and earth movers to widen the road to the top of the volcano. When they finished, it would be a two-lane route, thirty-five feet wide and nearly a mile long, with none of the incline steeper than ten percent. "From now on," Richard Newcomb wrote, "those too lazy to climb up could ride." Atop the crest now were radar, weather, and navigational equipment to aid B-29s and Mustangs in their strikes against the Japanese home islands.

A few Japanese were still in Suribachi's labyrinth of tunnels and caves. "But there was no fight left in them," Newcomb recalled. "They came out only at night, searching for food and water. Every day there were fewer left."

In his command post at the foot of the cliffs at the northern end of Motoyama Number One, General Erskine called a meeting of his staff and combat commanders. The Big E had decided now was the time to spring the pre-dawn attack on the Japanese. What he had in mind was not a small-scale foray before an assault in force, but a major push made in darkness—a surprise thrust that he hoped would catch the Japanese asleep, or at least catnapping and off guard.

Such a tactic hadn't been used on Iwo, and seldom had Marines employed it in earlier Pacific campaigns. It might work now, Erskine felt, as it had in France against the Germans in World War I. Maybe this could be the key to open the way for a breakthrough sweep, without heavy American casualties, that would carry to the island's northern shoreline.

Lieutenant Colonel Howard J. Turton, the Third Division's dour and shrewd intelligence officer, wasn't keen on the idea for a number of reasons. "Got its points," he said, "but it's risky as hell. We've already been shot to pieces, and we're at the bottom of the barrel of experienced people—officers and men." Besides, he continued, the troops weren't trained in the demanding skills of night fighting, the terrain was an open invitation to ambush, heavy bombardment had leveled so many landmarks that maps were next to impossible to decipher, and there was no assurance the enemy wouldn't be alerted by the first movement of Marines and be ready and waiting when they came.

Captain Oscar Salgo, the six-foot-four burly and gung-ho commander of the division's reconnaissance company, had some misgivings about the outcome of the venture. "I don't know what the hell will happen, General," Salgo said, "but we'll do our goddamndest, you can be sure of that."

Rain was beginning to fall as Erskine was on the field phone with General Schmidt for authority to attack at five o'clock instead of 7:30 as ordered. It didn't take long for the Third Division commander to outline his scheme. "Permission granted," Schmidt said, and Erskine was in business.

2

Two companies from Colonel Boehm's Third Battalion of the 9th Marines began moving into the lines at 3:20 A.M. to spearhead the attack. The objective, Hill 362C: 250 yards to the southeast. Its capture would remove the last strongpoint between the Marines and Iwo's north shore.

Company commanders tried to orient themselves in the light of parachute flares, but the steady downpour and black night practically obliterated the landscape. Radio silence was in force all along the line, and Marines moved as quietly as possible to launch the attack. At 4:50 A.M., all illumination of the front stopped as ordered, but at five o'clock an errant Navy star shell, fired from a destroyer, burst over the lines.

Apprehension swept Erskine's command post as the hushed, drenched troops froze in their tracks, fearful they would be slaughtered before the assault began. But the brightly burning flare was almost immediately extinguished in the pelting squall; once again the front was in total darkness.

Five minutes later Marine artillery fired a barrage of smoke shells to further screen the movement of the attackers, who began crawling forward again. They moved without detection for half an hour until a Japanese machine gun opened fire and gave the alarm. The position was silenced in seconds by a flamethrower. Now the enemy was aroused, but not before Marines had passed through the lines without being discovered and without suffering a casualty.

Dawn's light was cutting through the overcast, and the rain had stopped when Erskine began getting early reports. "I had a hunch it would work," he beamed at Turton, the doubting intelligence officer. "We caught the bastards asleep just as I thought we would."

Now radio silence was broken and circuits crackled with news, all of it good—or so it appeared. Assault troops still were meeting only scattered resistance, but the enemy was coming to life. Many Japanese had been killed in their foxholes and pillboxes. Colonel Boehm reported that K Company was atop Hill 362C. But euphoria was brief. At about 6:30 A.M., after a check of the terrain against maps and aerial photographs, Boehm found that the Marines were on Hill 331—not 362C. It was another 250 yards ahead.

The explanation was simple. Given ideal conditions of terrain and weather, and with experienced troops and commanders, a night attack is warfare's most difficult maneuver. On Iwo, with its jumble of escarpments nearly the same elevation, it was difficult in broad daylight to distinguish one hill from another, to determine one ridge from the next. In the darkness and rain, the wrong objective had been pointed out and taken.

Fortunately, the thrust was in the right direction. At 7:15, after ten minutes of heavy artillery fire against Hill 362C, Marines resumed the attack. But by then, the Japanese were fully awake and resistance was fierce. Not only were the attackers being hit from the front, but from positions bypassed in the silent sweep through the lines. It was late afternoon before 362C was finally in American hands.

Boehm's outfit wasn't alone in slipping through scores of slumbering Japanese before being detected. Lieutenant Colonel Robert E. Cushman's Second Battalion and Major William T. Glass's First gained several hundred yards before heavy fighting erupted around them at 7:30 A.M.. One instant everything was quiet; the next, the attack was in an enemy ambush. From directly in front, and from bypassed bunkers and pillboxes only yards away, Marines were caught in a hailstorm of bullets and mortars. Within five minutes, the assault was not only pinned down but both battalions were cut off from Marine lines.

Two of Cushman's companies—Easy and Fox—now were surrounded and in a roaring struggle for survival in an area that would quickly become known as Cushman's Pocket. Tanks and infantry from the 21st Regiment tried repeatedly throughout the day to extricate the embattled Marines, but without success. Fighting as fierce as any during the campaign would rage for six days in the narrow maze of ravines and ridges before the last Japanese gunner and his weapon was silenced.

Baker Company's commander, Second Lieutenant John H. Leims, had serious doubts that he or any of his men would make it through the first day. The outfit from Glass's battalion had lost twenty-three killed and twenty wounded by midafternoon in holding its position four hundred yards in front of the lines, and had lost contact with the rest of the bogged-down attack. Iwo was the first combat for the twenty-two-year-old Chicagoan, but he'd become battle-wise since D-Day and knew something drastic must be done if anyone in the company was to live.

"If we spend the night here by ourselves, we'll all be wiped out," Leims told his platoon sergeant. "I'm going for help." With that, the lieutenant sprang from behind the cover of a boulder and was spotted immediately by the Japanese. Sometimes crawling flat on the ground, other times ducking and darting in a scampering crouch, always under heavy fire from small arms and mortars, he zigzagged toward the rear. "I knew that every time I moved, it could be the last and that I'd probably die out there," he said later. "But what the hell else could I do? I was a Marine."

Fate was with the gallant shavetail on his perilous ten-minute trip across no man's land to the CP. He made it unharmed.

Minutes later, after showing Glass on an aerial photograph where the company was being systematically slaughtered, Leims headed back to his men. It was twilight, and he was dragging a telephone line along to call in artillery and mortars to cover the withdrawal of the shot-to-pieces outfit. He worked his way across the same terrain, was caught again in a cracking fusillade of enemy fire, and was amazed and grateful to be still alive and unwounded after dashing the last fifty yards like an upright Olympic runner to reach the outpost.

"Pass the word," Leims said in a voice loud enough to carry over the noise of a falling mortar barrage as he jumped into a foxhole occupied by two startled Marines. "Be ready to take our wounded and pull back to the lines when I give the signal." Still gasping for breath, he was immediately on the field phone he'd brought with him. "I'll give you map coordinates of where to deliver artillery and mortars so we can get the hell out of here," he told Glass. Shells were screaming through the gathering darkness five minutes later, their roaring explosions driving the Japanese to cover as the Marines began their desperate trip to the safety of the lines. Some carried wounded comrades on their backs, and it was nearly 10:00 P.M. before the pullback was completed without further casualties.

But Baker Company was on the brink of extinction, bled white and all but wiped out in nineteen agonizing hours since the predawn attack began. Fewer than two dozen men came back unhurt. To make matters worse, Leims found that several wounded had been left behind in no man's land, missed in the black night during the confusion of the pull-out.

With no thought except to do what he *knew* must be done, Leims crawled alone through the darkness and dragged one Marine back, then he went out again and brought in another. "They were my men, my comrades," he said the next day, "and they'd have been out there, come hell or high water, bringing me in if the situation was reversed."

Baker Company's commander would be wounded before Iwo was captured and would receive two medals for his part in the island's conquest—the Purple Heart and the Medal of Honor.

Cushman's Pocket was a dusk-to-dawn nightmarish battle for survival for Easy and Fox Companies, surrounded by fiercely resisting Japanese entrenched in a complex of caves, pillboxes, trenches, and dug-in tanks. First Lieutenant Wilcie A. O'Bannon was fearful that his Company F would cease to exist by daybreak. Captain Maynard Schmidt was no more optimistic about the prospects for his men in Company E.

Both units had been isolated and unable to move in any direction since midmorning, O'Bannon with forty-one troops and Maynard with forty-four. Tanks tried twice to extricate them, both times without success. The first attempt failed when the lead Sherman triggered a roaring chain of explosions when it hit a land mine, lost its treads, and blocked the narrow ravine that was the hoped-for escape route. Boulder-strewn terrain and intense fire from antitank guns stopped the second rescue mission.

Without hope of immediate help, Easy and Fox Companies did the only thing possible—they dug in and fought for their lives. "We were in one helluva mess and we knew it," O'Bannon recalled when he and nineteen survivors finally made it to safety after thirty-six hours in the deathtrap. Schmidt got back to the lines with nine men.

Japanese positions were so near on all sides that the enemy taunted the Marines when they weren't being cut down. "We couldn't see anything from our foxholes," O'Bannon remembered, "and sticking your head up meant losing it." From the Japanese came intermittent shouts: "Hey, stupid Marine! Tonight you die!" "Banzai!" "Charge!" O'Bannon was glad there had been no attack. "It would have been curtains for us," he said.

Except for Cushman's Pocket, where the Japanese were in firm control, March 7 had been a gratifying day for the Third Division. General Erskine's gamble on the predawn attack had paid off despite heavy losses to the 9th Regiment, the near debacle of taking the wrong hill in the darkness, and having to swarm 362C in broad daylight. "Although nearly all the basic dope was bad," Colonel Boehm noted in his battle journal, "the strategy proved very sound, since it turned out that the open ground taken under cover of darkness was the most heavily fortified of all terrain captured."

Marines had paid a high price for Hill 362C, nearly six hundred men killed or wounded. But now nothing could drive them from its crest, and its capture had removed the last major obstacle blocking the final breakthrough to Iwo's northern shoreline in the center of the island. "From now on, it's all downhill," Erskine said, "and the end, thank God, is in sight."

If anyone on Iwo was the epitome of a professional fighting man, it was one of the general's men—Sergeant Reid Carlos Chamberlain.

He had joined the Corps in the late 1930s and was a swashbuckling twenty-two-year-old corporal serving in the Philippines when Pearl Harbor was attacked. For five months his outfit fought side-by-side with outnumbered and outgunned American soldiers and sailors and a small and ill-trained Filipino army, before being smothered by a million-man Japanese invasion force.

Chamberlain was on Corregidor, wounded and plagued with malaria, when the island fortress in Manila Bay fell to General Masaharu Homma's troops on May 7, 1942. In the wild confusion of the final shots and surrender, he managed to evade the conquering Japanese, found a leaky boat, and escaped with three men to Mindanao Island where they somehow located a band of American and Filipino guerrillas who nursed him back to health.

During the next fifteen months, Chamberlain fought in—and then led—countless hit-and-run raids against the Japanese. Word of the corporal's leadership and daring reached General MacArthur in Australia, who commissioned him a second lieutenant in the United States Army.

American submarines by mid-1943 were making regular runs to supply the guerrillas with ammunition and medicine, and to collect firsthand intelligence. MacArthur ordered one of the missions to bring Chamberlain back to Allied Southwest Pacific Headquarters at Melbourne, where he was promoted to first lieutenant, awarded the Army's Distinguished Service Cross for "extraordinary heroism," and sent by air back to the States for a hero's welcome and to sell war bonds.

Like "Manila John" Basilone, this wasn't Reid Chamberlain's version of what a professional fighting man should be doing in wartime. He resigned the commission, rejoined the Marine Corps, traded his officer's bars and all that went with them for the stripes of a Leatherneck sergeant, and asked for combat duty. An obliging but confused personnel officer sent him to the Third Division in time for the Iwo campaign.

Now, in the late afternoon of D-plus sixteen, Sergeant Chamberlain and several men were making their way to the front from the 9th Regiment's command post. As a battalion runner, he'd made the trip several times during the day; each time using his combat skills to evade snipers who had been especially troublesome.

Alvin Josephy, the Marine correspondent, was among the group. He and the others believed that the area had been cleared of Japanese, although mortars still fell with uncomfortable frequency.

"We were picking our way among the stones and burned Jap bodies," he wrote, "when three shots rang out from the hillside." Startled Marines scrambled for cover behind boulders. Chamberlain snapped his Colt pistol from its holster, looking for the source of the enemy fire. "There was another shot," Josephy recalled. "We heard a thud. We thought the bullet had struck the curving side of the ridge." Suddenly there was bedlam as Marines sprayed the area, still unable to spot the sniper's nest.

Again Josephy: "A jeep ambulance driver and an automatic rifleman crouched behind nearby rocks, their teeth clenched, their hands gripping their weapons. We called Chamberlain but received no answer." Other men joined the fray, emptying their clips in a fury of futility. "One burly sergeant stood straight up without a helmet on," Josephy said, "and fired his carbine from the hip, moving directly at a hole as he fired."

The ambulance driver found Chamberlain slumped against a rock. A trickle of blood flowed from behind his left ear. His eyes were open, but he was dead. The "thud" the Marines had heard was the bullet that killed him. It remained for Josephy to write Chamberlain's epitaph. With minor variations, the same words could have been used for thousands of others who died on Iwo:

"There is nothing you can say or do when a good friend is suddenly killed in battle. You feel stunned, angry, sad, and frustrated. We could have fired point-blank the rest of the day at those holes. The Japs would only have laughed at us. In an instant they had claimed one of our best men. Chamberlain's wonderful war record had ended abruptly. After so many heroic deeds, it seemed an added tragedy that he was killed while doing nothing but walking. There was nothing anybody could do about it."

3

Business as usual was the pattern of D-plus sixteen along the Fifth Division's front. Colonel Graham's 26th Regiment moved out at daybreak without artillery support, not as a tactic to surprise the enemy but because Marine howitzers were short of shells from the previous day's bombardment. But the Japanese *were* caught off guard by the absence of pre-jump-off shelling, and the advance quickly made nearly two hundred yards, overrunning a defensive complex on a hill that had held up the previous day's advance.

Some Marines rested while others proceeded to surround the knoll, north of the rubble of Nishi Village. For the most part, things were quiet: only the occasional hiss of a flamethrower's jetstream of fire, and the explosion of a satchel charge, as demolitions men sealed bypassed cave entrances. In fact, things were *too* quiet to suit suspicious oldtimers. One man atop the ridge thought he detected the muffled sounds of hand grenades exploding beneath him.

Suddenly there was a gigantic blast that could be heard on Motoyama Number One and on the summit of Suribachi. A flash of flame shot into the air, followed by a series of rumbles and a chain of more explosions. The hill shuddered for an instant before its top blew sky-high. Dozens of men were swallowed in the mammoth crater. Others were blown into the air like rag dolls, stunned by concussion and wounded by cascading rocks and chunks of concrete.

Marines on the slopes scrambled to the top and frantically began digging out comrades. "Strong men vomited at the sight of charred bodies," one of the men later recalled, "and others walked crying from the dreadful scene." One Marine struggling down the slope saw Japanese trying to escape from caves, only to be buried in landslides that sealed up most of the holes in the ridge's sides.

What the enemy had done would happen repeatedly during the final phase of the battle. They had blown up their own command post, killing and wounding scores of Marines at the same time, in this instance claiming nearly half-a-hundred 26th Regiment casualties.

Colonel Liversedge's 28th Marines had easier going in their push

along the western shoreline. They jumped off at 9:05 A.M. against light
resistance that caused them less difficulty than the terrain.

With gunfire from destroyers paving the way, the assault had
little trouble moving five hundred yards toward Kitano Point. There
were several anxious minutes just before sundown: a poison gas alarm
that lasted less than a quarter-hour before it was discovered the alert
was caused by a strong breeze blowing sulphur fumes and the smell
of a smoldering enemy ammunition dump that had been hit by Marine
artillery.

But the advance was not without cost. Sniper fire, hand grenades,
and mortars took their toll. All things considered, however, it was one
of the best days the 28th had experienced since the flag-raising on
Suribachi.

Japanese infiltrators were active along the Fourth Division front
in the post-midnight hours of D-plus sixteen, making repeated small-
scale attempts to find a weak spot in the lines. Captain Headley's
battalion was the target of the first raid, but the intruders were spotted
and wiped out before they reached Marine positions.

Major Mee's battalion was hit by the next foray, a probing action
that began in silence and then erupted into a two-hour firefight before
it was over and the enemy destroyed. Point-blank rifle and grenade
duels flared along the two-hundred-yard front, a frantic battleground
lighted by star shells falling among the ridges and gullies.

Some of the fifty-man Japanese force were able to sneak around
outposts and jump into Marine foxholes before being discovered, only
to die in man-to-man combat fought with bayonets, pistols, knives,
entrenching tools—even rifle butts and rocks. A dozen Japanese,
hugging the sides of one ravine, were spotted in the glare of a parachute
flare and instantly killed by rifle and machine gun fire. "They looked
like little devils running through the gates of Hell," a corporal said
the next day. "All they needed were pitchforks."

When dawn came, Mee's men counted fifty lifeless Japanese
sprawled in and around the Marine positions. Arms and legs, blown
apart by grenade blasts, were strewn among the dirt and rocks. But
thirteen Marines also had been killed in the furious melee. "It was
too much to pay, even if we'd have killed a company of the fuckin'
Nips," a bitter platoon sergeant said.

Dry canteens were found on many of the riddled enemy, a sign that the Japanese were not only bent on killing Marines but also trying to find water. Others carried no ammunition to reload empty rifles. The only weapons of two infiltrators were anti-personnel mines strapped around their waists, suicide devices they'd been unable to use.

Elsewhere along the line were minor scrimmages, frequent and heated exchanges of close-in rifle and grenade fire that kept weary Marines awake and alert. Then, at 5:02 A.M., a large Japanese rocket made a direct hit on the command post of the 23rd Regiment's Second Battalion. It was one of the few instances during the battle that one of these missiles found its target, this time with devastating results.

Killed in the blast was the outfit's communications chief. Every other man in the CP was wounded: Major Robert H. Davidson, the outfit's CO; his executive officer, Major John J. Padley; Captain Edward J. Schofield, the operations officer; the battalion adjutant; and two sergeant clerks.

Lieutenant Colonel Edward J. Dillon, the regimental executive officer, took over from Davidson, stunned by concussion but otherwise unhurt. He was back on the front four days later and would lead the battalion for the rest of the campaign. But the battle was over for the others, evacuated to hospitals in the Marianas.

When the Fourth Division attack began at 7:30 A.M., it found the Japanese somewhat subdued—the usual enemy rifle and machine gun fire, the hand grenades and mortars, the sniper bullets pinging into advancing troops. The Japanese firepower around Turkey Knob had been, as the day's action report would say, "notably reduced."

Gains for the day were unimpressive along the front, but casualties were relatively light as the Marines fought to drive to Iwo's eastern shoreline. It was now only a matter of time until the savage sector no longer was an obstacle to the capture of the island; only a matter of time and more casualties until Marines no longer would be wounded or die in overwhelming strong points among the cliffs above the East Boat Basin the Monks of Makalapa had expected would be taken on D-Day.

4

Now that the Third Division had all but broken through to the coast in the center, and with the Fifth Division closing in on Kitano Point on the west, General Schmidt was ready to light the fuse for the final phase of the campaign.

He didn't expect the job to be finished that day, or even during the week. Cushman's Pocket remained a killingground for the Third Division, the Fourth Division still had its hands full with die-hard Japanese around Turkey Knob, and the Fifth faced an unknown number of deeply entrenched troops holding out with General Kuribayashi among the violence-infested rocks and gorges in its sector. But, like General Erskine, the Fifth Corps commander was certain that "the end, thank God, is in sight."

John Antonelli's battalion from the 27th Marines moved out at 7:30 A.M. to begin the push on the Fifth Division front. Easy Company, led by twenty-nine-year-old First Lieutenant Jack Lummus, was the spearhead and immediately came under scathing small arms and mortar fire. Despite the storm of resistance in the heavily mined area of caves and concrete emplacements, Lummus's men ground out an advance of some two hundred yards during the morning.

Then the attack bogged down, halted by a complex of bunkers and pillboxes. Oblivious to a torrent of machine gun bullets, grenades, and mortars, Lummus stood upright and was sprinting forward to rally the troops when a grenade blast knocked him to the ground.

Stunned by the concussion but otherwise miraculously uninjured, the lanky officer from Ennie, Texas, got to his feet and charged the position from whence came the grenade. He killed its occupants with a single sweep of his submachine gun, but fragments from another grenade ripped into his shoulder before there was time to take cover.

Hardly faltering despite his wounds, Lummus swarmed another emplacement and wiped out its three occupants. Only then did he motion for the company to follow. With himself twenty yards in front, shouting Marines were surging forward when the lieutenant vanished from sight in the thunderclap of an explosion that sent rocks and dirt skyward. The men could see Lummus when the debris settled.

"We thought he was standing in a hole," one of them said. A land mine had blown off his legs. On bloody stumps, the lieutenant waved and shouted: "Keep coming! Goddamnit, keep coming! Don't stop now!"

Several ragged, dirty, tired, cursing riflemen, some with tears now flowing down grimy faces, ran to his side to see if they could do anything. A comrade since the long-ago days when the division trained at Camp Pendleton wondered aloud whether or not to shoot him to end his agony—a not surprising reaction that immediately passed since Lummus continued shouting: "Goddamnit, keep moving! You can't stop now!"

Tears turned to raging fury as Easy Company swept ahead an incredible three hundred yards, overwhelming foxholes and pillboxes and bunkers, bolting across ravines and scrambling up ridges, blasting cave entrances and sniper pits. The spark that ignited the steamroller charge was the horrifying sight of their mortally wounded, indomitable commander and his fathomless courage. Seeing him, the men knew what they had to do.

Surgeons at the Fifth Division hospital were powerless to stop the massive bleeding draining Lummus's life away. All they could do was relieve his pain with morphine and give him blood transfusions, eighteen pints in all. But a determination to live and his stamina— he'd played football and was an All-American end at Baylor University—kept him alive for several hours, always conscious and sometimes smiling and talking to the doctors.

"I guess the New York Giants have lost the services of a damn good end," he said at one point to Lieutenant E. Graham Evans, one of the surgeons. Lieutenant Howard Stackpole, another doctor and a fellow Texan friend, stopped by in the late afternoon. Both knew the end was near. "He was smiling as he closed his eyes and died," Stackpole remembered.

Lummus's Medal of Honor was the twentieth earned in the eighteen days since the invasion began. That night what remained of Easy Company was atop the last ridge overlooking the ocean at Kitano Point. Jack Lummus's men had advanced another two hundred yards as he was dying. To them, he was still their leader. And always would be.

Private First Class James D. LaBelle also lost his life that day in the Fifth Division push. And he, too, would be awarded a posthumous

Medal of Honor. The action of the nineteen-year-old from Columbia Heights, Minnesota, didn't inspire a spectacular charge by his comrades, but it saved the lives of two of them. Like so many young riflemen in the 27th Regiment's Second Battalion, LaBelle was fighting his first battle—and his last.

Several times since D-Day, death had missed him by inches. In the push across the island at the base of Suribachi, machine gun fire killed three men next to him. Three days later, a mortar landed on the edge of a shell hole where he had been pinned down with four men. LaBelle was the only one who was unwounded. On D-plus ten, a sniper's bullet killed his best friend as they advanced side by side toward Nishi Ridge.

Now LaBelle's platoon was caught in the same firestorm of machine guns, grenades, and mortars ripping into Lummus's men. He and two others took cover behind a boulder near the mouth of a burned-out cave, waiting for things to get better.

LaBelle saw the silhouette of a Japanese in the mouth of the cave and watched as he lobbed a grenade. It landed too far away for the Marine to throw it back. Shouting a warning, he leaped to cover the explosion with his body and died instantly in the blast. LaBelle's luck had run out. This time it was his comrades who survived.

Third Division troops, meanwhile, whittled away at Cushman's Pocket and continued the drive to reach the northern shoreline. Artillery blasted enemy lines for ten minutes before the attack began at 7:50 A.M. Then tanks rumbled forward, firing into caves and pillboxes blocking the advance to the sea. At day's end, the push had carried to within three hundred yards of splitting Iwo across the highlands in the center.

The Fourth Division kept up its pressure to wipe out the last resistance around Turkey Knob. It was doubtful this could be done during the day, but there were encouraging signs that remaining enemy strongpoints were crumbling and would be silenced by the next day's assault.

General Cates was concerned about it all, wondering if he still had enough men and firepower to finish the job.

5

On D-plus eighteen, Cushman's Pocket showed few signs of losing its fury. In Iwo's familiar pattern, Marine artillery and Navy gunfire drove the enemy underground before the assault jumped off. When the attack began, it came under the usual torrent of Japanese fire—small arms and mortars from hidden strongpoints untouched by the bombardment.

Minor gains were made in the morning by tank-supported infantry. But the spearhead Sherman was knocked out by satchel charges, and the push ground to a halt. By midafternoon, it was obvious that the stubborn corridor would hold out longer and claim more Marines before it was finally overrun.

While the main thrust pounded the obstreperous pocket, a patrol from the 21st Regiment's First Battalion had skirted around the front and driven to the cliffs overlooking Iwo's north shore. Lieutenant Paul M. Connally and his twenty-seven men were amazed at how easily the final breakthrough had been made; they'd met only sporadic resistance and it had been quickly overcome without casualties.

"All of us just stood there for several minutes," Connally recalled years later, "staring at the waves lapping over the beach." The jubilant men scampered down the rocky bluff, moving rapidly past cave entrances and bunkers demolished by naval gunfire and air strikes. "It was eerie," the lieutenant said. "Not a sound except the gentle surf."

Several men walked nonchalantly into the water and scooped it up in handfuls to splash their faces. Others gingerly shed shoes and socks they'd worn for two weeks, and waded in the cool sea. "It was like a beach party in California," one of the men said, "but it didn't last long."

While most of the patrol frolicked in the surf or rested on the inviting beach, Connally was on the radio with regimental headquarters. He knew the surge to the sea was more significant to the conquest of Iwo Jima than the flag-raising on Suribachi, although not as spectacular. Nor had the scene been captured in a photograph for history to remember. But the Third Division had reached the island's northern shore and had at last split General Kuribayashi's rapidly dwindling force into two pockets.

"Bring back a canteen of sea water," an exultant Colonel Withers told the lieutenant. "I'd like to taste it and send the rest along to General Erskine," he said.

The "beach party" reverie lasted less than ten minutes, long enough for Connally to fill the canteen and start it on the way to the 21st Marines' CP. Bypassed Japanese watched the spectacle, and used the time to set up mortars and target them on the Marines. Shells were falling moments later among the unwary Leathernecks, wounding seven. They were carried to the crest of the cliff where the patrol dug in for the night.

Connally's outfit, Able Company of the 21st Regiment's First Battalion, had landed with nearly four hundred men. Only three of the original complement made it to Iwo's northern shore; the others of Company A were replacements.

That evening, as another brilliant sundown came to the island, a runner appeared at Erskine's command post with Connally's canteen. It was wrapped with white tape from a battle dressing that read: "Forwarded for inspection, not consumption." The Big E was gratified but misty-eyed when he saw the memento—pleased by the historic breakthrough, sorrowful over the cost. In its drive to the coast, the Third Division had lost more than half its original assault troops— 3,563 men killed, wounded, or missing in action.

Thursday night was hectic on the Fourth Division front. It was the eighth of March, exactly thirty-nine months to the day since the Pearl Harbor attack, and General Kuribayashi's troops were determined to make it a memorable anniversary.

Nearly a thousand Japanese, probably the largest single force still available to the enemy commander, began infiltrating Marine lines at 11:00 P.M., hitting the boundary separating the 23rd and 24th Regiments. It was a motley gathering, mainly survivors of naval units, well-organized but poorly armed. Many intruders had only bamboo spears. A few had small supplies of hand grenades and rifles. Some carried land mines strapped to their bodies, suicide squads with a common thought: to kill Marines as they blew themselves to smithereens. The heaviest weapons of the attackers were a few light *nambu* machine guns.

Easy Company of the 23rd Marines' Second Battalion was first to spot the enemy movement, shadowy figures crawling slowly and quietly down a ravine. Some of them, carrying stretchers and shouting "Corpsman! Corpsman!" in passable English, were within ten yards of Lieutenant Colonel Dillon's command post before the alarm was sounded. From then on, close-quarter fighting raged until dawn.

Shouts of *"Totsukegi!"* (charge) and *"Banzai!"* could be heard over the clatter of Marine machine guns and rifles. Grenades and mortars exploded among the Japanese, cutting them down in sickening numbers but not stopping the screaming attack. Parachute flares and star shells illuminated the roaring montage of man-on-man combat.

A captured Japanese, a Navy pilot, later said his orders were to break through to Motoyama Number One, steal a B-29, and fly to Tokyo. He didn't know how this would keep the Marines from taking Iwo Jima, but he was willing to try anything to get off the island alive and still save face.

One by one or in small groups, the attackers were wiped out. At daybreak, fewer than two hundred Japanese were able to crawl back to their lines. Marines tallied 784 enemy dead, although not without heavy losses to themselves: ninety men killed and 257 wounded. But the heaviest attack the Japanese would mount during the battle had been beaten back.

A measure of the ferocity of the nightlong melee was reflected in the amount of ammunition used by Company E: five hundred hand grenades, two hundred rounds of sixty millimeter mortars, two hundred star shells, and nearly 20,000 rounds of .30-caliber machine gun and rifle bullets.

Mopping-up operations went on until noon while other Fourth Division units continued the yard-by-yard push toward the eastern shoreline to quell the stiff resistance around the rubble of Turkey Knob. When General Cates's men dug in for the night, they could look down from positions on the ridge and see the ocean at the foot of the cliffs.

6

D-Day plus eighteen, cloudless and warm.

Kelly Turner, on the *Eldorado*, was ready to leave for Guam, taking with him most of the remaining ring of warships. The Navy's fighting role in the campaign was almost over, and all the seapower that could be mustered would be needed for the invasion of Okinawa, now just seventeen days away.

Without ceremony or a personal "farewell and well done" to General Smith and "his Marines," the admiral left Harry Hill as Nimitz's top commander on the scene. At this stage of the battle there wasn't much for him, or "Howlin' Mad," to do except play cribbage.

Only the cruisers *Salt Lake City* and *Tuscaloosa*, along with several destroyers, remained two miles offshore, on station and ready for fire missions when ordered. The *Enterprise*, the last of the big carriers, steamed away with six small flattops and their planes and pilots. From now on, Army P-51 Mustangs would fly air cover for the remaining ships and the Marines at the front.

Two thousand troops from General Chaney's Army Garrison Group came ashore from LSTs. When the Marines left, it would be the Army's responsibility to transform Iwo Jima into a mighty American base.

That night, 334 B-29s droned northward toward Tokyo in a sixty-mile-long formation from the Marianas, flying five miles above Iwo in moon-drenched skies. It had taken the armada three hours to lift off runways on Guam and Saipan and rendezvous for what would be the most destructive air raid in history, greatly surpassing anything in Europe—even the soon-to-come atomic bomb infernos of Hiroshima and Nagasaki.

Shortly after midnight, Superforts dropped the first of 1,665 tons of incendiary bombs on the heart of Japan. With Iwo no longer an early-warning station for incoming bombers, there was little opposition from fighter planes or antiaircraft batteries. A sea of flames, fanned by a strong wind, roared liked a typhoon, destroying sixteen square miles of the city by daybreak.

Eighty-four thousand Japanese died in the flames; more than 265,000 tinderbox buildings were destroyed, leaving a million people homeless. The A-bomb dropped on Hiroshima, 142 days later, would cause 24,000 fewer casualties and destroy less of the city.

"The holocaust exceeded any conflagration in the history of the Western World, including the burning of Rome in 64 A.D., the London fire of 1666, and the burning of Moscow in 1906," Richard Newcomb wrote of the fire bombing of Tokyo. Homeward bound B-29 crews said they could see the glow of flames for nearly two hundred miles.

Admiral Nimitz and General LeMay met with newsmen the next morning at CinCPac Headquarters on Guam. They reported that two damaged Superforts had landed on Iwo, and fourteen others had ditched at sea with their crews rescued by Navy Catalina flying boats based just offshore from Suribachi.

"We can take these losses," the 20th Air Force commander said, "but the Japanese sure as hell can't. With Iwo in our hands, you can be damned certain this is only the beginning." He paused to light a big Havana cigar and spoke again: "It's the absolute beginning of the end for Hirohito and his crowd of warlords."

Heavy and costly fighting still faced the Marines across the island on D-plus eighteen, especially in the convoluted terrain of the Fifth Division sector. So formidable were the natural defenses, so deadly and determined was enemy resistance in the zone, that less than fifty yards were gained during the next forty-eight hours.

Major obstacle was a long and low ridge jutting southeast from Kitano Point, a heavily fortified escarpment overlooking a deep draw manned by suicidal troops. It would take fifteen days to finally wipe out what would become the final pocket of organized Japanese resistance on Iwo.

Two battalions from the 27th Regiment—Justin Duryea's First and John Antonelli's Second—moved into the death-dealing maze shortly after daybreak. Both commanders were out of the battle by early afternoon, maimed by a land mine as, together, they were working their way to the front to see if anything could be done to spring the advance.

One of Duryea's men, Platoon Sergeant Joseph Julian, was doing everything imaginable to quell the firestorm of small arms and mortar fire from the ridge, and what Marines already were calling "the Gorge," a place name to rank in ferocity with the Fourth Division's Meat Grinder and Cushman's Pocket in the Third Division zone.

Julian was a twenty-six-year-old career Marine from historic Sturbridge Village in Massachusetts. Since D-Day he had defied the odds in countless rampages that reminded his platoon of the devil-be-damned attitude of his gung-ho friend, PFC Jacklyn Lucas. Now, with the attack less than fifteen minutes old, Julian's platoon was pinned down by machine gun fire from several caves.

Crawling forward some fifty yards into no man's land, the sergeant demolished one four-man strongpoint with two hand grenades, killing its screaming occupants in almost simultaneous explosions. Before Japanese in a nearby cave could swing their machine gun his way, Julian plunged to cover behind a boulder and emptied his carbine in a single burst, wiping out two more enemy troops.

At that instant, as the Marine got to his knees, another machine gun nest started firing from a position farther up the ridge's steep sides. While comrades on the line covered him with rifle and automatic weapons fire, Julian got to his feet and dashed back for more ammunition to continue the furious one-man assault. Snatching up a satchel of demolitions, a bandoleer of rifle cartridges, and a bazooka, he sprinted back into no man's land.

"You guys stay put until I take care of a few more Nip bastards," he yelled to the platoon, which watched incredulously as Julian again went to work.

Three hours later the sergeant still hadn't signaled the troops to move forward. But his intrepid determination had wiped out four more enemy positions, two with demolition charges, one with bazooka fire, and the other with hand grenades. Just when Julian thought the area was cleared enough for the men to advance with a chance of making it alive, a machine gun burst caught him in the chest. He died instantly.

His Medal of Honor would be the second in two days for Antonelli's gallant battalion. Like Private First Class James D. LaBelle, Platoon Sergeant Joseph Julian was now a Marine Corps legend of self-sacrifice and devotion to duty.

In fourteen days since the conquest of Suribachi, the Fifth Division had driven five miles up Iwo's western shore and could now look down on Kitano Point, its ultimate objective. But 4,292 more of its men had fallen: 1,093 killed, 2,974 wounded, 220 with combat fatigue, and five missing in action.

*

Except for continued and costly fighting in Cushman's Pocket, and bitter but scattered resistance from Japanese holding out in by-passed caves on the cliffs above the northern shoreline, the Third Division had completed its mission on Iwo. From now on, most of General Erskine's troops would be engaged in mopping-up operations with the Fifth Division around Kitano Point.

On the Fourth Division front, General Cates's weary survivors had put down the last resistance around Turkey Knob, the final jaws of the Meat Grinder. His troops, too, could now look down on Iwo's northern beaches.

Behind them were the two bloodiest weeks of fighting in Marine Corps history: fourteen days of relentless head-on assault, of yard-by-yard carnage—the price of the advance against defiant Japanese dying for their Emperor in the man-killing defenses of Charlie-Dog Ridge, Hill 382, the Amphitheater, Minami Village, and Turkey Knob. The two weeks in the Meat Grinder had cost the Fourth Division 4,075 men: 847 killed, 2,836 wounded, 391 with battle fatigue, and one missing.

LEFT - Fifth Division Marines zero in on enemy snipers holding out at northern tip of the island. (*Charles O. Jones*)

RIGHT - Wary Marine looks into mouth of cave that served as Japanese hospital and supply depot near Kitano Point. (*Mark Kaufman*)

Marine infantry and tanks attack enemy position three days before battle's end. The explosion is from a Japanese mortar shell that claimed three casualties in a day-long advance of less than a hundred yards, which cost thirty Marines. (*Charles O. Jones*)

Marines take cover as demolitions men blast a cave strongpoint. (*Charles O. Jones*)

Marine casualties get first-aid for corpsmen at frontline command post near Iwo's eastern shore, where enemy naval guns (*top center*) were zeroed-in on beachhead. (*Arthur J. Kiely, Jr.*)

Another charge closes a cave near Kitano Point at Iwo's northernmost point. (*Robert Wilton*)

One of the 1,083 Japanese taken prisoner, having survived the battle, is questioned by a Marine corporal interpreter. (*Louis R. Lowery*)

Captured Koreans from labor battalion cover bodies of Japanese dead as Third Division Marines look on. (*James Cornelius*)

PART TEN

The Final Phase

1

D-plus twenty-three, March 14. A day to remember.

Dawn-to-dusk fighting, at times heavy and costly, continued without letup in isolated sectors where fewer than two thousand disorganized and shattered remnants of General Kuribayashi's troops held out in the Gorge, Cushman's Pocket, and in the gullies and ridges east of Turkey Knob.

But it wasn't action on the front that marked the milestone.

This was the day when Admiral Nimitz would formally proclaim that Iwo Jima had been conquered. Marines, from privates to generals, later cynically and understandably questioned his timing as tragically premature; they would suffer more than six thousand additional casualties before leaving the island.

Ceremonies began precisely at 9:30 A.M., as Nimitz had directed, near the blackened rubble of a huge concrete bunker, incinerated by a flamethrower on D-Day, some two hundred yards north of Suribachi. Nimitz wasn't there. Final conferences with the admirals and generals, who would land and command the Marines of the First and Sixth Divisions in the invasion of Okinawa, had kept him at CinCPac Headquarters on Guam.

An honor guard of twenty-four riflemen, eight from each division, stood at parade rest. Dressed in dungarees they'd washed the night before but that showed the wear and tear of more than three weeks of front-line combat, they faced the assembled brass: Generals Smith, Schmidt, Erskine, Cates, and Rockey; Admirals Turner and Hill; and the Army's General Chaney.

Colonel David A. Stafford, General Schmidt's strong-voiced personnel officer, began reading 113 words that Nimitz personally had written the previous night:

"I, Chester William Nimitz, Fleet Admiral, United States Navy, Commander in Chief of the United States Pacific Fleet and Pacific Ocean Areas, do hereby proclaim as follows: United States forces under my command have occupied this and other of the Volcano Islands. All powers of government of the Japanese Empire in these islands so occupied are hereby suspended. . . ."

Four P-51 Mustangs roared across Motoyama Number One and peeled off to land, their first close-air support mission of the day completed. A suddenly brisk breeze carried the sound of artillery exploding in Cushman's Pocket, three miles to the north. A distracted Stafford paused for several seconds, then continued:

"All powers of government are vested in me as military governor and will be exercised by subordinate commanders under my direction. All persons will obey promptly all orders given under my authority. Offenses against the forces of occupation will be severely punished.

"Given under my hand at Iwo Jima this fourteenth day of March, 1945."

A three-man color guard, one rifleman from each division, snapped to attention and stepped off a dozen paces to an eighty-foot flagstaff embedded in concrete atop the demolished bunker.

Twenty-year-old Private First Class Thomas J. Casale handed the flag to Private First Class Anthony C. Yust, nineteen, who unfolded and held it for twenty-four-year-old Private First Class Albert B. Bush to attach to the lanyard. Field Musician First Class John C. Glynn, a twenty-one-year-old bugler, sounded colors. The notes were sharp and clear as Casale quickly raised the flag to the top of the pole, where it snapped in the warm wind.

At that instant the flag on Suribachi was lowered. The admirals and generals saluted. The honor guard responded sharply to the command: "Present arms!" Knots of nearby men—Marines, Seabees, Air Corps pilots, and ground crews—looked on in silence and saluted, many misty-eyed.

Everything was over in less than five minutes.

Iwo Jima was officially United States territory.

Someone heard "Howlin' Mad" Smith say to Erskine: "This is the worst yet, Bobbie." The Old Man wore dungarees, a sun helmet, and an aviator's flight jacket. His eyes were full of tears. Erskine was not quite sure of what he meant.

When word of the proclamation and official flag-raising reached President Roosevelt, he was on Capitol Hill to report to Congress on his historic meeting with Winston Churchill and Josef Stalin at Yalta. After detailing agreements reached by the "Big Three" to finish the war in Europe, FDR turned to events in the Pacific theater.

"The Japanese warlords know they are not being overlooked," he told the hushed audience of military leaders, cabinet members, Supreme Court Justices, lawmakers, foreign dignitaries, and newsmen jammed into the stifling chamber of the House of Representatives. "They have felt the force of our B-29s and our carrier planes. They have felt the naval might of the United States and do not appear very anxious to come out and try again."

Wagging his head in a vigorous, characteristic movement, he solemnly continued: "The Japs know what it means that 'the United States Marines have landed.'" The Commander in Chief's next words were followed by loud shouting and roaring applause: "And I think I may add, having Iwo Jima in mind, that the situation is well in hand."

This, too, was the day the cemeteries were dedicated.

Marines had been coming down from the high ground in the north since early morning, not because of the flag-raising ceremonies but to seek out graves of fallen comrades. The burial grounds by now had the appearance of hallowed dignity, and what was spoken at the ceremonies added to the aura.

"No words of mine can properly express the homage due these heroes," General Cates said of the Fourth Division dead, "but I can assure them and their loved ones that we will carry their banner forward. They truly died that we might live, and we will not forget. May their souls rest in peace."

Navy Lieutenant Roland B. Gittelsohn, a Jewish chaplain, delivered the eulogy for the Fifth Division: "Here lie officers and men, Negroes and whites, rich men and poor—together. Here are Protestants, Catholics, and Jews—together. Here no man prefers another because of his faith or despises him because of his color. Here there are no quotas of how many from each group are admitted or allowed. Among these men there is no discrimination. No prejudices. No hatred. Theirs is the highest and purest democracy."

Rabbi Gittelsohn spoke of high hopes for a postwar world, of "joining hands with Britain, China, and Russia in peace, even as we have in war, to build the kind of world you died for. Out of this, and from the suffering and sorrow of those we mourn, will come, we promise, the birth of a new freedom for the sons of men everywhere."

General Erskine was visibly moved, his frame ramrod straight as his tearful gaze swept the rows of markers in the Third Division resting place. "There is nothing I can say which is wholly adequate to this occasion," he began. "Only the accumulated praise of time will pay proper tribute to our valiant dead. Long after those who lament their immediate loss are themselves dead, these men will be mourned by the nation. For they are the nation's loss."

A gust of wind rustled the two pages from which he read. Another flight of Mustangs roared down the runway, some two hundred yards away, and lifted skyward for support missions against the Gorge and Cushman's Pocket. The dust from their take-off runs hadn't settled when a twin-engined Navy hospital plane landed for another load of casualties.

Now Erskine began again. "There is talk of great history, of the greatest fight in our history, of unheard-of sacrifice and unheard-of courage," he said. "These phrases are correct, but they are prematurely employed. The evidence has not sufficiently been examined. Even the words and phrases used by historians to describe the fight for Iwo Jima, when the piecemeal story of our dead comes to light, will still be inadequate.

"Victory was never in doubt. Its cost was. What was in doubt, in all our minds, was whether there would be any of us left to dedicate our cemetery at the end, or whether the last Marine would die knocking out the last Japanese gun and gunner.

"Let the world count our crosses. Let them count them over and over. Let us do away with names, with ranks and rates and unit designations, here. Do away with the terms—regular, reserve, veteran, boot, oldtimer, replacement. They are empty, categorizing words which belong only in the adjutant's dull vocabulary."

The general paused. "Here lie only," another pause, "only Marines."

The dedication of the last cemetery was over.

For the rest of the day, men who could be spared from the battle came down from the front for requiems of their own. They came singly, in pairs, in small groups. Most walked, but some hitched rides on jeeps or supply trucks. They moved reverently down the rows of markers, some walking less slowly than others: they were searching for a particular name, for a close buddy's grave. Others shuffled along. Virtually all were in grimy and ragged dungarees, steel helmets in hand, rifles slung over shoulders.

One man with a black beard and dirt-encrusted eyebrows hesitated before one grave, moved on, looked back for a fleeting second, and moved on again, crying to himself and cursing "this no good fuckin' island, this no good fuckin' war." At the edge of the Fifth Division cemetery nearest Suribachi, the engines of two bulldozers roared and treads clanked as they dug fresh trenches for more graves.

Marines still to be buried lay nearby in neat rows, their bodies covered with ponchos and blankets. Worn shoes and leggings stuck out here and there from under the make-do shrouds. A jeep ambulance pulled up with three more bodies. The two-man burial detail quickly, gently lifted them to a bank of volcanic ash and drove away, back to the fighting on another unending trip.

With most of General Kuribayashi's troops bottled up in three small but savage pockets, the pattern of assault had changed. No longer were attacks preceded by heavy naval and artillery bombardment; the danger was too great that shelling would kill more Marines than Japanese. Thus the cruisers *Salt Lake City* and *Tuscaloosa*, their missions completed, steamed away to rendezvous with the fleet for the invasion of Okinawa. Six destroyers remained on station to light the front at night with parachute flares and star shells.

P-51 Mustangs still flew close-air support missions when they could unload explosives or napalm on Japanese strongpoints without hitting Marines. Flamethrowing tanks, their fire-spitting muzzles spewing as many as 10,000 gallons of flame oil daily, were now the major heavy weapons spearheading the final phase of the campaign.

But, more than ever, the burden of the battle was on the infantry: riflemen, demolitions squads, and back-pack flamethrowers smashing head-on against Japanese, whose only reason to survive another day was to kill Marines.

Attrition was terrible beyond belief. Colonel Tom Wornham's 27th Regiment had ceased to exist. The Second Battalion, Major Antonelli's old outfit, now was commanded by Major Gerald F. Russell. But so few men were left that the unit was pulled off the front, so shredded that it never fought again. The First Battalion lost its third CO in nine days when Major William Tumbelston's left arm was all but severed by machine gun fire.

Fewer than five hundred men were all that remained of the regiment's D-Day roster of three thousand. Lieutenant Colonel Donn Robertson was the only original battalion commander still in action.

For the rest of the campaign he led a special Composite Battalion, all that was left of the 27th Marines, in the fighting to wipe out the last Japanese in the Gorge.

Two Medals of Honor would be awarded for deeds of valor the day Admiral Nimitz proclaimed Iwo Jima United States territory. One was posthumous.

It went to eighteen-year-old Private George Phillips from Rich Hill, Missouri, a frightened replacement who had been in the lines for two days. But boot camp had embued him with Marine Corps esprit de corps and a devotion to his comrades. When a hand grenade landed near the mouth of a bypassed cave where he had taken cover with three men, the teen-ager smothered the blast, sacrificing his life for men he hardly knew.

Private Franklin E. Sigler wasn't a replacement, but Iwo was his first campaign. Every day had been a frightening one for the twenty-year-old from Little Falls, New Jersey. Now, in the bedlam of battle to silence the Gorge, he showed his mettle. "Taking command of his leaderless squad," his Medal of Honor citation would read, "he led a bold charge, then, disregarding his own wounds, he carried three comrades to safety and returned to fight on until ordered to retire for treatment."

Marines on the front settled in for a night of relative quiet. They expected few fireworks—possibly some Japanese stragglers looking for food and water, but that was all.

Twilight had been magnificent, the brilliance of the setting sun burning through scattered cumulus clouds like dying embers in a fireplace. Three miles to the south, near the "official" flag, movies had begun to flicker on the screens of three makeshift outdoor theaters now on the island.

Fires burned in steel barrels where men heated coffee or water to wash clothes and shave, some to bathe as best as they could. Others talked over the day's events. Some wrote letters home. Radios in communications jeeps were tuned to Tokyo Rose or shortwave broadcasts from Guam and the States, their speakers blaring with the pleasant sounds of dance music.

Motoyama Number One was heavy with sundown traffic: sinister-looking Army P-61 Black Widow night fighters taking off on patrols between Iwo and Japan, the last of the day's flights leaving Iwo with wounded Marines for the Marianas, P-51s setting down from final low-level sweeps over enemy positions near Kitano Point. Three Super-forts, hit in an attack on Nagoya but now airworthy, awaited clearance to roar down the north-south runway and fly to Saipan for further repairs, then to stand by for their next mission.

Along the western beaches, just north of Suribachi, two men were on security patrol. Marines later said they were Army troops—but the evidence is that they were bored Leathernecks. Moving in opposite directions, both had walkie-talkie radios.

One man began to fantasize and, in his mind, he became an on-the-spot radio reporter covering the biggest story of his life. What would be his words, he asked himself, if his job was to broadcast the first news of an Allied victory in Europe? Before realizing what he was doing, he switched on his set and said the fateful words: "Flash! An official statement from Radio Berlin announces that Nazi Germany has accepted terms of unconditional surrender! The war in Europe is over!"

Now the incredible happened. Not only was the transmission heard by the other walkie-talkie, but also in the communications center at Fifth Corps headquarters and in the radio shack of an offshore ship where an operator was monitoring news reports from the mainland. Without a second thought, he blared the announcement over the vessel's loudspeaker system and relayed it to the rest of the fleet.

Within minutes pandemonium erupted across the island. Rifles and machine guns cracked and chattered on the lines in joyful cele-bration. Star shells and parachute flares from the destroyers illumi-nated every yard of the front. A destroyer sent a cascade of rockets screaming across Kitano Point with no target in mind, only a thun-derous and brilliant display of jubilation. Transports and LSTs let go with antiaircraft batteries, firing hundreds of shells lighting the skies thousands of feet above the fleet and over the island.

Movies broke up in bedlam. Men leaped into the air, cheering and yelling and slapping one another on the back. This was it! Victory in Europe! Now Japan soon would feel the full force of military power that had battered Hitler's Europe into submission. Men crawled from foxholes and tents to join in the raucous festivities, some not knowing what they were celebrating but certain it was something historic.

General Schmidt, fuming at the undisciplined Marine and Navy firing, was on the radiotelephone with Admiral Hill on the *Auburn* to find out what the hell was happening. By then all hands aboard the flagship knew the report was false. Only after fifteen minutes, when a Condition Red alert was flashed ashore and to the fleet, did the firing cease.

Private First Class Alvin J. Doyle, a Third Division correspondent from Brooklyn who had covered New York's City Hall for *The Daily Mirror*, wrote the next day: "It was a great feeling while it lasted, but it was a dirty trick." His story and those by civilians were killed by Navy censors; the brass was too embarrassed to let the people at home know about what Harry Schmidt later called "the incident of the false surrender."

Aid stations treated a dozen minor casualties, victims of falling shell fragments from the short-lived celebration. The identity of the Marine culprit who caused it all remains one of Iwo's lost secrets.

General Kuribayashi, in his cave headquarters deep in the Gorge, learned that night of Admiral Nimitz's proclamation in a special broadcast from Japan. It glorified the surviving defenders and exhorted them to "hold out to the last man as valiant Sons of Nippon, killing repugnant Americans as you die for Emperor and Homeland."

Schoolchildren from the general's birthplace, a small village on the outskirts of Tokyo, closed the program with prayers for the doomed garrison and by singing "The Song of Iwo Jima," specially written for the occasion. The enemy commander must have felt deeply moved at the words; even hard-bitten Navy interpreters, monitoring the transmission in the combat information center on the *Auburn*, were touched by the tiny voices of the boys and girls as they sang:

> Where dark tides billow in the ocean,
> A wink-shaped isle of mighty fame
> Guards the gateway to our empire:
> Iwo Jima is its name. . . .

Kuribayashi responded with an eloquent message of thanks to "the gallant and brave people of Japan." He vowed to continue the battle, saying: "I am pleased to report that we still fight well against the overwhelming material odds of the enemy, and all my officers and men deserve the highest commendation. I humbly apologize to my Emperor that I have failed to live up to expectations and have to yield this key island to the enemy after seeing so many of my officers and men killed."

General Rockey, in his revetment command post two miles away, pondered the next move to silence the Gorge and end the battle in the Fifth Division sector. He wondered if his feeble assault battalions still had the manpower to finish the job. Orders went out for ten percent of all rear-echelon men to be ready on one-hour's notice to bulwark the onerous shortage of riflemen on the front.

Nearly two hundred cannoneers from the 15th Regiment went into the lines the next morning along with fifty-five men from the division's amtrac battalion and 105 truck drivers from the 5th Motor Transport Battalion. More than sixty percent were casualties within forty-eight hours.

2

March 17, D-plus twenty-six, was another red-letter day in the official chronology of the battle.

Admiral Nimitz issued a special communiqué, the last of the campaign, announcing that Iwo had been "officially secured" at 6:00 P.M., and that organized Japanese resistance had ended. The announcement lauded all branches of the armed forces for their roles in the terrible fighting, particularly the Marines. He reported that 24,127 had fallen: 4,189 killed in action and 19,938 wounded during twenty-six days and nine hours of combat, the costliest battle in 168 years of Marine Corps history. The communiqué concluded:

"Among the Americans who served on Iwo island, uncommon valor was a common virtue."

To the Marines at the front—especially those hacking away against stubborn resistance in the devilish sandstone buttes of Cushman's Pocket and those ensnared in the seemingly endless struggle for the Gorge—it appeared the admiral again had been too hasty in writing off Kuribayashi and what remained of his troops, organized or not.

When a Third Division machine gunner heard about the communiqué, he shook his head in disbelief. "If this damned place has been secured, I wonder where in the hell all the Nip fire is coming from?" he said. It was a common reaction among the troops, many of them bitter over the fact that the home front now most certainly believed the battle was over even as Marines still were being wounded and killed.

The final phase of the campaign would last another ten days and claim another 1,724 American casualties before the island was, in fact, secured and the fighting finally was over.

General Kuribayashi long since had abandoned all hope of driving the invaders from the island, or of his own survival. But he was still alive and planning one desperate final attack before dying leading his troops in battle—or committing hara-kiri with his ancestral samurai sword.

"The situation is now on the brink of the last," his farewell message to Imperial General Headquarters in Tokyo said. "At midnight I shall lead the final offensive, praying that our empire will eventually emerge victorious and secure. . . .

"Unless this island is wrested back, our country will not be secure. Even as a ghost, I wish to be a vanguard of future Japanese operations against this place. Bullets are gone and water exhausted. Now that we are ready for the final act, I am grateful to have been given this opportunity to respond to the gracious will of the Emperor. Permit me to say farewell."

Premier Kuniaki Koiso and his cabinet of warlords had anticipated the fall of Iwo for some time. But they were shaken, nonetheless, by the loss of the bastion, knowing that Japan's front door now was open to invasion. That night the prime minister went on Radio Tokyo to tell the Japanese nation the mournful news. He said the defeat was "the most unfortunate thing in the whole war situation," but promised the conflict would continue.

"There will be no unconditional surrender," Koiso said, his voice choking. "So long as there is one Japanese living, we must fight to shatter the enemy's ambitions. We must not stop fighting until then."

If Kuribayashi heard the broadcast, he did not acknowledge it. Nor did the Japanese high command again hear directly from the doomed general.

Fifth Division men, when they finally snuffed out the last stragglers in the Gorge, found what probably was the samurai's last order. It apparently was issued the night of Kuribayashi's farewell message. In strong, classic Japanese characters, it read:

All surviving officers and men:

The battle situation has come to the last moment.

I want my surviving officers and men to go out and attack the enemy tonight.

Each man! Go out simultaneously at midnight and attack the enemy until the last. You have devoted yourselves to the Emperor. Don't think of yourselves.

I am always at the head of you all.

Since there was no banzai that night, it is most probable that the order never left the general's headquarters, an ill-ventilated and candle-lighted cave beneath a huge camouflaged concrete blockhouse at the head of the Gorge. But Marines two days later discovered evidence that Kuribayashi, and what was left of his staff, moved through tunnels that night with four hundred men to a last-stand cave nearer Kitano Point.

Where, when, or how the Japanese commander died was never determined. Nor was his body found. Some survivors, taken prisoner by Third Division mop-up troops, said he committed hara-kiri shortly after midnight of March 25. Other POWs said he died leading a pre-dawn banzai the next day, a doubtful probability, since the attack was made two miles from the general's last known command post.

What is known is that on the night of March 21 Kuribayashi sent a final message to the garrison on Chichi Jima.

"My officers and men are still fighting," it said. "The enemy front line is two hundred meters from us and they are attacking with flame-throwers and tanks. They have advised us to surrender by leaflets and loudspeakers, but we only laughed at this childish trick.

"All officers and men on Chichi Jima, good-by." It was the last transmission from the Japanese on Iwo Jima. But it was still not the finale of the battle.

"Howlin' Mad" Smith came ashore from the *Auburn* and left Iwo the day it was declared secure. So did a handful of Fourth Division troops, a shallow trickle of thousands who had swarmed the D-Day beaches. Some stopped off at the cemetery to pay final homage to dead comrades before boarding beached LSTs for the five-thousand-mile voyage back to base camp in the Hawaiian Islands.

The general left in style. Admiral Nimitz had sent his personal plane, a four-engined Douglas transport, to fly the Old Warrior back to Pearl Harbor. It was the least the CinCPac could do for the man who had led "his Marines" in an unbroken chain of victories across the central Pacific to the doorstep of Japan's home islands.

A press conference was held at Makalapa.

"We showed the Japanese at Iwo Jima that we can take any damn thing they've got," Smith told rear-echelon newsmen.

"Watching the Marines cross the island reminded me of Pickett's charge at Gettysburg. Mortar, artillery fire, and rockets fell among the troops, but they closed. In thirty-seven minutes after the first wave hit the beach we were on the southern end of the airfield. I say again, this was the toughest fight we have had so far.

"If there had been any question whether there should be a Marine Corps after this war, the battle of Iwo Jima will assure that there will always be a Marine Corps."

B-29s filled the skies over Iwo that night: 307 Superforts in a sixty-mile-long armada heading for a massive fire-bomb assault on Kobe. They left Japan's sixth largest city an inferno; nearly three thousand killed, twelve thousand-plus wounded, 240,000 homeless, and 66,000 buildings destroyed.

And Iwo Jima, because it was there and in American hands, saved the lives of another 150 fliers. Thirteen bombers, crippled by anti-aircraft fire over the target, landed on the island. On Saipan, General LeMay briefed newsmen. "Iwo Jima is really making the job easier," he said. The 20th Air Force's top commander spoke with firsthand knowledge. He had piloted the pathfinder bomber on the mission.

Back in Washington, Secretary of War Henry L. Stimson wrote Navy Secretary Forrestal to congratulate the Marines on the capture of the island. "The price has been heavy," the Army's representative in President Roosevelt's cabinet said, "but the military value of Iwo Jima is inestimable. Its conquest has brought closer the day of our final victory in the Pacific."

3

Fighting in Cushman's Pocket was coming to its violent end.

On D-plus twenty-five the last hard core of resistance had been squeezed into a deep gorge roughly two hundred yards long, but the enemy continued to determinedly hold out. Fierce small arms and machine gun fire came from caves, spider traps, and dug-in tanks.

Artillery could no longer be used for fear of landing on the Marines. Tanks were unable to maneuver in the narrow ravines. So Fifth Corps engineers built four specially-designed sleds, each mounting twenty rocket-launching tubes that could deliver 640 pounds of TNT in a single salvo. They were winched forward in an attempt to put an end to the fighting.

"Ten barrages smashed the pocket area," an official report on the day's action said, "and although the effect could not be directly observed, no miracle had taken place. Enemy resistance continued undiminished as the Marines moved in." By midafternoon, tank bulldozers had carved paths for flamethrowing Shermans to sear every target they could find.

At sundown, there was no answering fire as Marines advanced to the end of the ravine. It had taken six days to accomplish what a battalion of crack troops might have done in a day—two, at the most. But the task had fallen to a handful of surviving oldtimers and inexperienced replacements to finally overrun Cushman's Pocket. When it fell, there was nothing left of Kuribayashi's defenses in the Third Division zone.

About the same time Cushman's Pocket was silenced, a series of blasts shook the island. They came from the Gorge, where Fifth Division engineers detonated 8,500 pounds of TNT in a chain of five thundering explosions that ended organized resistance around Kitano Point.

The Fourth Division, too, swept through the last enemy strongpoints in its sector. From now on, it was a matter of mopping up; of another ten days of costly work for patrols of riflemen, flamethrowers, and demolitions teams wiping out bypassed bunkers, caves, pillboxes, and stragglers hiding wherever they could find concealment.

*

Private First Class Walter Josefiak, nineteen, of Detroit, Michigan, was at the point of one six-man Third Division mop-up patrol with Rusty, his war dog. The detail had cleaned out two pockets of stragglers, killing seven, and were moving warily toward the mouth of another cave.

Josefiak and Rusty were some fifteen yards ahead when a low growl came from the Doberman pinscher. His alerted handler spotted a sniper about to fire from behind a large rock guarding the entrance; he killed him with a carbine burst. With a savage snarl and a loud bark, the dog signaled the presence of another Japanese, who fell in an immediate fusillade.

Another sniper popped up. Josefiak fired again, wounding him. But as the enemy fell forward, he let loose with two rounds that thudded into the PFC's shoulder and chest. By now the air was full of hand grenades hurled by other Japanese.

Rusty darted to his wounded master and was lying at his side, between him and the cave mouth, when a grenade exploded nearby and its fragments tore into Josefiak. He shouted for someone to call the dog to safety, and motioned back two corpsmen who had started forward to give him first aid. Another grenade roared. Rusty took the full blast in a vain attempt to shield Josefiak. He died without a whimper.

Josefiak managed to roll to the cover of several boulders. Marines on a ridge above the cave threw a rope. Grasping it, he was pulled from the ledge. A jeep ambulance carried him and Rusty's body to the Third Division hospital. Josefiak died that night and was buried the next day. Not far away, in a tiny and special section of the Third Division cemetery, a small marker carried the stenciled words:

CORPORAL RUSTY
3D WAR DOG PLATOON

More Marines came down every day from the battlefield: grime-encrusted men in ragged dungarees; mostly unsmiling men with blank stares that mirrored the raw fighting; men inwardly proud of what they had accomplished but bitter over the awful losses; men with a smoldering hatred for the Japanese, but with a measure of grudging respect for the suicidal determination of the foe.

Shadow platoons, shot-to-pieces companies, battalions with a handful of survivors, regiments that couldn't muster a thousand men, made their way to the black sand of the beachhead. The stark, appalling, brutal, tragic fact was that of *all* the Marines who landed on Iwo, nearly thirty percent were casualties. But the *average* losses of assault units, the troops who fought on the front, were sixty percent.

Some outfits covered the three miles on foot, men too weary and disheartened to move at more than a slow and laborious shuffle. Jeeps and trucks carried others to the re-embarkation points. For many there was a grim, final farewell stop at the cemeteries to bid fallen comrades a last good-by.

On March 19, one month after D-Day and at almost the same hour the first troops hit the beaches, the last Fourth Division survivors boarded transports and LSTs to begin the long journey back to Maui, back to the base camp on the volcano, there to fill depleted ranks with new men, and shortly to begin training for the invasion of Japan.

The Fifth Division was gone by March 27, sailing in convoy for Hawaii, the Big Island, and for the inevitable preparation for what was expected to be the final climactic campaign of the war. It would be April 12 before the last Third Division troops departed for Guam, to refit and gird to spearhead the planned million-man invasion force against the enemy homeland.

On D-plus thirty-five, General Schmidt closed the Fifth Corps command post and flew to Pearl Harbor. Seabee battalions would remain on Iwo Jima to help complete its build-up into a forward base with striking power unimagined by the Marines who conquered shrewd General Kuribayashi's island fortress. General Chaney's 147th Army Regiment, recently arrived from New Caledonia in the south Pacific, would finish the mop-up and take over occupation duties.

In the dark predawn stillness of March 26, exactly five weeks after D-Day, between two and three hundred Japanese launched a final suicide attack—not a drunken, shouting banzai charge, but a well-organized and silent raid that bore every sign of Kuribayashi's cunning and determination. The first indication of trouble came at 5:15 A.M. when a sudden, sharp outburst of small arms fire broke out in a bivouac area just west of Motoyama Number Two.

Peacefully at sleep in a complex of tents were nearly three hundred men, a mixed bag of Marine shore parties and supply troops, Air Corps crewmen, Army antiaircraft gunners, and Seabees. All had bedded down believing there was no danger within miles. After all, organized resistance had ceased; the island was officially secured.

Things might have been different if the Americans were all combat troops. But most were unaccustomed to the bitter business of man-to-man fighting, and the enemy commander, whoever he was, had picked shrewdly the spot where the Japanese could expect to inflict maximum destruction before their certain annihilation.

Moving grimly and silently, the enemy struck from three directions. Within seconds Japanese were everywhere, slashing tent walls, knifing sleeping men who never knew what hit them, throwing hand grenades, swinging ceremonial swords, firing automatic weapons.

By a stroke of fortune, the brunt of the attack hit the Fifth Pioneer Battalion. The unit had finished its shore party work and was ready to leave the island that day. Like all Marines, they were combat troops first, specialists second, and they knew what to do in such circumstances.

First Lieutenant Harry L. Martin of Bucyrus, Ohio, threw up a scrimmage line manned largely by black troops, who coolly beat back one attack, then another, by screaming Japanese firing wildly as they came. It was now light enough to see what was happening, and Martin moved forward to help other Marines in a foxhole and was wounded twice. Then the thirty-four-year-old reserve officer overran a machine gun position, killing four Japanese with his pistol.

Fifth Division infantrymen, standing by to head for the beach and board ship, heard the fury and joined the melee. The attack was beaten back in furious fighting. Wounded and dead, friend and foe, littered the scene. A company of men from the Army's 147th Infantry Regiment appeared with a flamethrower tank shortly after 8:00 A.M., nearly three hours after the first shots were fired.

By then Iwo's last battle was over.

In the blood-spattered tents were forty-four dead airmen and eighty-eight wounded. Nine Marines were killed and thirty-one wounded, the last of 25,851 to fall in thirty-six days. Strewn grotesquely about the battleground were 262 Japanese bodies. Eighteen were taken prisoner, the last of fewer than two hundred captured by Marines.

No one knows the name of the first Marine killed on the awful island.

But the name of the last was First Lieutenant Harry L. Martin. He gave his life fighting for his comrades, his Corps, his country. And he had earned the last Medal of Honor to go to the valiant men of Iwo Jima.

D-plus twenty-three: March 14, 1945. The three division cemeteries are dedicated while the fighting still rages less than four miles away. Near the base of Suribachi, the Stars and Stripes rise above the graves of the Fourth Division dead. (*U.S. Marine Corps*)

Flag flies at half mast in center of Third Division cemetery, not far from beachhead below Motoyama Number One. (*U.S. Marine Corps*)

A Fifth Division Marine smooths the dirt around the cross over the grave of Gunnery Sergeant John Basilone, the first Marine to be awarded the Congressional Medal of Honor during World War II. (*U.S. Marine Corps*)

Fifth Division cemetery on D-plus twenty-five. Its row on row of crosses, and those in nearby Fourth and Third Division burial grounds, marked the battlefield resting places for 6,821 Marines. Ten years later, all bodies were exhumed and returned to American soil for final interment. (*Louis R. Lowery*)

Cast in bronze and weighing nearly one hundred tons, the statue commemorating the battle of Iwo Jima is situated on a gentle rolling slope near Arlington National Cemetery, across the Potomac River from Washington, D.C. Dedicated on November 10, 1954, the 179th anniversary of the Marine Corps, it honors Marines of all wars. Carved in the polished marble base are the names of the battlegrounds where Leathernecks have fought during the past two centuries, and the words of Fleet Admiral Chester W. Nimitz in tribute to the men who were at Iwo Jima: "Uncommon Valor Was a Common Virtue." (*U.S. Marine Corps*)

PART ELEVEN

Epilogue

1

Was General Kuribayashi mortally wounded leading the final predawn suicide attack of March 26? Or did he die the ceremonial death of a samurai warrior by committing seppuku in his cave redoubt deep in the cliffs around Kitano Point? What happened to the other ranking Japanese officers of the Iwo Jima garrison?

The questions will remain forever unanswered.

Speculation about the final hours and ultimate fate of the general and his commanders is based almost entirely on hearsay rumors, with only vague and piecemeal documentation and a handful of eyewitness survivors to support them.

All battle records on Iwo were burned, along with regimental battle flags, by Kuribayashi's aides before they died. He was determined the Americans would have no memorabilia by which to remember their victory and his disgrace. And most documents that existed at Imperial General Headquarters were lost in the fire bombings of Tokyo or in the shambles of Japan's final days before the downfall and surrender.

Major Mitsuaki Hara, whose battalion was wiped out on D-Day atop the terraces inland from Yellow Beach 2, was the highest-ranking Japanese to survive. Captured by Third Division troops on March 25 in a cliffside cave at the northern end of the island, he knew nothing of what happened to any of the last-ditch defenders.

During all the fighting, Marines took just 216 prisoners, many of them noncombatant Koreans from a labor battalion. During April and May, General Chaney's 147th Army Regiment captured another 867 POWs and killed 1,602 Japanese in the final mop-up. But a year later, emaciated foragers, unaware the war was over, still were being captured or slain in ambush as they crept at night from caves in search of food and water and to kill Americans if they could.

One far-fetched account of Kuribayashi's last hours puts him at the point of the banzai that ripped through the tents of the sleeping Americans, being hit by machine gun fire after Lieutenant Martin organized the Marine scrimmage line, and then being dragged by three of his own men to a cave where the general bled to death.

Another version is more in keeping with Kuribayashi's known character and ancestral background. It was pieced together by Marine intelligence officers after interrogating two badly wounded and frightened enlisted men captured in the Gorge after it was overrun:

General Kuribayashi died shortly after dawn on Sunday, March 18, after issuing his last order to the remaining trickle of troops to "go out simultaneously at midnight and attack the enemy until the last." At the mouth of what American and Japanese military personnel stationed on Iwo in 1984 still called the "General's Cave," Kuribayashi knelt and bowed three times, facing north toward the Imperial Palace, 650 miles across the sea. Begging forgiveness from Emperor Hirohito in a final prayer, the general plunged a hara-kiri knife into his abdomen. At that moment a trusted aide, standing over him with a sword, brought it down across his neck. The traditional *coup de grâce* severed Kuribayashi's head.

While Admiral Nimitz had his first team of admirals and generals at Iwo, General Kuribayashi's high command was a strange mixture of the lame and the halt, of officers too old for promotion, and even a high-living winner of an Olympic Games gold medal for horsemanship.

The 22,000-plus defenders were a hodgepodge of airmen aloof from the rest of the garrison, of unhappy sailors serving as infantrymen, of army troops confused by the fact that the general's second in command was an admiral. After his first inspection of the island's defenses and the men who would man them, Kuribayashi told Colonel Kaneji Nakane, his most experienced combat commander and the officer who supposedly wielded the sword that killed the general:

"These are no soldiers, just poor recruits who don't know anything. Their officers are superannuated fools. We cannot fight the Americans with them." Kuribayashi appealed to Tokyo for better trained troops and more guns. "Give them to me," he asked the Imperial General Staff, "and I will hold Iwo." When no help came, the hapless general knew the bastion would fall.

Rear Admiral Teiichi Matsunaga, who had met Kuribayashi at the East Boat Landing when the general arrived on Iwo, was relieved as second in command two months before the invasion. He was a brilliant pilot whose squadron earlier in the war had sunk the British battleships *Prince of Wales* and *Repulse* off Singapore.

Matsunaga's courage and qualities of leadership were unquestioned, but with Iwo's air force virtually wiped out, and because of poor health, he was recalled to Japan. He was happy to leave; he found Iwo's water so bad that he drank sake all the time.

Rear Admiral Toshinosuke Ichimaru, who succeeded Matsunaga, was another airman, and wondered why he'd drawn a billet on the godforsaken island.

He still limped from the lingering and painful effects of a leg injury suffered in the crash of an experimental fighter plane in 1926. Since Pearl Harbor, he had commanded aviation training units, mainly kamikazes, and had constantly pleaded for combat. He wanted to die in battle—whether it was in the skies or on the ground. Ichimaru got his wish leading sailors fighting as infantry against the Fifth Division on the western front.

In an emotional last meeting with some fifty survivors of an original force of two thousand, he told them: "The loss of this island means that Yankee military boots soon will be treading on our motherland." He then wrote a bitter tirade in Japanese and English that was addressed to President Roosevelt. "All we want is for you to return to the East that which belongs to the East," it said. Marines found the letter. Today it is part of the history of World War II in the Naval Academy Museum at Annapolis.

Captain Samaji Inouye, under Ichimaru, commanded naval forces manning antiaircraft batteries and big coastal defense guns. He was a stern disciplinarian and his spirit was packed with *Bushido*. He also was an accomplished swordsman: colorful, profane, hard-drinking, and known as a ladies' man.

Inouye's men feared his storming wrath. He had threatened to personally behead a wounded naval lieutenant who had made his way north, escaping from Suribachi after its fall to continue the fight. "Why didn't you die at your post like a samarui should?" he ranted at the bewildered man.

Two weeks after the volcano was conquered, Inouye was still obsessed with the idea of replacing the Stars and Stripes with the flag of the Rising Sun on its summit. It was the determined captain who led the thousand-man predawn attack on D-plus eighteen against the

Fourth Division, the well-organized banzai during which the Japanese pilot hoped to overwhelm a crew of a B-29 and fly the plane to Japan. Inouye probably died in the attack.

Major General Sadasue Senda was the highest-ranking Japanese army officer on the island. He was an artillery man who had fought the czar's troops in the victorious Sino-Russian war and had helped slaughter hundreds of thousands of Chinese at Nanking and Canton in Japan's glory days of conquest on the Asiatic mainland. At Iwo he commanded the Second Mixed Brigade, five thousand troops who battled the Fourth Division in the Meat Grinder.

Most of Senda's troops were from Tokyo: former street urchins from the sprawling slums of the city, men not considered among the Emperor's finest. But they were savage and skillful fighters on Iwo, and fewer than a dozen survived the battle.

Late in the afternoon of March 14, the day the Marines dedicated their cemeteries, Senda held a solemn ceremony with the last of his doomed brigade. With fewer than fifty men still alive, and many of these badly wounded, he assembled the officers and men in a cliffside cave above the eastern shoreline.

Iwo Jima was lost, the general said, and he was going to kill himself rather than surrender to the heathen Marines. He offered hand grenades to all wanting to join in committing hara-kiri. Many accepted and held the explosives to their stomachs, dying in the sickening blasts.

Others looked on, frightened and confused and undecided, while Senda unholstered his pistol and calmly fired it into his temple. Death would have come more easily and less painfully if all had joined in the grisly mass-suicide ritual. Nearby Marine patrols heard the string of muffled explosions, located the cave, and captured two wounded privates guarding its entrance.

Then demolitions men sealed the mouth with satchel charges. Those inside slowly suffocated or died of their wounds.

Colonel Masuo Ikeda was commander of the 145th Infantry Regiment. Kuribayashi thought Ikeda was his best officer, and his 2,500 men the best trained and most competent of the defending force. In the general's battle plan they held down the main defense line in the center of the island north of Motoyama Number Two, where they battled General Erskine's Third Division to a bloody standstill for more than a week.

Some flimsy evidence was discovered placing Ikeda with Kuribayashi when the general died, and indicated that the colonel vowed to carry on the battle to the last man. Whatever the obscure facts, General Erskine on March 16 undertook a determined but futile attempt to induce Ikeda to surrender with what remained of his command.

Two prisoners of war, both privates, said they knew the location of Ikeda's command post and agreed to deliver the offer—a document that filled two sheets of stationery, typed in English on the left and hand-lettered in Japanese characters on the right.

"Our forces now have complete control and freedom of movement on the island of Iwo Jima except in the small area now held by the valiant Japanese troops just south of Kitano Point," the message said. "The fearlessness and indomitable fighting spirit which has been displayed by the Japanese troops on Iwo Jima warrants the admiration of all fighting men.

"You have handled your troops in a superb manner and we have no desire to completely annihilate brave troops who have been forced into a hopeless position. Accordingly, I suggest you cease resistance at once and march, with your command, through my lines to a place of safety where you and all your officers and men will be humanely treated in accordance with the rules of war."

A final paragraph dealt with specifics about effecting the surrender, where the Japanese were to pass through Marine lines, and setting 8:00 A.M. the next morning as the deadline for accepting Erskine's offer.

Whether Ikeda ever received the document was never learned. But the POWs and a Marine patrol made a valiant try at getting it to the colonel. Although the cave was less than six hundred yards from the Marine lines, it took six hours to find it.

Lieutenant Colonel Howard Turton, Erskine's chief intelligence officer, led the mission and was convinced they had found the enemy command post. One of the POWs disappeared with the surrender document into the darkness of the unguarded cave mouth. He returned half an hour later, reporting that the place was packed with troops, many of them wounded. He had been unable to get to the colonel but had located his orderly, a friend, who promised to deliver the message to Ikeda.

Then the Marines and the Japanese messengers returned to the lines, occasionally ducking fire from both sides. The eight-o'clock deadline came and went with no response. Two days later, Third Division troops swarmed the area, seared the cave entrance with flamethrowers, and closed it with a fifty-pound charge of TNT. Whether Colonel Ikeda was inside, and how he died, was never learned. Nor was his body ever found.

Colonel Kanehiko Atsuchi, at fifty-seven the oldest Japanese officer on Iwo, had been passed over for promotion because of his age. Nonetheless, he had drawn General Kuribayashi's most impossible assignment: defend and hold Mount Suribachi for at least ten days while artillery and mortars bled the Marines white on the beachhead.

After three days, when Atsuchi knew he could no longer keep Chandler Johnson's men from the summit, he asked Kuribayashi's permission to die at the head of a banzai. The general refused.

Atsuchi died the morning the flag was raised, mortally wounded by shell fragments. A seriously hurt private captured by Johnson's men told interrogators that the colonel's dying orders were for survivors to sneak through American lines, escape to the north, and continue fighting.

Of all the Japanese on Iwo, including General Kuribayashi, the best known to the homeland was Lieutenant Colonel Takeichi Nishi, who commanded the 26th Tank Regiment.

He was a baron, the scion of an ancient, extremely wealthy and influential family with a direct line to Emperor Hirohito and the imperial family. He had traveled the length and breadth of the United States, spoke impeccable English, doted on fast and expensive American-made automobiles and high-powered racing boats. He had won an Olympic Games gold medal for horsemanship in 1932. While competing in Los Angeles, he was entertained by and photographed with the reigning stars of Hollywood: Spencer Tracy, Douglas Fairbanks, and Mary Pickford.

He had also toured Europe, a handsome and dashing twenty-eight-year-old captain participating in horse shows and becoming involved in numerous and well-publicized extramarital affairs despite his devotion to a beautiful wife and two children, who stayed home at their lavish estate on the outskirts of Tokyo with a sweeping view of Mount Fuji. His was not an unusual lifestyle for a Japanese nobleman of extreme wealth.

Above all, the baron was dedicated to the blood-oath code of *Bushido*. When most of his tanks were destroyed, he ordered those that remained buried to their turrets and used as artillery. When the dug-in weapons had exhausted their ammunition or were overwhelmed, he and the handful of survivors fought as infantrymen, resisting to the last.

Colonel Nishi was a paradox, a man of strange contradictions for a Japanese officer and nobleman. He mingled freely with his men and once stopped them from murdering a captured Marine, a flamethrower who later died of his wounds. Yet he was a stern disciplinarian, a fearless samurai who could, and did, kill Marines in hand-to-hand combat.

Actual circumstances of the flamboyant officer's death will never be known for certain. One survivor said he killed himself after being wounded by machine gun fire in a post-midnight attack in Cushman's Pocket on March 22. Virtually blinded by an artillery blast two days earlier, he was said to have led the raid with his longtime orderly pointing the way. Before putting his revolver to his head and pulling the trigger, the baron supposedly told the aide: "Turn me toward the Imperial Palace."

According to another account, Nishi committed hara-kiri in the surf off the northernmost tip of Iwo, the point nearest Japan, and his body swept out to sea. This version has it that he had a lock of mane from Uranus, his favorite horse, in his breast pocket, and that he carried his Olympic Games riding crop in one hand as he shot himself in the head with a revolver in the other.

An ironic twist of fate befell Colonel Shizuichi Hori, Kuribayashi's chief of staff, and Major General Kotau Osuga, commander of the 2nd Mixed Brigade. Both had been removed from command just before the invasion and ordered back to Tokyo. But by then there was no way to leave the island and they died there—either by hara-kiri or in battle.

2

Victory in Europe came twenty-five days after the last contingent of Third Division troops left Iwo Jima for their base camp on Guam.

Half a world away, in midmorning of May 7, emissaries of Adolf Hitler's crushed Third Reich entered a small schoolhouse in Reims, France, where General Eisenhower had his headquarters. There they signed the official document of unconditional surrender ordering cessation of all fighting on all fronts in Europe at 11:01 P.M. that night.

Now the men of Iwo Jima could celebrate victory in Europe without waking up the next morning and finding their jubilation had been for nothing.

And celebrate they did. Not as boisterously as the millions of United States and Allied servicemen in Europe and other millions of civilians on the United States mainland and in the liberated continent across the Atlantic, but just as joyfully and with a greater sense of gratitude.

Henceforth the mightiest military machine in history could be shifted from the European theater and unleashed against the Japanese homeland: additional millions of soldiers, tens of thousands of bombers and fighters, a vast armada of naval firepower and troop and supply transports; unlimited stockpiles of ammunition—anything and everything in the Allied arsenal to bring about the final downfall of Emperor Hirohito's crumbling empire.

Marines training on Guam and on the Hawaiian Islands to spearhead the invasion were given special beer rations and a two-day break from rigorous schedules to commemorate the end of the Nazi stranglehold on Europe.

But there was no let-up on Okinawa, where Marines had established a beachhead against light opposition on Easter Sunday, April 1. Here, along with soldiers from General Buckner's Tenth Army, they were locked in a desperate battle against an aroused 80,000 Japanese defenders, a costly struggle that would continue until June 21.

"Maybe Nimitz, Spruance, and Turner learned something from Iwo•Jima," a caustic "Howlin' Mad" Smith later told a friend. "They bombarded and bombed Okinawa for nine days before Marines hit the beaches, six days more than we got at Iwo."

By early May, General LeMay's Superforts were making full use of Iwo Jima, not only as a haven for disabled B-29s but as a base for daily raids on virtually every major target in Japan. P-51 Mustangs flew cover missions from the island and added their firepower to the devastation being rained down by the bombers on the enemy's home islands.

American submarines moved unmolested in Japanese coastal waters, laying mines and sinking and shelling merchant ships and naval vessels within sight of shore. Carrier planes ranged over southern Japan, bombing and strafing war plants, rail transportation, and coastal shipping.

In late June, Japan's largest battleship, the *Yamato*, was sunk by carrier planes in a futile attempt by the enemy fleet to challenge the irreversible tide of American naval power.

Within days the remnants of the once indomitable Japanese armada no longer posed a threat—the United States Third Fleet roamed unopposed in Japanese home waters, its battlewagons, cruisers, and destroyers closing to within a few miles of shore and blasting at will key targets with thousands of tons of high explosive shells.

Throughout the tumultuous days of July, as the Navy's guns ravaged Japan's naval bases and coastal cities, as many as 1,000 American aircraft systematically bombed and burned out the reeling empire's major cities in nonstop around-the-clock attacks.

Instead of bombs, some B-29s dropped millions of leaflets urging the Japanese to surrender. Powerful radio transmitters broadcast the same message from the Marianas.

But there was no outward indication that the warlords had any intention of surrendering. While some members of Prime Minister Suzuki Kantaro's cabinet secretly favored laying down arms and ceasing the senseless struggle, they kept their views to themselves.

And so the empire continued to muster its still formidable manpower and what remained of its military resources to meet the invasion: 2,350,000 soldiers of the regular army backed up by 250,000 garrison troops; the remnants of the navy and all the aircraft in Japan, including training planes, numbering about seven thousand; 4,000,000 civilian employees of the armed services; and a civilian militia of 23,000,000 men, women, boys and girls sworn and determined to fight to the death, even with bamboo spears.

July 16, 1945.
Alamogordo, New Mexico.

Predawn darkness above the desert sands of Yucca Flats vanished in an unbelievable flash of blinding light, the likes of which man had never before witnessed. With the incredible destructive force of 20,000 tons of TNT, the United States had successfully detonated the first atomic bomb in an historic test of the most powerful weapon the world had ever seen.

When the results were flashed to Washington, there was tense debate among the scientists who had developed the bomb, the military high command, and members of the President's cabinet about whether or not to drop it without warning on Japan. Without hesitation, Harry S Truman ordered its use against the enemy as quickly as possible.

Exactly three weeks after the test, on August 6, a lone B-29 dropped an atomic bomb on Hiroshima. Three days later, Nagasaki was seared in a second nuclear blast.

Premier Suzuki sent a team of medical experts and military men to the scene for a firsthand inspection of the holocaust. When it reported back to Tokyo with its awful findings, Emperor Hirohito decreed that the warlords accept unconditional surrender.

On August 14, the recorded voice of the Son of Heaven, high-pitched and faltering, was heard in an emotional broadcast from Radio Tokyo. He told his stunned and bewildered subjects that the time had come when they must bow to the inevitable, and announced to the world that Japan would fight no more. "A continuation of the war will result in the ultimate collapse and obliteration of the Japanese nation," the Emperor said.

There would be no invasion.

World War II was over.

All that remained was the formal surrender.

September 2, 1945.
Aboard the *U.S.S. Missouri* in Tokyo Bay.

Surrender ceremonies began at 7:59 A.M. with the ship's band playing "The Star-Spangled Banner."

General MacArthur and Admiral Nimitz stood at attention a few feet in front of a ten-foot-long table covered with a gold-trimmed green cloth, where the instruments of surrender were ready to be signed.

Two paces behind the irreconcilable commanders were their lieutenants: fifty Army generals and colonels, fifty senior Navy officers, and three Marine generals. Beside them were thirty-six hastily assembled representatives of the Allied Powers and more than two hundred correspondents, photographers, and radio newsmen.

Nearly two thousand sailors and some one hundred Marines, members of the *Missouri*'s crew, jammed every foot of the fore and after decks of the 45,000-ton battleship to catch a glimpse of history.

Foreign Minister Mamoru Shigemitsui and General Yoshijiro Umezu, chief of staff for Imperial General Headquarters, headed the disspirited Japanese delegation. All appeared dazed, even stupefied in their shabby and ill-fitting uniforms or disheveled formal cutaway coats and striped trousers.

Uniforms of the day for American officers were starched and pressed khaki. No one wore decorations or sidearms. The Japanese were also without ceremonial swords or other trappings of rank as they listened stoically to MacArthur stridently intone the litany of capitulation.

Looking every inch the elegant "American Caesar," as author William Manchester would later call him, the general spoke eloquently into a battery of five microphones that carried his measured words on loudspeakers to the onlookers, and via shortwave radio to millions of listeners throughout the world. When he finished, he moved four steps to the big table.

Using six pens, one a bright red fountain pen carried in his left breast pocket, he placed his bold signature on the historic documents, signing as the representative of the Allied Powers. Nimitz signed for the United States, Shigemitsui and Umezu for the shattered Japanese Empire.

World War II ended officially at 9:18 A.M. with MacArthur's ringing words: "These proceedings are closed."

Two minutes later bright sunshine broke through the low overcast. One observer likened it to "an omen of future peace for mankind." On signal, three hundred carrier planes and forty-six Superforts roared overhead in V-for-victory formations. The American flag Commodore Perry had carried ashore ninety-two years earlier, when he opened

Japan's doors to Western civilization and foreign trade, was in a glass case overlooking the *Missouri*'s quarterdeck. The emblem had been flown from Navy headquarters in Washington for the occasion.

Anchored a hundred yards to starboard was the battleship *Iowa*; sister battlewagon *South Dakota*, just astern. Sweeping to the horizon and beyond were aircraft carriers, cruisers, destroyers, troop transports, and supply ships ready to put in motion the first phase of Japan's occupation.

"Howlin' Mad" Smith, the highest-ranking Marine in the war zone, was the only three-star United States officer in the Pacific theater not on the *Missouri*'s quarterdeck. Stunned and heartsick, he listened to the broadcast of the ceremonies in his Quonset hut headquarters at Pearl Harbor, five thousand miles from the momentous event he'd done so much to bring about.

Admiral Hill had petitioned Admiral Nimitz to invite the general. But the strongly worded written request was returned with the word "NO!" scrawled across it in CinCPac's unmistakable handwriting.

Nimitz never made public why Smith was not among the American dignitaries. Years later, the general told a friend that personal animosity was involved as well as "the fine hand of the highest brass" in the ignoble affair. They'd never forgotten, he said, that he had sacked two Army generals "who weren't fighting hard enough, or didn't know how to fight hard enough, to beat the Japs."

Not only was the Old Warrior personally embittered, but he felt Nimitz's callous action, for whatever reason, was an unforgivable affront to the Marines, to what they had done, and to the price they had paid for the ultimate triumph in the Pacific.

In less than three years "his Marines" had forged an unbroken chain of victories unsurpassed in global military history—and always at heavy cost. Beginning at Guadalcanal and ending at Okinawa, their sweep of 10,000 miles was nearly twice the distance marched by Napoleon's army from Paris to Moscow and Genghis Khan's from Mongolia to the Mediterranean.

3

Iwo Jima today is hallowed ground to the Japanese, a haunted memorial to General Kuribayashi and his garrison. It also is a backwater airbase for a squadron of air-sea rescue helicopters and one hundred men of the Japanese Maritime Self Defense Force.

To most Americans, it is a vaguely remembered and remote place where Marines fought a bloody battle in World War II, and where the Stars and Stripes was photographed being raised on the summit of a volcano whose name they can't recall. But to twenty-seven United States Coast Guardsmen operating a LORAN navigational aids and weather station for civilian and military aircraft, it is a dismal, lonely, and uncomfortable outpost where a duty tour is one year.

Vegetation now hides most scars of the struggle of four decades ago, but not all of them. Just off Green Beach the rusty remnants of a sunken ship still haven't surrendered to the inexorable pounding of the surf. Creeping pealike vines, rich in dainty blue flowers, envelop the skeletons of countless bunkers and their long-silent guns.

A narrow, pot-holed asphalt road circles the island and snakes upward to the top of Suribachi. Dense clouds of stinking vapor frequently steam from the crater, and the bowels of the volcano occasionally rumble and threaten to erupt, but it no longer dominates the skyline.

Not far from Nishi Village, where the Fifth Division fought for its life, the antenna of the Coast Guard's LORAN station towers 1,350 feet over the island.

An American flag flies from dawn to dusk in the constant breeze on Suribachi's summit, the imposing centerpiece of a well-kept stone Fifth Division memorial to its dead. Nearby are two monuments erected by the Japanese in memory of Kuribayashi's troops entombed in Iwo's miles of still undiscovered tunnels and caves.

Earthquakes are frequent and their shock waves sometimes open fissures leading to underground installations. Hospitals have been found exactly as they were when Marine demolitions units sealed them in 1945. Skeletons lie on cots or litters; plasma bottles hang alongside them; splints are in place although mortal flesh has gone; surgical instruments and drugs are neatly arranged on treatment tables with the remains of doctors and attendants close by.

To inspect one of these caves is not an excursion, but it would be good medicine for anyone prone to forget the horrors of Iwo Jima. Where rice and other rations had been stored, the roof rustles with the crisp sound of thumb-sized roaches. Rusted weapons lie beside skeletons. Gas masks, empty and rotted wooden ammunition cases, rice bowls, ragged shreds of uniforms are silent sentinels of the battle.

Even in peace Iwo aboveground is grim. Hundreds of unexploded shells lie across the island, undiscovered in the undergrowth covering the countless crevices and ravines. Water is a constant problem, and the supply can only be replenished by rainfall collected in giant cisterns. Typhoons strike several times a year, almost without warning. Nights are chilly; days are hot.

Reaching the island is next to impossible for civilians, American or Japanese, wanting to visit for whatever purpose. There is no scheduled commercial air service, and the infrequent small supply ships that anchor offshore must put cargoes and passengers on the beach the same way Marines came in—by landing craft or small boats.

A Coast Guard C-130 Hercules transport makes a weekly round-trip flight from the U. S. Navy Base at Yakota on Honshu Island. The four-engined prop-jet ferries mail, supplies, and an occasional visitor-for-a-day from the States. Other than the complex of single-story cinder-block barracks and operations buildings of the LORAN station, there are no permanent structures on the American part of the island.

Japanese facilities are a half-mile away at the north end of the 9,000-foot-long runway paved four decades ago by Seabees and Army engineers for Superforts and Mustangs. A twelve-foot-high chain-link fence surrounds the buildings that house the LORAN transmitter and the base of its tower. But otherwise there are no man-made obstacles to free movement anywhere on the island.

Members of the Association of Iwo Jima, an organization of Japanese survivors and the families of those who died in the fighting, come to the island each spring and fall. In groups of fifty, they fly in chartered vintage planes from Tokyo for a week-long religious pilgrimage to honor the thousands of entombed through the ceremonial cremation of skeletons, and by dedicating memorial obelisks to units and individuals.

*

High-flying aircraft pass over Iwo several times a day. Most are commercial jets jammed with Japanese tourists and newlyweds on flights to and from Guam, called "the Niagara Falls of the Pacific." An occasional Air Force or Navy transport will drop from its regular altitude to circle Suribachi and take a close look at the pear-shaped battleground.

Less frequently a plane, short of fuel from the buffeting of strong Pacific headwinds or with mechanical problems, still finds a haven on Iwo as hundreds of Superforts did in 1945.

It is an incredible and little-known footnote to history that General Eisenhower might not have lived to become president had it not been for the island. In November, 1952, two weeks after his election, the propellor-driven four-engine Lockheed Constellation carrying him to Korea for a personal inspection of the battlefront had serious engine trouble halfway to Japan from Guam.

"All of us aboard breathed a collective sigh of relief, grateful that the ugly island was there," Bob Considine, the International News Service correspondent and columnist for the Hearst newspapers, wrote of the incident.

4

Even before V-J Day was official, the six Marine divisions in the Pacific were being broken up.

In the nineteen tumultuous days between Hirohito's broadcast accepting the terms of total capitulation and the surrender ceremonies on the *Missouri*, thousands of men boarded LSTs and transports. They sailed for occupation duty with full combat equipment, not knowing whether the Japanese in the field would follow the Emperor's edict or continue the fight.

Some units went to Japan and were met with sullen silence by the civilian population, but with no resistance from Japanese troops. Others landed in north China, where they were greeted by hundreds of thousands of wildly cheering people in the port cities of Tientsin and Tsingtao. Less fortunate outfits found themselves on bypassed islands and atolls populated by natives overjoyed at being freed from the yoke of the Japanese.

By early winter thousands of men had returned to the States for discharge under a point system that gave priority to those with the longest overseas service, for combat landings, and for battle wounds. Within a year the total manpower of the Marine Corps was less than a third of what it had been on V-J Day.

One general and a colonel who were at Iwo later became Marine Corps commandants. Many career lieutenants, captains, and majors would attain high rank as they followed their profession in Korea and Vietnam. Some enlisted men would stay in the Corps and become officers. Others would serve the necessary hitches to retire.

But most junior officers and enlisted men, members of the Marine Corps Reserve who had enlisted "for the duration of the war plus six months," would become civilians again as soon as possible: some to find jobs for the first time; some to attend college and carve out careers; others to pick up the threads of lives interrupted by their country's call to duty.

In the years to come, and with varying degrees and depths of emotion, all would recall from time to time the awful fighting and what it was like to be one of the men of Iwo Jima.

On the evening of February 23, 1985, forty years to the day after the raising of the Stars and Stripes atop Mount Suribachi, some four hundred American survivors of the battle met at the Marine Corps Base in Camp Pendleton, California, to commemorate the historic occasion.

Most were veterans of the Third, Fourth and Fifth Marine Divisions. There was a sprinkling of former Navy medics and Seabees who had fought side by side with the Marines to conquer the terrible island. Now, in the autumn of their lives, they assembled once again to pay homage to comrades who had fallen in combat four decades earlier.

There was the usual quota of emotional speeches that mark such affairs and bring on moist eyes and lumpy throats. There was a re-enactment by five Marines, all in their teens, of the scene captured atop the volcano so many years ago by Joe Rosenthal in his unforgettable photograph; a tableau greeted with cheers.

Then a lanky, erect, bespectacled man made his proud way to the podium. He was Walter J. Ridlon, Jr., a much-decorated and retired Marine colonel who, as a valiant young company commander on Iwo Jima, earned the Navy Cross for valor.

Now, in crisp phrases delivered in the strong voice of a man who had often commanded amid the sounds and smells of battle, he told of a more recent time on Iwo Jima. He spoke of an event that had taken place just four days earlier—February 19, 1985, the fortieth anniversary of D-Day—when he and some three hundred Americans had returned to the island for the first time since they had faced the enemy in do-or-die battle.

Colonel Ridlon didn't dwell on the horrors and brutalities of the fighting. He didn't talk of the savage combat that had marked the Marines' march from Guadalcanal to the front door of the Japanese homeland. Nor did he speak of the horrible losses—to friend and foe—of the war in the Pacific.

He spoke, instead, of a hope that what happened on Iwo Jima will never happen again. He told of the dedication of a statue on Mount Suribachi; a memorial to the living and the dead—American and Japanese—and its words of reconciliation and the mutual respect of men who did awful battle against each other at a now-distant time on a fly-speck Pacific island.

These were not words that would have been acceptable in the heat of combat at Iwo—nor in the time immediately after the horrendous loss of Marines during the bloody battle. To some Americans, they must be unsettling to this day.

Colonel Ridlon read the inscription to a hushed audience, a smattering of whom had been with him on the pilgrimage: "On the fortieth anniversary of the battle of Iwo Jima, American and Japanese veterans meet again on these same sands, this time in peace and friendship. We commemorate our comrades, living and dead, who fought here with bravery and honor, and we pray that our sacrifices on Iwo Jima will always be remembered and never repeated."

Then he introduced a Japanese dressed in the ceremonial robes of a Buddhist priest, the Reverend Taunezo Wachi, now eighty-five. As Captain Wachi of the Imperial Japanese Navy, he had commanded the enemy garrison on Iwo until a few months before the invasion.

Few of the Americans knew of Wachi's background; that he had been relieved of his command because, among other things, he had ordered that the island's meager stockpile of food and supplies be shared equally. They were told only that Wachi was now a Buddhist priest, that he was founder and president of the Association of Iwo Jima, a Japanese organization composed of the handful of survivors of the fighting and the kin of the living and dead, and that he was the organizer and leader of the Japanese who had joined the Americans in the recent ceremonies on the island.

Reverend Wachi spoke briefly. His voice had the thin timbre of an octogenarian; the words faltering, but packed with force and easily understandable. He said that, since 1952, he had gone frequently to Iwo Jima to conduct Buddhist ceremonies for the more than twenty thousand Japanese killed during the battle and still entombed in the island's maze of caves, tunnels and unmarked graves.

"In the spirit of reconciliation," he said, "I also pray for the American Marines who died there. I pray, as Colonel Ridlon did, for the living and dead who fought on Iwo Jima, and that our sacrifices will always be remembered but never repeated."

There is a postscript. After Reverend Wachi finished his remarks and was escorted by Colonel Ridlon to his table, he asked to speak with me. We had been introduced earlier in the day by the colonel.

"I understand, Mr. Ross," he said in passable English, "that you have written a book about the battle of Iwo Jima." I answered that I had. Wachi turned to Betty Asako Tsutsumi, a Japanese-American, who, as a representative of Japan Air Lines, had served as the Americans' interpreter on their journey of memory from the United States to the historic World War II battleground some six hundred miles from Tokyo Bay.

"If Mr. Ross cannot fully understand what I say, will you please interpret for me?"

Then, partly in English, but largely in Japanese, Reverend Wachi asked if I would do for him and his fallen comrades of Iwo "a most important favor for which I and the Japanese will be forever grateful."

At times searching for the right words, he recounted how, on his trips to the island to conduct religious ceremonies, he had found that the skulls of many Japanese killed in battle had been severed from skeletons and, presumably, had been sent or carried back to the States as souvenirs. Equally as disturbing, "but not as grisly," he said, was that three different pairs of statues of Kannon, the Buddha goddess of mercy, had been stolen.

Reverend Wachi's words through Betty Tsutsumi: "Marines who fought at Iwo Jima were not involved. Their legacy of valor on the island is the legacy of honor of the United States Marine Corps. These unpleasant matters were done by other American servicemen who visited or were stationed on Iwo Jima long after the battle."

I was puzzled. I told him that, in researching the book, I had heard of such desecrations elsewhere in the Pacific war but not on Iwo Jima. "So what is the favor you request? What can I do?" I asked.

Again the voice of Betty Tsutsumi and the words of Tsunezo Wachi, the Japanese military commander of a long-ago time and distant place:

"I appeal to you to plead with anyone who has the skull of a Japanese from Iwo Jima—or one of the statues of Kannon—to return same to me so that I can then return them to the island where, in the name of humanity and the honor of warriors, they belong and can rest in eternal peace. If even a token—just one Buddha and a few skulls—are returned, I will ask no questions about where they came from, and I will proclaim to all the Japanese war widows and relatives and survivors that the issue is closed."

And so I pass along Reverend Tsunezo Wachi's appeal. His address is:

Reverend Tsunezo Wachi,
President, Association of Iwo Jima,
2-24-23 Higashicho, Kichijoji,
Musashinoshi, Tokyo, Japan, 180

Acknowledgments and Postscript

This book owes much of its being to an abandoned project to write with Graves B. Erskine a first-person account of his experiences and brilliant career as a Marine officer in two world wars. He was then a retired sixty-year-old four-star general serving President Eisenhower, under a special act of Congress, as Director of Special Operations in the Department of Defense.

Press of duties in the highly sensitive and demanding post made it impossible for him to devote the time he felt necessary to complete the venture, and so it was dropped. But during our times together, his deep feelings for the Marines, particularly those who were at Iwo Jima, made me determined to someday write this book.

Through the years I have talked to scores of veterans—from privates to generals and admirals—about the battle.

There were illuminating and gratifying conversations, some brief and others lengthy, with Admirals Nimitz and Turner; with Generals Smith, Rockey, Cates, and MacArthur.

There were talks with civilian newsmen who landed with the assault forces. And there were hundreds of joyful hours of reminiscence with Marine Corps combat correspondents and photographers, my wartime comrades of fondest memory, whose frontline writing and pictures rank with the best battle coverage to come out of World War II, not only at Iwo, but wherever Marines fought in the Pacific.

All the photographs in the book, with the exception of those by Joe Rosenthal of the Associated Press and the aerial views of Suribachi and the assault waves hitting the beaches, are the work of Marine Corps photographers. Where available, their credit lines are beneath the pictures.

Special thanks are given to Arthur J. Kiely, Jr., who was assigned to General Smith as his personal photographer, and who has permitted the use of the best shots in his collection of Iwo pictures. And to Charles O. Jones, who was in the assault with the Fifth Division and provided many rare combat photos he made under fire.

Brigadier General Edwin H. Simmons, Director of Marine Corps

History and Museums, and his staff provided valuable assistance in securing other photographs and Tom Dunn's drawing. I am especially indebted to Regina Strother, the indefatigable photo researcher, and to Jack Dyer, the curator of Marine Corps art.

Coast Guard Lieutenant M.J. Lewandowski, who was commanding officer of Iwo's LORAN station in 1984, was the source of photographs and firsthand information on what the island is like today.

And special thanks go to Colonel Raymond Henri, my commanding officer four decades ago and my friend through the years, for permission to use the excerpt from his volume of poetry *Dispatches from the Field*.

John Shotwell, Michael Imsick, and the staff of the Marine Corps Public Affairs Office in New York, were most helpful in countless ways. To the memory of the late Brigadier General Robert L. Denig, who fathered the idea of Marine Corps Combat Correspondents, and to Gladys McPartland, who kept track of them for nearly four decades after World War II, deep appreciation is expressed.

In early summer of 1984 as Bernice Woll, Vanguard's editor-in-chief, worked her magic on the last pages of this book, I received a letter from Gene Jones. The teen-aged flamethrower and combat photographer of the long-ago days of Iwo Jima, now in his fifties, was personally cited for bravery by General Cates after the battle, and has a jagged scar across his throat—a perpetual reminder of his service as a young Marine with the 24th Regiment.

Through the years, Gene has been an unfailing fountain of constant encouragement, unstinting assistance, and always meaningful advice as words that ultimately became this book were set to paper. His letter likened the *ultimate meaning* of Iwo Jima to what the survivors of the Union and Confederate Armies must have felt at the end of the Civil War. I am grateful for his permission to pass them on:

"At dusk on the day that long, tragic war ended, the regiments of the Blue and Gray came together to share food and talk of tomorrow. In the glow of thousands of campfires spreading across blood-soaked terrain, they must have seen everywhere the faces of old comrades; weary but resolute, the living and the killed.

"These men had fought for what they believed in, and for each other. Even though they had been caused to leave their dead thickly on terrible battlefields, there was probably in them on that night a conviction that somehow it had all been worth it. Many of them, even then, had a perception of what they had done and why, and in this they found meaning to their ordeal and merit in their sacrifice. I think that of Iwo Jima.

"My thoughts have to do with something far more elemental beyond the raw, violent horrors of combat. They have to do with our nation's cause and the uncommon valor that is the legacy of our Corps, and with memories of Marines, memories that are like bugles on the wind, true to our credo of *Semper Fidelis*.

"Iwo Jima drew us from our homeland in the sunlit springtime of our youth. Those who did not come back alive remain in perpetual springtime—forever young—and a part of us is with them always."

To these "forever young," I acknowledge an everlasting debt I can never repay.

—B. D. R.

MEMORIAL DAY, ARLINGTON

Does it really matter where your wreath
is laid? or who it is who lies beneath,
who lies below it letting time erase
him at the maggot's slow but certain pace?

Why must some registrar point on his list
precisely where each man does not exist?
Cannot you claim a random plot to be
the one—they're all alike—you came to see?

Suppose the diggers erred and skipped one grave—
interred some body where they shouldn't have—
how odd to pray exclusively for Jones
upon the sod that covers Smithers' bones!

Worse yet: suppose some bumbling crew
had somehow used a list containing you...
embarrassing to be in vigorous health
and caught in lamentation for yourself.

Forget the names! Just fling your wreathed bouquet—
whatever stone it rings, there stop and pray.

— COL. RAYMOND HENRI
UNITED STATES MARINE CORPS (RET.)

BIBLIOGRAPHY

ARNOLD, HENRY H. *Global Mission*. New York: Harper & Brothers, 1949.

ARTHUR, ROBERT A. and COHLMIA, KENNETH. *The Third Marine Division*. Washington, D.C.: Infantry Journal Press, 1948.

BARTLEY, WHITMAN S. *Iwo Jima: Amphibious Epic*. Washington, D.C.: Historical Branch, U.S. Marine Corps, 1954.

BLAKENEY, JANE. *Heroes, U. S. Marine Corps, 1861–1955*. Washington, D.C.: Historical Branch, U. S. Marine Corps, 1957.

BROOKS, WALKER Y. *Engineers on Iwo*. Washington, D.C.: *Marine Corps Gazette*, October, 1945.

CANT, GILBERT. *The Great Pacific Victory*. New York: The John Day Company, 1945.

CARTER, WORRAL REED. *Beans, Bullets and Black Oil*. Washington, D.C.: U. S. Government Printing Office, 1953.

CHAPELLE, DICKEY. *What's a Woman Doing Here?* New York: William Morrow & Co., 1962.

CHAPIN, JOHN C. *The Fifth Marine Division in World War II*. Washington, D.C.: Historical Branch, U. S. Marine Corps, 1945.

CHAPMAN, GUY. *A Passionate Prodigality*. New York: Holt, Rinehart and Winston, 1966.

CONGDON, DON. *Combat: Pacific Theater*. New York: Dell Publishing Company, Inc., 1958.

CONNER, HOWARD M. *The Spearhead: The Fifth Marine Division in World War II*. Washington, D.C.: Infantry Journal Press, 1950.

COSTELLO, JOHN. *The Pacific War*. New York: Rawson, Wade Publishers, Inc., 1981.

CRAIG, WILLIAM. *The Fall of Japan*. New York: The Dial Press, Inc., 1967.

CRAVEN, WESLEY FRANK and CATE, JAMES LEA. *The Army Air Forces in World War II, Vol. V*. Chicago: University of Chicago Press, 1953.

CUSHMAN, ROBERT E., JR. *Amphibious Assault Planning: Iwo Jima*. Washington, D.C.: *Infantry Journal*, December, 1948.

FANE, FRANCIS DOUGLAS and MOORE, DON. *The Naked Warriors*. New York: Appleton-Century-Crofts, Inc., 1956.

FORRESTAL, JAMES. *The Forrestal Diaries*. Edited by WALTER MILLIS with E. S. DUFFIELD. New York: Viking Press, 1961.

GALLANT, T. GRADY. *The Friendly Dead*. New York: Doubleday & Company, Inc., 1964.

GARAND, GEORGE W. and STROBRIDGE, TRUMAN R. *Western Pacific Operations: History of U. S. Marine Corps Operations in World*

War II, Vol. IV. Washington, D.C.: Historical Branch, U. S. Marine Corps, 1971.

HALSEY, WILLIAM F. and BRYAN, J., III. *Admiral Halsey's Story.* New York: McGraw-Hill, Inc., 1947.

HAVASHI, SABURO and COOX, ALVIN D. *Kogun, The Japanese Army in the Pacific War.* Quantico, Va.: U. S. Marine Corp Association, 1959.

HEINL, ROBERT D., JR. *Dark Horse on Iwo.* Washington, D.C.: *Marine Corps Gazette*, August, 1945.

——. *Target: Iwo.* Annapolis, Md.: *U. S. Naval Institute Proceedings*, July, 1963.

HENRI, RAYMOND. *Iwo Jima: Springboard to Final Victory.* New York: U. S. Camera Publishing Corporation, 1945.

——; BEECH, W. KEYES; DEMPSEY, DAVID K.; JOSEPHY, ALVIN M. JR.; LUCAS, JIM G. *The U. S. Marines on Iwo Jima.* Washington, D.C.: Infantry Journal Press.

HOWARD, CLIVE and WHITLEY, JOE. *One Damned Island After Another.* Chapel Hill, N.C.: University of North Carolina Press, 1946.

HOYT, EDWIN P. *How They Won the War in the Pacific.* New York: Weybright and Talley, 1970.

HUIE, WILLIAM BRADFORD. *From Omaha to Okinawa.* New York: E. P. Dutton & Co., Inc., 1945.

HUNT, GEORGE P. *Coral Comes High.* New York: Harper & Brothers, 1957.

——. *The Hero of Iwo Jima and Other Stories.* New York: Signet Books, 1962.

ISELY, JETER A. and CROWL, PHILIP A. *The U. S. Marines and Amphibious War.* Princeton, N.J.: Princeton University Press, 1951.

JENSEN, OLIVER. *Carrier War.* New York: Simon and Schuster, Inc., 1945.

JOSEPHY, ALVIN M., JR. *The Long, the Short and the Tall.* New York: Alfred A. Knopf, Inc., 1946.

KIRBY, W. WOODBURN. *The War Against Japan.* London: Her Majesty's Stationery Office, 1965.

LARDNER, JOHN. *D-Day, Iwo Jima.* New York: *The New Yorker*, March 17, 1945.

LECKIE, ROBERT. *Strong Men Armed.* New York: Random House, 1962.

MARQUAND, JOHN P. *Iwo Jima Before H-Hour.* New York: *Harper's Magazine*, May, 1945.

MATTHEWS, ALLEN R. *The Assault.* New York: Simon and Schuster, Inc., 1947.

Medal of Honor, 1861–1949. Bureau of Naval Personnel, U. S. Navy Department, 1951.

MERRILL, JAMES J. *A Sailor's Admiral,* A Biography of William F. Halsey. New York: Doubleday & Company, Inc., 1976.

MILLER, BILL. *Hot Rock, The Fight for Mt. Suribachi.* Washington, D.C.: *Leatherneck Magazine*, May, 1945.

MICHENER, JAMES A. *Tales Of The South Pacific.* New York: The Macmillan Company, 1947.

MORISON, SAMUEL ELIOT. *History of United States Naval Operations in World War II, Vol. XIV.* Boston: Little, Brown & Co., 1960.

NALTY, BERNARD C. *The United States Marines on Iwo Jima: The Battle and the Flag Raising.* Washington, D.C.: Historical Branch, U. S. Marine Corps.

NEWCOMB, RICHARD F. *Iwo Jima.* New York: Holt, Rinehart and Winston, Inc., 1965.

O'SHEEL, PATRICK and COOK, GENE. *Semper Fidelis: The U.S. Marines in the Pacific, 1942–1945.* New York: William Sloane Associates, Inc., 1947.

POTTER, E.B. and NIMITZ, CHESTER W. *The Great Sea War.* Englewood Cliffs, N.J.: Prentice-Hall, 1960.

PROEHL, CARL W., editor, and DEMPSEY, DAVID, text. *The Fourth Marine Division in World War II.* Washington, D.C.: Infantry Journal Press, 1946.

PYLE, ERNIE. *Last Chapter.* New York: Holt, Rinehart and Winston, 1946.

ROSENTHAL, JOE and HEINZ, W.C. *The Picture That Will Live Forever.* New York: *Collier's Magazine,* February 18, 1955.

RUSSELL, MICHAEL. *Iwo Jima.* New York: Ballantine Books, 1974.

SCOTT, F.A. *Ten Days on Iwo Jima.* Washington, D.C.: *Leatherneck Magazine,* May, 1945.

SHERROD, ROBERT. *On to Westward: War in the Central Pacific.* New York: Duell, Sloan and Pearce, 1945.

——. *History of Marine Corps Aviation in World War II.* Washington, D. C.: Combat Forces Press, 1952.

SMITH, HOLLAND M. and FINCH, PERCY. *Coral and Brass.* New York: Charles Scribner's Sons, 1949.

SMITH, S. E., editor. *The United States Marine Corps in World War II.* New York: Random House, 1969.

SNYDER, LOUIS L. *Masterpieces of War Reporting.* New York: Julian Messner, Inc., 1962.

TOLAND, JOHN. *But Not In Shame.* New York: Random House, 1961.

——. *The Rising Sun: The Decline and Fall of the Japanese Empire, 1936–1945.* New York: Random House, 1970.

WALLECHINSKY, DAVID and WALLACE, IRVING. *The People's Almanac.* New York: Doubleday & Company, Inc., 1975.

WALTON, BRYCE. *D-Day on Iwo Jima.* Washington, D.C.: *Leatherneck Magazine,* November, 1945.

WHEELER, KEITH. *We Are The Wounded.* New York: E. P. Dutton & Company, Inc., 1945.

WHEELER, RICHARD. *The Bloody Battle for Suribachi.* New York: Thomas Y. Crowell Company, 1965.

——. *Iwo.* New York: Lippincott & Crowell, Publishers, 1980.

WILLIAMS, R. H. *Up the Rock on Iwo the Hard Way.* Washington, D.C.: *Marine Corps Gazette,* August, 1945.

World Book Encyclopedia. Chicago: Field Enterprises, 1952.

Index

ABOUT THE AUTHOR

BILL D. ROSS saw action on Iwo Jima as a twenty-three-year-old Marine sergeant combat correspondent. After V-J Day he volunteered for an additional six months' duty in North China. In 1946 he joined the Washington staff of the Associated Press, covering government agencies, Capitol Hill, and the White House. In July 1950, he was sent to Korea as a correspondent for the Associated Press, landing with the first wave of Marines at Inchon. Since then he has written for several metropolitan dailies and numerous national magazines, as well as for television and motion pictures. He is presently working on *Trenchcoat Brigade*, a book about war correspondents and photographers.